PUERTO RICO
A Political and Cultural History

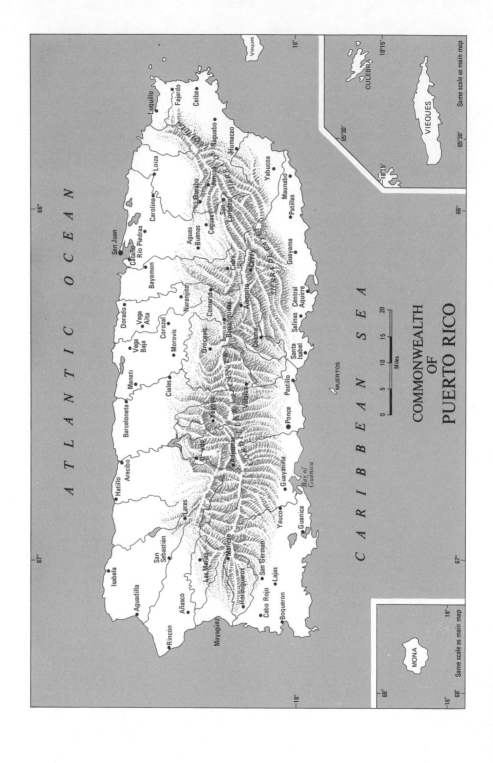

COMMONWEALTH
OF
PUERTO RICO

PUERTO RICO

A Political and Cultural History

Arturo Morales Carrión

Chapters by
María Teresa Babín
Aida R. Caro Costas
Arturo Santana
Luis González Vales

W. W. Norton & Company, Inc.
New York

American Association for
State and Local History
Nashville

Photo credits: Photographs collected by Jack Delano. C. M. Colon Torres: p. 119, above left; The Library of Congress, pp. 174, 217, 218; Puerto Rico Office of Information, Photo by Rosskam, pp. 181, 254, 259, 323; Caperic Studios, Inc., p. 260. *Cartographer:* B. Andrew Mudryk.

Published and distributed by
W. W. Norton & Company, Inc.
500 Fifth Avenue
New York, New York 10110

Library of Congress Cataloguing-in-Publication Data
Main entry under title:

Puerto Rico, a political and cultural history.

Bibliography: p.
Includes index.
1. Puerto Rico—History.   2. Puerto Rico—Civiliza-
tion.   I. Morales Carrión, Arturo.   II. Caro Costas,
Aída R.   III. American Association for State and Local
History.
F1973.P83   1983   972.95   83–2655
ISBN 0-393-01740-0

Printed in the United States of America
2 3 4 5 6 7 8 9 0

Contents

Part Three
EPILOGUE
María Teresa Babín

Invitation to the Reader

The American Association for State and Local History is pleased to present this major new study of the history of Puerto Rico, written by Arturo Morales Carrión with the help of four other specialists.

From the beginning it was our intention to produce a serious and substantial history of the island, as free as possible of the political biases that have colored too many other accounts, but written with general readers in mind—thoughtful citizens in the States and the Commonwealth itself, who through this work could find help in understanding a place whose political status and aspirations have raised, and continue to raise, policy questions of great national and international concern. We believe this book offers a source of enlightenment—and a fascinating reading experience.

For that we are indebted to Dr. Morales, whom we asked to serve as general editor and principal author of the work because of the great respect he enjoys, in both Puerto Rico and the States, as a judicious historian, an esteemed educator, and a dedicated public servant. He recruited the other distinguished scholars whose special expertise, presented in signed chapters or sections, contributes much to both the depth and the objectivity of this work.

Even so, both we and the authors are regretfully aware of how much could not be included because of space limitations. Much more might have been said, for example, of the different migrations of Puerto Ricans to the mainland of North America. But notes in the back of the book will guide the interested reader to titles of other books and articles on such subjects, so that this work may serve beyond itself as a reference to dependable sources.

Finally, we are eager to acknowledge our collaborators in the publication of this special study. The National Endowment for the Humanities—which in so many ways has been so valuable in helping make

vii

available to the public objective sources of historical background for understanding contemporary situations—made the editorial work possible through a grant to the American Association for State and Local History. We in turn contracted with W. W. Norton and Company, who, as co-publisher, invested its own funds in the manufacturing and distribution of the book.

But the authors and the Association alone are responsible for opinions expressed in the book and the content of it—and proudly so!

—The Editors

Introduction

As noted in the text, Robert T. Hill, an American geologist who had finished writing a book on the West Indies shortly before the Spanish-American War broke out in 1898, observed that Puerto Rico was less known to the United States "than even Japan or Madagascar. . . . The sum total of the scientific literature of the island since the days of Humboldt would hardly fill a page of this book."

Over three quarters of a century has elapsed since Hill wrote those words, and numerous studies and books have been written in the interval about Puerto Rico. With regard to the island's socioeconomic development or to its political and constitutional relationship with the United States, the bibliography is impressive. A growing bibliography is also available about Puerto Ricans in the United States—their profile, problems, and aspirations. Puerto Rico is no longer a Caribbean Madagascar waiting to be discovered by American curiosity or scholarship.

It is questionable, however, whether the current American reader knows and understands who Puerto Ricans are as a people, as a historical entity, within the varied ethnic and cultural canvas of the Caribbean. Few realize that Puerto Rico has had a long past as one of the earliest European establishments in the New World, that its evolution is closely linked with the power struggles which have taken place in the Caribbean from the time France and England challenged the Spanish claims to make the region a *Mare Clausum,* a sea closed to outsiders, to the contemporary American concern about Soviet penetration in what the United States has considered its own "backyard." Others have thought that while Puerto Rico as a colony of Spain had a past, little of interest happened before 1898. The contours of Puerto Rican history have been blurred as a result. To this lack of perspective should be added the almost total absence of references to Puerto Rico in American history books. Beyond the fact that the island was ceded to the United States by Spain in the Treaty of Paris of 1898, the average textbook hardly mentions the social, political, and cultural factors that have shaped Puerto Rico and given it a distinctive character. The island, to most North Americans, is but a geographical expression or a geopolitical fact. In view of the nation's continental and world concerns, Puerto Rico looks like a minute speck, a Caribbean outpost, and a link in a strategic chain forging the rise of U.S. globalism.

A prime consideration of this book is to establish a more balanced perspective of what Puerto Rico constitutes as a people, a cultural nationality, or a distinctive Caribbean entity. It is not a book written by Puerto Ricans for Puerto Ricans, but by Puerto Ricans who wish to bring their outlooks and scholarship to the attention of the reader in the United States. The historians here represented have worked long and hard with the substance of Puerto Rican history, have taught courses on it for many years, or gone into archives and private collections in search of new materials on the island's social, institutional, and cultural evolution. Rather than a single author, it was thought convenient to bring together, in essay form, the gist of many research efforts, providing a variety of views on the more than four centuries of Puerto Rican history. Each author is, of course, responsible for his or her interpretation, and the views here expressed have been highly respected by the editor. But at the same time, there has been broad consensus on the contents of this book and the approach to the subject.

It has been agreed, for instance, that while the North American reader may naturally wish to learn about the U.S. role in the island since 1898, proper attention should be given to the preceding era, which shaped to a very high degree the culture, the institutions, and the mores of the people. In this sense, the pre-1898 period is no mere prologue; it is rather the key to understanding the roots of the folk culture; the attachment to the Spanish language; the origins of an ethnically mixed society; the literary and artistic expressions and the modalities of thought and feeling that, in spite of many dramatic social changes, are at the bottom of the Puerto Rican personality. That Puerto Rico has been profoundly affected by American ways, values, and influences there is no doubt. But the pull of a long past has also to be realized. 1898 was not simply a *tabula rasa,* in spite of the efforts then undertaken at what President William McKinley called "benevolent assimilation." The crucial cultural forms prevailed, including the language, for by 1898 a people composed of nearly one million inhabitants of variegated ethnic extraction had already emerged with a budding sense of its identity. Puerto Rico in 1898 had not only a population density but a historical density as well.

The events of 1898 form a watershed between two eras in the island. The arrangement of the material in this book conveys that conviction. There are two main divisions. The first, "The Emergence of a People," deals with the formative centuries. There is a bird's eye view of the Indian inheritance, based on the findings of the new Puerto Rican school of archaeologists, headed by Professor Ricardo Alegría. The succeeding periods, involving the arrival of the Spanish type of western civilization, are summarized in two key chapters by Professor Aida Caro Costas, who has labored in the Spanish archives, especially those at the Archivo General de Indias in Seville, and has written several books and articles on the institutional development, particularly at the municipal level. She has also emphasized the critical strategic role Puerto Rico began to play as a defensive outpost of the Spanish empire in the first half of the sixteenth century. The basic historical dichotomy, the clash between the strategic demands and the gradual and silent growth of an ethnically diversified human community are highlighted in Dr. Caro Costas's contribution.

In the eighteenth century, the West Indies, particularly the French and British settlements, gained a significance beyond their geographical limitations. These islands and keys were bitterly contested and stubbornly held. European wars originated in clashes taking place in the Caribbean. Saint Domingue, later known as Haiti, became the richest sugar colony in the world. British West Indian planters were an influential power elite in London. By the end of the century, after Saint Domingue collapsed in a revolutionary maelstrom, Cuba became the great sugar magnet. Puerto Rico followed suit, on a much more limited scale, and entered into a new phase as a plantation economy, while, politically, it became a haven for royalists and pro-Spanish elements.

Professors Arturo Santana and Luis González Vales have analyzed the impact of the Atlantic revolutions on Puerto Rico. Both writers have stressed the changes brought about in colonial administration and trade by the Spanish Enlightenment and particularly by anarchical, chaotic conditions in the Caribbean as a result of the revolutionary struggles and the old powers' ambitions in the area. The advent of the United States as a young nation committed to aggressive trade and Caribbean political hegemony is also taken into account, but considerable space is devoted to the Puerto Rican struggle for self-determination in the light of Spanish colonial policies and attitudes. Since colonialism has been a predominant element in the island's history, with key decisions on the island's development and way of life taken by a remote metropolis, the political and cultural struggles have been highlighted against the socioeconomic background and the prevailing colonial policies.

The second division of the book deals with the twentieth century. Here two main aspects are stressed: first, the complex colonial or dependent relationship with the United States, especially as it influenced not only material events but a whole range of values and attitudes; and second, the evolution of Puerto Rico's cultural profile, including the literary and artistic traditions, *vis-à-vis* the pressure for cultural absorption.

The editor, Professor Arturo Morales Carrión, has devoted considerable space to explaining the nature and course of American policies regarding the island, the strategic interest behind its acquisition, and the framing of a colonial tutelage, influenced by the ideas of the time and British imperial traditions. The clashes with the native political elite are explained against a socioeconomic backdrop, as Puerto Rico was subject to an intense expansion of the sugar industry by American corporate capitalism.

The serious economic and political plight of the 1930s is analyzed, as well as the Puerto Rican response in the postwar period, when a profound social, economic, and political transformation took place. The story covers what may be considered the Luis Muñoz Marín era, in view of the towering impact of his political personality in the island's history. The consensus of values and interests developed at that time (1940–1968) as a foundation of economic and political action is brought into focus, as well as the factors, both internal and external, which gradually undermined it. This section ends with a look into the present Puerto Rican crisis and the trend towards increased polarization and confrontation, both in relations with the United States and in the economic and social cleavages.

A full section, written by the well known critic, Professor María Teresa Babín, is devoted to Puerto Rico's cultural expression, its folk traditions, its art and literature. This essay takes into account the many trends influencing both the popular culture and the culture of the elite, from the Indian heritage to the present. It is not only concerned with Puerto Rican creativity within the island, but also embraces the artistic and literary expression of mainland Puerto Ricans, growing out of their struggles as a minority, suffering in many areas from discrimination and prejudice.

The scope of this book is vast and complex, for over the centuries the trials of Puerto Ricans have been many. An effort has been made to provide a coherent picture, although many facets have been left out, particularly social history. Each author, while holding to his or her personal views, has tried to be fair in the handling of the historical material, eschewing purely ideological polemics. There is room in historical writing for divergent interpretations. But together with a respect for fact, there has to be a sense of fairness in judging personalities and events and the interplay of conflicting cultural and attitudinal values.

This has to be the case in writing about Puerto Rico for American audiences. Understanding the island and its people involves transcending the confines of American nationalism in an effort at empathy and insight. The reader is cordially invited to this exercise. Only through mutual understanding and respect will the United States and Puerto Rico face with hope and creativity the many baffling and thorny issues of the present.

The authors are particularly grateful to the American Association for State and Local History for their interest in publishing this book, which emphasizes the distinctiveness of Puerto Rican history within the Caribbean and New World setting, and the long political and cultural odyssey of its people.

Arturo Morales Carrión

Part One

THE EMERGENCE OF A PEOPLE

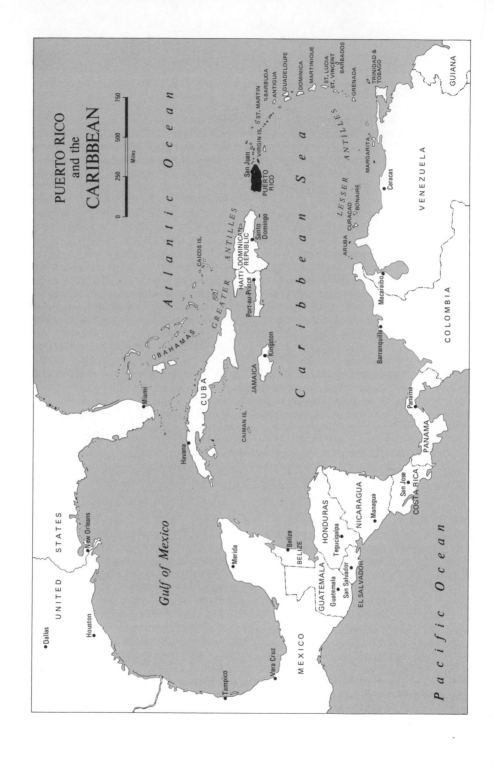

PUERTO RICO
and the
CARIBBEAN

0   250   500   750
Miles

Atlantic Ocean

UNITED STATES

•Dallas

Houston •

New Orleans •

Miami •

Gulf of Mexico

MEXICO

Tampico •

Vera Cruz •

Merida •

Havana •

CUBA

BAHAMAS

CAICOS IS.

GREATER ANTILLES

CAIMAN IS.

JAMAICA

Kingston •

HAITI
Port-au-Prince •

DOMINICAN
REPUBLIC

Santo
Domingo •

PUERTO
RICO

San Juan •

VIRGIN IS.
ST. MARTIN
ST. MARTIN

BARBUDA
ANTIGUA

GUADELOUPE

DOMINICA

MARTINIQUE

ST. LUCIA
ST. VINCENT
BARBADOS

GRENADA

TRINIDAD &
TOBAGO

Caribbean Sea

LESSER ANTILLES

MARGARITA

GUIANA

BELIZE

Belize •

GUATEMALA

Guatemala •

San Salvador •

EL SALVADOR

HONDURAS

Tegucigalpa •

NICARAGUA

Managua •

San Jose •

COSTA RICA

PANAMA

Panama •

ARUBA

CURACAO

BONAIRE

Maracaibo •

Barranquilla •

Caracas •

VENEZUELA

COLOMBIA

Pacific Ocean

1

An Island Is Settled

Arturo Morales Carrión

The Indian heritage of Puerto Rico is closely connected with the ethnic history of the pre-Columbian West Indies. It has left its marks in the rich historic sources of the Spanish chronicles and accounts of the island's discovery and conquest, now supplemented by intense archaeological work. New evidence in this field is constantly being uncovered.

Radiocarbon dating has enabled scholars to establish a tentative chronology of man's first presence in Puerto Rico. The earliest archaeological remains so far discovered are at a large limestone cave near Loíza Aldea, close to the northeast coast. This cave, known locally as Cueva María de la Cruz, was excavated by the Puerto Rican archaeologist Ricardo Alegría in 1948. It yielded artifacts related to a preceramic culture which was estimated to go back to the first century A.D. For nearly 2,000 years, therefore, man has inhabited the island.

This early migration is related to the Archaic culture of the West Indies, which persisted throughout the centuries and even left some vestiges in the ethnohistoric accounts of the early years of colonization, although no reference is found in the Spanish chronicles on Puerto Rico. As revealed by archaeology, this Indian tradition was noted for its absence of agriculture and pottery; its seminomadic living; its use of caves for shelter and burial; and its crude artifacts made of conch shells or stones. Some of these are pebble choppers of striking simplicity.

The Archaic Indians relied on hunting and fishing for their food; their settlements were usually near the seashore and the mangrove areas. Their artifacts were rudimentary and utilitarian. Evidence found in other

3

places suggests the possibility that they went from Florida to Cuba and from Cuba began a migration to the other islands of the West Indian chain, reaching as far as Antigua, although no evidence has been found of their presence in Jamaica. In Puerto Rico, at least three sites are known to be related to the Archaic tradition. These Indians also seem to have inhabited the island of Vieques, to the east. Further archaeological excavations may reveal more data on the original settlers, whose simple nomadic life was adjusted to the island's tropical habitat.

Of much greater significance in Puerto Rico's pre-Columbian period is the Arawak cultural tradition. It is derived from the migratory movements which, starting in the Orinoco basin, sailed to the islands adjacent to the Venezuelan mainland and from there continued, by skillful navigation, to explore and settle the whole West Indian chain.

These Indians probably moved from the Venezuelan mainland into the archipelago during the first centuries after Christ. There were other migratory waves that left their imprint on the archaeological map of the islands.

The first wave to reach Puerto Rico, according to the radiocarbon dates, was that of the Igneris or *Saladoids*. They had already settled in Loíza, on the north coast, around 120 A.D., and are known for their pottery making. They used beautiful and exotic designs, finely polishing their vases and dishes and painting them with red and white colors. Their stone artifacts, however, are few: they were mostly petaloid or rectangular hammerstones.

Little is known of the Igneris' social organization. They relied mostly on hunting and fishing and fed on crabs and shells. They seem to have settled in Puerto Rico until the sixth century A.D. Archaeological opinion is divided as to their fate. While some archaeologists think that the Igneris gradually changed their cultural pattern into what is called Ostionoid culture, others believe that a new migration from South America conquered the Igneri tribe and took over some of their cultural traits. But no other cultural tribe excelled, as the Igneris did, in ceramics.

As the art of pottery making declined, becoming more coarse and utilitarian, new skills were developed in handling stones. The Ostionoids learned how to polish and use them as axes and grinders and as tribal amulets. These Indians moved into the interior of Puerto Rico, carrying with them their stone and shell artifacts.

They exhibited a rising concern for religious ceremonies and objects. Small three-pointed idols or *cemíes,* made of shell or stone, are found in their archaeological remains. The Ostionoids made a distinctive contribution to the Indian heritage of Puerto Rico by developing their first ceremonial courts, where the earliest ball games were played and the first *areytos* or ceremonial rites were sung and danced.

By 1000 A.D., the Ostionoids had evolved a more complex social and material organization. From then on, they would be more associated with the *Taíno* culture—the culture found by the Spaniards when they discovered America in 1492.

The *Taínos* spread throughout the West Indies, but they reached their maximum cultural development at Santo Domingo and Puerto Rico. They had certain outstanding traits including a common universal language; the development of agriculture as well as hunting and fishing; the erection of villages; and a prevailing social organization based on the *cacique* or chieftain. The *cacique* ruled over the higher class of *nitaínos* and the lower class of workers, called *naborias*, and there were regional *caciques*, as well as an insular *cacique* at the top of the social pyramid.

With the passing of time, the *Taínos* developed a religious cosmology, with ceremonial rites which were carefully observed and recorded in the Spanish chronicles. They believed in supernatural deities who inhabited the sky. *Yocahú* was to them the Supreme Maker; *Juracán* was the angry god of the destructive winds. There was an afterlife which demanded that the dead should be buried with their weapons, their utensils, even their favorite wife; for the dead were then to turn into tutelary spirits, worshipped in the form of *cemíes*, or idols made of stone or wood. Through the inhaling of tobacco, the *caciques*, as well as the priests or *behiques* or *bohiques*, communicated with the gods.

The myths, stories, and traditions of the tribes were transmitted in ceremonial dances called *areytos*. Drums, made from hollow trunks, and *maracas* and *güiros*, carved out of gourds, helped to produce the needed accompaniment. The *areytos* were danced at the *batey* or plaza, surrounded by the native thatched huts, called *bohíos*. They were impressive tribal events, feeding the Indian collective memory. Large *bateyes* or courts were used for another activity of socioreligious significance: the ball game, played with a rubberlike ball by two teams, each made up of ten to thirty players. The game was more than a social bond within the Indian tribe. It had a religious meaning connected with fertility rites. As the *Taínos* moved inland they built more and more courts and took their rites, dances, and games to the upper valleys. At Caguanas, in the central mountainous region, they built a most impressive court, marked by rows of great stone blocks or monoliths—a real feat of Indian engineering, which they repeated at Tibes, near Ponce.

A peaceful, sedentary people, the *Taínos* were adept at hunting and agriculture. They were expert canoe makers and good sailors. Familiar with the maritime currents between the myriad islands of the archipelago, they moved easily from one island to another. Women cultivated the land with primitive hoes and learned the techniques of preparing cassava bread from the *yuca* and of harvesting tobacco and a pepper called *ají*. The *caciques* lived in peace but, by the time the Spaniards arrived, their hold on eastern Puerto Rico was being challenged by the Caribs, a new migratory wave from northern South America.

The Caribs were a warlike tribe that, according to the chronicles, practiced ceremonial cannibalism on their victims. They fought with poisoned arrows and raided the island for women whom they took to the Lesser Antilles. They posed a real threat to the *Taínos* by the end of the fifteenth century, and were to challenge with bravery and ferocity the Spanish domination of Puerto Rico.

The *Taínos* called the island *Boriquén*—the land of the brave lord. Many of the island's names have remained to this day as part of the Indian heritage: Humacao, Caguas, Mayagüez, Utuado. Although the Indians lost not only their possessions but their ethnic cohesion as a result of the Spanish conquest and colonization, the peasantry that came after them inherited their legacy. The *bohíos*, the *hamaca* or hammock, the *maracas*, the *güiros*, the cassava bread, the *ají*, the myths, the many words that dealt with aspects of everyday life, passed into the Spanish period. This heritage was and is a significant imprint on the Puerto Rican culture.

This was the neolithic Indian world that Christopher Columbus found on November 19, 1493, on his second momentous voyage, in the island he then called San Juan Bautista. Several years were to elapse before colonization was attempted. A permanent foothold was finally established in 1508, when Juan Ponce de León led a group of settlers from Hispaniola, and after initial friendly contacts with the island *cacique*, Agueybaná, founded the town of Caparra not far from the site of the present capital, San Juan.

As in other parts of the West Indies, the early Spanish colonizing thrust led to a period of great social turmoil. It was evident in the internal squabbles among the settlers, the struggle for power and authority, the frantic search for gold, the subjection of the Indians, and the evangelizing fervor of priests and missionaries.

The Spaniards had to endure the hardships of a sudden adaptation

First encounter between Europeans and Indians as depicted by Theodore de Bry.

to the American tropics. It was, of course, even worse for the Indians, who now became a subject labor force. In 1511 they rebelled, but their stone axes were no match for Spanish firearms. The rebellion was promptly quelled by Ponce de León, and the proud *Taínos* were forced to surrender or flee. Some joined the Caribs, who now challenged Spanish attempts to colonize the east coast. It was, however, a lost cause. Whatever was left of the aborigines gradually merged with the native inhabitants; this ethnic heterogeneity eventually gave a peculiar flavor to the folk heritage. Some Indian villages remained in the social mosaic until the late eighteenth century. But the Indian role as a laborer was soon taken over by the Africans, who were brought by the early settlers and later by the slave traders.

By 1521, the Indian *Boriquén* had become another Spanish settlement in an expanding empire. It was no longer governed by Ponce de León, who had left to discover Florida in 1512. After returning to Caparra, he made a second trip to the mainland where he was mortally wounded in a skirmish with the Indians, and died in Havana in 1521. Against Ponce de León's opposition, Caparra had been transferred to an islet at the entrance of a spacious bay, a fine natural port. The city's name became Puerto Rico and it became a center of the Spanish colonizing venture. In time, the port came to be called San Juan and the island Puerto Rico. As the Spanish empire in the New World grew, and faced rivals and foes, Puerto Rico's strategic location overshadowed its economic significance. For the growing empire, Puerto Rico was to become a Caribbean "Christian Rhodes" a bulwark ready to repel intruders and infidels into the new Spanish *Mare Nostrum;* and, as the crown officials stated, "the strongest foothold of Spain in America."

2
The Outpost of Empire

Aida R. Caro Costas

The sixteenth century saw Spain become the leading European power of its day. The discovery of the New World by Christopher Columbus and other discoveries by intrepid Spanish explorers set off a tremendous overseas expansion, which eventually became the mighty Spanish empire. The power of the Catholic Church stood firmly behind the gigantic enterprise. In May 1493 Pope Alexander VI bestowed upon the Catholic Kings and their heirs the exclusive jurisdiction, authority, and absolute rights over the discovered lands and those still to be discovered. The papal bull clearly prohibited all persons "regardless of rank, estate, degree, order or condition" from entering those lands without a special license granted by the kings.

The concessions Spain received from the Pope disrupted the political and economic balance of the Old World. Other nations, especially France and England, soon expressed their resentment. The French monarch Francis I scornfully demanded to be shown the "will of Father Adam leaving all the world to Spain and Portugal." Action followed. France and England were not only determined to seek footholds in the New World but to challenge Spain's commercial exclusivism in the Indies and to undermine the power of Castile. Bold sea rovers preying upon Spanish ships and attacks on budding towns along the coasts became the order of the day. In time widespread smuggling also struck at the Spanish trade monopoly in the New World.

The attention of Spain's rival nations focused on the West Indian archipelago, where the Castilian colonizing process began and from which

9

the overseas expansion was further extended. That remote region felt the first foreign blows in the struggle for hegemony in Europe. Puerto Rico's frontier location gave it a significant role in the Spanish defensive system. Caribs, Frenchmen, and Englishmen were the islanders' three enemies in the sixteenth century.

Puerto Rico: Key to the Indies

As this struggle for power in Europe intensified, pirates and privateers intercepted Spanish vessels traveling to or from the Indies, and plans were made to plunder Spain's possessions in the New World. Since Puerto Rico was the "key to the Indies," the first port of call for all Spanish ships heading toward the newly discovered islands, orders were issued in 1522 for its defense. This action was prompted by reports that a French force of three warships and seven hundred troops was being prepared to attack Puerto Rico and the rest of the Greater Antilles. Though this expedition never reached the island, its anticipation moved local authorities to order the construction of San Juan's first defenses, a bulwark at the "point of entry to the port." Started and finished in 1522, the wooden bulwark was hardly effective. Years later another defensive structure was built, this time by the descendants of Juan Ponce de León. They framed the wooden family house as a "defensive cube" in order to provide shelter to city dwellers in case of attack. Toward 1530 this house, better known as *Casa Blanca,* was replaced by a stone building; but even this could not be considered adequate defense for San Juan.

In spite of its importance as a key to the Indies, Puerto Rico in 1530 still had no effective fortifications. Spain delayed action in spite of urgent requests in 1529 and 1530 by Puerto Rican authorities, who reported that "the island's defenseless conditions caused the people to emigrate." Not until 1532 was construction of a fortress in the interior of San Juan Bay begun; the work was completed in 1540. This fortress was known as *Santa Catalina* or *La Fortaleza.* Its location, however, was not well chosen—a "poor place" according to Gonzalo Fernández de Oviedo, the early Spanish historian of the Indies. Thus, shortly before it was finished, the Crown officers and the settlers of San Juan requested a fort to be built at the entrance to the harbor. Construction began in the 1540s on a rocky promontory overlooking the entrance to the bay. *El Morro,* as this fort was named, received special attention during the sixteenth century. These two fortifications, gradually improved in the decades to follow with soldiers, guns, ammunition, artillery, and gunpower, augmented the defensive capacity of San Juan.

But, while the capital was protected, the rest of the island was completely defenseless. French privateers took advantage of this weakness. The *Villa de San Germán,* founded on the west coast as the second center of colonization, became a frequent target for the Frenchmen. Though the Frenchmen were beaten off by courageous resistance, the *Villa* could not escape plundering and devastation. These bitter experiences account for its many changes of site until it was finally established in 1573 on its present site of *Lomas* (hills) in the southwestern part of Puerto Rico. In spite of these raids, except for a fortress begun in San Germán in 1540 but left unfinished in 1542, no provision was made for the protection of the coast.

Ironically, while the Crown ignored the need for coastal fortifications in Puerto Rico it was so deeply concerned with the defense of the Florida coast that in 1565 a royal decree ordered the Governor of Puerto Rico to assist Pedro Menéndez de Avilés, en route to Florida by way of Puerto Rico, with fifty men, twenty horses, artillery, and a vessel. In this way the island contributed to the foundation of San Agustín in Florida.

The French assaults on San Germán marked the beginning of foreign aggression on Puerto Rico. The role played by French corsairs, however, lessened toward the 1570s. France's internal religious strife forced her to give up commercial and territorial pretensions within the Spanish empire in America. Yet Frenchmen continued to engage in smuggling and exchange of local products such as cattle and hides for slaves.

The end of the French depredations did not assure the island's peace during the ensuing decades. By the time France ceased to be a feared enemy, Spain was already facing the English menace. Queen Elizabeth's sea dogs defied Spanish commercial exclusivism in the Indies and engaged in "aggressive commerce" in the Caribbean. John Hawkins' voyages of 1563, 1564–1565 and 1567–1568 are clear examples of such activities, which introduced slaves and manufactured goods to the islands. English sea rovers also intercepted Spanish vessels traveling to or from the Indies. Private reprisals opened the path to hostile relations between Spain and England, leading to war in 1585. Queen Elizabeth's ambitious plan to destroy Spanish power in America, which would finally entail the fall of Spain as a first-rank power in Europe, was embodied in Francis Drake's "Indies voyage" of 1586. The outcome of this enterprise was

tremendous. The fort of San Agustín in Florida was destroyed; Santo
Domingo and Cartagena were devastated; and local authorities and
inhabitants underwent the humiliation of having to ransom their cities.
The defeat of the *Armada Invencible* in 1588 posed a grave problem for
Spain in protecting her American domains. Since 1586, the Council of
the Indies in Spain had realized the need for a broad defensive plan for
the Caribbean area, especially including fortifications in vital areas. To
this effect a commission was given to Field Marshal Juan de Tejeda and
military engineer Bautista Antonelli. The defeat of the Armada made
this plan even more essential. The rise of England as a maritime power
increased the danger of further assaults on Spanish commerce and strategic possessions in the New World.

The Presidio, the Captaincy General, and the Situado

Needless to say that under such expectations, Puerto Rico, as the key
to the Indies, deserved special attention from the Crown. Even before
the war broke out between Spain and England and the Armada was
defeated, important military reforms were under way on the island.
Within the defensive scheme of America, Puerto Rico was considered a
presidio; that is, a place whose strategic location demanded skillful fortification, a strong garrison, and the needed artillery. These would enable
it to repel any attack, thus assuring not only the protection of the island,
but of the rest of the West Indies and of the continent as well.

However, actual military conditions were depressing. For defenses
the island depended upon two very poorly garrisoned fortifications: *La
Fortaleza* and *El Morro.* The defense of both was entrusted to a small
garrison: fifty soldiers in want of guns, ammunition, and artillery, and
islanders who volunteered as guardsmen. The maintenance of these soldiers was shared by the royal treasury of the island and, to a great extent,
by its inhabitants. However, the extreme poverty of the settlers and the
meager income of the treasury more than once prevented the soldiers
from receiving the money needed for their own support. The inadequate fortifications and lack of soldiers and funds to support them made
it impossible for the island to perform as a *presidio.*

Aware of this situation, the crown and the governors acted to improve
the defensive conditions of the island between 1580 and 1595. The title
of captain general as the leading military officer in Puerto Rico was created in 1580 and thereafter conferred upon the governor. Increased

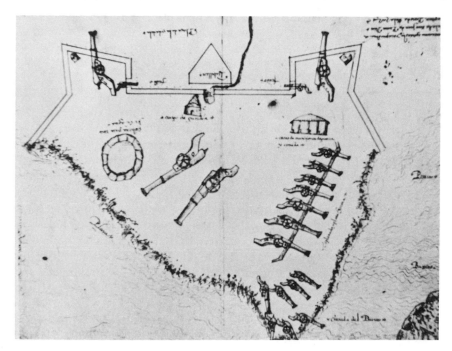

Plan of El Morro *fortress* (*1591*).

military powers were given to the then Governor Diego Menéndez de
Valdés in 1583. Under his strong military and civil leadership (1583–
1593), new fortifications were constructed in vulnerable areas. Outstanding among them were the bulwarks of *El Boquerón* in the eastern
part of San Juan, and *Santa Elena,* which was located between *El Morro*
and *La Fortaleza.* Some changes were made in *La Fortaleza* to provide
adequate shelter for the soldiers. The *Puente de los Soldados,* a land bridge
known today as *Puente de San Antonio,* was also strengthened.

The most impressive defensive work started during Menéndez's term
of office was the construction of a new fort on the site of *El Morro,* following plans that had been drawn between 1588 and 1589 by the military engineer Bautista Antonelli and Field Marshal Juan de Tejeda. In
the opinion of Governor-Captain General Menéndez de Valdés,
expressed in a letter dated November 20, 1590 and addressed to the
Council of the Indies, this strong fort

standeth in a good situation, and in a convenient place on a high mount which doeth lye upon the entering in of the harbour . . . leaving in the fort as much space as wil containe 3,000 persons without joyning thereunto any part of the coast . . . when it is ended will be the strongest that his majestie hath in all the Indies. And now the people of the country sleepe in security. For commonly before the Englishmen would come and beard us to the havens mouth.

Menéndez de Valdés's prediction eventually came true. The city depended for its defense upon this solid and complex structure.

Intimately related to these defensive improvements, other measures were adopted to assure the island's effectiveness as a *presidio*. Artillery, ammunition, and guns were sent. The garrison was increased from fifty to 209 soldiers, whose salaries and expenses for food, clothes, medicines, and ammunition were paid by the *Situado,* a sum the king ordered in 1582 to be sent annually from the royal treasury of New Spain, now Mexico. The first *Situado,* however, reached the island in 1587: coin shortage, lack of a ship to transport it, and fear of piratical seizures accounted for this delay. Originally, the amount set for the *Situado* was enough to cover salaries and expenses for fifty soldiers; however, whenever the garrison was increased the sum was raised. The *Situado,* which from 1643 to 1683 was to be sent from the Peruvian treasury instead of from New Spain, was seldom received. Thus the captains general and the royal officers on the island not only had to borrow money from well-to-do citizens, but to issue credit notes to pay the soldiers.

A Coveted Island: English and Dutch Attacks

Menéndez de Valdés's remark in 1590 makes it clear that at that time the English were the island's most dreaded enemies. In previous years the English had sporadically engaged in interloping trade with the islanders, but beginning in 1583 events led to growing suspicion of England's ill designs toward Puerto Rico. In that year Englishmen reconnoitered on the island's southwestern coast; they claimed they were looking for victuals. Two years later, under the same pretext, Sir Richard Grenville's expedition bound for Virginia landed at Mosquito Bay on the southern coast and built a fort which they burned shortly afterwards before sailing away. In 1586, when England and Spain were already at war, Sir Francis Drake's raids in Santo Domingo, Cartagena, and Florida led the islanders to fear that the same fate would eventually befall Puerto Rico. This fear grew as news reached the island that a powerful English fleet was being organized to attack Spain's overseas domains.

In 1587 Sir Francis Drake and John Hawkins had submitted to Queen Elizabeth a daring plan intended "entirely to ruin the Spaniards." In 1593 Drake was still insisting on an attack upon the West Indies, but the queen had not yet made up her mind. She feared that while the fleet was engaged in the West Indies, the Spaniards would invade England or Ireland. In 1595, upon learning that a highly prized treasure (two million ducats' worth of gold and silver) had been deposited in *La Fortaleza* by the damaged flagship of a Spanish fleet, the queen's vacillation came to an end. A fleet, commanded by Drake and Hawkins and made up of six royal ships, twenty-one other vessels of different sizes, and 4500 men, was sent toward Puerto Rico. It was the declared intention of both admirals to take the island "with all speed."

The English fleet sailed from Plymouth on August 28, 1595, and made its way to the Canaries. Having failed to take Gran Canaria, it headed toward the West Indies. At Guadeloupe another unfortunate experience befell it: the bark *Francis* was captured and sunk by five Spanish frigates bound for Puerto Rico to transport the treasure in *La Fortaleza* to Spain. These incidents were but the prelude to more trouble the English expedition had to face before reaching the island.

The English intended to take Puerto Rico "with all speed." This, of course, could only be accomplished if the island were poorly defended. To the surprise of the Englishmen, the island's defenses were in good condition, and its inhabitants determined to repel any aggression. First, there had been the improvements in the defenses dating back to the governorship of Menéndez de Valdés. His successor, Pedro Suárez, having learned of a possible English attack from King Philip II and received more immediate news from Admiral Pedro Tello de Guzmán, the commander of the five Spanish frigates, worked out a plan to repel the attack.

To prevent Drake's entrance into the harbor, the dismasted flagship and another vessel were sunk, while the five frigates remained anchored behind them. The defense of the port was entrusted to Tello de Guzmán. Governor Suárez and General Pardo de Osorio strengthened the land defenses. Seventy pieces of artillery were planted in exposed or strategic areas. The island defenders, 750 Puerto Rican and Spanish fighting men and 800 Spanish seamen, were distributed on shore and inside the forts. The frigates had at least 300 men on board. All the women, children, and persons unable to participate were sent into the woods. With their religious fervor stirred up by Bishop Antonio Calderón, together with the sound defensive measures, the defenders looked anxiously toward the big moment to come.

The wait was not long. Nine days after the arrival of the five Spanish frigates with the news about the proximity of the English fleet, the ships were sighted at daybreak on November 22. Immediately the call to arms sounded and everybody ran to his post "joyfully and willingly to fight." Much to the disappointment of the English, who on that day had already suffered a great blow with John Hawkins' death, it became clear that their plan to take the city rapidly could not work. The alertness of the defenders was shown by the fact that as soon as an English launch approached the front of *El Boquerón* it was "hailed" by a cannon shot. After this hot reception, on the same afternoon, the whole fleet anchored eastward of the city, in front of the forts known as *Caleta del Cabrón* and *El Morrillo* from which it was subjected to strong bombardment. Twenty-eight great shots were fired; one reached Drake's cabin while he was at supper, "stroke the stoole from under him," and mortally injured Sir Nicholas Clifford and Master Brown. Unable to land his forces and aware of the aggressiveness of the city defenders, Drake looked for a position out of range of the artillery on the forts. He thus moved to the *Isla de Cabra,* at the bay entrance, in the late afternoon; from there the following night (November 23), he led an attack against the harbor. With twenty-five launches, each carrying fifty to sixty men and benefiting from the darkness, the English tried to force their entry into the harbor and set fire to the frigates. For an hour the fight went on between the men on board the frigates and the English who, at the same time, had to endure a heavy fire from the forts of *El Morro* and *Santa Elena.* Both English and Spanish documentary sources describe the fight as "resolute," "hard," and "hot." Victory went to the Spanish. One frigate was completely burned, forty men killed, some others were wounded and a few made prisoners. The English suffered heavier losses, with nine or ten launches destroyed and more than four hundred dead and wounded.

Having failed to take the city or to get the treasure deposited in *La Fortaleza,* Sir Francis Drake wandered for some days in the vicinity of the harbor and finally moved his fleet to the western part of the island near Aguada. There he secured meat, water, and wood and finally sailed away early in December.

It was believed that after such a defeat and the deaths of Hawkins in November and of Drake in late January 1595, England would attempt no further attack on the island. However these events did not change the English plan for Puerto Rico. England continued to covet the island and, in the following years, worked out a careful secret plan of attack. Queen Elizabeth did not hesitate in planning the assault. The man to undertake this enterprise was the experienced seaman George Clifford, third Earl of Cumberland.

In Puerto Rico the main concern was defensive forces and structures. At the request of both insular and municipal authorities, the king increased the garrison from 209 to 409 soldiers by 1596. The *Situado* provided additional funds to continue work at *El Morro*. These improvements in the city defenses suffered a setback when an epidemic killed many of the soldiers, slaves, and citizens who were building the defensive works. The significant losses in the military and civilian population reduced the number of defenders available for the rest of the military posts. Thus, the city faced a critical situation in 1598, when the English attack was made.

On Tuesday, June 16, a powerful English fleet approached the eastern coastline of San Juan. On the same day Cumberland ordered the landing after exhorting his men to be courageous, "assuring your selves you have the maydenhead of Puerto Rico and so possesse the keyes of all the Indies." The landing place, a beach four leagues from the city, had no defenses at all; thus the thousand men in the party encountered no difficulty whatsoever. Marching along the sea side while the fleet covered their advance, Cumberland's men reached the Soldier's Bridge, which connected the mainland to the islet where the city stood, only to find that the bridge had been destroyed. Beyond was a barricaded gate and the *Boquerón* bulwark with six pieces of artillery, blocking the way to the islet. A handful of natives, together with a few Spanish soldiers, defended this vital area where, for the first time, both forces met. A courageous fight took place as the English tried to force their way through the gate and the defenders of the fort repelled the assault and made them retreat. Doctor Layfield, the earl's chaplain, wrote, "For though the assailants left no way in the world unattempted, yet no way could they finde to enter the Gate." Cumberland "was (by the stumbling of him that fore his Forget) overthrowne even to the danger of drowning; for his armour so overburdened him" and it was the sergeant major who got him "from under the water." Later Sir John Berkeley, Cumberland's second officer, also nearly drowned.

After this assault, in which he lost two lieutenants and about fifty soldiers dead or wounded, on the next day, June 17, Cumberland landed two hundred pikes and fifty musketeers on the *Salemas* beach at an unguarded point between the *Escambrón* and the *Boquerón* bulwark. Outnumbered by the English, the defenders of the fort were faced with a difficult situation, since the enemy was now positioned behind and in front of the bulwark. After a short resistance, the defenders gave up and the English proceeded to San Juan.

At daybreak on June 18, Cumberland's forces reached the city, which was completely desolate. Women, children, and the elderly had sought refuge in the interior of the island. The able men, Puerto Rican and Spanish, soldiers, and officials (including the former governor, Pedro Suárez, and the current governor and captain general, Antonio Mosquera) quartered themselves in *El Morro*. In all, about four hundred men were inside. Cumberland immediately demanded the deliverance of the fort. On Governor Mosquera's refusal Cumberland laid siege. The defenders resisted courageously but as the days went on could not withstand the strong English offensive. Within the fort famine, shortage of ammunition, and the almost continuous bombardment exhausted their endurance. On July 1, after fifteen days of resistance, Governor Mosquera surrendered *El Morro*. English flags were immediately flown and the defenders were imprisoned in *La Fortaleza*. Mosquera and some soldiers escaped with the help of an island mestizo, Juan Pérez, but Suárez and the remaining defenders of *El Morro* were sent to Jamaica.

With the capitulation of *El Morro*, Puerto Rico came under English jurisdiction. Cumberland intended to keep it at all costs, since he was convinced that the island was "the very key of the West Indies which locketh and shutteth all the gold and silver in the continent of America and Brasilia." Yet he did not succeed in making Puerto Rico a permanent English colony. Nature and the islanders prevented it. Many English soldiers were lost during the assaults on the *Boquerón* bulwark and *El Morro*. Afterwards, the same epidemic that had recently ravaged the inhabitants also hit the English. It soon claimed more than four hundred lives and weakened the remaining forces. The situation was worsened by the hostility of the inhabitants, who defied the earl's orders and harrassed the English in the countryside. Fights occurred, men were killed, and finally Cumberland decided to leave the island. His hurt pride, however, would not allow him to depart without doing all the harm he could. He burned two sugar plantations and most of the houses in the city and its surroundings, destroyed the crops, asked for a ransom (which he never got) and finally, upon leaving on August 27, took with him a strange assortment of loot: two thousand slaves, all the bells from the churches, an organ, a marble window torn from a private house, and "All the Hides therefore, and Ginger and Sugar which either was alreadie . . . All the munition in the Towne, all the Ordnance . . . which amounted in all and of all sorts very neere the full number of fourscore coast peeces, some of them the goodliest that ever I [Doctor Layfield] saw." This brief but destructive English occupation—65 days in all–came to an end on September 5 when Sir John Berkeley, just recovering from the epidemic and aware of the precarious situation of the English, followed Cumberland and left the island.

For a second time England had failed to get the outpost so desired for strategic reasons. This failure was a blow to the overseas expansion within the Spanish dominions as planned by Queen Elizabeth. Her death in March 1603 brought the accession of a King James I, who made peace with Spain. Puerto Rico experienced a respite from English aggressions. However, Cumberland's successful attack clearly demonstrated that the island still needed defenses and stern military discipline. The Spanish authorities on the mainland and in Puerto Rico dealt with the problems of defense during the early decades of the seventeenth century. King Philip III and the Council of the Indies provided funds to continue the fortifications at *El Morro,* to build new defenses such as *El Boquerón* on the eastern part of the islet, the fort *San Juan de la Cruz* or *El Cañuelo* across the bay and opposite *El Morro;* and to reinforce the Soldier's or San Antonio Bridge. Ammunition, artillery, and guns of all sorts were gradually assembled between 1600 and 1625, and efforts were made to provide an adequate garrison.

In spite of all these efforts, the island sporadically faced shortages of soldiers. Recruiting men in Spain to volunteer for service in Puerto Rico was not easy. In addition, once the men reached the island there was no assurance that they would remain, for desertions were frequent. Tropical diseases and epidemics in 1602, 1608, and 1609 also significantly reduced the defensive forces, leaving the island thinly garrisoned during some years.

In 1625, defensive improvements in *El Morro* were still under way and local authorities were worried about pirate attacks on Spanish vessels, particularly on those conducting the *Situado,* and illicit trading in the Caribbean. Now Puerto Rico also had to face the growing ambition of Holland. The Dutch merchants, organized in small and large trading companies under franchises and privileges given by the Estates General, had developed a very aggressive policy toward the Spanish possessions in which commercial interest and the desire to gain a foothold in the New World combined to undermine Spanish rule over America. These factors must be considered in order to understand the Dutch attack launched in 1625 against Puerto Rico by Boudewijn Hendrikszoon, or Balduino Enrico as the Spanish called him, a general in the service of the powerful West India Company.

On September 24, 1625, eight vessels of Balduino Enrico's fleet were sighted. Early in the morning of September 25, the fort *El Cañuelo* was taken. The whole fleet of seventeen ships now menaced the city. Fearing a Dutch landing east of San Juan, the governor-captain general, Juan de Haro, an experienced soldier, quickly took measures to defend the *Boquerón* and *Cambrón* areas, the two most exposed sites along the shore next to the city. However, the Dutch had no intention of landing there. Instead, on September 25, Enrico had the fleet sail boldly into the harbor, "with as much confidence as if they were entering a port in Holland or Zealand." Once the Dutch held that vital area it was almost impossible for the Puerto Rican and Spanish defenders of the city—330 men altogether—to prevent their landing, especially under fire from Dutch artillery. Governor de Haro immediately ordered his forces to retreat to *El Morro*. During September 26 and 27, the enemy landed; on the following days, after reconnoitering the fort's surroundings, the Dutch dug trenches and placed six pieces of cannon at a strategic point known as *El Calvario,* just in front of *El Morro*. A siege was laid. Through heavy cannonading and starvation Enrico intended to force the fort to submit.

But Enrico underestimated the courage of the defenders and the military experience of Governor Juan de Haro. The governor was the leading figure in organizing and directing the resistance at *El Morro*. Rationing the scarce food supply, carefully planning the firing since powder was scanty, and providing for sorties of small groups of soldiers who conducted surprise assaults on the trenches and captured guns and food from the enemy, all helped to withstand the siege. Governor de Haro's refusal to surrender *El Morro* provoked the Dutch into a desperate barrage against the fort and a tightening of the siege. The defenders were even more determined to fight and continued to resist with great courage, even increasing the sorties in which Dutch soldiers were beheaded and equipment and food obtained. Outstanding among these performances was that of Captain Juan de Amézquita who, on October 5, led a group of fifty men to attack the trenches and slash the throats of more than sixty Dutch soldiers including a captain and a sergeant major.

This exploit was followed by a successful surprise night attack that drove the Dutch from *El Cañuelo*. Then news reached the enemy that forces from the interior of the island, mainly from San Germán, were marching toward the city. This forced Enrico to make a critical decision.

In a letter to Governor de Haro dated October 21, Enrico boldly
announced his intention of burning the city if no understanding was
reached. On the same day Enrico received a sternly worded note in which
de Haro stated:

the settlers have enough courage to rebuild their houses, for there is timber in
the mountains and building materials in the land. And here I am today with
people enough in this fortress to wipe out yours; and do not write any more such
letters for I will not reply; and this is what I choose to answer. And concerning
the rest, do as you please.

Making good his threat, on October 22 Enrico burned down the town.
The civil and ecclesiastical archives, Bishop Bernardo de Balbuena's house
and library, by then the most renowned in America, fifty-two wooden

Dutch engraving of San Juan harbor at the time of the Dutch attack (1625).

houses, part of the convent of *Santo Tomás,* and part of *La Fortaleza* were reduced to ashes, while forty-six stone houses were badly damaged. Highly incensed, but still firm in holding *El Morro,* the governor ordered Captain Amézquita to lead a sortie of 150 soldiers against the Dutch. In addition, Captain Andrés Botello was set to organize the incoming countrymen from the interior of the island. Both parties assailed the Dutch in their trenches and forced them to flee in such haste that they threw themselves into the water to reach their vessels. Finally, on October 22, the siege was lifted, although the Dutch did not sail away immediately. Subjected in the following days to almost continuous fire, which greatly harmed the flagship and some other vessels and caused the death of more soldiers, the Dutch fleet finally left in disarray on November 2. They left behind a stranded ship, guns, and pieces of artillery, and numerous dead; two hundred according to the chronicler of Enrico's fleet, or four hundred as noted by the Spanish source. From San Juan the Dutch sailed to Aguada in the western part of the island, where they stayed for about a month to repair their vessels before leaving for the island of Martinique.

A Major Defensive Structure: Circumvallation Walls

The Dutch siege forcibly reminded the Spanish Crown of the need to develop a far-reaching scheme of defensive improvements in Puerto Rico. Although *El Morro* had proved to be the strongest fort in the Indies, as Governor-Captain General Diego Menéndez de Valdés had predicted in 1590, it was very risky to leave the whole defense of the island to one military structure. The growing might of England, France, and Holland was successfully challenging the declining Spanish empire. Their hostile attitude toward her overseas domains and commerce, expressed in assaults, privateering, freebooting, and interloping trade, clearly showed that if Spain wanted to keep her possessions and trade in the Indies she had to provide her colonies with the necessary naval and land defenses. After Enrico's assault on Puerto Rico, the island's pressing need for effective defensive measures was evident. The French, the English, and the Dutch had been swarming into the Lesser Antilles, building up fortifications on their islands. This potential menace to Puerto Rico, of course, generated great concern among its governors and among the islanders, who threatened to leave Puerto Rico if no effective defensive measures were adopted.

King Philip IV considered several plans to improve the defenses of

San Juan. Most of them favored constructing a fort at *La Puntilla,* in the southwestern part of the city, which would make defense of the port much more effective. The king finally chose a plan that comprised the walling of the city. This was not a new idea. Since 1584 the city council of San Juan had proposed such a plan, and during the ensuing decades at least two governors, as well as members of the Spanish War Board, had backed it. Yet priority had been given to the building of forts and bulwarks in exposed areas. Not till 1632–1633 was the project revived by Governor Enrique Enríquez de Sotomayor, and finally approved by the king.

The plan was to surround the city by a line of mounded walls covered by stones held together with mortar. These walls would join bulwarks, and would have openings or gates at intervals. The western part of the wall, or bay section, was started in July 1634. It covered the area from *Caleta de Santa Catalina* to *La Fortaleza.* In this area, about 300 feet north of *La Fortaleza,* the first gate, *Puerta de San Juan,* was constructed by 1635. It still exists. In the years 1636–1638 Governor Iñigo de la Mota continued the work along the southern part, from *La Fortaleza* to *La Marina,* or bay side, where the second gate, *Puerta de San Justo,* was built. Next he extended the wall toward the eastern section of the city to connect with fort *San Cristóbal.* In this area the third and, for the time being, last gate, *Puerta de Santiago,* was built in front of the space that today corresponds to the northeast corner of *Plaza de Colón.* Since it was the only gate to face land—the other two looked to the bay or port—it was commonly known as *Puerta de Tierra* (land gate).

In four years (1634–1638) the impressive walls had been finished on the southern and eastern flanks of the city; they stood seven and a half meters high and about six meters wide. Their completion to the west, from *Caleta de Santa Catalina* to *El Morro,* and to the north, along the rugged coastline from *El Morro* to fort *San Cristóbal,* was not to be achieved until the eighteenth century. This work was included in fortification plans submitted in 1765 to King Charles III by Field Marshal Alejandro O'Reilly and military engineer Tomás O'Daly. These plans, developed between 1765 and 1783, brought the city defenses to their greatest splendor.

The city walls comprised seven bulwarks. They also included the three gates and the existing castle of *El Morro* and *La Fortaleza.* San Juan could rely on these complex defenses to resist any attack. However, there was a weak point. The garrison was too small to man the defenses. After the walling, even though in 1645 King Philip IV stressed the strategic importance of the island by declaring her "front and vanguard of all my Western Indies and, consequently, the most important of them and most coveted by the enemies," the garrison was not increased. The city still had only the assigned 400 professional Spanish soldiers to carry out the greatly augmented defensive tasks. The situation worsened, since for some time during the second half of the seventeenth century the island garrison was incomplete. There were several reasons: Spanish negligence for not sending all the needed soldiers; tropical epidemics, which caused havoc; and late pay since the *Situado* did not come annually and thus motivated many to give up their military career. Some returned to Spain while others escaped to the interior of the island.

As an immediate solution to the shortage of soldiers some governors filled military vacancies with natives, an initiative which the Spanish Crown condemned. In peacetime, only Spanish soldiers and the few natives to whom the king by royal decree had conferred the grace, or *merced,* of holding military posts were to render regular services at the garrison. In the event of an attack, natives voluntarily assisted the defensive force, and performed very delicate tasks with great courage.

Eventually the natives were voluntarily organized into a local militia, better known as the *Milicias Urbanas,* one in each of the existing *Partidos* or territorial districts: San Germán, Arecibo, Aguada, Coamo, Loíza, and Ponce. Under the command of newly created officers, first a *Capitán a Guerra* and afterwards a *Teniente a Guerra,* the militia men or *milicianos* undertook the defense of their home towns and of the city when necessary. They lacked training, pay, uniforms, and even weapons—their arms consisted of *machetes,* wooden sticks, and knives. But the *milicianos'* most valuable assets, as many governors attested, were their love of country, their courage, and their loyalty. In spite of the material limitations, they performed their defensive tasks with excellence and made an outstanding contribution to Puerto Rico's role as the *presidio* and the "front and vanguard" of the Indies.

3

The Organization of an Institutional and Social Life

Aida R. Caro Costas

Puerto Rico, besides its defensive role as a *presidio,* developed a community life under Spanish patterns, laws, and institutions. In distant Spain the king and the Council of the Indies determined the island's structure of government, defined the powers of each institution, and set rules to govern social and economic development. Within the walled city were established the institutions that shaped the island's evolution under the Spanish regime. We will examine briefly these developments during the first two centuries of Spanish rule.

The Political-Administrative Core

The Governor.—The governor stood at the head of a highly centralized governmental structure. The provisions for this important post underwent some changes during the sixteenth century because of three main factors: the legal claims of the heirs of Christopher Columbus, the crown's endeavor to set up a suitable form of government, and the strategic position of the island. Neither in the sixteenth nor in the seventeenth century was any democratic procedure for the selection of a governor devised.

At the earliest stage of colonization, the appointment of the governor was the king's prerogative. Thus in 1509 Ferdinand the Catholic named Juan Ponce de León as the first governor. The king soon lost this privilege; in 1511 the Council of Castile ruled that Diego Columbus and his descendants were to appoint the officials. Accordingly, from 1511 to 1536 these appointees served with the title of governor. At the end of their term, the officials were subjected to the *juicio de residencia,* a careful examination of all their acts in office, conducted by a judge designated by the monarch who was empowered to level charges against them. In general, however, the office of governor did not provide the political stability the island so badly needed.

In 1536 the Columbus family sold its political rights over the islands to the crown. This eventually changed the local system of government. Puerto Rico was no longer ruled by a governor. Once the appointing power reverted to Emperor Charles V, he bestowed the governmental functions upon the two *Alcaldes-Ordinarios,* or municipal judges, of the two existing *Cabildos* or municipal councils, San Juan and San Germán. These *Alcaldes* were elected annually by the *Cabildos.* Once elected, they became the governing body, or *Alcaldes-Gobernadores,* and for a year exercised full executive and judicial powers within the territory. This system met with opposition long before it was put into practice and did not work. Most of the settlers and local authorities clamored for the appointment of a governor to rule over the entire island. They strongly favored the appointment of a *letrado* or judge, and "a man of education and conscience," and urged that the decision be made in Spain. Finally, in 1545 the king agreed. The *Alcaldes-Gobernadores* were abolished. A *gobernador letrado* was designated, and until 1564 Puerto Rico was ruled by judge-governors appointed either by the king or by the *Audiencia* of Santo Domingo.

This government proved effective in maintaining peace and order, in restoring faith in the administration of justice, and in stimulating economic development. However, the growing military importance of Puerto Rico as a key to the Indies and the expectation of foreign attacks forced the king to change the criteria for the governorship. From 1564 to 1898, the post was filled by officers of the Spanish infantry or cavalry, practically all with impressive military careers. The military character of the governorship was further stressed with the creation in 1580 of the post of captain general, which, as already noted, was held by the governor.

This military emphasis gave the island a highly centralized and strong-handed government. The governor-captain general, who was usually appointed for a five-year term, exercised the fullest authority as direct representative of the king. Through the *juicio de residencia,* the king ensured the governor-captain general's performance of his duties.

The governor's power reached all sectors of the island's life. By various means he imposed his political-administrative mandate over the entire island. To control the *Partidos,* or territorial divisions, the governor relied not only on the *Teniente a Guerra,* but also on special commissioners vested with the power to deal with certain matters.

The governor was responsible for the general welfare of the community; in his annual visit to the sparsely populated *Partidos* he learned of local problems and provided accordingly. On these visits he also acted as judge since, as the highest judicial authority over the island, he could try and sentence civil and criminal cases both in first instance and in appeal. The governor, a professional soldier untrained in the law, was assisted in this work by a law counselor selected from lawyers on the island or in Santo Domingo.

The governor's political influence also extended to the *Cabildo,* or municipal council, in which he had significant powers. He acted as president of the city councils of San Juan and San Germán and also appointed *Regidores* or aldermen as well as minor officers. He also determined which offices were to be auctioned, as provided by law, and confirmed the annual elections and municipal ordinances.

Likewise, the governor had wide authority over economic and social life. Through such legislative acts as the *Bandos de Policia y Buen Gobierno* (Administrative Government Edicts), the governor regulated economic matters such as land use in agriculture and cattle raising, price fixing, and the system of the *reparto de pesa* (distribution of weights devised to assure the city's daily meat supply). He also regulated social activities such as public amusements, cockfighting, card games, and festivities in honor of patron saints. The repressive character of the *Bandos* was clear from the rules they established and the penalties they prescribed, which ranged from fines to corporal punishment.

However, the *Bandos* regulating economic matters were only part of the governor's complex and far-reaching economic power. Uppermost among the edicts were those aimed at defense, and the preservation and increase of the royal interest or patrimony, including administration of the *real hacienda* or royal treasury; taxation; control over the circulation of currency; and the protection and fostering of a Spanish trade monopoly. The crown's economic interests were involved in all of these sensitive areas, so they came under the governor's jurisdiction.

The curbing of illicit trade became an important duty for the governor. This commerce with foreigners had gone on since the sixteenth century, undermining the Spanish trade monopoly and thus reducing royal revenues. Although the governor was commanded to cut down smuggling activities, some governors were involved in the forbidden trade and merited severe punishments, from removal from office and confiscation of property to confinement in jail.

Within the social context, the governor performed other tasks with a direct bearing on community development. Through land grants he fostered colonization of the island. However, as land concessions were generously made with no definite settlement pattern, the direct outcome was a widely scattered population. This dispersal, together with the lack of means of communication and transportation, accounts for the island's slow urban development during the early centuries of Spanish rule.

In the ecclesiastical sphere the governor enjoyed certain powers derived directly from his position as vice-regal patron of the church. While the king required that the governor preserve good relations with the bishop, he also had the duty to protect and defend royal interests and rights in church matters. It was the governor's responsibility to see that only Papal Bulls and *Breves* (letters) approved by the Council of the Indies were observed on the island. Nor was the construction of any church, convent, monastery, or hospital allowed without royal license. The upkeep of all religious buildings was another of the governor's responsibilities. He was also empowered to see that the bishop and clergy received their salaries, partly from the *Situado* and partly from the inhabitants of the *Partidos*. Pastoral visits, the behavior of the religious orders, and the general conditions of religious life in the island were matters about which the governor periodically informed the king. As a devout Catholic and vice-regal patron, the governor enjoyed special privileges at the cathedral, where he usually attended services.

The governor was also the island's leading military figure. As captain general, he had full jurisdiction over military structures and procedures, defensive plans and forces (Spanish regular troops and local militia), the organization of expeditions against foreigners on adjacent islands or against pirates, and the distribution of the *Situado*. The governor's handling of military and defensive problems was usually scrupulous; this was not always true of the *Situado*. Some governors, in connivance with relatives, royal officers, and even high-ranking military officers, used the *Situado* for their own benefit.

Tenientes a Guerra.—In San Juan, the seat of the central government, the governor issued *Bandos* and military orders, met with his subordinates, and performed his civil and military duties. In the distant *Partidos*, or territorial divisions, he was represented by the *Teniente a Guerra*. This office appeared in the island's institutional scheme in the second half of the seventeenth century when five *Partidos* were created: Coamo, Arecibo, Ponce, Aguada, and Loíza. It was through this officer that the governor, who appointed him, imposed his authority over the urban districts of the island. Commonly the *Tenientes a Guerra* were members of prominent Spanish or Puerto Rican families.

Appointed for a term that varied from two to four years, although the governor could remove or transfer him at any time, the *Teniente a Guerra* had political-administrative, judicial, economic, and military powers. As the governor's highest representative in the *Partido,* he enforced the *Bandos,* maintained peace and order, acted as judge in some cases, and pursued smugglers. Within the *Partido* he commanded the *Milicias Urbanas,* volunteer local defense forces made up of white men between the ages of sixteen and sixty.

Social Dynamics

The Church.—The spreading of the Catholic faith among the aborigines—a duty imposed on the Catholic monarch by Pope Alexander VI in 1493 for all Indians in the New World—and the preservation of the faith among the colonists were the church's endeavors in the Indies. The Bishopric of Puerto Rico was created in 1511 and Alonso Manso was appointed the first bishop. The creation of the island's diocese and the arrival of Bishop Manso at Caparra on December 25, 1512, laid the foundations of the Roman Catholic Church in Puerto Rico. Under its spiritual, moral, and cultural guidance the island lived. Puerto Rico was the first episcopal see in the New World; it turned out to be the first see of the Holy Inquisition as Bishop Manso was designated Inquisitor of the Indies in January 1519. Puerto Rico served this function until the early 1590s when the seat of the Inquisition was transferred to Cartagena.

Even before the establishment of the bishopric, both Ponce de León and King Ferdinand were concerned about evangelization and the religious needs of the colonists. As early as 1509 Ponce de León asked for priests to be sent and had built a small wooden hut to serve as a church at Caparra. In 1511, King Ferdinand provided for the establishment of a Franciscan monastery and for the construction of a chapel commemorating San Juan Bautista. He took an active interest in the conversion of Indians to the faith and also imposed definite Christian obligations on the *encomenderos* who had been granted lands and Indians. These included religious instruction, the sacraments, Christian burials, and the building of a church. Most of these duties were also required of sugar mill owners with Negro slaves.

Yet it was the church that led the missionary effort and looked after the spiritual welfare of the Indians, the Negro slaves, and the Spanish colonists. Catholicism prospered. It began in *Caparra,* where Bishop Manso settled and where Franciscan monks, who arrived in 1512, built a humble convent. When Caparra was moved to the islet where San Juan was founded in 1521 (the same year Dominican monks settled there), religion prospered. The city was thinly populated and rustic but it soon held three religious centers. The original cathedral, built of wood and *tapiería* (mortar) and roofed with straw, was replaced in the 1520s by a solid stone building. In 1523 the Dominican monks began to build their stone and brick convent, which was almost finished by 1530. Two years later work had begun on the convent church, which, however, was not completed until the late 1630s. In the meantime the city dwellers showed their religious devotion by established hermitages such as *Santa Bárbara, Santa Ana, San Sebastián,* and *Santa Catalina.* In the seventeenth century, while the city was still underpopulated, the clergy was strengthened by the arrival of Franciscan monks, who built a church and a convent from 1642–1670. From 1651 onward, women with a religious vocation could enter the Carmelite convent established in that year.

While San Juan enjoyed an abundance of clergy and churches, conditions were different in the rest of the island. San Germán, the second urban center, had been organized under a vicar and had a *sacristán* (sexton), but was short of priests and had only a very small and primitive parish church. Conditions did not change until the seventeenth century. Early in the century religious life was highly stimulated by the establishment of the Dominican *Porta Coeli* convent. By 1688 San Germán at last had a stone parish church. On the other hand, the budding settlements of Coamo, Arecibo, Ponce, and Aguada still had very primitive parish churches.

In an island as poor as Puerto Rico was, the church's income was meager. Its main revenue, the tithes, was not enough to meet its expenses. The Spanish kings, whom the pope had made patrons of the church in America, allocated a fixed amount annually from the *Situado.* In addition, the crown occasionally helped the island's convents and churches through special grants. Occasionally wealthy private citizens made substantial donations to the church.

The church went far beyond its spiritual mission to play a significant role in the sociocultural development of the island. The care of the indigent in hospitals was linked to church action. The *Hospital de San Alfonso* and the *Hospitales de la Concepción* in San Juan and San Germán, all built in the sixteenth century, attest to this achievement.

The church also assumed educational leadership. Early in the colony's history, King Ferdinand had ordered that the Indians be taught to read and write for religious reasons; this task was performed by the clergy and the *encomenderos*. Bishop Manso was also deeply interested in the education of the settlers. He founded the *Escuela de Gramática* (Grammar School), dependent on the cathedral, for youths with a religious vocation and other interested persons. This was the first school in the island where Latin grammar was taught without charge. Toward the mid-seventeenth century education reached the elementary level. Franciscan monks taught the children in their convent not only the catechism but how to read, write, and count as well. In 1685–1687 Bishop Francisco Padilla founded a similar school in San Juan. No fees were charged in either school; in Bishop Padilla's school, the bishop paid for the books, the rent of the schoolhouse, and the teacher's salary. He believed so strongly in elementary education that he favored penalties for parents who failed to send their children to school. Since many children did not attend school because their parents were too poor to buy their clothes, he petitioned the king in 1688 to provide the pupils' clothes.

Higher education was considered equally important; the Dominican monks taking the initiative in developing advanced studies. In the 1520s a *Casa de Estudio* (house of study) or *Estudio General* (general studies) was established to teach grammar, liberal arts, and theology to students for the priesthood, clergymen, and laymen. This education was free of charge. The intellectual capacity of the Dominican teachers, the quality of their teaching, and the students' achievements are highly praised in documentary sources.

Two libraries, the Dominicans' and Bishop Bernardo de Balbuena's, contributed much to the cultural formation of the islanders. Both were burnt when the Dutch set fire to the city in 1625, but the Dominicans succeeded in replacing their library, which thus continued to be available to the community.

Population.—The Papal Bulls of May 3 and 4, 1493 granted Spanish monarchs the exclusive right to issue travel permits to the newly discovered lands. Thus, settlement in the Indies depended on the crown. It promoted Puerto Rico's settlement through the *cédulas de vecindad*, official permits for vassals who wanted to establish themselves as colonists.

Settlers were mainly Castilians, with a few Italians, Portuguese, and
Flemish. Parallel to the white settler influx, the Negro came to constitute
a strong racial element in the colonization of Puerto Rico. Under licenses
from the crown, Negro slaves were introduced into Puerto Rico from
the beginning of colonization. As the Indian population dwindled, the
Negroes came to supply the labor for mining and agriculture; they
became the most important asset in the development of the sugar industry.

After Juan Ponce de León and his companions began colonization at
Caparra in 1508, settlers from Spain or from *La Española* (Hispaniola)
moved into Puerto Rico. In 1512, San Germán was established on the
west coast. Early in its colonization, the island's good mining prospects
and Indian labor attracted colonists to Puerto Rico. Eventually, conditions changed. The low yields of the mines, the dwindling of the Indian
population, the high prices for slaves, Caribs' depredations, lack of
defenses, plagues, and hurricanes, all discouraged new settlers and drove
many colonists away.

Toward 1531 the Spanish population numbered at least 426. However, as the influx of new settlers stopped and migration from the island
increased, a trend toward depopulation began. In 1534, news of the
wealth of Perú reached the island. To the heavily indebted colonists who
had bought slaves on credit and found gold mining unprofitable, Peru
looked promising. An exodus followed. Lieutenant-Governor Francisco
Manuel de Lando's prompt action and the crown's eventual economic
concessions put an end to the migration. The king provided for loans to
build *ingenios* (sugar mills), the emerging sugar enterprise was encouraged, and colonists became optimistic. In 1549 the city council informed
the king that with the loans "the island had kept itself out of depopulation." Local authorities began to hope for new settlers for the largely
uninhabited island. Throughout the second half of the sixteenth century
the governors and the municipal councils of San Juan and San Germán
requested colonists. Canarians and Portuguese settlers were preferred
for their agricultural skills. However, no economic incentives were offered
and the island did not attract all the needed human resources. Nor did
foreign attacks, epidemics, and hurricanes encourage new settlers. Colonists from Spain preferred Perú and México, lands of wealth.

However, in spite of at least three epidemics, the white population of
the island, though still small, increased between 1581 and 1647. This
may be attributed to the arrival of a few farmers, the settling down of
government officials who stayed on the island at the end of their term

of office, and, most significant, to natural population growth. San Juan had the highest demographic concentration; it increased from 170 *vecinos* (settlers) in 1581, to 500 in 1647. The garrison for its walls also increased from fifty in 1582 to 400 in 1647. San Germán, the second urban center, had barely 200 *vecinos* in 1647.

Population also increased slightly in the rural interior, where prior to 1581 Spaniards and their island-born descendants had established two settlements. Coamo, which had twenty *vecinos* in 1581, had 100 by 1647. Arecibo increased from about ten in 1581 to forty in 1647. Three new towns, Ponce, Aguada, and Loíza, also contained a few inhabitants.

Yet white inhabitants were still scarce in the second half of the seventeenth century. For example, San Juan had a population of only 820 whites in 1673. The king responded to petitions for more settlers by permitting 200 Canarian families to settle in the island in 1683 and 300 more in 1691. The population still suffered a setback in 1689–1690, when epidemics of smallpox, measles, and *tabardillo* (spotted fever) claimed the lives of 631 whites and slaves. In spite of attempts to increase the white population, the seventeenth century ended with the island still in want of white inhabitants.

Information on the number of slaves and the mulatto population (offspring of Spanish and Negro mixture) is scant. Both groups were found in the cities and in the island settlements where they cultivated the land, worked as domestic servants and, above all, constituted the labor force of the *ingenios*.

By 1531, the African slave population had increased by leaps and bounds. The census of that year listed 2,264 slaves. Of these, 1,047 were introduced illicitly, on a license for only 500. Such irregularities incurred by license holders who brought more slaves than authorized and the contraband trade undertaken by foreigners—mostly Portuguese, English, French, and Dutch—were responsible for bringing the large majority of slaves to the island during the sixteenth and seventeenth centuries. The island depended heavily on slaves and since the crown did not always approve the numbers requested, foreigners often smuggled in the coveted slaves. It is impossible even to estimate the volume of this trade and the numbers introduced under royal licenses.

Economic Trends

Land Distribution: Agriculture, Industry, and Cattle Raising.—The Papal Bulls made the Spanish kings the sole owners of the New World. The monarchs then granted land to the earliest settlers, who owned their land upon fulfillment of definite requisites: construction of houses, use of land for agriculture or cattle raising, and continuous residence for four to five years.

These land grants were generous in size, from one to seven *caballerías* (200 acres). Thus the kings rewarded their vassals for undertaking colonization.

Later on, the monarchs authorized the island's governor to sell lands at public auction and to distribute them among the landless. In practice, however, the municipal councils of San Juan and San Germán assumed most of the tasks of land distribution.

The gold mining period was almost over in 1540. The island then made the transition from a mining-based economy to an agricultural one. Settlers eager for land requested grants from the island councils. As colonists were few and land was available, the councils first distributed lands free; eventually they charged two ducats for each *caballería*. No plan was followed in this distribution. Land grants or *mercedes de tierras* were made for different locations in the island, in sites requested by the settlers. Naturally, this scattered the island's population, though it paved the way for the founding of settlements which would eventually turn into *Partidos,* or territorial districts.

Grants made by the councils or by the governors did not entail land ownership. Lands were only given on a usufruct basis; grant recipients were to profit by the use of the land and its fruits. The kings continued to own the lands. Not until 1778 was land ownership vested in Puerto Ricans.

Devoted to agriculture and livestock production, lands were worked by the colonists, their slaves, and mulattoes. Subsistence farming was developed in the *haciendas de labranza* (farm property), with cassava, corn, tobacco, vegetables, plantains, rice, ginger, cocoa, cereals (and for a while wheat and barley). The island also raised tropical fruits, a variety of medicinal plants and flowers, and woods of high commercial value.

However, by the mid-sixteenth century, the backbone of the island's economy was sugar cane cultivation and a new industry: sugar production. Sugar mills required large investments in machinery and in human and animal resources; the industry could not have developed without royal assistance. The settlers were rich in ideas and in initiative but very poor in material resources. Royal loan grants for sugar mill building, facilities for transporting the sugar to Spain, and credit for purchasing slaves helped to create a flourishing sugar industry. In 1550 Alonso Pérez

Martel, owner of a sugar mill, reported to the king that the island already had ten sugar mills. In 1564, their output was 20,000 *arrobas* (25-pounds weights).

In time the bright future of the sugar industry darkened. There were frauds in loan grants and some loan recipients failed to honor their payments, thus losing their sugar mills and slaves to royal officers. Labor shortages were serious; the crown did not send as many slaves as requested and the smuggled slaves were too expensive. Lack of ships to transport sugar to Spain made the situation still worse. All these factors contributed to the decline of the sugar industry. The output and number of sugar mills was significantly reduced. In 1582 eleven sugar mills produced 15,000 *arrobas;* in 1602 only eight were in operation and their output was limited to 3,000 *arrobas.* By 1647 only seven were left.

The drawbacks of the sugar industry led sugar mill owners to look for other means of living, primarily ginger planting and cattle raising. Both these enterprises were well known to the settlers but primarily done by those too poor for the sugar enterprise.

When ginger replaced sugar cane as the main crop, the king retaliated with strict orders. In 1598 and 1602 he forbade the growing of ginger and urged the islanders to raise sugar cane. The sugar mill owners were threatened with such punishment as burning the crop and the loss of all their privileges. They continued to plant ginger since, as they wrote to the Council of the Indies in 1601, "They did not care about losing those privileges."

Encouraged by illicit trade, ginger planting flourished and mill owners exchanged the product for slaves. A ginger surplus soon followed, bringing a price drop in both the legal and the illicit trade. To make things worse, the government raised the import tax on ginger. All this led to a significant reduction of the crop. During the second half of the seventeenth century, the colonists gave up ginger for two other crops, tobacco and cocoa. In spite of government restraints and taxes, some farmers tried hard to make tobacco an important crop. Tobacco crops spread as the demand increased among the islanders; in 1690 Bishop Francisco Padilla wrote, "The use of tobacco is such, that it prevails over the necessity of eating." Domestic use and illicit trade made tobacco an important agricultural product in the eighteenth century. Cocoa yielded temporary profits mainly in San Germán and its vicinity.

To the settlers, cattle raising offered better economic prospects. Good grazing areas and climate helped to promote livestock development; horses, cows, oxen, sheep, pigs, and goats were raised. Horses bred here played an important role in the conquest of Perú and Central America and in the settlement of *San Agustín* in Florida. Locally, they were of the utmost importance since mills were driven by horses, oxen, and slaves. Each sugar mill had an *hato* (cattle ranch) to raise the needed stock for beef, agriculture, and industry. Encouraged by the governor and city council, the *hato* was a means of assuring the daily supply of beef for the garrisoned soldiers and civil population of San Juan. Each year the distribution authorities fixed the amount of stock the *hato* owner had to bring to the city slaughterhouse. The price of meat was set by the governor and municipal council. Livestock also brought an additional income from hides, which were traded in quantity, both legally and illegally.

Impact of Spanish Mercantilism: Commerce and Interloper Trade or the "Plague and Misery" of the Island

Commercial exclusivism was the salient feature of Spain's economic policy towards her overseas possessions. Thus trade with America was exclusively reserved for the metropolis, which made all regulations for import and export. Through the *Casa de Contratación* (House of Trade) in Seville and the fleet system adopted by the crown to enforce commercial exclusivism, Spain exerted full control over American trade. Commerce with foreign nations was expressly forbidden and severely punished.

Puerto Rico, accordingly, could only trade with Spain. Commercial activity was limited to San Juan, the only *puerto habilitado* or open port. Furthermore, local products were exported only to Seville, which enjoyed the trade monopoly with America.

Early in the sixteenth century, as Castilian merchants licensed by the *Casa de Contratación* brought goods in, the island was allowed to trade with *La Española*. Vessels bound for the Indies or returning to Spain stopped at the island, and thus the settlers' needs and the shipment of the meager local products to Spain were taken care of. However, from 1533 on, the colonization of México and Perú meant that the island could no longer count on the regular arrival of Spanish vessels. The islanders thus lacked regular supplies of food and merchandise. In addition, there were no ships to transport sugar to Seville.

By the middle of the sixteenth century, Spain instituted the fleet system to supply its American possessions, but Puerto Rico received little benefit from it. Under the fleet system, only one or two vessels were assigned to commerce with the island.

Throughout the second half of the sixteenth century, the city council complained about the inadequate shipping and very irregular schedule, which caused shortages of basic commodities such as wheat, oil, wines, clothes, as well as the slaves and implements needed for the sugar industry. The council asked for another vessel to be added to the fleets and special licenses for one or two inhabitants to take a shipload of island products to Seville or the Canaries and return with Castilian goods. But no permanent concession was granted and no permanent improvement was made.

This perennial crisis (from 1651 to 1662 not a single ship arrived at the island) led the islanders to look for a more dependable source of supply. Illicit trade with foreigners was their only recourse. Beginning in the sixteenth century, they smuggled goods first with the Portuguese, who brought coveted slaves, and afterwards with the French and the English. During the following century, as the foreigners settled in the Lesser Antilles, smuggling flourished. By then Dutch traders spearheaded the illicit but lucrative slave trade. Most of the illicit commerce was conducted by barter: local goods such as sugar, hides, tobacco, livestock, ginger, and wood were traded for slaves, wheat, clothes, agricultural implements, tools, household utensils, and other basic supplies.

Smuggling was punished, but nothing curbed illicit trade. Political, administrative, and military authorities, priests and friars, and even the island's governors, were involved.

The Royal Exchequer.—The *real hacienda* (royal treasury) in Puerto Rico was organized almost immediately by the Spanish crown. Tax collection and the administration of royal revenues were assigned to special officers. A simple bureaucratic structure was devised for fiscal matters. Between 1511 and 1513 the crown appointed the four *oficiales reales* (royal officers) who administered the *real hacienda:* the *Contador* (accountant), the *Factor* (commissioner), the *Tesorero* (treasurer), and the *Veedor* (overseer).

The *Contador* and the *Tesorero* collected taxes and administered the revenues; they also oversaw the *Caja Real,* where the money was deposited. Periodically judges sent from the *Tribunal de Cuentas* of Havana and the island governor inspected the accounts and reported to the Council of the Indies. The governor and the royal officers also constituted the *Tribunal de Real Hacienda* (tax tribunal), in which contraband and *comiso* (seizure) cases were judged. Like the governor, the *oficiales reales* were subjected to the *juicio de residencia.*

Revenue reached the *real hacienda* from several taxes and a variety of special sources, among them revenues from mining production and ecclesiastical taxes. In addition there were commercial sales taxes of several types. Extra income derived from the sale of some municipal posts, fines, interest paid on loans, *composición de extranjeros,* paid by foreigners who had settled on the island, and the sale of slaves, goods, and ships confiscated from smugglers.

In spite of these sources, the island's revenue did not cover its expenses. The governor often had to apply to the king for special funds from the *Situado* to meet governmental obligations.

Traditions of Municipal Life

The Municipal Council or Cabildo.—As previously noted, the central government in Puerto Rico was represented by the governor who through the *Teniente a Guerra* established his authority over all the *Partidos* or territorial districts of the island. Still another institution played an important role in community life. This was the *Cabildo,* the municipal government established early in the colonizing process. However, the *Cabildo* existed only in the two main centers: Caparra, which later became San Juan, and San Germán. Towards 1515, on the orders of the king, Juan Ponce de León established the territorial jurisdiction of both *Cabildos* by tracing a demarcation line from the Camuy River in the north to the Jacaguas River in the south. The eastern territory, the *Partido de Puerto Rico,* came under the jurisdiction of the *Cabildo* of Caparra while the western zone, or *Partido de la Villa,* was assigned to the *Cabildo* of San Germán. Thus the *Cabildo* of San Juan ruled over the city and the *Partidos* of Coamo, Arecibo, and Loíza. The *Cabildo* of San Germán had under its jurisdiction the city and the *Partidos* of Aguada and Ponce.

Structure and Oligarchic Composition.—Organized and regulated by the laws of the Indies, the *Cabildo* was not a democratic institution. The governing body for San Juan and the *Villa* of San Germán was composed of two *Alcaldes Ordinarios* (municipal magistrates) and a variable number of *Regidores.*

The inhabitants did not participate in the government. The two *Alcaldes* were elected annually by the *Regidores.* For some time during the sixteenth and seventeenth centuries the King appointed the *Regidores* for both councils or the posts were sold at public auction. Commonly the governor annually designated two *Regidores* for each *Cabildo.*

Both *Cabildos* were dominated by a small economic oligarchy of sugar mill owners or *hacendados,* and *ganaderos* (cattle breeders), who monopolized the municipal posts. For this situation the governor was mainly

responsible, since he always chose the two *Regidores* from among the two
or three richest families in San Juan and San Germán. These officers
elected their relatives or members of other distinguished families as
Alcaldes (mayors). The *Regidores* and the *Alcaldes* had the power to elect
or appoint the rest of the municipal officers. Such abuses were specifically forbidden by law, but violations were normal in both *Cabildos*. The
outcome of all these irregularities (which the governor permitted and
even encouraged) was that the municipal posts were held by relatives
and friends of the *Regidores* and *Alcaldes* who belonged to the elite group.

*The Council as "Father of the Republic" and the Welfare of the Commu-
nity.*—Documentary sources called the *Cabildo* the Father of the Republic
or the local government of the municipality. The councils met weekly or
monthly, the former under the presidency of the governor or of an
Alcalde Ordinario and the latter under this officer. At these meetings they
dealt with matters relating to the community. In addition to these regular meetings, they also held extraordinary ones and *Cabildos Albiertos* (open
meetings) when pressing municipal problems demanded them. These
open meetings were the only council gathering in which community
members participated. However, those who attended were not elected
by the citizenry but selected by the council itself.

The *Cabildo* also dealt with a myriad of major and minor problems
(widow subsistence, disputes over personal belongings, failures to pay
debts). A paternalistic attitude was evident in the council's handling of
these cases.

The Cabildo in Action.—Though it was not democratic, the *Cabildo* met
its responsibilities toward the community, setting and enforcing municipal ordinances. The ordinances, however, had to be approved by the
Audiencia of Santo Domingo and confirmed by the Council of the Indies.
The citizenry had the right to protest an unfair law before the council
and even seek action against the *Cabildo* from the *Audiencia*, the King, or
the Council of the Indies.

Within its territory, the council enforced the royal orders, the regulations set by the governor or by *Bandos*, and the judicial decisions issued
by the *Audiencia* of Santo Domingo. The *Cabildo* also examined the credentials of anyone who hoped to fill any post in the island. It was before
the *Cabildo* of San Juan that the governor, the *Juez de Residencia*, and the
Oficiales Reales presented their titles and were officially recognized.

Among the council's most important tasks was the adoption of a policy assuring the *abastos* (provision of basic foodstuffs to the community)
and the distribution of lands. Within the *abastos*, the meat and flour supply were given special attention. For the meat supply the council devised

the *reparto de pesa,* which obliged all cattle owners to bring a set amount of livestock to the city slaughterhouse. The flour provision was guaranteed either through the monopoly held by the government or by a particular merchant. Whenever this system failed, the council demanded the governor to introduce foreign flour. This only encouraged smuggling, which was the only solution to the flour shortage. The *abastos* also controlled the site of marketplaces, the supervision of quality, price controls, and the establishment of units of weight.

In open violation of the law that prohibited land distribution by the *Cabildo,* the island's councils gave land to those who asked for it for agriculture or cattle breeding. Needless to say, the members of the *Cabildo* and their relatives and friends profited from these concessions. Land grants were the most important source of income for the city council, as two ducats were charged for each *caballería.*

The *Cabildo* not only distributed land, but tried all cases involving property. This too violated the law, which only empowered the council to serve as a court of appeal.

The council was always short of money for vital community services. The municipal income was scant and irregular. Year after year the *Cabildo* requested grants from the crown; these were granted for a limited time. Still the *Cabildo* had to find other sources of money, such as the sale of municipal land and the *derrama* (a special contribution authorized by the monarch), which could only be used for repairing bridges and fountains.

The *Cabildo* was responsible for matters related to public works and public health. It provided for repair of the two main bridges, maintained the streets, the slaughterhouse, the meat shop, the cemetery, the fountain of Aguilar and the *aljibes* or wells (both related to the city's water supply) as well as the town hall. In health matters, the council built a *casa de degredo* or a *tinglado* (shed) to confine lepers and smallpox victims and provided for their needs. The *visita de sanidad* (health inspection) was instituted for ships that transported slaves and also periodically for private houses.

In spite of its heavy expenses, the *Cabildo* was always eager to celebrate traditional festivals and social activities ordered by the crown. A shortage of funds never prevented the council from paying for several religious festivities each year. The crown also ordered festivities to honor the advent of a new monarch, the *Jura* or oath of the prince of Asturias, royal birthdays and weddings. To meet expenses, the council went so far as to borrow money from its own members or from wealthy merchants.

4

The Eighteenth-Century Society

Luis González Vales

The eighteenth century saw a quickening in the tempo of the island's history, particularly during the last third of the century. In America the eighteenth century witnessed the birth of a new era. Ideas, institutions, and daily activities underwent dramatic changes. Population grew substantially, commerce multiplied, and the pace of city life quickened. The Caribbean islands, Puerto Rico included, were increasingly affected by their crucial role in the struggle for trade and power among the western European states. Puerto Rico, with its strategic location, was thrust into the center stage.

The differences between San Juan, site of the military presidio, and the rest of the island was intensified by armed struggle in the Caribbean. The walled city, seat of the colonial government, remained a bastion of Spanish might while the rest of the island was left pretty much to its own devices.

Anglo-Spanish rivalry would dominate the century and greatly influence the history of Puerto Rico. The century began with the war of Spanish Succession and ended with the failure of the last British attempt to conquer the island in 1797. Between these events, the island struggled to make the most of the situation and began to develop a distinct society, which would crystallize in the nineteenth century.

Socioeconomic Structure and Privateering

Although Puerto Rico continued to play a minor role in official Spanish trade with its colonies, its location in the heart of the Caribbean placed
it at the center of an ever-increasing colonial trade. The British had succeeded in establishing sugar production on some of their islands in the
Lesser Antilles and trade between them and British colonies in North
America became increasingly active. Tropical products from the islands
found their way into the markets of New York, Boston, and Philadelphia
in exchange for manufactured goods from the north. The French colony of Haiti became one of the world's leading producers of sugar and
the Danes transformed the island of Saint Thomas into a commerical
center.

Spain continued, on the other hand, to see Puerto Rico primarily as
a military bastion; therefore, little was done at first to develop its agricultural potential. Throughout the century, the island continued to
depend on the *Situado* to support its bureaucracy and military forces; at
the same time, ever increasing contraband trade provided almost the
only outlet for the island's products and source of needed goods.

Increasing trade in the Caribbean encouraged the growth of privateering, which led to a state of intermittent warfare in the waters adjacent to Puerto Rico. In this struggle Spain used sea raids against her
enemies, just as French corsairs and British sea dogs had been used
against her. Settlers in search of adventure were drawn to these under-
takings and soon outdid the Biscayne privateers who until then had led
Spain's struggle for control of the West Indian sea lanes.

Privateering was originally envisioned as an urgent measure to protect imperial trade routes and to defend the exposed coasts of the island
settlements. But Puerto Rican privateers, like their counterparts elsewhere, combined plundering and trading with their defensive tasks. The
local privateer, according to Morales Carrión, "found in his new occupation a most attractive though risky road to wealth and distinction."
This opportunity often came with the blessing or at least the tacit approval
of the local authorities, reflecting a society already accustomed to nomi-
nal observance of the laws. In this period the top colonial authority, the
governor, was sometimes involved in privateering and shared in its profits. Under the protection of the crown's commissions, privateers often
went far beyond the letter of the law and verged on piracy.

While privateering went on in the shadow of San Juan's mighty fortresses, cattle ranchers and farmers miles away from the capital contin-

ued to trade with the interlopers, who took advantage of the island's many harbors and coves. Penalties and threats were useless; practically the whole island's economy was based on contraband. Clandestine trade, centuries old, became the normal way of commerce for Puerto Ricans.

Among the island's privateers none commanded more respect or fame than the mulatto Miguel Henríquez, a thorn in the side of foreign traders in and around the island. As Morales Carrión wrote, "He stood as a typical example of the rustic colonial society, where class distinctions were still fluid, and bold and unscrupulous men, no matter the color of their skin nor their humble origins, could gain wealth and recognition serving the king in the dangerous business of privateering." Henríquez, a former shoemaker, in a few years gained such a reputation that Philip V in 1713 named him *Capitán de Mar y Guerra y Armador de los Corsos de Puerto Rico* (Captain of Sea and War and Provider of the Corsairs of Puerto Rico). The king subsequently made him *Caballero de la Real Efigie* (Knight of the Royal Image). Henríquez distinguished himself in the Spanish attack on Crab Island in 1718 and during the next decade wielded great influence in the affairs of the colony, his power many times surpassing that of the governor.

Puerto Rico's location gave the local privateers a marked advantage. Nor did they consider themselves bound by the crown regulations issued in 1674 and 1718 to govern their conduct. The *guardacostas* (coast guard), as they came to be known, seized almost all the ships that came near the island's waters, making British vessels their favorite prey and creating several serious incidents. Gradually they extended their range beyond their territorial waters, to the "irreparable damage of all vessels that trade to the West Indies."

On October 5, 1730 the British government officially protested the hardship suffered by English shipping in the West Indies. In this period, governors involved in privateering encouraged attacks on British commerce as far south as Tobago in the Lesser Antilles. The year 1734 was particularly violent: in February alone six British ships were taken into Puerto Rico.

Hostilities between Spain and England led to the War of Jenkins's Ear in 1739. Admiral Edward Vernon's fleet was active in the Caribbean and an attack on Puerto Rico was rumored. San Juan's fortifications were strengthened, but the attack never came. The war only intensified privateering, which continued unabated throughout the war.

The first half of the eighteenth century was dominated by privateers and contraband trade, but a significant development occurred on land:

in 1736 coffee was introduced to the island from Santo Domingo. It did not surpass sugar in commercial importance until the nineteenth century, but by 1765 Puerto Rican coffee was already an item of contraband trade.

From a Poverty Stricken Island to Threshold of Progress

The accession of Charles III to the Spanish throne signaled change in the imperial system's entrenched bureaucratic tradition. "The fight against the dislocation of trade was a major consideration of the new reformist attitude particularly with regards to the sensitive Antillean area where the island settlements were exposed to contact with one of the richest commercial regions anywhere in the world."

Privateering had embroiled Spain in serious conflicts with the English but had failed to diminish contraband trade, which flourished during the late 1750s with the English and the Danes boldly calling at the island's ports in spite of the *guardacostas*.

As an experiment the crown authorized a trading company, the *Compañía de Barcelona,* on March 24, 1755. It soon proved to be a great disappointment. Few ships were sent to the Antilles and they also succumbed to the temptations of smuggling. However, this company was only part of the crown's plan to increase the island's commerce and, more important, to foster its economic and social development.

Paramount in these reforms was Captain General Felipe Remírez de Estenós, who assumed that position in 1753. During the four years of his mandate, he promoted a series of significant measures affecting the island's development. Among these was the encouragement of coffee growing. The hinterland, with its humid climate, was ideal for coffee. Its cultivation thus made new areas attractive to settlers. During the balance of the century, population patterns changed as new settlements sprang up in the mountainous interior and drew some of the population away from the coast.

Remírez de Estenós' efforts were directed toward increasing the island's production, developing trade with Spain, and settling the island. To encourage settlement and revitalize agriculture, he proposed dividing the large *hatos* (grazing lands) and issuing titles for the land. Unfortunately, Estenós was removed before he could do much to implement his plan and the notion created such an uproar that his successor, Esteban Bravo de Rivera, abandoned the idea in 1759.

The Report of the Royal Commissioner, Alejandro O'Reilly

The crown, distressed by the prevalence of contraband and the offenses of the British, in 1765 sent a trusted representative to the Antilles to report on the situation.

The selection of Marshal Alejandro O'Reilly was felicitous. O'Reilly was thorough and precise, and his report went far beyond its scope to analyze the island's situation. It has gone down in Puerto Rican history as one of the most perceptive views of the island.

O'Reilly arrived at San Juan in April 1765. The most important finding of his *Memoria,* or report, was the crucial role of smuggling in the island's history. He raised three major issues: volume and nature of the island's trade revenues; the importance of contraband trade; and the state of the island's defenses.

Hardly anything of significance escaped O'Reilly. He was remarkably objective and took pains to document his observations. One of his first acts was to make a census of all the inhabitants of the island which showed a total population of 44,883, of whom 39,846 were free and only 5,037 remained slaves. Of the twenty-four towns or villages in existence, the vast majority were coastal towns; the northern and western coasts were more densely populated than the southern and eastern coasts. The census data does not divide the population by races, although it does give information on age. With 34,991, or 77.96 percent of the total free population below forty, the island's population was clearly young. It is also clear that the majority of the laboring population was free since slaves only amounted to 11.22 percent of the total population.

O'Reilly made the census mainly to appraise more accurately the volume and value of trade and revenues. Trade with Spain was insignificant. Imports were limited to oil, wines, flour, and a small number of other commodities, which were exchanged for money, hides, and *achiote* (annato, a food-coloring seed). The marshal learned that revenues from the *Situado* amounted to 80,000 pesos a year, while the total of all taxes added up to 10,804 pesos and three *reales.* The evidence indicated that a substantial part of the island's bullion was drained off through illegal channels.

Searching for an explanation of these distressing conditions, O'Reilly reflected on the island's social development. In his view, the peculiar growth of its population, coupled with the lack of a progressive policy, were the fundamental causes for the island's social backwardness. Much

of the population consisted of soldiers with little or no inclination for
farming and runaways and sailors who deserted the ships and took to
the mountains. These people were more interested in evading the law
than in working to develop the island. The mild climate and abundance
of easily obtained food provided little if any inducement to till the soil.
Other needs could easily be supplied through smuggling in exchange
for cattle, horses, mules, dyewood, coffee, hides, and a few other products. To some degree O'Reilly found that the contraband exchange stimulated progress. He stated in his *Memoria:* "this illicit trade which in the
rest of America is so detrimental to the interests of the King and of
Spanish trade has been useful here. The King owes to it the increase in
the products of the Island, and the vassals although poor and lazy are
doing more work than could otherwise be expected."

The society O'Reilly described was predominantly rural. People lived
in the country and mixed freely. Formal education was limited since only
two schools were available and time was measured in terms of a change
of governor, a hurricane, the visit from the bishop, or the arrival of the
Situado. Land grants to the poor, encouraged by the crown particularly
since the mandate of Remírez de Estenós, had only dispersed the population and increased its rusticity. Local markets and internal trade were
almost nonexistent and only one twentieth of the land had been cleared
for cultivation.

In spite of its rural nature, Puerto Rico was not isolated from the rest
of the world, thanks to the contraband with foreign colonies that provided its material needs. Everywhere O'Reilly found the same pattern:
fruits, livestock, and woods went to the smugglers in exchange for tex-
tiles, hats, agricultural tools, flour, and even *aguardiente.* So generalized
was the practice that in spite of the absence of records the marshal was
able to report on prices, merchandise, and distribution pattern throughout the island.

The established trade was very well organized. All orders were
promptly filled from England and Holland. "Those engaged in this traffic
are very punctual," O'Reilly remarked in his *Memoria,* "and I have been
told that any complaint of a breach of faith would be immediately taken
care of on account of their intent in preserving this trade."

The marshal proposed that royal policy toward the island be mod-
eled on the policy of other colonial powers, for example, the Danish
administration of flourishing Saint Croix. The island needed urgent economic measures to increase its revenues so that it could cease to be "a

perpetual and heavy burden to the Royal Treasury." Laws governing trade and property rights should be revised. All uncultivated lands should return to the crown for distribution to new farmers and the state should stimulate the immigration of men of capital willing to invest their money and talent in the construction of sugar mills. The revamping of the sugar industry was a primary goal which would require crown financing. O'Reilly considered state aid and guidance essential to change the island's economic structure.

O'Reilly also urged reorganization of the island's military forces to improve its defenses. First and foremost a soldier, he studied the situation thoroughly. The soldiers stationed in the island had adopted the carefree attitude so typical of the settlers. Discipline was lax, while graft and corruption prevailed among the officers. The marshal spared no efforts to remedy this situation. He heard the troops' grievances, encouraged them to meet their military obligations, fined the officers for their dereliction of duty, and reorganized the native militia to protect the coasts against enemy privateers and foreign invasion. The timeliness and thoroughness of these reforms helped considerably in defending the island when the English made their last assault on Puerto Rico in 1797.

The historian Arturo Morales Carrión in *Puerto Rico and the Non-Hispanic Caribbean. A Study in the Decline of Spanish Exclusivism* has very aptly summarized the marshal's report:

[it] marked, therefore, the first serious attempt to provide the basis for an eightened administration in Puerto Rico. The reorientation of trade through legal channels, increased productivity by means of state aid and selected immigration and the strengthening of colonial defenses were its cardinal principles. The objective was to change Puerto Rico into an asset rather than a liability in the balance sheet of the empire. Royal paternalism in government and protectionism in trade and agriculture were advocated as the desired instruments for the implementation of the program.

Political and Administrative Reforms

The crown's new interest in the affairs of Puerto Rico contributed visibly to its growth and development. The spirit of reform up to now evident in the actions of some of the captains general received new impetus with the measures adopted by the metropolitan government. The aim was to transform Puerto Rico into a prosperous colony capable of contributing to its own subsistence. Agricultural prosperity through a larger slave population, better defenses, a more enlightened administration, and a lucrative commerce with the peninsula were the elements of this reform.

The defenses of the island were immediately bolstered. A *Junta de Guerra* (war council) convened in Madrid in June 1765 to consider a program to upgrade the island's fortifications, drafted by O'Reilly and Tomás O'Daly with the support of Governor Benavides and the officers from the garrison. By January 1766 a vast effort to make San Juan a stronghold was underway.

The necessary funds were made available from the Royal Treasury of New Spain. From 1766 to 1771 100,000 pesos yearly were assigned to finance the work. In subsequent years the *Situado* rose to 225,000 pesos. This influx of money affected the economy, revitalizing commerce and stimulating contraband.

Work on the fortifications of *El Morro* and *San Cristóbal* required manpower. The laborers, from the most varied walks of life, indirectly helped population growth.

In 1769 Don Miguel de Muesas became governor and captain general of the island. During his seven years as governor, he left his imprint on the political and administrative organization of the island as well as its social and economic development.

Among his most notable administrative reforms was the *Directorio General,* which provided precise new instructions for the *Tenientes a Guerra.* They were also charged with improving education in their areas. They were not only to make qualified teachers available but also to see that parents sent their children to school regardless of color or station. Schools were to be ethnically integrated.

Muesas implemented O'Reilly's recommendation that people be gathered into towns rather than dispersed throughout the countryside by founding seven new towns, some in the interior.

He promoted construction of roads and bridges and the general improvement of the island's means of communication. His *Directorio* gave the *tenientes* the responsibility for road and bridge building and maintenance within their jurisdictions.

The intendant system, designed to strengthen the treasury operation, was introduced in 1764 to improve fiscal administration. At first the title and responsibility were ascribed to the governor and captain general. Not until the nineteenth century did the *intendencia* develop into one of the island's most important institutions.

Social and Cultural Mobility

Three visitors to Puerto Rico toward the end of the eighteenth century provided a good description of social and cultural conditions. Two of them, Fernando Miyares González and Fray Iñigo Abbad y Lasierra, made long stays; the third, Andre Pierre Ledrú, a member of a French scientific expedition, was in Puerto Rico only for a short visit.

Abbad, who lived in Puerto Rico between 1771 and 1778, came to the island as secretary to Bishop Manuel Jiménez Pérez. As he traveled about the island with the bishop he recorded his observations. His *Historia Geográfica, Civil y Natural de la Isla de San Juan Bautista de Puerto Rico* (Geographic, Civil and Natural History of the Island of San Juan), written after his return to Spain and published in 1788, is the first published history of the island. It offers useful information about the island's past and a vivid description of Puerto Rico during the 1770s.

Fernando Miyares González, a Cuban in the Spanish army, lived in Puerto Rico between 1769 and 1779. Like Fray Iñigo, he traveled extensively through the island and left us his observations in the form of his *Noticias Particulares* (Special Reports).

Ledrú, the Frenchman, was in San Juan during the last British attempt to seize Puerto Rico. His *Viaje a la Isla de Puerto Rico* (Voyage to the Island of Puerto Rico) is also an important testimony of conditions in Puerto Rico at the end of the century.

All three writers saw Puerto Rico as a changing society. Fray Iñigo remarked a stark contrast between the island's potential and its development. His analysis of the situation agreed in many respects with O'Reilly's. To foster development, he proposed three measures: the liberalization of commerce, the distribution of land and the issuance of titles to the rightful owners, and the encouragement of immigration. He considered the Spanish commercial system restrictive and outdated, repressing the island's development. With less restriction and fewer taxes, commerce would flourish and make the island a profitable colony. Abbad viewed distribution of uncultivated lands as essential for agricultural development. The large *hatos* should be broken up and the *agregados* (squatters) should be made owners of their own land as an inducement to increase agricultural production. These two measures, in his view, would eventually increase revenues and make the colony productive. The land reforms might also attract immigrants, leading to more production and more wealth.

During this period, San Juan continued to be the center of power and the most important urban community. Life became more refined, with better housing, more ornate furniture, and new public buildings. The cathedral was imposing and the convents of the Dominicans, the Franciscans, and the Carmelite Sisters were prime examples of colonial architecture. José Campeche, the foremost colonial painter, produced religious paintings for the churches and convents of the city, while his portraits adorned some of the city's finest houses.

Country life continued to be frugal, centered in the *haciendas* growing coffee or sugar. Ledrú described its beautiful women, dancing, and feasting. The growing society already showed a distinctive West Indian profile.

5

Puerto Rico in a Revolutionary World

Arturo Santana

The Bourbon Reforms

Late in the eighteenth century neither Puerto Rico's socioeconomic process nor its institutional framework had been able to catch up with the intensive demographic growth of the previous five decades.

Population growth was discernible from the early years of the century, although it quickened during its latter half. Various factors contributed: deserters from Mexican fleets; an expanded garrison; a new labor force brought in to work on the fortifications; fugitive slaves from neighboring European colonies; and the royal decree of 1778 allowing certain categories of foreign immigration. From the beginning of colonization to the early eighteenth century only five urban centers had been established in Puerto Rico. By 1760 there were eighteen; by 1800 there were thirty-nine. Population also grew impressively. In 1765 Marshal O'Reilly had estimated the total population at 44,883; by 1775 it had risen to 70,200; by 1787 to 103,051; and in 1799 it had jumped to 153,232. The older coastal regions continued to grow, but there was a heavy penetration into recently settled areas like the east coast and the mountainous interior. The second half of the century saw the emergence, among others, of such important coastal urban centers as Ponce (1752), Mayagüez (1760), Fajardo (1760), and Humacao (1793).

The inevitable result of this expansion was the gradual transforma-

51

tion of Puerto Rico into a more complex society, no longer a mere military outpost.

In the second half of the eighteenth century, social and economic reforms were launched by metropolitan and insular authorities, but at the end of the century the island's socioeconomic structure still lacked a viable foundation. The reforms, aimed mainly at curbing contraband trade and stimulating productivity and commerce, were still conceived within the traditional Spanish spirit of monopoly over the colonial economy and were never part of a sustained or all-embracing program; they thus fell quite short of their goal.

The period from Marshal O'Reilly's visit in 1765 to the outbreak of the revolutionary struggle in America and Europe saw the most important of these early reform measures. O'Reilly, as noted, had underscored the island's unorganized production economy, its scanty trade with the peninsular metropolis, and the crucial role of smuggling in almost every phase of insular life, particularly in drawing off through illegal channels a substantial part of the island's bullion. Soon after he submitted his report the first reform measures were drafted. A royal *cédula* of November 8, 1765, opened the trade of the Spanish West Indies to seven additional Spanish seaports besides Seville and Cádiz. The reforms, however, did not open additional ports to legitimate trade in Puerto Rico, nor did they provide for the coastal commerce so essential to the development of the interior. San Juan remained the only legal port and legal trade with the non-Hispanic world was still forbidden. Measures enacted during the next years pursued similar limited goals. The slave trading contracts awarded in 1766 and 1760 specifically permitted the introduction of clothing, salt, meat, and flour into Puerto Rico, the latter product being allowed to enter in foreign vessels, a significant landmark in the history of Spanish colonial trade. Although these enactments did not produce the expected results, they did originate a modest increase in exchange, the harbinger of a more significant future growth. Customs revenues increased from 1200 pesos in 1765 to 16,000 in 1778. The reform reached its peak in 1785 with the creation of the *Real Factoría,* a royal trade monopoly for direct export-import trade to the Netherlands, based mostly on tobacco and other insular agricultural products. This was a serious effort to reorganize trade and agriculture along more productive lines and brought considerable increase in revenues during its early years. Although it still existed toward the end of the century, the *Factoría* had by then fallen short of early expectations. There was a widespread feeling that the greater part of the profits went to the crown, sole owner of the monopoly, with only a minor fraction reaching the insular producers and traders. However, during the 1790s effects of the French Revolution disrupted Spanish maritime lines of communication and colonial trade, thus undermining the *Factoría*. A remarkable upsurge in contraband trade considerably reduced the *Factoría's* share in the island's commerce. By 1794 illegal exchange was estimated at more than 500,000 pesos a year.

Obviously, these reforms had not laid appropriate economic foundations for a colony in transition from an economically dependent naval and military outpost to an increasingly more populated and more complex agricultural society. Visitors to the island and the Madrid authorities agreed that Puerto Rico had great potential. However, its trade and agriculture had not been appropriately encouraged and its contraband trade flourished despite all attempts to curb it. The revolutionary wave that swept Europe and the Americas in the 1790s brought the Puerto Rican situation to a crisis. Spanish imperial lines of communication were disrupted, leaving the overseas empire, notably the West Indies, in isolation from Spain. In the case of Puerto Rico the crisis brought out two vital facts: first, the dependence of its economy on the *Situado,* irregular and now sometimes missing; and second, the disorder of the island's trade with its metropolis and other parts of the empire. Clearly, new sources of revenue, trade, and supply were urgently needed; the island had to be opened at last to legal trade with foreign ports, which implied the eventual abrogation of one of the most obnoxious remnants of the old imperial commercial exclusivism.

Fin de Siècle—A War Interlude.—Before the end of the century, Puerto Rico suffered the most important and best organized British onslaught in its history. This episode encouraged those bonds and elements that were already defining the insular population as an organized society and spurring colonial authorities to create needed socioeconomic and fiscal structures.

During the second half of the eighteenth century, Puerto Rico had become gradually more significant to British interests in the Caribbean. British diplomacy during the 1780s and 1790s was already tending toward acquisition of the island; this goal became a determining factor in naval and military policies and operations at the turn of the century. When in 1796 Spain joined France at war against Great Britain, the Admiralty prepared to send an expedition to the Spanish West Indies, either to Trinidad or to Puerto Rico. Trinidad was initially the preferred goal, among other reasons for its excellent location for a future offensive against Spanish trade and naval communications in the Caribbean area. Trinidad, without fortifications and with a foreign population, was easily captured on February 17, 1797. The British commands thus decided to proceed immediately against Puerto Rico. But Puerto Rico was not as easy a target. Two centuries of work on the ramparts and fortresses of San Juan and, above all, the rapid completion of the comprehensive defense plan submitted in 1765 by O'Reilly had made the capital city, the obvious focus of any foreign attack, into one of the major strongholds in the Spanish imperial network. British authorities, by their own account, had no trustworthy intelligence on the island's defenses. Furthermore, the British forces were an incongruous, heterogeneous group, including German, Irish, and even French emigré soldiers. On the other hand, Puerto Rico was commanded by Governor Don Ramón de Castro, a military leader of rare capacity with an outstanding record in Mexico and Florida. Although the regular Spanish garrison at San Juan was not up to the required muster roll, Governor de Castro could depend for the immediate defense on around 5000 men, including regular soldiers, militias, and a number of French privateers temporarily on call at San Juan.

Having picked up reinforcements in the Lesser Antilles, the British fleet anchored off Cangrejos Point, a few miles to the east of San Juan, on April 17, 1797. It totaled sixty vessels and carried between 8000 and 10,000 men. After his demand for surrender had been rejected, General Abercromby landed the main part of his forces, overpowered Spanish opposition, and occupied the greater part of what is now Santurce, the present central urban area of metropolitan San Juan, east and southeast of the ancient walled city. From there the British commander concentrated on an attempt to force the eastern approaches to the city. This brought him into violent collision with the first line of advance defenses, dominated by the Castle of San Jerónimo and a fortified bridge that connected the main island with the islet on whose western extremity the capital city was located. These fortifications had to be overcome before proceeding toward the city; the fleet meanwhile blockaded the harbor entrance to isolate the city. The Spanish defense strategy recognized that the key to the contest was the city of San Juan and concentrated all efforts on its first line of defense, hoping to stop the enemy there or, if not, at least to blunt his thrust considerably. It was thus in this area that the most important hostilities took place, characterized by almost constant British artillery activity and assaults. The defenders held their ground, organized devastating counterassaults, and prevented the enemy from outflanking the defense through the channel connecting Santurce with San Juan Bay. In the meantime, by order of Governor de Castro, militia units from all over the island were assembling in the towns surrounding San Juan, to join in the defense and the apparently approaching Spanish counterattack. This, however, never came. The invaders now faced growing adversity: their advance appeared indefinitely blocked, losses in men and material were rapidly mounting, and now emerged the increasingly grave risk of annihilation at the hands of a superior Spanish counterattack. The British commanders therefore abandoned the siege and left with their army on May 1 and 2. A massive onslaught by the first naval power of the age had been defeated without outside resources, by an army made up mostly of local militia. The invaders had undoubtedly

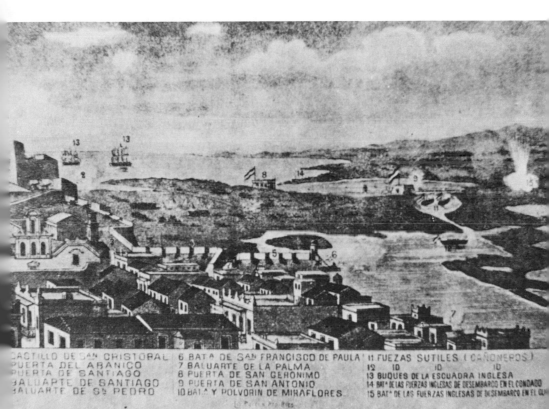

1 CASTILLO DE SAN CRISTOBAL
2 PUERTA DEL ABANICO
3 PUERTA DE SANTIAGO
4 BALUARTE DE SANTIAGO
5 BALUARTE DE S? PEDRO

6 BAT? DE SAN FRANCISCO DE PAULA
7 BALUARTE DE LA PALMA
8 PUERTA DE SAN GERONIMO
9 PUERTA DE SAN ANTONIO
10 BAT? Y POLVORIN DE MIRAFLORES

11 FUEZAS SUTILES (CAÑONEROS)
12 ID   ID   ID
13 BUQUES DE LA ESCUADRA INGLESA
14 BAT? DE LAS FUERZAS INGLESAS DE DESEMBARCO EN EL CONDADO
15 BAT? DE LAS FUERZAS INGLESAS DE DESEMBARCO EN EL GUI

Engraving based on the painting by José Campeche of the British attack (1797).

underrated the strength of the fortifications and the capacity and determination of the defenders. Practically the whole island had contributed
men and material to this efficient and successful effort, an obvious culmination of recent demographic growth. The epsiode fereshadowed a
new day in Puerto Rico. The new sense of social cohesion revealed by
the war led in the favorable circumstances of the years ahead to the
development of new institutions to serve a renovated socioeconomic
structure.

The Development of Legalized Foreign Trade

Toward the end of the eighteenth century, a complex sequence of
political and economic circumstances in the Spanish overseas empire,
the Atlantic, and the Caribbearn affected favorably Puerto Rico's production and commerce, thus preparing for the island's development of
its own economic and fiscal structure. During the second half of the century some of Spain's American colonies had been developing their trade
and economic activity impressively: Cuba in sugar, Venezuela in cacao,
and Buenos Aires in hides and salted meats. They now shared the main-
stream of Spanish colonial economic life with the already rich precious
metal producing colonies of Mexico and Peru. The wealth and trade of
Cuba, above all, now attracted worldwide attention. The Cuban sugar
industry from 1760 to 1790 grew nearly four times as fast as the economy of the other European Caribbean colonies. By 1762 sugar exports
reached 5,000 tons; they were up to 8,160 tons in 1777 and 15,423 tons
in 1790, a most significant increment by Caribbean standards. In
contrast, Abbad wrote of the comparatively minor role still played by
sugar cane in Puerto Rican economic life. In the late 1770s he
commented:

The farming of sugar cane is very common throughout the island: there is scarcely
a farmer who does not have some portion of his land dedicated to this product,
very few, however, make it their principal crop. The larger number of slaves
needed and the great costs entailed in the establishment of a sugar mill, with the
necessary machinery, prevents the development of this crop.

The earliest available figures after Abbad, those for 1803, indicate that
the island's sugar production toward the end of the eighteenth century
was still almost immaterial compared to Cuba's. Puerto Rico in the 1790s,
like Cuba before the 1760s, remained underpopulated, a settlement col-

ony of small cattle ranches, tobacco farms, emerging towns, some rudimentary plantations, and few slaves. This, of course, was apart from the military establishment in San Juan, supported by the Mexican *Situado*. Cuba began to leave this stage during the 1760s; by the 1790s it had already entered the initial phases of the sugar plantation economy. Puerto Rico was to evolve at a slower pace.

This extraordinary growth of the Cuban and Venezuelan economy, based on bulk shipments of sugar and cacao, greatly disrupted the Spanish colonial shipping organization, based mostly up to now on the mineral economy of Mexico and South America. It was already evident by 1790 that the Spanish maritime and mercantile machinery was inadequate to transport and market this colonial production. Besides, Spanish merchant vessels were, on the average, much smaller than their British or United States counterparts. External factors soon complicated this crisis, while stimulating Cuban sugar production. In 1792 the Haitian slave rebellion eliminated French Saint Domingue as the world's foremost sugar producer, removing close to 80,000 tons per year from the international sugar market. Though the British West Indies desperately increased their production, Cuba was considered the likeliest candidate to supplant Saint Domingue. In a few months the price of sugar skyrocketed to the highest level ever attained and Cuban planters feverishly expanded their production and scrambled to ship it as rapidly as possible. Spanish shipping was already stretched to its limits; also, the war with France, declared in 1792, was hamstringing a considerable portion of the Spanish merchant marine. The heavy Cuban demands completely overwhelmed the shipping system and threatened to paralyze the expanding Cuban economy. The planters were thus forced to use foreign shipping which, under the circumstances, meant the British and the Americans. Great Britain, though an ally of Spain, was also at war, so the Americans, much closer geographically, were obviously a better choice. At this time the United States merchant marine was the second largest in the world (after the British) and the largest among the neutral powers. Cuban planters started to ship a large proportion of their sugar and molasses illicitly in foreign bottoms, at the same time exerting heavy pressures (mostly, according to some historians, in the form of bribes) on Spanish colonial officials to legally allow this foreign traffic. Permission soon came, and though it was partially revoked in 1794, the new order was not entirely obeyed. There followed a series of contradictory decisions about trade with foreigners, typical of a government under heavy contradictory pressures and already lacking the power to impose its will on the economic life of its most prosperous colonies.

Although this concession of 1793 did not apply to Puerto Rico, the Spanish diplomatic agents in the United States and the governor of Puerto Rico, taking advantage of the precedent and acting under traditional discretionary powers, occasionally permitted shipment of foodstuffs and war material to the island, with the consequent return of the vessels to American ports laden with Puerto Rican produce. In 1795 San Juan urgently requested foodstuffs from the United States for the use of Spanish war vessels calling there. The arrangement was concluded, but since the naval forces never arrived, the provisions were used during the British attack and siege of San Juan in April and May of 1797. During this period (1795–1796) Spain had made peace with the French Republic and, as a result, closed Cuban and other colonial ports to foreign neutral trade. Spain's enjoyment of commercial exclusivism and peace was brief. In a diplomatic maneuver culminating in the Treaty of San Ildefonso (August 18, 1796) Spain established an alliance with the French Republic, resulting in war with Great Britain, declared on October 6, 1796. The British navy now became an insurmountable obstacle. Much of the Spanish merchant marine was soon bottled up in the Mediterranean. Communications between the Spanish Caribbean and its European metropolis, already poor, were now completely disrupted, with immediate disastrous consequences for the colonial economy. Spain responded in 1797 by opening the Caribbean and South Atlantic ports of the empire to neutral trade and shipping. This measure has been hailed by historians as the prelude to Spanish American independence. For the first time since the conquest, Spain legally opened a considerable part of her empire to foreign trade, finally recognizing the impossibility of channeling this traffic through the imperial monopoly.

The United States, first among the neutral maritime powers, was again the chief beneficiary of the new decree. American traders benefited from their geographical location and the relations they had already established throughout the Caribbean. Trade developed rapidly between the United States and the Spanish West Indies. Official American statistics for this period show an impressive upsurge in this trade. Exports from the United States to the Spanish West Indies during the calendar year 1795 amounted to $1,389,219. During the calendar year 1798 the total was $5,080,543. Imports the United States received from the Spanish West Indies showed a similar increase.

One reason for this growth was the development of the American carrying trade as a result of the deficiency in Spanish tonnage and the complications of the war in Europe. Not all of the Spanish West Indian products exported by American vessels were for the American consumer. Since the outbreak of war in Europe, British naval superiority had made shipping between the European enemies and their colonial possessions extremely hazardous, if not impossible.

The French, Dutch, and Spanish had to depend upon neutral nations for trade between them and their colonies. Under the circumstances this almost always meant the United States. Export and import from the Spanish West Indies now moved in American bottoms, usually with a re-export stopover in the United States. Thus began, among other things, a triangular trade between the Spanish West Indies, the United States, and the Baltic region (particularly Russia) that was to become important during the first half of the nineteenth century. Carrying and re-export trade formed the basis of American commercial relations with the Spanish West Indies, more important than the direct imports of the domestic American sugar market. By contrast, the United States was already the main consumer of Spanish West Indian molasses, importing more than 90 percent of production. Not until a few decades later did the American sugar market become essential to the Spanish islands.

Even though these favorable circumstances were unrelated to Puerto Rico and most American trade was with Cuba, Puerto Rico benefited from the situation, developing its own legal commercial relations with the United States. Wide differences in the trade volume between Cuba and Puerto Rico at this time can be attributed to the well-known disparity in geographic, economic, and demographic resources, and to Cuba's importance by the early 1790s as a source of sugar and molasses for American shipping. Havana, moreover, had become the foremost commercial port in the Spanish overseas empire.

While new channels of legal trade were opened, the age-old smuggling trade continued. To escape certain Spanish prohibitions, duties, and bureaucratic snags involved in commercial voyages to the United States, regulations were not strictly observed. As a result, smuggling continued in the Spanish West Indies during the first decades of the nineteenth century. In Puerto Rico smuggling was encouraged by the time-honored but impractical legislation recognizing San Juan as the only legal port for the island. Because of inadequate communication and transportation on the island, the producer of goods in the interior and coastal parts of the colony was often forced into an illegal exchange to earn his livelihood. In 1797 the French botanist and traveller Pierre Ledrú stated that "a considerable part of the foodstuffs consumed in the island are imported from outside: the United States supplies it with flour." In the same year the chief pilot of the Royal Spanish Navy declared that the American traders were chiefly responsible for the illicit trade in the Caribbean and the West Indies.

Smuggling strengthened Spanish opposition to the trade concessions of 1797, which deprived them of their traditional lucrative monopoly. In this they were backed by their correspondents in the West Indies and Caribbean. West Indian planters and local merchants had profited greatly from the trade concessions, but their influence was ineffectual; the peninsular interests were closer to the Madrid ministry. Spanish opposition was supported by France, Spain's ally and, to some extent, master at that time; the French began a quasi-war with the United States to keep Americans out of West Indian ports. Consequently, in 1799 Madrid closed the Atlantic ports of the Spanish Empire in America to neutral trade.

This step, however, did not end legal trade between the United States and the Spanish West Indies, for the order was not as restrictive as it appeared. Its purpose was to keep British trade out of the Spanish American colonies, for the neutral merchant vessels from northern Europe were taking cargoes of British wares to the Spanish colonies. Since the order was directed against British manufacturers, not against United States flour, Spanish colonial authorities were directed to allow the importation of provisions from the United States wherever necessary. Evidently this also entailed (perhaps it was the pretext for) the export of Spanish colonial products in the returning American vessels. Authorities in Cuba, anxious to ship their increasing sugar production, had apparently decided to continue permitting American trade even before receiving instructions from the metropolis. Thus, the commerce between the Spanish West Indies and neutral nations, mostly the United States, was not seriously hampered. The revocation had little discernible effect, although other circumstances discouraged American trade with the Spanish Caribbean.

Spain's policy on the Spanish West Indies had come to be based more and more on pretense. Repealing the concessions to neutral trade could not be enforced in view of the prevailing European situation and the scarcities in the colonies. In addition to Spanish opposition, American trade to the Spanish West Indies encountered other obstacles. During the state of quasi-war between the United States and France, from 1797 to 1801, French privateers attacked American trade in the West Indies on the pretext that the Americans were carrying contraband to the British West Indies. In these activities the French, as Spain's allies, had the use of Puerto Rican ports and, often, the cooperation of Spanish privateers operating out of Puerto Rico. Other obstacles included British seizures of Spanish vessels and crews; Haitian privateers who extended their activities to France's ally, Spain, and its colonial trade; and the Spanish restriction of overseas maritime trade only to San Juan. In spite of all this, however, trade between the United States, the most important foreign neutral nation, and Puerto Rico continued to expand. In some areas, such as flour and foodstuffs, the island developed a state of semi-dependency on the United States. Thus, during the late eighteenth and early nineteenth centuries, exports from the United States to the Spanish West Indies show no significant decline.

1798	$5,080,543
1799	8,993,401
1800	8,270,400
1801	8,437,659

The Decree of 1799, then, did not end legal trade between the United States and the Spanish colonies. Food was excepted from the decree; thus the trade in provisions continued whenever it was deemed necessary. Some colonial officials even refused to enforce the decree, claiming urgent necessity in their jurisdictions. Every port along the Atlantic coast of the Spanish Empire protested, causing Spain to institute, in 1801, a system of special licenses sold to neutrals to permit entry into certain Spanish American ports for general trade. At the end of the war, in 1802, the special license system was abolished and an attempt made to restore the old Spanish monopoly. Some colonial authorities, however, invoking discretionary and emergency powers and alleging scarcity of foodstuffs and sheer necessity, continued to admit neutral vessels, mostly American, to Spanish colonial ports. Even this token return to imperial monopoly was of short duration. In May 1803 war broke out again between France and Great Britain. In December 1804, Spain entered the war as the ally of France. Within a few weeks the Spanish Caribbean and Atlantic colonies were officially reopened to neutral trade, which, under the circumstances, meant predominantly American trade. The right to issue licenses for neutral trade was farmed out to a number of court favorites and other individuals who, through their agents, sold the licenses to the highest bidder. This was the situation when Napoleon invaded Spain in 1808. During the uncertain months and years that followed, the enforcement of Spanish trade regulations varied from colony to colony, and the supervision of colonial trade was at the discretion of local authorities.

For a brief period after 1801 trade between the United States and the Spanish islands suffered a setback; in peacetime neutral carriers were less necessary. Between 1801 and 1803 the entries of vessels from Cuba into Philadelphia dropped from 98 to 20, while those from Puerto Rico disappeared altogether.

According to the contemporary commentator Pedro Tomás de Córdova, in 1803 the only foreign vessels trading in San Juan were American. The exports of Puerto Rican sugar to the United States in that year amounted to 263,000 pounds, valued at 15,790 pesos. Official records for 1804 show that imports in foreign (mostly American) vessels were foodstuffs, household goods, and, ominously, 150 Africans. Insular exports consisted mostly of sugar, coffee, molasses, tobacco, hides, and indigo.

The slump, however, was temporary. With the renewal of war in 1803, communications with the overseas metropolis were again disrupted, and the island's situation was complicated by frequent failures to receive the Mexican *Situado* to cover government expenditure.

The actions of the governor and captain general, Field Marshal Don Toribio de Montes, exemplify the powers of colonial authorities in emergencies. Montes reported to the crown that when he arrived on November 12, 1804, there was only enough flour for ten days, a dangerous shortage since all flour had to be imported from outside, mainly from the United States. He anticipated paying the soldiers and government employees out of the duties to be charged on the sale of flour and other goods brought by neutral vessels "for which, out of necessity and following a *Junta de Real Hacienda* to have opened the port, but as the natives absolutely do not have any money, the ships are compelled to return without selling their cargo." In pleading his special case, the governor omitted that much neutral trade was on a barter basis. However, the absence of the *Situado,* with the resulting monetary scarcity, had undoubtedly brought insular finances to a crisis.

By 1805 exports from the United States to the Spanish West Indies had reached a total value of $7,690,888. This commercial development was hampered during this period, however, by the renewed activities of French and even of Spanish privateers. After the Louisiana Purchase and several American gestures toward Florida, Spain was more apprehensive than ever of the United States' designs upon Spanish colonies in the Caribbean, especially the West Indies. Spanish colonial authorities were thus more disposed than ever to be friendly to France. With Spain and France as allies, the Spanish islands were again open to French vessels which, after the resumption of war in 1803, renewed the seizures of American vessles. From 1803 to 1811, on the other hand, Great Britain did what she could to hamper American shipping to the Caribbean. Vessels trading with Havana, Puerto Rico, and Puerto Cabello, among others, were seized and taken to British ports, frequently to Halifax, Nova Scotia, where the British government maintained a vice admiralty court.

American export trade to the Spanish West Indies from 1795 to 1805 increased from $1,821,000 to $10,867,000. The statistics also show that in 1806 reexported foreign goods constituted only 23 percent of its exports to Spanish America; thus the overwhelming bulk of this traffic was with the Spanish West Indies. American agricultural and industrial producers expected the Spanish islands to become an increasingly lucrative market, heavily dependent on the United States for foodstuffs and other commodities. The Spanish government, nevertheless, viewed the concessions to foreigners in colonial trade as a mere transitory evil, refusing to recognize the Americans sent from Washington as consular agents to assist in matters of trade. These obstacles did not deter American merchant vessels from active trade with the Spanish West Indies. Records for 1807 show that vessels from Philadelphia traded with Cuba, Puerto Rico, Venezuela, Veracruz, and the Río de la Plata. Also in 1807, the first American consular agent was appointed to Puerto Rico, an undoubted sign of increased American interests in the island. Although the agent seems to have arrived at his post, there is no documentary evidence of Spain's reaction to his appointment or of his functions in office.

Commercial exchange between the United States and the Spanish West Indies seems to have been considerably affected by the Jeffersonian embargo of December 1807. According to Federalist politicians from New England, the embargo had wiped out the lucrative American carrying trade with the Spanish West Indies, cutting exports in half and reducing sugar imports from 87,763,464 pounds in 1806–1807 to 34,657,330 pounds in 1808–1809. After the Napoleonic invasion of the Iberian Peninsula in 1808 and the resulting Anglo-Spanish alliance, Spanish West Indian ports were opened to British merchant ships. Like the Americans, however, they were only admitted because of food shortages. The trade was tolerated in certain ports by local regulation but had no treaty basis. It was of little help at this time in Puerto Rico. Great Britain, engaged in a titanic struggle in Europe, could not meet even the needs of her own West Indian colonies. Metropolitan Spain had almost disappeared as a supply and buyer's market; it was fighting for survival in Europe and could not supply even bare necessities to the colonies. In Puerto Rico, the result was a severe shortage of food and other prime necessities.

The lifting of the Jeffersonian embargo in 1809 was followed by an increase in trade with the Spanish West Indies. On April 7, 1809, the governor again opened the ports of Puerto Rico to neutral vessels

because of the scarcity produced by the glorious struggle against the French in the Peninsula and because of the entrance into the ports of the island of several American vessels loaded with foodstuffs and several others being expected, the Congress at Washington having again opened the ports of the American Republic.

United States customs records for 1809 show a significant increase in the number of vessels from Puerto Rico.

After the Napoleonic invasion of Spain in 1808, American interests had new concerns in the Gulf-Caribbean region. The historian Samuel Flag Bemis described the apprehensions of American leadership at this time:

The security of American territory, achieved by President Washington's foreign policy, could have vanished if, during the European wars and alliances at the end of the eighteenth century and beginning of the nineteenth, adjacent Spanish territory had suddenly passed into the possession of a stronger European maritime power. . . . The initial Latin American policy of the United States had been to make sure that during the disruption of the Spanish Empire, a more powerful European rival monarchy should not step into Spanish provinces contiguous to or close to the United States in such a way as to threaten its independence and vital interests.

President Thomas Jefferson, having all this in mind, had asserted that decadent Spain should be left in possession of her American colonies, since they could not be in better hands until the United States was ready to take those that it needed. Of his Gulf-Caribbean policy, as it had developed by 1808, Bemis adds: "We can say little more than that he had begun to cast speculative glances at Florida, Cuba, and Mexico, that he was ready to oppose the transfer of an American colony from one European power to another, and he was more disposed to use government agencies for the promotion of foreign commerce than adherents of the agrarian-capitalist philosophy seem willing to admit."

Aroused by the Napoleonic invasion of Spain and its repercussions in the Spanish overseas empire, President Jefferson and his cabinet in October 1808 instructed American agents in Cuba and Mexico to express unofficially to influential persons there the main lines of American policy towards the region. Such was the mission undertaken to Havana during the spring of 1809 by General James Wilkinson. He was to emphasize that Spain's American colonies were to remain loyal to Spain or free themselves, but must not fall under the domination of Great Britain or France. Such overtures only alarmed Spanish officials, increasing their long-standing fears of American designs on Mexico, Florida, and the Spanish West Indies. Although Puerto Rico was much less important to Jeffersonian diplomacy than Cuba, Mexico, and Florida, the Spanish authorities were also worried about its future security.

The Spanish *chargé d' affaires* in the United States wrote to his superiors that Wilkinson was under instructions to negotiate "a reunion of the Kingdom of Mexico and the islands of Cuba and Puerto Rico under these United States." In spite of these qualms, circumstances continued to compel Spanish authorities to allow trade with foreign neutrals, mainly Americans, in the Caribbean colonies. War and necessity thus overruled a secular tradition of exclusivism in shaping the immediate future and ushering in new economic, financial, and administrative policies.

Toward the Disintegration of the Spanish Colonial Trade Monopoly

The alliance with Great Britain that resulted from the Napoleonic invasion of the Peninsula in 1808 relieved the Spanish Caribbean from the pressures of the blockading British navy, but it did not significantly improve conditions. Spain, struggling for her life as a nation, could not attend to the economic needs of her colonies. Thus the Spanish islands continued to depend on foreign neutral trade. The revolt of the Spanish continental colonies, which started in 1810, compounded this difficult situation. When the newly established revolutionary governments unleashed numerous privateers to prey on Spanish commerce and naval power in the Caribbean and Atlantic, Puerto Rico soon felt the disastrous effects. Communications and trade with Spain remained disrupted, as they had usually been since the 1790s; in addition, rebels raided the island's coastline.

The damage to the island's economy became critical as the island's

meager resources were called upon to help the Spanish authorities subdue the continental rebellion. In the words of Cuban historian José Luci-
ano Franco, during this period Cuba and Puerto Rico were "the barns
and bastions of the metropolis in the New World . . . and . . . all, or
almost all the Spanish expeditions against Venezuela left from these two
West Indian islands."

The War of 1812 was a serious setback to the development of American trade generally and particularly with the Spanish West Indies, which
it had gradually developed since the 1790s and which had but recently
recovered from the Jeffersonian embargo. After war with Great Britain
broke out, the foreign trade of the United States declined alarmingly.
Exports to the Spanish West Indies in particular dropped from
$3,972,140 in 1812 to $2,020,294 in 1814. Total American imports of
sugar from the area declined by more than half between 1812 and 1814.
The rigid British blockade of the American coastline had disastrous consequences for American ocean-carrying trade.

A curious and important development during this period of Anglo-
American struggle was that the Spanish islands surpassed the other foreign colonies in the West Indies as sources of supply for most of the
tropical products imported by the United States. Although the total
amount of these products was much less than in previous years, the proportion coming from the Spanish islands was greater than ever. During
1812 the Spanish West Indies were the main suppliers of sugar to the
United States. Traffic in this product with the French and British West
Indies had been almost wiped out. The only other competitors, and not
serious ones, were the Swedish West Indies. In coffee and molasses the
Spanish islands were the first sources of supply for the United States,
closely followed by the French West Indies. The same situation prevailed
in 1814, for in that year the Spanish West Indies were the main sources
of supply of sugar to the United States, far ahead of any other region in
America and the world.

The Spanish West Indies shared in the general trade recovery following the end of the War of 1812, becoming an even better market for
American products, especially flour. In 1815 United States exports to
the Spanish islands were greater than exports to the French or British
West Indies. During this period the United States imported almost all of
its sugar from the Caribbean area. In 1815 the United States imported
16,337,587 pounds of sugar from the Spanish West Indies, second only
to the 17,635,821 pounds exported to the United States by the French
West Indies. In 1815 the Spanish West Indies also exported to the United

States 2,345,206 gallons of molasses and 11,204,392 pounds of coffee. The Spanish islands were the United States' principal source of these products.

A series of economic reforms inaugurated in Puerto Rico during the second decade of the nineteenth century paved the way for closer and regular commercial relations with foreign countries, culminating in statutes that put this exchange on a permanent legal basis. These reforms, which are discussed in detail elsewhere in this book, were the result of the efforts of Ramón Power, deputy from Puerto Rico in the Spanish Constituent *Cortes,* or Parliament, then assembling at Cádiz. The most important of these measures was the creation of the civil intendancy of Puerto Rico in 1811. The new intendant was to administer financial and economic affairs, which until then had been part of the all-inclusive jurisdiction of the captain general; it was he who implemented the reforms decreed by the Cortes. For the first intendant, Power proposed and the Spanish Regency appointed Alejandro Ramírez y Blanco, a distinguished Spanish colonial administrator and economist. A zealous and untiring worker, he put into effect the decreed reforms and inaugurated some of his own. As a result of his measures, other ports besides San Juan were opened effectively to trade, taxes that had impeded trade and economic development were abolished, and permission was granted for the export of cattle to the foreign West Indian islands.

Since Ramírez's internal measures are discussed in the next chapter, this chapter deals solely with the impact of his administration on foreign trade, particularly with the American market. On April 1, 1815, Ramírez issued a proclamation intended to encourage trade and economic relations with the United States. Since peacetime made it possible to resume commercial relations with the United States, the intendant prescribed several regulations to stimulate it. Tariff duties were considerably decreased. All agricultural and husbandry implements, seeds, specie, machinery, and "instruments to assist labour or to promote the arts and sciences and horses for labour or pleasures," were to enter the island free of duty. The intendant emphasized the new attitude toward the United States in the proclamation when he wrote: "Every protection and assistance will be extended to American citizens trading here, and should any doubts hereafter arise on the construction of these regulations, the decision shall be in favor of the American citizen." Encouraged by this new atmosphere, on November 27, 1815, the United States appointed a second agent for San Juan.

As noted, the Spanish crown had made many exceptions to the

monopolistic rule, frequently licensing foreigners, including citizens of the United States, to take munitions, foodstuffs, and general merchandise to colonial ports. The colonial officials also used their discretionary powers to admit American trading vessels into port on the plea of an emergency, and renewed these admissions again and again. Finally, there was the forbidden but inviting contraband trade, which seemed considerable at this time.

As a rule, the exceptions in favor of American commerce were most numerous in colonies whose need for munitions and foodstuffs was most pressing and where the local colonial officials, who sometimes accepted favors from foreign merchants, could allege the need without overstraining the credulity of the home government. Also, these exceptions in favor of the United States were most numerous in the colonies near it. These two rules gave the United States an exceptionally favorable position in the Spanish West Indies during this period.

A very important relaxation of the Spanish monopoly for Puerto Rico was the Royal *Cédula* (the *Real Cédula de Gracias*) granted to the island on August 10, 1815. In this decree, King Ferdinand VII bestowed a series of concessions on the island to reward its people for not joining the rebellion then raging in the continental colonies and for helping the royal government subdue the rebels.

The chief objectives of the *Cédula* were the promotion of foreign colonization and the promotion of foreign trade. In trade, it granted the Puerto Ricans a fifteen-year permit to trade directly with foreign ports where Spanish consuls resided, providing all shipments were registered before these consuls. The concession, however, was limited to traffic in Spanish vessels; hence Puerto Rican ports continued legally closed to foreign vessels as far as permanent trade concessions were concerned. The decree empowered the governor and the intendant, in cases of extreme necessity, to allow direct trade with the foreign colonies in the Lesser Antilles. This article provided the governor and intendant with the pretext they needed in thier efforts to adjust the Royal *Cédula* to the social and economic realities of Puerto Rico.

Colonization provisions tempted prospective permanent settlers with one hundred seventy acres of land plus half that amount for each slave. In addition, slaves and agricultural implements were declared free of duty.

In efforts to adjust the *Cédula* to the economic necessities of Puerto Rico, the governor and intendant undoubtedly interpreted the decree more liberally than its makers intended. During the last weeks of 1815 and January, 1816, they issued a number of *Acuerdos* (agreements) to implement the *Cédula*. In view of pressing needs, commercial exchange was allowed with the Lesser Antilles and admission of vessels from the United States and Europe was granted for one year. Ramírez, in a report sent to the home government, recognized that the admission of foregin vessels was not in accord with either the letter or spirit of the *Cédula* but justified the measure in light of special circumstances in Puerto Rico:

Concerning the principal question, I rendered the viewpoint which seemed to me most expedient for the moment being of the opinion that for the present time we should imitate the conduct of the other powers which, according to the needs and the circumstances, refuse or allow the entrance of foreign vessels into their colonies, limiting the period of their stay and the articles or merchandise for import and export. Once the time period specified in the aforesaid *Acuerdo* has elapsed, we shall proceed according to Article I to examine again whether it is convenient to abolish or to continue such a permission; that is, unless a Crown decree to the contrary is received before. This inquiry into the matter should be repeated frequently according to any change in the circumstances and progress of our national trade in this island, encouraged as it is with a 12 percent preference in the tariff duties, total exemption of the tonnage duties, and in addition the other concessions which it widely enjoys by the Royal *Cédula* of August the 10th.

This statement clearly summarizes Ramírez's position on foreign trade in the colonies. He advocated strong protection of Spanish vessels and commerce, but as long as necessity and scarcity prevailed in the island, he defended the admission of foreign vessels under the best possible terms. Apparently the action he and the governor took in continuing to admit foreign vessels, as well as his other measures of economic rehabilitation, gained the approval of the crown, for Ramírez was promoted soon afterward to the much more important position of intendant of Havana.

The benefits of the new regulations were soon apparent. The volume of legal trade in Puerto Rico, which in 1813 totaled $269,008, increased to $1,082,299 in 1816 and to $2,103,498 in 1818. From this time, Puerto Rico's foreign trade increased steadily, mainly with the United States but also with the British, Danish, and French West Indies. Among products introduced from the United States were machinery for grinding rice and corn and medicines for the military hospital.

The growth of foreign trade in Puerto Rico, as in other parts of the Spanish empire, came to be tolerated by a crown that could ill afford to insist on its outdated monopoly. The Council of the Indies came to believe that the foreign trade allowed in wartime emergency had saved and was, saving key strategic colonial possessions from the revolutionary debacle.

Thus permission for American and other foreign vessels to enter Puerto Rican ports, granted by the governor and the intendant on January 31, 1816, was renewed yearly for the rest of the decade and the beginning of the next one, with the crown's approval. As demonstrated in Puerto Rico, Cuba, and Panamá, Madrid tended to yield, reluctantly but inevitably, to circumstances and gradually to open the colonial ports in America that were still in Spanish hands. In 1818, Cuba was finally granted the permanent admission of foreign vessels and freedom to trade with foreign nations, subject, of course, to heavy duties and a protectionist policy toward the commercial interests of the metropolis. The measure considerably boosted trade between Cuba and the United States. In January 1923, the *Cortes* of Spain decreed that the privileges already accorded to Cuba should be extended to all other colonies under the control of the crown, for a term of ten months, in favor of all those nations which the government might think proper to include. This policy reached its climax with the royal decree of Ferdinand VII issued on February 9, 1824, by which foreigners were permitted *ad perpetuam* to trade with the Spanish colonies in America. By this time, of course, the order applied for practical purposes only to Puerto Rico, which with Cuba was the only Spanish colony left in America. Before the end of the decade, the last remnants of Spanish mercantilistic monopoly in the islands disappeared when Spain finally allowed foreign nations official consular representation in Cuba and Puerto Rico. The importance of American trade to Puerto Rico was summed up by George Dawson Flinter, an Irish Army officer in the service of Spain; after commenting on Puerto Rico's favorable balance of trade with the United States, he added:

The trade which is carried on between the United States and Puerto Rico is more advantageous to the latter than that of any other nation. . . . The American trade embraced in 1830 27 percent of the total imports and 49 percent of the exports. The importations from America are not in luxuries, but in the necessities of life—such as salt, fish, flour, butter, lard, grain, lumber, staves, and articles of furniture. . . . The chief articles with which this island supplies America are sugar, rum, molasses, and coffee. From this hurried survey of the exports from this island to the American continent it is obvious that the United States, besides affording an inexhaustible and cheap supply, is also the best and surest market for the disposal of the planter's productions, for which there is not a sufficient sale either in the Peninsula or in the rest of Europe.

The development of these trade outlets added vitality to Puerto Rican economic life, particularly after maritime peace returned to the Caribbean with the success of the Latin American continental revolutions in the mid-1820s. Most of the insular economy benefited: agriculture, internal and external commerce, incipient industry, and, above all, the island's public finances all entered a period of unparalleled growth. Puerto Rican society, whose population had been growing since the early eighteenth century, had lacked the modern economic and fiscal structures necessary to support such growth. Such structures, with their concurrent public and private institutions, now began to take shape, solidly rooted in the new commercial and economic development. Socially, economically, and administratively, Puerto Rico had at last come of age.

Puerto Rico and Latin America's Struggle for Independence

Early in May 1810, as Napoleon was invading Spain, alarming news from Venezuela reached San Juan: a serious revolt in Caracas and other cities had overthrown peninsular Spanish authorities. It was soon learned that the revolt had spread to contiguous Spanish colonies, notably Nueva Granada (now Colombia). Soon numerous refugees, mostly expelled military officers and government officials, started arriving in Puerto Rico. A new period was at hand in the complicated history of the Spanish Caribbean. It was a revolutionary era, perhaps more important in the area's evolution than the era around 1789. But this time the challenge to the Spanish colonial monopoly was reinforced by the revolt of the Spanish colonials themselves. The Spanish West Indies were to remain faithful to the mother country during this stage, although they were not to escape the immediate effects of the continental revolutionary upheaval. The nationalist spirit of the South American Creoles had also been evident, though much more faintly, among some groups in Puerto Rico since the 1790s. Historians have recorded the subversive activities and public outbursts of Puerto Rican partisans of the era's revolutions. These feelings were strengthened by Puerto Rico's links with Venezuela through cultural, social, religious, and educational ties.

The South American revolutionary spirit thus evoked sympathy as well as some echo among parts of the rising insular Creole class. This spirit pervades the Instructions given in 1809 by the *Cabildo* (Municipal Council) of San Germán to the first delegate to the Spanish Constituent *Cortes*, Ramón Power. Though recognizing the sovereignty of French-held Ferdinand VII, San Germán maintained that if Spain were defeated by Napoleon, "this island should then be independent and free to choose the best ways to preserve in peace its inhabitants and their enjoyment of the Christian religion." The *Cabildo* also demanded the creation then, as in war-torn Spain, of a temporary provincial *Junta* that would assume the supreme military and civil powers in the island, a revolutionary step that had already been unsuccessfully attempted in some other continental colonies and was to be generally adopted after 1810. In the same vein, when in late 1810 the special commissioner sent by the Spanish Regency to negotiate with the Caracas rebels, apparently proposed in San Juan that Puerto Rican militia be used to reinforce Spanish Royalist forces in South America, Puerto Rican separatists warned him in a stern anonymous note. "This country," they wrote, "compliant enough to obey its recognized authorities will never allow a single American being taken away from the island to fight against his Caracas brothers." Historian Francisco Morales Padrón, quoting unpublished Spanish archival sources, has pointed out that as soon as revolt broke out in Caracas in 1810 and 1811 the new revolutionary currents began to be felt among certain prominent Creole groups in San Juan and San Germán. Discontent with the regime, in many degrees, was rife and came to the fore at the time of the election of Ramón Power as insular *diputado*. At the same time, Venezuelan revolutionary leaders corresponded with members of the insular Creole elite, keeping the island abreast of the political and military situation in South America. Many Puerto Ricans now publicly expressed their opposition to local peninsular authorities and urged the creation of a provincial *Junta*. This agitation seems to have culminated in San Germán in 1811 in a widespread but rather unorganized and rapidly quashed separatist conspiracy which involved many members of that region's Creole landed gentry.

However, the revolutionary, separatist spirit was not shared by the majority of the island's inhabitants at this time, and thus, as in the case of Cuba, it would not be the decisive historical force at this stage. A liberal reformist tendency was to emerge, instead, to oppose the conservatives who were unconditionally loyal to Spain. From the start the members of the *Cabildo* of San Juan took an anti-revolutionary line. In 1810, when the *Cabildo* of Caracas invited them to follow its revolutionary program, they ratified, instead, their loyalty to local peninsular officials and the Spanish Regency Council. The widespread economic and political discontent went no farther than liberal reform; this attitude prevailed in insular public opinion and was clearly exemplified in the words and actions of Ramón Power, its foremost exponent at this time. Various theories have been suggested to explain this attitude. Some historians have noted the country's strong loyalty to Spain and its representatives, carefully nurtured among the local residents in a military *presidio* such as Puerto Rico had been since the late sixteenth century. These bonds were reinforced during the revolutionary conflict as the island became Spain's anti-revolutionary bastion in the Caribbean and welcomed successive waves of South American loyalist refugees. Others have stressed the Creole landholders' fear of a revolutionary climate that would promote Haitian-type slave rebellions in a colony which, like contemporary Cuba, was now in the early stages of a sugar cane, slave-operated, plantation economy. Others have underscored the inherent economic weakness of the local Creole landholding class which prevented it, in contrast to its South American counterpart, from generating a revolution to promote its own economic and political power.

In spite of this pervading anti-revolutionary spirit, insular Spanish authorities were plagued during these years by the manifold activities of local revolutionary sympathizers, conspiracies, and the presence in the island of agents of the South American insurgents. Throughout this period, Puerto Rico was Spain's principal counter-revolutionary bastion in the eastern Caribbean for the struggle in northern South America, especially Venezuela. Many expeditions were fitted out in Puerto Rico and sailed from its ports to suppress the continental rebellion. A notable example was the expedition sent from Puerto Rico under Captain Domingo Monteverde and reinforced by royalist partisans there, that in 1812 swiftly put an end to the first Republic of Venezuela. Puerto Rico was also the supply and auxiliary base for the forces of General Pablo Morillo during his long struggle, from 1815 to 1822, to reestablish royal power in northern South America.

In reaction to this role, the South American revolutionaries intensified their subversive actions in and around Puerto Rico. Perhaps the most notable was the increased activity of insurgent privateers in Puerto Rican waters and even along the coastline. From 1814 on these irregular naval forces flying the flags of various insurgent regimes—New Granada, Mexico, Venezuela, and even the far-off Río de la Plata—menaced Spanish power in the West Indies.

From the early days, United States citizens and residents played an important role in these activities. Unable to assemble the necessary naval and human resources in their own territories, the insurgent regimes sent agents to the United States to sell privateer's licenses there. Thus, fitted and equipped in American ports, often financed there, and manned in many cases by American crews, insurgent privateers swarmed around the West Indies to attack Spain's most vital interests and lines of communication, completely disrupting the latter. For Puerto Rico the results were disastrous, both indirectly in the effects on trade and directly in the insurgent raids on the coasts. This activity reached a climax when on January 25, 1817, various Buenos Aires privateering vessels, mostly manned by American crews and led by Amercian-born Thomas Taylor, landed at the port of Fajardo on the eastern coast and raided the town. According to Governor Salvador Meléndez, they wanted plunder: foodstuffs, arms, and gunpowder. The local militia attacked the invaders and after a time forced them to retreat to their boats. There was a heavy loss of life on both sides. Governor Meléndez was forced to deal on a semiofficial basis with Taylor and on February 12 agreed with him to an exchange of prisoners.

For a long time Puerto Rico was kept semi-blockaded by the Buenos Aires, Venezuela, and New Granda privateers. Even official correspondence to Spain was intercepted; several important communications from the governor of Puerto Rico to the Ministry at Madrid were given wide publicity, making it necessary to use a code. According to the chronicler Pedro Tomás de Córdova, the privateers continued their attacks on Puerto Rico up to the end of the decade, raiding coastal establishments, disrupting maritime trade, kidnapping people and exacting a high ransom for their return. Coastal settlements like Humacao, Guayama, Ponce, and Aguadilla suffered most. For a time the privateers established themselves at Caja de Muertos Key, off the southern coast of the island, and from there made occasional raids on the Puerto Rican mainland.

Puerto Rico's economic life suffered as a result; trade and communications in the Spanish Caribbean and West Indies almost ceased. In 1817 London insurance rates on vessels navigating under the Spanish flag had become almost prohibitive, to the benefit of neutral shipping, especially British and American. By June 1817, according to the contemporary press, Spanish Caribbean trade was again carried on mainly in neutral vessels. Ship owners in Spain transferred their vessels to foreign neutral registry and the Spanish government tried in vain to raise money for an adequate naval force to confront the privateers. Both government officials and the civil population became further disheartened at each new turn for the worse in the chaotic situation, as the privateering noose tightened. The privateering naturally extended and intensified the contraband trade that had characterized the economic life of the Spanish West Indies since the sixteenth century. Although most of the cargoes and merchandise captured in and around Puerto Rico were sent to be sold in the Lesser Antilles, the privateers occasionally traded part of their captured merchandise in secret recesses along the coast of Puerto Rico. Between the disruption of legal trade and the expansion of contraband, the economic and administrative reform program inaugurated by Intendant Ramírez did not produce the expected immediate results. With the export trade so highly disrupted, the insular authorities had to keep the ports open to friendly foreign vessels, mostly American and British, one of the main goals of the Intendant's program. Not until the next decade, when maritime traffic had returned to a somewhat more normal state in the Caribbean, was the island to witness the full result of those early reforms.

As the 1820s approached, circumstances became more complicated and volatile throughout the West Indies and Caribbean as privateering rapidly degenerated into open piracy. Throughout the revolutionary period, pirates had profited from the disruption of maritime order. Many of the so-called privateers were no more than disguised pirates, using the privateering licenses as a cover for their illegal activities. Since privateering was never closely regulated, many privateers oscillated between privateering and piracy. When European naval powers and the United States put pressure on these practices, the insurgent regimes began to regulate their privateers, thus decreasing their profits and curtailing their field of action, as did the newly created Republic of Gran Colombia, or abolished privateering altogether, as did the government of Buenos Aires in 1821. As a result, most of the international adventurers who had flown privateer's flags became flagrant pirates after 1820.

Another factor soon complicated the situation further. As the insurgents gained control of northern South America after 1819, Spain instituted a naval blockade of the region; however, it did not have the power to enforce it. The new, independent governments opened their trade to all friendly nations and very soon vessels from Europe and North America flocked to their ports. To Spain, however, these new nations were still rebellious colonies and she tried by all means to counteract this growing exchange. Her main weapon was the authorization of Spanish privateers, who after 1820 increasingly operated all over the Caribbean out of Cuban and Puerto Rican ports. Thus, Puerto Rican-based Spanish privateers, operated mostly by insular crews, attacked European and American ships passing near the island on their way to the newly opened Venezuelan ports. Needless to say, Spain could not control completely her privateers and many swiftly turned to piracy. Naval warfare in the Caribbean thus took a turn for the worse and American interests were adversely affected. American authorities, under pressure from maritime and business interests, began to build up American naval strength in the Caribbean. Early in 1822 the United States Navy created a permanent West Indies Squadron to protect American trade in the region. By dint of constant patrolling and activity, between 1822 and 1826 the United States Navy, with the negotiated assistance and collaboration of local Spanish authorities, ended international piracy in the area. At the same time the Spanish government was prodded into a closer supervision of its privateers.

Incidental to this action, however, in 1824 the American Commodore David Porter embroiled himself in a situation that was to have adverse international repercussions. Claiming that local authorities in Fajardo, a port in Eastern Puerto Rico, had been disrespectful towards American naval officers who had landed there to search for pirates, Porter landed part of his forces there, threatened to destroy the town, and extracted an apology from the local officials. Both the Spanish captain general of Puerto Rico, Miguel de la Torre, and the Madrid ministry protested; Porter was court martialed and suspended from the service. However, these joint United States-Spanish naval actions led to the capture of several international pirates. Notable among these, and later executed, were the Puerto Rican Roberto Cofresí, still today a controversial figure among Puerto Rican writers, many of whom view him as an early national hero, and the Portuguese-American José Joaquín de Almeida, a former American privateer during the War of 1812, and later in the service of Buenos Aires and Venezuela. The American naval intervention underscored Spain's incapacity to control maritime anarchy in the West Indies and the Caribbean and brought to the fore the early presence there of the adjacent North American republic as the power who undertook this task.

After 1820, when the Spanish royalist cause seemed doomed in the continent, frequent attempts were prepared in the United States to invade the insular Spanish possessions and wrest them from their metropolis. A notable example, affecting the relations between Puerto Rico and the United States, was the expedition outfitted in New York and Philadelphia in 1822 by Louis Du Coudray Holstein, a German-French soldier of fortune who had previously collaborated with Simón Bolívar in Venezuela. With a group of European and American adventurers, he planned to invade Puerto Rico and proclaim the so-called Republic of Boricua. The attempt was financed by residents of Puerto Rico, mostly foreigners who had sent funds to the United States and made that country the main base for their conspiracy. The expedition failed. The local Puerto Rican counterpart fizzled when the conspiracy was denounced to the Spanish authorities; the main conspirators were arrested and executed. Du Coudary Holstein, who had sailed from the United States with his expedition, learned in the Lesser Antilles that his Puerto Rican confederates had failed. He sought refuge from bad weather in Curacao and ended up, with his companions, arrested and tried on piracy charges by Dutch West Indian authorities.

Another result of the defense of the Spanish cause was the mass migration of royalist partisans to the Spanish West Indies, their only remaining haven in America. Although the subject has never been adequately studied, a large number of these refugees arrived and settled in Puerto Rico, both in the urban and the rural areas. Their establishment has been, for historians, a double-edged issue. On the one hand, while most arrived penniless, their superior education and their knowledge and experience in agriculture, trade, and industry became a dynamic element in the development of the island. On the other hand, their conservative, anti-separatist outlook may have exerted a deleterious influence on nineteenth century insular political life.

Between 1819 and 1823, as the insurgents consolidated their control over northern South America and Mexico, colonial authorities in the Spanish West Indies lived in fear of an invasion of their territory by the forces of the new nations. In Puerto Rico this feeling was perhaps exacerbated after 1822, when Miguel de la Torre, the defeated Spanish commander in chief in Venezuela, was appointed captain general. Another factor aggravating these misgivings was the presence in South America and Mexico of many Cuban and Puerto Rican separatists, some of them military men, who had collaborated in the continental struggle as a preamble to the independence of the islands, and were now actively pushing in that direction. A notable example was the Puerto Rican Antonio Valero de Bernabe, a native of Fajardo, who after years as an officer in the Spanish army and serving the independent governments of Mexico, Peru, and Gran Colombia, attained the highest ranks in the latter. After 1824, when the continental struggle culminated triumphantly in the Battle of Ayacucho in Peru, reports and rumors of an impending Mexican and Colombian invasion of the islands multiplied. This development reached its heights with the assembling of the new independent republics at Panama in 1826 to consider forming a confederative alliance. The invasion never materialized, however, and the islands were to remain throughout the nineteenth century in the hands of Spain. Various factors were held responsible for this situation, notably the early rivalries among the new states, their internal conflicts, and the outspoken opposition of Great Britain and the United States, both with their designs on the area, to the islands' changing hands at this juncture.

As the struggle ended, naval warfare subsided over the Caribbean and trade and economic activities resumed. There was a return to something approaching normal conditions in the Spanish West Indies. From the 1820s on, the islands were permanently opened to foreign commercial exchange and permission had been granted to establish foreign consulates. It took a long while for fears to quiet down completely, even after Spain and her once rebellious daughters established formal diplomatic relations during the 1830s. Politically, Puerto Rico was now, with Cuba, the last New World bastion of a conservative Spanish colonial regime, but conditions now favored the full operation of previously granted reforms and the initiation of a new stage of economic growth which under increasing foreign control would gradually but relentlessly draw insular interests away from their metropolis.

6
Towards a Plantation Society

Luis González Vales

The British attack on San Juan in 1797 signals the end of an era and the dawn of one of the most significant periods in the island's history. The failure of Abercromby's expedition closed the cycle of major aggressions that marked the island's history during its first three centuries.

During the British attack native Puerto Ricans, or *Criollos,* played a significant role in the defense. The self-reliance this experience generated helped speed the development of a national consciousness. The islanders had a sense of community. Left behind was the era of a military *Presidio.* Puerto Rico was more than just a fortified outpost. The island was on the way to becoming a thriving colony.

The administrative system was based on the Laws of the Indies, which, for the most part, dated back to the reigns of Philip II and his successor, Philip III. The *Nueva Recopilación* (new compilation) of 1795 supported a conservative and absolutist monarchy, reflected in the absolute power of the colonial captain general. The governor was virtually omnipotent. He continued to exert broad executive and legislative powers and was supreme commander of the island's military forces. As intendant he controlled the Royal Treasury, thus wielding tremendous economic power. He was also the top judicial officer and, as vice regal patron, exercised powers over the church. In contrast, the colonists had no representation in any governing body and no way to check the power of the governors.

Due to the island's strategic importance, the practice of naming soldiers to the governorship persisted. Unfortunately, these candidates were rarely qualified in government and administration; thus their performance was in many ways detrimental to the colonists and to the general development of the island.

The colonial economic system considered the island as a mere dependency to be exploited to the advantage of the mother country. Like the political regime, it offered little opportunity for the islanders to prosper. Commerce still struggled under a myriad of discouraging restrictions and local production was heavily taxed. What little commerce existed with the metropolis was to the advantage of the peninsular entrepreneurs. Agriculture languished and exports were insufficient to offset the importation of countless badly needed manufactured goods.

In spite of the fertility of the land and the importance of the island, which moved Reynal to consider it "an asset to an active nation," agriculture was in bad condition, discouraged by many restrictions and prohibitions and the heavy taxes levied on land and production.

Only sugar and coffee could be considered major commercial crops. The Haitian revolution had stimulated Puerto Rican sugar production, which found a ready market and benefited from the increased demand and the rise in prices in the international market.

Industrial resources, aside from those devoted to sugar production, were limited to small factories that helped supply the domestic market with fiber goods, pottery, furniture, livery equipment, sails, tobacco, and small powder. This limited industrial development was primarily the result of protective legislation favoring peninsular industries and prohibiting the establishment of any type of factory that would compete with those in Spain. Even the sugar industry suffered from such restrictions, some of which date back to the first half of the sixteenth century, and occasionally had to bear excessive taxes. Fray Iñigo Abbad, in his history referring to rum production, wrote: "If the extraction of this product is allowed and used to supply the demands of the 'Tierra Firme' markets, even if it is heavily taxed so that it does not compete advantageously with those produced in Spain, this would alone suffice to insure the well being and happiness of this island." However, the tribute of *saca* or distillation kept the product from competing with imported rums even in the local market.

The cattle industry was close to ruin because of the *abasto forzoso*, which required all landowners to contribute, in proportion to the land held, to the supply of fresh meat for the population of San Juan. Those who had no cattle had to pay for the purchase of enough heads of cattle to fill their quota.

The treasury was in chaos. Total annual income from revenues amounted to 60,000 pesos. The government depended on the *Situado*, instituted in 1582, to cover perennial deficits. A suspension or delay in the receipt of this money from the Mexican treasury created a crisis in the island's finances at the beginning of the nineteenth century. Accountability for funds was at best spotty, for records were seldom audited. Revenues from the extremely complicated tax system could not be determined. Accounts were never closed out and balance sheets were never prepared. If entries were made, they were more likely to conceal misuse of public funds than to prevent it.

Public works were rarely begun. "The roads of this island," records Fray Iñigo Abbad, "are so rough, soggy, narrow and dangerous that they seem more fitted for birds than for human beings." Sanitary conditions were extremely poor and public schools were scarce. The French botanist Pierre Ledrú, a visitor to the island in 1797, wrote that "seven tenths of the population did not know how to read due to lack of schools." In 1805 Governor Toribio Montes complained that the education of adolescents, both male and female, was practically nil because of the need for schools where they could be taught the basic skills. San Juan had only two elementary schools, subsidized by the *Ayuntamiento* (City Council), and a few other private schools, not enough to meet the city's needs.

Secondary education was limited to schools established in the Convents of Santo Domingo and San Francisco in San Juan. Higher education was restricted to philosophy and theology courses given at the Convent of Santo Domingo primarily for candidates to the priesthood. To obtain a university education, students had to go abroad, usually to Spain, Santo Domingo, Mexico, and Venezuela. Events in the early nineteenth century further limited these opportunities.

The judicial system was still in the hands of the *Tenientes a Guerra*, who served as judges of first instance in the towns of the interior. These officers, appointed by the governor, in many cases lacked the judicial expertise to exercise their functions. Appeals could be made to the *Audiencia* of Puerto Príncipe in Cuba, but this was a slow and expensive process and did not guarantee justice.

Socially, the situation was not much better. The island's population was approximately 158,000, less than one inhabitant per square mile. The lack of incentives and opportunities encouraged a very quiet and uneventful existence. The vast majority of the people were content to produce the bare essentials to meet their immediate needs. The *penin-*

sulares or Spaniards enjoyed a privileged position. To them went the choice posts in the colonial administration and many of them controlled the principal commercial enterprises.

For Spain, the first decade of the nineteenth century was a period of political turmoil and military disasters, which eventually brought about the collapse of its American empire. Since 1796 the Spanish nation had been virtually a satellite of revolutionary France. This brought Spain into conflict with England, which was at war with the French. Spain enjoyed a temporary respite when Napoleon made a short-lived peace with England, but in 1804 hostilities broke out again with Spain once more on the side of the French. War with England was disastrous for the Spanish interests. The defeat of the Spanish fleet by Lord Nelson at Trafalgar left England in nearly absolute control of the sea lanes and disrupted communications between Spain and its American colonies. Commercial relations between the two came to a standstill.

The virtual suspension of trade with the American colonies and the ever-increasing burden of the war brought Spain to an economic and political crisis, worsened by some of the government's attempts to raise the revenues to finance the war. Government expropriation of some ecclesiastical properties aroused the displeasure of the powerful Catholic church. The introduction of large quantities of paper currency fed inflation and increased popular discontent. The opposition rallied around Crown Prince Ferdinand; and in 1808, faced with open rebellion and popular rioting, Charles IV abdicated in favor of his son, who became Ferdinand VII.

Napoleon now injected himself into the situation, intending to replace the Spanish Bourbons with one of his brothers as king. While Ferdinand was being hailed as the new king, Napoleon's armies marched into the peninsula. By the end of the year Charles IV, María Luisa, and their ministers were in exile in Italy, Ferdinand was Napoleon's virtual prisoner, Joseph Bonaparte had been declared king of Spain, and Spain's major cities were occupied by French troops.

The Spanish people rebelled against the French occupation; their resistence led to the coexistence of two governments in Spain. The government of the French invaders was led by King Joseph I, Napoleon's brother; the other, a symbol of the resistance, consisted initially of many local and regional *Juntas* (Boards), which gave way eventually to a *Junta Central* (Central Board), the Regency, and the Cortes.

These events had important effects for the American continent. Many of the Spanish American colonies claimed independence. The movement that began under the guise of preserving Ferdinand VII's rights later became open rebellion against Spanish rule. As former possessions proclaimed their independence one by one, three centuries of Spanish domination came to an end.

The first news of the events in Spain reached Puerto Rico on July 24, 1808, with the arrival of two representatives of the *Junta* of Seville, visiting the American colonies to raise funds for the war. In Puerto Rico, allegiance was publicly sworn to Ferdinand VII and the occasion was celebrated with gun salutes and church services. Shortly after, a representative of Bonaparte arrived at San Juan to invite Governor Montes to pledge allegiance to Bonaparte. Montes declined, and the emissary had to be locked in *El Morro* to save him from being stoned to death by the people.

By far the most significant news from Spain was the decree issued on January 22, 1809 by the *Junta Suprema y Gubernativa de España e Indias* (Supreme Governing Council). This document recognized the equality of the colonies with the Spanish provinces and made them integral parts of the monarchy with the right of representation before the *Junta*. This decree entitled Puerto Rico to a representative at the *Junta,* who was to be elected by the process specified in the decree.

Governor Montes sent immediate instructions to the five *Ayuntamientos:* San Juan, San Germán, Aguada, Arecibo, and Coamo. Each town council was to select three candidates of known reputation and suitable qualifications; one would be chosen by lot as the candidate for that *Ayuntamiento.* The name of the candidate with all the pertinent data was to be sent to the governor. The election was to be witnessed by all the most outstanding members of the community.

The decree raised Puerto Rican's hopes for a better understanding of their problems by the metropolitan government. Naturally, the concession holders and favorites of the old regime took steps to maintain the status quo and their privileges. Two opposing tendencies emerged at this time: a liberal tendency represented mainly by the *Criollos* or Creoles, and a conservative one represented by the Spaniards.

On May 4, 1809 the *Ayuntaminentos* met to elect their candidates. Next came the meeting of the Provincial Electoral Board to select the island's representative from the five candidates. The Electoral Board met in July 1809 at *La Fortaleza,* under the presidency of the governor, and elected Navy Lieutenant D. Ramón Power y Giralt. Born in San Juan in 1775, he had been educated abroad and had traveled extensively throughout America. He was well known as a man of liberal ideas. Power's election would bring about a series of reforms, culminating in the establishment of the Intendancy separate from the office of the captain general and the appointment of Alejandro Ramírez as first intendant for Puerto Rico.

An Experiment in Constitutional Government

Power's election was received with great joy, and his short sojourn at San Juan before leaving for Spain was marked by public celebrations demonstrating the feelings of the people of Puerto Rico. In a ceremony at the Cathedral of San Juan, Juan Alejo de Arizmendi, the first Puerto Rican to serve as bishop, presented Power with his episcopal ring, which as he put it, would remind him of his "commitment to protect and sustain the rights of our fellow countrymen, as I myself am willing to die for my flock." The bishop's gesture and Power's speech in response, are early indications of a nascent spirit of nationalism in Puerto Rico.

Governor Meléndez and other members of the island's Spanish community were displeased by this outburst of nationalism. Meléndez wrote to the *Junta Suprema* denouncing Power's election, even though he had previously proclaimed that Power was the best qualified candidate. In the governor's colonial mentality the nationalistic sentiments of Arizmendi and Power clearly indicated disloyalty to Spain.

Events in Spain changed the situation. The *Junta Suprema* was abolished and a regency was installed on October 31, 1810, thus invalidating Power's election. The new government, however, followed the pattern of the *Junta Suprema* and instructed the colonies to elect representatives to the *Cortes*. Power was elected again and confirmed in his post of *Diputado a Cortes* or representative for Puerto Rico.

The *Instrucciones:* The *Cabildo's* Assessment of the Island's Problems

Before his departure for Spain, Power received instructions from the five island *Ayuntamientos* to guide his action at the *Cortes*. These instructions revealed most of the grievances against the system and contained a number of petitions for reforms. They can be compared to the *cahiers de doléance* drafted by French cities during 1789.

The *Ayuntamientos* proclaimed their allegiance to the Spanish crown but described the contemporary regime as "oppresive, arbitrary and tyrannical" and asked Power to take steps for its immediate reform so that "the chains that weigh us down and prevent our development be broken," as demanded by the "laws of humanity." This amounted to an assertion of their natural rights. The *Ayuntamiento* of San Germán went a step further, instructing Power that if Spain should be lost to Napoleon, the island would be free to select the best way of "preserving the Christian faith and insuring the peace and tranquility of its inhabitants." (Power is said to have rejected this recommendation as contrary to the oath he had taken.)

The *Ayuntamientos*, concerned for intellectual conditions in Puerto Rico, requested more public schools with capable teachers and sufficient equipment, as well as a university with offerings in the arts and sciences. To improve health conditions, they proposed the establishment of hospitals and a sanatorium. To prevent delinquency, the reformers suggested that a mechanical arts school for both sexes be organized.

The *Ayuntamientos* urged the construction of roads and bridges to improve communications with the towns of the interior. This would foster economic development by allowing for more active commerce between San Juan and the other towns, which the poor roads had rendered virtually nonexistent. The *Ayuntamientos* recommended the creation of a *clase de jornaleros* (paid laborers) to improve the moral and economic conditions of the working class. All the uncultivated lands that belonged to the state were to be distributed and *gremios* or craft guilds should be formed like those existing in Spain.

The *Ayuntamientos* also addressed the conditions of the judicial system. They requested that the *Tenientes a Guerra* and their deputies, who administered justice in the towns, be elected by the people instead of appointed by the governor. They also suggested that Puerto Rico be put under the jurisdiction of the *Audiencia* of Caracas because of its convenience and proximity.

To improve agriculture, the principal source of income, it was requested that the *abasto forzoso* be abolished. The *Ayuntamientos* also wanted restrictions on wheat farming lifted since this was an essential product for the island which Spain could not supply. They requested the right to introduce, free of duty, agricultural equipment, seeds, fertilizers, and other needed items to improve agricultural production. Several decreases in taxes were also requested.

In industry and industrial development, the first priority was the abolition of taxes on distillation of rums. To improve commerce, franchises for the island's commerce, freedom of trade with foreign nations for fifteen or twenty years, and the opening of new ports to such commerce were requested, as well as an end to the government monopoly on the flour supply.

To stimulate the cattle industry, the *Ayuntamientos* demanded free trade with foreign nations. They also requested a new tax system based on income and, finally, that talented Puerto Ricans be given an opportunity to occupy important positions in the island's administration.

These instructions reflect the liberal ideas common to Spanish jurists, intellectuals, and theologians of the sixteenth, seventeenth, and eighteenth centuries, the democratic ideals of the North American reformers, and those of the representative authors of the Enlightenment—especially the French—ideas that came via Spain or were disseminated by Puerto Ricans educated in universities abroad.

Armed with these instructions, Power left for Spain aboard the corvette *Príncipe de Asturias* in April 1810.

Power at the *Cortes de Cádiz*

The *Cortes* opened its sessions on September 24, 1810. Next day Power was unanimously elected first vice president. One of the first actions of the *Cortes* was to restate the principle that the colonies were an integral part of the Spanish nation with rights and privileges equal to those of other provinces of Spain.

Colonial reforms were eagerly awaited. Ships from Spain brought news of the works of the *Cortes*. Newspaper accounts and the Minutes of the *Cortes* were widely circulated. As has been mentioned, the island's population was divided into two sectors. The conservatives consisted of the civilian and military government employees, and the influential businessmen, generally Spaniards, who controlled trade and local production and who, with their intermediaries, made up the island's most important economic force. The liberals and reformists included the majority of the professionals, small farmers, cattlemen, industrialists, and Creole businessmen (some of whom turned conservative later on). The liberals thus comprised the majority of the middle and lower classes and its most important social element. The first group clung to tradition, the other saw change and development as the source of happiness. The conservatives took a paternalistic stance that saw society as a mere dependency of the crown; the liberals believed in the sovereignty of the people. The former considered regionalism and Spanish imperialism incompatible; the latter saw them as perfectly harmonious. The conservatives desired more state intervention in local affairs; the liberals aspired to more individual freedom. The conservatives considered economic matters more important while the liberals gave priority to political and social matters. To accomplish their objectives, the conservatives adopted the position of loyal vassals and true friends of the government. The liberals adopted the legalistic approach and tried to achieve reform through peaceful means.

Meanwhile, Venezuela, taking advantage of the demise of the *Junta Suprema* and its replacement by a regency in 1810, proclaimed its independence three days after Power's election. This had a twofold effect on Puerto Rico. Loyal Spaniards migrated from Venezuela to the island to avoid persecution, creating more difficulties for the Puerto Rican economy. More important, however, the Regency, without waiting for the meeting of the *Cortes,* on September 4 granted the governor of Puerto Rico dictatorial powers. This was a gross error. Puerto Rico had given enough proof of its loyalty to the Spanish crown, including its successful resistance to the British assault in 1797. Rather than being praised for its loyalty, Puerto Rico was being punished. The regency was acting to preserve the island for Spain, but the method did more to alienate than to strengthen loyalty toward the mother country.

The convening of the *Cortes* had far-reaching effects. Between September 1810 and March 19, 1812, the period in which the *Constitución de Cádiz* (Cádiz Constitution) was drafted, fundamental changes were made in Spain's political history. The Spanish historian Luis Sánchez Agesta describes two events which accentuate the political significance of that period: "The absolute monarchy that had reached its zenith towards the end of the eighteenth century suffered a violent transformation giving way to a constitutional monarchy of liberal and democratic tendencies" and further adds that "the social and economic evolution begun in the seventeenth century is accelerated and strengthened by political revolution."

On December 16, 1810 the American and Asian deputies presented to the *Cortes* a document comprising eleven propositions that would make the promised colonial equality a reality. The document requested the most ample freedom of commerce, the suppression of all government monopolies, the free exploitation of the quicksilver deposits, equal opportunity for Creoles, Indians, and Mestizos in government, and the return of the Jesuits to the Indian missions.

Almost two months later, on February 15, 1811, Power presented the case of Puerto Rico before the *Cortes*. He analyzed the effects of the

September 4 decree, labeling it untimely, a repudiation of all the promises made by the defunct *Junta Suprema* and by the regency, and contrary to the rights of the Puerto Ricans. The order was reversed by a decree of the *Cortes* on that very day.

For Puerto Rico, the most significant result of Power's efforts at the *Cortes* was the decree of the regency scantioned by the *Cortes* on November 28, 1811, in which many of Power's petitions for the development of the island's agriculture, industry, and commerce were addressed. The main reform was the separation of the intendancy from the office of the governor and the appointment of Alejandro Ramírez as the island's first intendant. The so-called *Ley Power* (Power Act) ordered the opening of the ports of Aguadilla, Cabo Rojo, Ponce, and Fajardo to commerce and appointed an administration for all of them. The law also called for the abolition of the *abasto forzoso,* authorized free trade in flour, granted freedom of export of cattle with only a modest duty and provided for the establishment of a *Sociedad Económica de Amigos del País,* an economic society patterned after those already existing in Spain.

Even though this law did not address all the aspects of the *instrucciones,* it was considered adequate for the time being. Some of the *Ayuntamientos'* requests had been filled. The separation of the intendancy from the governorship meant that a movement toward decentralization and balance of power was underway.

The constitution approved by the *Cortes* in March was proclaimed in Puerto Rico on July 15, 1812. It extended to the Puerto Ricans the basic rights of inviolability of house, person, and property, and freedom of speech, work, and voting. The island was authorized to have a *Diputado a Cortes* to be seleceted by a system of indirect vote at three levels, the parish, the district or *Partido,* and the province. The election of the *Diputado* was for a two-year period. After two years out of office he was eligible for re-election.

The *Diputación Provincial,* a provincial delegation authorized by the new constitution, consisted of nine members. The governor, who presided, and the intendant were *ex-officio* members; the other seven members and three alternates were elected by the five electors who chose the *Diputado a Cortes.* The main functions of the *Diputación* were to determine the taxes to be paid and distribute them by towns; examine the accounts of the *Ayuntamientos;* regulate the use of public funds, organize new *Ayuntamientos;* supervise the operation of the hospitals and other public institutions; promote public works; stimulate agriculture, industry, and commerce; and promote education. The *Diputación* could be dissolved only by the king with the approval of the *Cortes*.

The executive power was vested in the governor, who was always appointed by the king. Everything not covered by the constitution was governed by the statutes contained in the new compilation of the Laws of Castile.

Even though the constitution gave more autonomy in local administration, it left many of the old economic problems unresolved. In political matters the main drawback was that the *Cortes* still ruled on affairs of importance to small communities thousands of miles away about which it knew nothing.

Parochial elections started in October 1812. The process was very slow, especially because of the rivalry between liberals and conservatives. José Maria Quiñones was elected *Diputado a Cortes* on February 21, 1813, and the first *Diputación Provincial* had its first meeting on May 5, 1813.

The Puerto Ricans took full advantage of the *Diputación Provincial* during the year of its existence. It provided a forum for the new experience in government just when the people were beginning to define their identity. The members of the *Diputación* behaved with suitable discretion. Inexperienced in self-government, they were timid and uncertain. Nevertheless, their actions showed signs of an incipient political maturity. The efforts of the *Diputación* were as varied as its responsibilities. The limits of its authority were broad and matters that had to be submitted to the central government for approval generally received it.

The *Diputación Provincial* was abolished by Ferdinand VII on May 4, 1814, upon his return from captivity and his re-establishment as absolute monarch. It was revived in 1820 during the second Spanish constitutional period.

Alejandro Ramírez and the Intendancy

Power's selection of Alejandro Ramírez as the island's first intendant was a wise one; in his previous posts Ramírez had given ample proof of his administrative capacity, his devotion to duty, and his commitment to the interests of those he served.

When Ramírez was appointed on January 14, 1812, he was serving in Guatemala. On his way to Puerto Rico he visited Havana, where he took time to familiarize himself with the operation of the Intendancy and the *Tribunal de Cuentas* and to observe the operations of nearby coffee and sugar plantations. On December 14 he was sworn in by his friend Captain General Juan Ruiz de Apodaca.

Ramírez arrived in Puerto Rico on February 11, 1813 and two days later assumed his new responsibilities. Puerto Rico was fertile ground for economic reforms. The island's finances lacked organization. In large measure the existing conditions were the result of the island's dependency on the *Situado*. Collected revenues were barely enough to cover a very minimal part of the current expenses. This parasitic condition was aggravated by the fact that the governor held all economic power. In summary, the economy was rudimentary and lacked controls.

Ramírez faced two pressing problems. First and foremost, he had to balance the budget and secure the necessary funds to sustain government operations. Another urgent priority was to organize the island's finances and make a basis for future economic development.

A critical aspect of the economy was its tax system, both the variety of taxes and the collection system. Tax collections were assigned to individuals who advanced the money and received a percentage of the sums collected, a method that lent itself to abuses. Taxes included a land tax, a sales tax, tithes, a rum tax, an *abasto forzoso,* and many others. The system was so disorganized that, for example, the tithes and *primicias* that were collected were not used for church expenses and the taxpayers had to make another payment to support the church. A royal order of April 22, 1804 had granted exemption from tithes and sales tax on coffee, cotton, and sugar produced in new plantations, but it took several years to go into effect.

One of Ramírez's first reforms was to implement a decree of the *Cortes* of September 13, 1813, establishing a new system of direct taxation. This measure abolished all indirect taxes and interior customs, enabling products to circulate freely without taxation for being transported from one market to another. The decree also did away with tax farming. The new tax was to be based on an estimate of the wealth of the towns, the provinces, and the individuals. Wealth was classified as territorial, industrial, or commercial.

Although Ferdinand VII abolished this decree upon his return to the throne, the assignment of taxes was permanently discontinued. A royal decree of June 14, 1814 provided that taxes would be based on agricultural wealth. Even though precise figures for agricultural wealth were lacking and had to be estimated, the new system succeeded in reducing administrative expenses increasing considerably the amounts collected.

The new tax was paid by all without exception; the assessment was based on the taxpayer's income. The revenues were used to pay government officials, the garrison expenses, and other salaries, formerly paid by the *Situado*. The new system nearly doubled revenues for the Treasury.

More funds were still needed and Ramírez had to re-establish several taxes that had not been collected for a long time and institute two new taxes, one on houses for rent and another on slaves.

During this period, as a result of the war of independence in Venezuela, many Venezuelan loyalists took refuge in Puerto Rico. These immigrants came without their possessions and wealth and, therefore, required government assistance. To build a fund for needy immigrants, additional taxes were imposed on cacao, cotton, tanned leather, and indigo destined for export.

The *Ayuntamientos* had more autonomy on fiscal matters and the taxpayers were freed from government surveillance. Ramírez instituted the practice of making public the accounts of the Royal Treasury, thus discouraging abuses and enabling citizens to seek redress when they felt their rights had been violated.

Since Puerto Rico suffered from a shortage of metallic currency, Ramírez proposed that the circulation of the *moneda macuquina* (Venezuelan currency) be allowed. These silver coins had been brought in large amounts by the refugees from Venezuela. Although this measure was considered a provisional one, the *macuquina* was not retired from circulation until 1857.

With the suspension of the *Situado*, Governor Meléndez had authorized the circulation of paper currency on August 31, 1812 in order to meet the government's financial obligations. By the time Ramírez assumed the intendancy, the amount in circulation had reached 350,000 pesos and was rising rapidly. Paper currency suffered from inflation and devaluation. Speculators began to deal in paper money, which was sometimes exchanged at a rate of 300 to one.

Ramírez used diverse methods to deal with this critical situation, and this multiple approach saved the day. The shortage of metallic currency precluded the withdrawal of paper money from circulation, so it was imperative to restore confidence in the soundness of the measures taken and to contain the inflationary run. Ramírez therefore initiated an orientation campaign in the *Diario Económico de Puerto Rico* to enlighten the island's population on the advantages of paper money. The *Diario* carried more than thirty articles on the subject. Ramírez also had printed and circulated a pamphlet containing the minutes of meetings of the *Junta de Hacienda* and the *Diputación Provincial* in which currency problems were discussed.

Ramírez stressed that the money in circulation was adequately backed by the expected funds from the *Situado* and by pledged revenues. However, to begin retiring paper money from circulation, he established a special commission to redeem the paper in existence and withdraw it permanently from circulation. In addition, a number of taxes were to be paid in paper money; the amounts collected would be taken out of circulation. A royal lottery was established with the same end in view for its proceeds.

This varied approach allowed Ramírez to announce before he left the island that all 500,000 pesos had been retired from circulation.

The *Diario Económico de Puerto Rico*, edited by Ramírez, was only the second newspaper published in the island, the first being the *Gaceta Oficial* (Official Gazette). The publication of the *Diario* was part of the intendant's efforts to enlighten the people on economic, agricultural, and commercial techniques that would promote the island's development.

The newspaper also served to disseminate directives from the intendancy, giving Ramírez's policies the widest possible circulation. The paper also included treasury reports of revenues collected and expenses authorized and reports of customs revenues and maritime movements through the authorized ports. Thus Ramírez kept the islanders informed and, by so doing, helped restore confidence in the Royal Treasury.

Part of Ramírez's charge as intendant was to establish an economic society similar to those already existing in Spain and in Spanish America. *The Sociedades Económicas* were not new to Ramírez, who had been among the founders of the one in Guatemala and was also a member of the Havana Society. Ramírez drafted the first statutes for the local society, which were sanctioned by the king on July 2, 1814.

The society played an important role in the economic and educational development of Puerto Rico during the nineteenth century, particularly during its second half. It encouraged agriculture by importing and distributing new and better seeds and by teaching more effective modern methods. In education, Ramírez was responsible for the establishment of courses on geography, commerce, and mathematics. In later years the *Sociedad* was instrumental in establishing the *Instituto de Segunda Enseñanza* (institute for secondary education).

The Real Cédula de Gracias

The news of the restoration of Ferdinand VII as absolute monarch reached Governor Meléndez in San Juan on June 30, 1814. He immediately ordered the restoration of the absolutist regime and dissolved all constitutional bodies in accordance with a royal decree abolishing the Constitution of 1812.

Ferdinand VII, hoping to isolate the island from the turmoil in other areas of the empire and to insure the continued loyalty of the Puerto Ricans, on October 10, 1814 asked the *Ayuntamiento* of San Juan to make recommendations on how to promote the development of the island's agriculture, industry, and commerce, as well as any other measure they considered necessary to the islanders' welfare.

As a result on August 10, 1815, the king issued a royal decree aimed at promoting development of the island's commerce, industry, and agriculture, which has come to be known as the *Real Cédula de Gracias*.

The *Cédula* addressed many of the liberals' principal economic demands as they were expressed in the *instrucciones* of 1810, such as freedom of commerce with Spain and with foreign nations, introduction of agricultural equipment free of duty, and others. Manuel Hernaiz, who drafted the report, had been a principal contributor to Powers' *instrucciones* and thus included in the document sent to the king most of the unfulfilled requests. Nevertheless, Ferdinand VII and his ministers should be credited for the *Cédula's* ample economic and demographic reforms as well as for granting nearly free commerce, which the *Cortes* and the constitutional regime had not done.

To increase the population of the island the *Cédula* declared that any foreign subject of a friendly nation, provided he was a Roman Catholic, could freely settle in Puerto Rico with all his possessions and slaves. The same applied to mulattoes or freedmen who wanted to settle. The only requirement was that the settler swear loyalty to the Spanish king and promise to obey the laws of the land.

To stimulate white immigration the government offered free land. The amounts varied, with an average grant of six acres for each family member and half that for each slave. The new settlers were granted tax exemption for ten years, at the end of which they were taxed one peso per slave yearly. The mulattoes and freedmen settling in the island were given approximately three acres of land per family member and a proportional amount for slaves. The only tax exemption granted to this group was on slaves, with an exemption period of five years. This exemption was to be effective at all times except during times of war or in an emergency.

Any settler was allowed to leave the island during the first five years with all his belongings provided he paid a 10 percent tax on all profits he had made during his stay. This clause was modified to cause the settler's land to revert back to the state.

After the initial five-year period the immigrant and his family could become naturalized citizens. They then received permanent title to their land, and could acquire additional lands. The new settler could move freely about the island provided he secured permission in advance from the local authorities.

Immigrants were free to establish industries or trade; at the end of the five-year period they could engage in maritime commercial enterprises, own warehouses or stores, and be shipowners.

The *Cédula* gave the new settler the right to leave the island to visit friendly countries so long as he had permission from the authorities. He was allowed to bear arms and was expected to help defend the island in case of war. On the settler's death, his properties would pass to his legal heirs provided they settled on the island. This was later modified to allow the owner to dispose of his estate freely.

The *Cédula* contained several provisions on commerce. It authorized free trade between the island and Spain for fifteen years starting August 10, 1815, so long as the trade was carried on with Spanish ships. Exchange with other Spanish colonies was also authorized subject to a 2 percent tax and under the same conditions as trade with Spain.

Trade with friendly countries was liberalized, it was authorized for fifteen years subject only to a 6 percent tax on exports. Yearly extensions were to prolong this measure beyond the original fifteen-year period. Freedom of importation was granted except for sugar, rum, molasses, and tobacco. To protect local production, these products could only be brought into the island for transshipment to other foreign ports, and only through San Juan, unless special dispensation for another port was granted.

Manufactured goods from the United States, Europe, and foreign islands of the Caribbean imported in foreign bottoms were taxes at 15 percent. Food products (except flour, which continued to be taxed at its old rate) were taxed at 10 percent. Farm equipment and industrial machinery were taxed at 3 percent while Spanish goods imported in foreign bottoms paid 2 percent. Tonnage charges for American vessels were set at eight *reales* while other foreign ships paid half that amount. Puerto Rican fruits and products going to foreign countries in foreign ships paid a 5 percent duty while those destined for Spanish ports paid only 2 percent.

The *Cédula* provided that in case of emergency, as determined by the governor and intendant, free trade be authorized between Puerto Rico and other foreign islands in the Caribbean. As already noted, the two officials immediately decreed a state of emergency and authorized free commerce with the neighboring islands. Puerto Rican products exported were taxed at 5 percent while imports from foreign ports would pay a 12 percent duty for manufactured products and 8 percent for food. To protect Spanish shipping, goods transported in foreign vessels paid a 15 percent tax.

Finally, the *Cédula,* authorized the establishment of a shipbuilding industry in Puerto Rico. Foreign ships bought during a three-year period would be considered Spanish vessels and enjoy tax exemption.

To promote agriculture and industry the *Cédula* authorized the introduction, tax-free for fifteen years, of farm equipment manufactured in Spain. In case of emergency such equipment could be bought from foreign suppliers with only a 3 percent duty. New settlers enjoyed a fifteen-year exemption from the *diezmo* (tithe) and the sales tax; afterwards they would pay one fourth of the *diezmo* and a 2½ percent sales tax. They were also allowed to introduce slaves from neighboring islands by paying a 3 percent duty, a provision extended to all Puerto Ricans by the governor and the intendant.

To facilitate administration of the *Cédula,* the island was divided into six districts: San Juan, San Germán, Humacao, Arecibo, Coamo, and Aguada. In each district, a subdelegate of the intendant was appointed to rule on matters pertaining to the four departments of the intendancy, justice, war, police, and treasury; preside over the town councils, execute orders of the intendancy or the government in general; and promote agriculture and industry.

The relationship between the island's development and the *Cédula, de Gracias* has never been seriously studied; however, there are certain indications of the *Cédula's* impact on the economy. To put them in perspective, it may be useful to compare the situation prior to 1815 to conditions several years after the implementation of the *Cédula.*

By 1814 the overall value of insular property was fixed at 1,490,021 pesos. The actions of the *Cortes* and the intendant brought a noticeable increase in agricultural production. There were 5,765 acres of land devoted to sugar cane. The tobacco crop amounted to 1,123,400 pounds and coffee production reached 4,446,100 pounds.

During this period a new variety of sugar cane, the Otahiti, was introduced into Puerto Rico. Agriculture was modernized and more extensive use was made of fertilizers. Uncultivated lands were distributed and some larger estates were divided and parcelled out. These measures helped to create a group of small farmers and increased the value of land. Ramírez was committed to creating a large group of landowners who would serve as the basis for economic development and also become a stabilizing element in society.

Industry was primarily limited to sugar cane. Sugar, molasses, and rum were in great demand in world markets because of the destruction of French sugar plantations in Haiti and the increased demand for sugar from the United States for domestic use and for re-export. Lack of protective legislation hampered development of other inudstries. The island's few shops and factories could barely supply the local market.

The cattle industry was greatly favored by the Power Act. Cattle was either exported legally or smuggled to neighboring islands, particularly to Saint Thomas and Saint Croix. Local mules were highly esteemed.

Maritime trade amounted, by the end of the period, to 484,648 pesos, a limited increase from the beginning of the century. Two factors were responsible: Spain's reluctance to liberalize the commerce statutes and the impact of the War of 1812 on American trade with the island.

Treasury receipts rose to 587,616 pesos annually, approximately eight times the revenues at the beginning of the century. This notable progress was primarily the result of Ramírez's policies as Intendant. But money was still short. The suspension of the *Situado;* the Anglo-American war; the abolition of several taxes; the economic assistance the island furnished during the insurrenctions in Santo Domingo and Venezuela; the cost of assisting needy Venezuelan immigrants; and the expenses of fortifying the island against possible attack by the Venezuelan rebels, all contributed to the tight situation.

Public services suffered and showed little improvement since the turn of the century. Communications were still difficult, most roads remained impassable during the rainy season, and public sanitation was still neglected.

Public administration had improved little or not at all. The new regime could not eradicate many of the old practices. Nepotism was common. Many public offices were filled by Spaniards whose sole aim was to get rich, thus depriving the Creoles of opportunities for public service and advancement.

Although the introduction of the *moneda macuquina* helped to solve the crisis created by the devaluation of the paper currency, in the long run it created new problems. The value of the coins could not be fixed because the silver content diminished with constant use, leading to speculation, with adverse effects on the economy.

For lack of banking or credit institutions, usury was rampant. The establishment of a bank to collect taxes and make loans was proposed in 1812 and again in 1814, but the idea never prospered.

The population of the island grew significantly. From 174,902 inhabitants in 1803 it rose to 183,014 by 1811 and stood at 220,982 in 1814. Part of the increase consisted of immigrants from Haiti and Santo Domingo, fleeing the unrest in Hispaniola. Immigrants also arrived from Spain and the Canary Islands, driven by the Napoleonic Wars, as well as from Venezuela, where revolution was well under way.

In the long run the influence of the immigrants was great. Politically, many took sides with the conservatives, thus strengthening them while the liberals weakened. Some of the French immigrants, on the other hand, were noted for their heterodoxy and anticlericalism. Since the Catholic church was the only church in Puerto Rico, the islanders resented attacks on it. However, many Puerto Ricans educated abroad brought back the liberal ideas of the French Revolution and a large clandestine commerce in books banned by the censors soon developed.

Life among the wealthy became more luxurious. Elaborate furniture and tableware came into general use for wealthy families. Styles in female and male attire changed. Houses, especially in San Juan, were now built of brick, with ornamented balconies and tiled roofs. The construction of country houses for the hot summer months also became common.

Rural life was still as primitive and uncomfortable as it had been when Fray Iñigo Abbad described it. Hours were long and equipment and methods had changed little in fifty years. The spade, the wooden plow, and the *machete* (cutlass) were the principal tools. Only the sugar cane industry had been somewhat modernized, with the introduction of new techniques brought by French immigrants.

The effects of the *Cédula de Gracias* on agriculture, industry, and commerce can be seen in the period from 1815 to 1819. By the end of the period the overall value of property in Puerto Rico had risen to 16,472,304 pesos, fourteen times the value during the previous period. This dramatic increase was due mainly to the growing demand for tropical products and to the peace in Europe and the United States.

Agriculture developed rapidly and was tending to specialize in three major commercial crops: sugar, coffee, and tobacco. The plantation system had been widely adopted.

Industrial development centered on the sugar and rum industry. Several distilleries were set up and sugar production increased to approximately 15,000,000 pounds yearly.

Under the *Cédula* and the measures approved by the governor and intendant, immigration continued to increase. Attracted by these provisions, 656 foreigners and their families settled in the island. To these one must add the Spanish immigrants, primarily from the Canary Islands, who came to Puerto Rico because of the liberal provisions of the *Cédula*.

Summing up the results of immigration, Puerto Rico's second Intendant, Morales, wrote:

The flow of new colonists, be they artisans or farmers from other countries, has brought the benefits of new ideas, and the introduction of new machinery to process sugar, rice, cotton and to facilitate other industrial and agricultural processes that were cumbersome and outdated. Everyone is interested in importing machinery and bringing technicians from the United States to improve production.

Alejandro Ramírez left the island in July 1816 to become intendant in Havana. In his appointment the king observed:

I confer upon you the direction of the Intendancy of Havana because of your outstanding achievements and your unquestionable loyalty to my Royal Person, and because of the flourishing state that, thanks to your knowledge and activity has been achieved in agriculture, commerce and the Royal Treasury of the Island of Puerto Rico.

Ramírez's work set the bases for the economic development of Puerto Rico during the nineteenth century. He did much to improve agriculture, industry, and commerce. He organized the fiscal system and enabled Puerto Rico to make the transition from a nonproductive colony dependent on a *Situado* to a substantially self-sufficient one.

Slave Trade under the Anglo-Spanish Treaty

The political turmoil in the Spanish colonies continued as the local governments set up during Ferdinand's captivity opted for independence. Open rebellion against Spanish domination was prevalent almost everywhere in the Spanish Empire. The activities of privateers in and around Puerto Rico affected the area's commerce and kept the island on constant watch against attack or invasion by rebel forces. Puerto Rico continued loyal to the Spanish cause and became an important base of operations in the crown's efforts to regain control of the rebellious colonies.

At this point a new trend appeared that was at cross purposes with plans for Puerto Rico's development. British pressures to abolish slave trade had persuaded other European nations to follow their lead. Sweden abolished its slave trade in 1813 and Holland did so a year later. In 1814 France reluctantly agreed to put an end to the trade in five years. In Vienna, British diplomats secured a declaration condemning the trade on February 8, 1815. This left only the southern states of the United States, Brazil, Cuba, and Puerto Rico, to a lesser degree, as the focus of the slave trade.

British pressure on Spain to abolish the trade coincided with Spain's plans to develop Cuba into a major sugar producer to replace Haiti. On a smaller scale, Puerto Rico was also struggling to expand its agricultural output and therefore required an abundant work force.

Spain was finally forced to capitulate to England on this issue and agreed in 1817 to sign a treaty suppressing the trade in all Spanish territories by May 30, 1820.

All efforts to end the slave trade failed because, as Arturo Morales Carrión has aptly put it, "there was no national purpose or firm desire for compliance. It was merely a response to external pressures." In Puerto Rico the authorities showed little inclination to comply with the ban on the trade. During the long term in office of Governor Miguel de la Torre particularly, slave imports increased considerably. The French consul in San Juan reported in November 1825 that during the preceding six months more than 6,000 slaves had entered the island. This thriving trade in Puerto Rico made the treaty meaningless. Such blatant disregard forced the British to act. Its West Indies squadron was considerably reinforced in an effort to end the violations.

The provisions of the *Cédula de Gracias,* which, as noted, implicitly ran contrary to the international commitments of the crown, included a loophole for the slave trade, which the governor used effectively. Although he claimed that no slaves had been introduced from Africa during his tenure, he admitted that slaves had been introduced from neighboring islands "in view of the need for hands to work in agriculture and to offset those that die annually."

Thus backed by Madrid and availing himself of the *Cédula,* de la Torre established a system of licenses to authorize the introduction of slaves from friendly neighboring islands. Slaves from Saint Bartholomew, Saint Thomas, and the French Lesser Antilles met the needs of plantations in the eastern part of the island; those needed in the *haciendas* of the western end came primarily from Saint Thomas and Curaçao.

For Puerto Rico, then, the treaty was no impediment to the importation of slaves. No doubt the extent of the commerce was determined by the purchasing power of the local *hacendados,* not by the treaty.

De la Torre's Enlightened Despotism

After Ferdinand's restoration to the throne and the reestablishment of absolutism, Puerto Rico returned to rule by governors with unlimited power; there was little or no Creole participation in government until the advent of the second constitutional period.

Once more, events in the metropolis dictated changes in the island's structures. The first army *pronunciamiento* for liberal ends was a call to revolt on January 1, 1820 by Colonel Rafael del Riego, commander of the Asturias battalion stationed near Cádiz. Riego proclaimed the Constitution of 1812, perhaps "just to give the rebellion an honest appearance." Gradually other regions, led by disaffected army officers, aligned themselves with the Constitution of 1812.

Ferdinand gave way and on March 9 formally pledged allegiance to the Constitution of 1812, thus signaling the beginning of a second constitutional period. The *Cortes,* met initially on July 9, 1820. It was dominated by the men hounded out of public life in 1814.

Puerto Rico again had the right to elect a Deputy to the *Cortes;* once again the liberals elected their candidate, Marshal Demetrio O'Daly, a supporter of Riego.

As was customary, O'Daly requested instructions from the San Juan *Cabildo* to orient his efforts on behalf of the island. Once again the petitions dealt with improvements in commerce, more and better educational facilities, reduction of taxes, and the establishment of welfare institutions.

The most significant legislation during this second constitutional period was a project presented by José María Quiñones, the *Diputado* elected in 1822–1823, and the Cubans Félix Varela and Leonardo Santos Suárez. Based on the Constitution of 1812 but amended to fit the circumstances of the island colonies, it provided for a high degree of autonomy in internal affairs. Although it became law, the return to absolutism prevented its implementation.

Late in this period the island's government was entrusted to Francisco González Linares as civil governor and to Marshal Miguel de la Torre as military governor. This separation of power was short-lived. A veteran of the Venezuelan revolt, de la Torre was bent on saving Puerto Rico for Spain. His determination extended from bolstering the island's defenses to developing an effective spy network. When the constitutional government collapsed in Spain in 1823, Ferdinand VII made de la Torre governor and captain general, with unlimited powers to rule Puerto Rico as if under siege.

De la Torre's fifteen-year term in office was the longest in the island's history. Although some historians have disparaged his means of preventing rebellion, these criticisms do not recognize de la Torre's ability and his many activities. In several aspects, his administrative efforts were comparable to those of Alejandro Ramírez. De la Torre can better be described as an enlightened despot.

De la Torre centralized the administration and kept a tight rein on all matters of government, striving for more efficiency in public administration. To keep informed, he revived the *visita* (visit or inspection), an old institution that served him well in his efforts to keep the island secure. It also enabled him to learn of the most pressing problems and needs of the island's towns and constituencies. Under his auspices a *Junta de Visita* was established in every town to inform the governor on matters of interest to him.

In spite of the Anglo-Spanish treaty of 1817, which was to end the slave trade, the slave population increased significantly during de la Torre's government. Availing himself of the provisions of the *Cédula de Gracias,* he issued a number of licenses to import slaves from friendly neighboring islands. The substantial increase went hand in hand with an increment in sugar production. Fostering the plantation economy was a key element in de la Torre's government.

Public works were greatly stimulated by de la Torre. Churches, bridges, roads, cemeteries, armories for the local militia, paving of streets, were some of the most common projects. During this period the Municipal Theatre of San Juan was constructed and inaugurated, thus enriching the island's cultural life.

Determined to preserve Puerto Rico for Spain, de la Torre spared no effort to improve the island's defenses. In this he was obviously successful. The military forces at his command, both regular and militia, numbered over ten thousand. He did much to improve the forces' armaments and equipment.

De la Torre's mandate cannot be dismissed lightly, for it was a period of great changes in the island's history. While preserving Puerto Rico as a Spanish colony, de la Torre laid the basis for the authoritarian economic and political system that characterized most of Spanish rule over the island in the nineteenth century.

Sugar and Coffee

The political and social life of Puerto Rico was deeply influenced by the emerging plantation economy. Of all the efforts to turn the island into a productive colony, the most significant were the achievements in agriculture and commerce.

Until the early nineteenth century, local production was primarily for subsistence. However, population growth and increased immigration brought about by the *Cédula de Gracias* fostered a gradual expansion of commercial agriculture. Sugar, its production encouraged by the destruction of the flourishing sugar economy of Hispaniola, became for most of the nineteenth century the most important commercial crop. Its natural market was the United States.

The cultivation of sugar on a commercial scale had a decided impact on the patterns of land tenure. Gradually large *haciendas* developed, displacing small landholders and turning them into *agregados* (squatters).

To understand this turn of events, it is essential to analyze land distribution and tenure at the end of the eighteenth century. A royal decree of January 14, 1778, marked an important milestone in island agriculture. Its purpose was to bring rationality and legality to the distribution and possession of land. In spite of its efforts, very little was accomplished. A master plan for land distribution and tenure was still lacking at the turn of the nineteenth century. The *instrucciones* given to Power evidenced general dissatisfaction with the existing situation and called for a rapid solution to the problems of land distribution and the issuance of titles to the holders of land whose only claim was based on the continued cultivation of a tract.

In January 1813 the *Cortes* passed legislation mandating the distribution of uncultivated lands, except those needed for the expansion of towns. However, the law left the implementation of the measure up to the *Diputación Provincial*.

Alejandro Ramírez identified the fundamental difficulties in land distribution. The first was conflict in the laws, which created doubt about how to proceed. Furthermore, several extensive holdings were not cultivated. In addition, the Ordinance of Intendants of 1786 made the intendant responsible for the disposition of royal and uncultivated lands, called *baldíos*.

The *Real Cédula de Gracias* envisioned the development of a large class of small landowners as a means of promoting agricultural development. Ramírez considered this the most suitable approach. However, the conflicting legislation and struggles among officials for primary jurisdiction over land distribution produced numerous disputes, particularly between governors and intendants, which definitely hindered the development of agriculture.

The large sugar estates were developed in this period. Sugar plantations flourished in the coastal plains, because of good growing conditions for cane and because of their relative proximity to the ports. At that time, the relatively low population density meant that land was readily available. By 1820, the earliest date for which reliable figures exist, only 5.8 percent of the land was under cultivation. This proportion remained small throughout the century; by 1897, approximately 14.3 percent of the land was under cultivation.

The land devoted to sugar production, however, increased significantly throughout the century. Between 1820 and 1896, the amount of land devoted to producing sugar increased threefold, while the tonnage grew from 17,000 to 62,000 tons. This increase in production was due in part to important technological changes, particularly in the last third of the century. The development of large and more modern mills (*centrales*) was a decisive factor. Administratively, some of the *centrales* established by French capitalists and local businessmen were organized on a corporate basis, thus making the venture more profitable. Increasing amounts of sugar cane were required to keep the mills operating at maximum capacity and improve their chances of making a profit. José Ramón Abad described this tendency in his *Puerto Rico en la Feria Exposición de Ponce en 1882* (Puerto Rico at the Fair of Ponce in 1882): "There have been established in the island factories known as *centrales* . . . which have become centers for the concentration of lands and have thus reduced the number of landowners. . . . Property, before distributed in small holdings, is being accumulated in fewer hands." Other contemporary accounts suggest that by 1832 there clearly was a trend away from the small independent peasant producer, toward an *hacienda* economy.

The development of the sugar industry had to overcome a number of adverse circumstances. A solid financial base was lacking as capital was always in high demand; shortages of labor, high taxes, and unfavorable commercial conditions were also present. In the nineteenth century, these factors were somewhat offset by technical developments, dramatic changes in the relationship patterns of the labor force, and other factors. During the last quarter of the century, however, coffee replaced sugar as the island's major commercial crop.

Coffee production centered in the hinterland. Indroduced initially in 1736, it spread fairly rapidly. When the *Compañía de Barcelona* was founded in 1758 to promote commerce in the island, coffee was already one of the products to be promoted. O'Reilly in 1765 indicated that coffee was an item of contraband trade. By then San Germán and Guayama had become two centers of coffee cultivation.

By the end of the eighteenth century, coffee had become a favorite drink in Europe and was in great demand. To profit from the expanding market, the Spanish crown encouraged coffee production. By the time Abbad wrote his history, there were nearly 2,000,000 coffee trees in the island and in the six-year period before his writing, coffee production had increased by 50 percent.

Coffee thus became one of the principal crops in the nineteenth century, eventually surpassing sugar in value. By 1818 the island produced 70 million pounds of coffee; twelve years later production was over 130 million pounds, with nearly nine million coffee trees in production.

While sugar prices fluctuated throughout the nineteenth century, creating havoc among the producers, the value of coffee production in the second half of the century showed almost constant gains. By the end of the century, coffee had replaced sugar as the principal commercial crop.

Coffee plantations tended to be small to medium in size, centered on family holdings that grew depending on the variations in the coffee market and the relationships between the *hacienda* owners and the commercial entrepreneurs who advanced the always needed capital guaranteed by upcoming coffee production.

While Brazilian coffee was sold in the North American market, Puerto Rican coffee went in ever-increasing quantities to Europe. Britain, France, Germany, and Italy absorbed 40 percent of the coffee production by 1881 while Cuba and Spain accounted for approximately 43 percent of the coffee exports. The United States purchased little Puerto Rican coffee; with one exception, it never consumed more than 2 percent of the island's coffee exports.

The Labor Force: Slavery and Free Labor

The expansion of commercial agriculture during the nineteenth century stepped up the demand for labor to work on the sugar, coffee, and tobacco plantations. Slaves played a significant role in the economic life of the island. The agricultural expansion was paralleled by an increase in the number of slaves imported into the island. By 1846 the slave population had peaked at slightly over 51,000. Lack of capital and stronger British efforts to enforce the treaty abolishing the slave trade prevented the local slave owners from importing more slaves. By 1845 the Spanish authorities began to take action to end the slave traffic; from then on, the number of slaves entering the island illicitly was greatly reduced. Unlike the situation in other areas of the Caribbean, the slave population in Puerto Rico during the nineteenth century was a relatively small portion of the total population, between 11.5 and 14 percent at its peak. Many slaves were domestic servants and therefore not engaged in productive activities. As on the other islands, however, in Puerto Rico slavery was closely linked to the sugar industry.

The ever-increasing demands for labor resulting from the expansion of commercial agriculture forced the landowners to turn to the island's free population for labor. The ever-growing free black and mulatto population outnumbered the slaves; there were also "poor whites" who lived mainly as subsistence farmers on lands to which they had no legal title. This sector of the population kept growing, thus constituting an important potential labor source. However, since land was plentiful and food and shelter were easily obtained, the poor were not readily persuaded to work as wage earners in the commercial establishments. By 1830, only 6 percent of the total area was under cultivation; in 1897, in spite of the expansion of commercial agriculture, the figure had risen only to about 14 percent.

Since most of the free subsistence farmers could not be persuaded to work for wages in commercial agriculture, a campaign was launched in the nineteenth century to force them to do so. In 1831, Governor Miguel López de Baños issued his famous *Bando de Policía y Buen Gobierno,* which compelled all unemployed landless peasants to work on local plantations and farms. Yet the measures failed to achieve the expected results. Efforts were renewed in 1849, when Governor Juan de la Pezuela established a system requiring the workers to carry *libretas* (passbooks). In these books the employers were to record the services rendered by the holder and describe how the services were performed. The regulation imposed severe penalties on those found without the *libretas* and thus created a system of compulsory labor.

Contemporary reaction was mixed. The landowners were much in favor of the measure, but the workers and the more enlightened sectors of the Creole society opposed it. In retrospect, it is clear that the system did not benefit agricultural development. Landowners clung to cheap labor rather than modernizing production methods. Moreover, the dissatisfied work force did not produce as much as the landowners expected.

The Anglo-Spanish Treaty of 1817 banning the slave trade was an early manifestation of the abolitionist movement. The more enlightened members of the island's Creole class became outspoken advocates of abolition. In spite of the opposition of the Spanish and Puerto Rican slave owners, the movement gained momentum with the abolition of slavery in the British West Indies in 1833 and in the French Antilles in 1848. Among the most active abolitionists by midcentury were Ramón Emeterio Betances, Segundo Ruiz Belvis, José Julián Acosta, Román Baldorioty de Castro, Julio Vizcarrondo and Eugenio María de Hostos. In spite of their efforts the abolitionists made little headway in Puerto Rico. The lack of progress caused some of the leaders to carry the struggle to Spain. In the Spanish press they attacked slavery as barbaric and outdated. In Madrid, Puerto Rican and Cuban abolitionists joined with Spaniards to found the *Sociedad Abolicionista Española* (Spanish Abolitionist Society) in 1865. Julio Vizcarrondo, the society's permanent secretary, founded the newspaper *El Abolicionista Español* (The Spanish Abolitionist) which became the voice of the Antillian abolitionists. Despite these efforts, the time was not ripe for abolition; several years passed before slavery was abolished.

The Unfulfilled Promise: Las Leyes Especiales

The death of Ferdinand VII in 1833 was significant for the island's political development. Under the regency of Queen Mother María Cristina de Borbón important changes occurred in Spain's political makeup. In an effort to curb Spanish liberalism, the regency decreed the *Estatuto Real,* which established a national parliament of two estates (*estamentos*). As in the two previous constitutional periods, Puerto Rico was granted representation by two elected *procuradores* (representatives). Once more the islanders chose two liberals: José Saint Just and Esteban de Ayala. As before, these representatives requested reforms to promote the island's development.

The new regime was short lived. On August 12, 1836, the regency was forced to proclaim once more the Constitution of 1812, and to call the *Cortes* into session. In this constitutional period, however, the *Diputación Provincial* was not restored and the system for selecting the representative to the *Cortes* was significantly altered. Selection of the *Diputado* now fell to the *Cabildo* of San Juan and the island's principal taxpayers.

The *Cortes* drafted a new constitution, which was approved on May 22, 1837. It contained two articles directly ralated to the overseas provinces. One of these provided that Puerto Rico, Cuba, and the Philippine Islands would be ruled by *Leyes Especiales* and that their representatives were excluded from the *Cortes*. However, the metropolitan government apparently had no intention of implementing this article, and the *Leyes Especiales* were never put into force.

From 1836 on, the island was deprived of a voice in the Spanish parliament and settled once more under a regime of absolutist governors who ruled with an iron hand.

Puerto Rico under the *Pax Romana*

The period between 1837 and 1864 saw little or no participation by the Creole elite in island affairs. Although the conspiracy of 1838 and several minor slave uprisings hinted at unrest, in general the governors' overwhelming powers imposed a "Pax Romana," or a forced peace.

To maintain their control, several governors banished Creoles who criticized the Spanish system or were suspected of desiring more Creole participation in island affairs. Those who expressed separatist sentiments, like Betances and Ruiz Belvis, were especially vulnerable to persecution and exile.

These conditions did not improve until the 1860s, when the Spanish government again invited Cuba and Puerto Rico to send representatives to Spain to report on social, economic, and political conditions in the islands and to propose the *Leyes Especiales* (special laws) needed to promote their development and well-being.

7
The Challenge to Colonialism

Luis González Vales

The Junta Informativa de Reformas (*The Inquiry Board*)

For nearly thirty years, since 1837, the Puerto Ricans had been patiently waiting for autonomy promised by the *Leyes Especiales.*

Finally, on November 25, 1865, Antonio Cánovas del Castillo, the overseas minister, invited representatives of Puerto Rico and Cuba to Madrid to propose special laws governing the composition and extent of local administration.

The time was ripe to take this step. Demands for reform in the Spanish Antilles were coming from a number of sources, metropolitan and colonial. The topic was frequently discussed in newspaper articles written by noted intellectuals and politicians from both sides of the Atlantic.

In spite of the limitations of the decree, Puerto Rican liberals welcomed the opportunity to press their demands. Most conservatives, however, were against the decree, although a select minority favored some moderate reforms. Even the separatists gave their support to the quest for reform.

Election of the island's six commissioners fell upon the *Ayuntamientos* of San Juan, Ponce, San Germán, Arecibo, and Mayagüez together with an equal number of the principal contributors of each district. Three of the six representatives were liberals: José Julián Acosta for San Juan, Francisco Mariano Quiñones for San Germán, and Segundo Ruiz Belvis for Mayagüez. Two commissioners, Manuel Valdés Linares of San Juan and Luis Antonio Becerra Delgado of Ponce were moderate conservatives; while Manuel de Jesús Zeno y Correa of Arecibo was one of the ultraconservatives or *puros* (purists). Valdés and Becerra chose not to make the trip to Spain, leaving Zeno y Correa as the only spokesman for the island's conservatives.

The commission began its work on October 30, 1866. Although the government tried to limit the scope of the discussions, this did not inhibit the island's representatives, especially the liberals, from demanding far-reaching social, political, and economic reforms.

A Critique of the System

Acosta, Quiñones, and Ruiz Belvis drafted the report on social conditions, which condemned slavery and called for drastic reforms. The *Proyecto para la abolición de la esclavitud en Puerto Rico* (Bill for the Abolition of Slavery in Puerto Rico) is one of the most enlightened documents in Puerto Rican history. It called for the immediate abolition of slavery with or without indemnization to the owners. This position created a rupture in the unity of the Antillean liberals since the Cuban representatives considered it too radical and inappropriate to Cuba's particular slave problem. In spite of these objections the three liberal Puerto Rican commissioners pressed their point with vigor. A report on economic conditions drafted by the Spanish economist Luis María Pastor with the help of Acosta and the Cuban Pedro Sotolongo gave priority to free trade between the Antilles and Spain and free entry of foreign ships to the island's ports. The commissioners proposed abolishing customs duties; to compensate for them a 6 percent additional tax on net incomes from agricultural, commercial, and professional activities was suggested. As a substitute measure, the Antillean representatives demanded reforms that would liberalize commerce and reduce existing tariffs as well as grant tax exemptions for basic foods. The only report backed by the conservative Zeno y Correa was the stimulation of the fishing and marine industry.

The third report dealt with the political question and was fully endorsed by Quiñones, Ruiz Belvis, and Acosta. It began with an indictment of the existing system. After a detailed analysis of the colonial experience, it condemned the regime as absolutist, despotic, and unfair.

The report demanded reforms that would take into account the special circumstances of the island, its distance from Spain, and the differences to be expected in its form of government. The basis for the proposed new order had to be the recognition of equal rights for Puerto

Ricans as Spanish citizens: the inviolability of human dignity, of home, the right to petition, and the right to work would be guaranteed. The report proposed an autonomous form of government along the lines advanced in 1823.

The *Junta Informativa* was closed on April 27, 1867, with a solemn promise that the Spanish government would pursue the question of reform and that the often promised *Leyes Especiales* would finally appear. Once more the promise was not to be kept. Events overtook the situation and autonomy receded far into the future. The island liberals chose to work for political assimilation and made this their objective for the next two decades, particularly after 1870, when political parties were first organized in Puerto Rico. The separatists, disillusioned with Spain, became convinced that revolution was the only recourse.

Three Revolutionary Movements: The *Gloriosa*, Lares, and Yara

In less than a month, between September and October, 1868, three unrelated revolutionary movements shook the Spanish world both in the Peninsula and in its Antillean colonies. Each would bring about important changes.

The first revolution to occur was the *Gloriosa*. It began on September 18, 1868, when the commandant of Cádiz, Admiral Juan Topete, issued a *pronunciamiento* (pronouncement) that caused insurrectionary juntas to be formed in cities all over Spain. Influential military leaders soon joined the movement. Although Isabella II made feeble attempts to resist the inevitable, she finally gave in and exiled herself in France. She did not abdicate legally, nor was she really dethroned by force. Instead, she simply gave up for personal reasons. On other occasions, she risked death to keep the throne, but in 1868 she preferred to lose her crown rather than be separated from Marfiori, her lover. Isabella's departure brought five years of turmoil to the country and eventually contributed to the events leading to the Franco-Prussian War.

General Francisco Serrano and General Juan Prim, count of Reus, emerged as the revolution's strong men. By June, 1869, the *Cortes* had approved a new constitution, much like the Constitution of 1812 in its limitation of royal powers. While Serrano headed the provisional government, Prim's agents searched the European courts for a suitable replacement for Isabella II. Amadeo of Savoy was chosen to reign (but not to govern) until his abdication February 11, 1873. The First Spanish

Republic followed briefly and the Bourbons returned in 1875 when Isabella's son, Alfonso XII, was crowned king of Spain.

El Grito de Lares. The *Grito de Lares,* on September 23, 1868, was the second of the three revolutionary movements and the most serious challenge to Spanish domination in Puerto Rico. The nineteenth century had witnessed several pro-independence movements, none of any consequence.

By the mid-nineteenth century, Ramón Emeterio Betances had established himself as the leader of the independence movement in Puerto Rico. Because of his political ideas as well as his decided pro-abolitionist stance, he was banished from the island on several occasions. A physician trained in France, he had gained notoriety during the 1855 cholera epidemic ministering to the poor and needy in the Mayagüez area and was exiled for his involvement in the abolitionist movement.

On June 7, 1867, the artillery garrison rose to protest the inequities between them and artillerymen in Spain. This incident provided the governor with an excuse to expel a number of liberals including Betances and Ruiz Belvis, leaders of the separatist faction.

Betances and Ruiz Belvis went to New York to begin a pilgrimage to promote Puerto Rican independence. Ruiz Belvis went on to Chile, where he soon died, while Betances settled for a while in Santo Domingo and began to set up a revolutionary movement to free the island, organizing the Puerto Rican Revolutionary Committee. Men were recruited and material was gathered while contacts were made with separatist elements in western Puerto Rico in preparation for a revolution. This group's leaders were Manuel Rojas, a native of Venezuela, who owned a farm near Lares; Mariana Bracetti, Rojas' sister-in-law; and Mateo Bruckman, a native of the United States who had lived in Puerto Rico for many years and was a close friend of Betances. The revolutionaries were motivated by the dissatisfaction of planters in their area, who were heavily indebted to Spanish merchants, and by hatred of the *libreta* system.

Early in 1868, Betances moved to Saint Thomas and stepped up his propaganda campaign, issuing his famous "Ten Commandments of Free Men." These called for the abolition of slavery; the right to determine taxes; basic individual and collective freedom such as freedom of worship, freedom of the press, freedom of speech, and of assembly, and freedom of commerce. The document also demanded the right to bear arms.

Betances's revolt was to start on September 29, 1868. However, Spanish authorities discovered the plot, causing the Puerto Rican leaders to advance the date. On September 23, several hundred men left Rojas's farm and occupied the town of Lares. There they declared the independence of Puerto Rico and set up a provisional government. The next morning, a column left Lares for San Sebastián, the closest neighboring town. There the insurgents met organized Spanish resistance and the revolution fizzled.

The revolt was localized and had no repercussions elsewhere in the island, so the Spanish authorities who had been alerted to the movement were able to deal with it swiftly and efficiently. The support the revolutionaries expected from without as well as from within never materialized. The Spanish military broke the revolt within twenty-four hours. Some of those implicated were exiled, while others were jailed for several weeks. Finally, amnesty was declared by the new Spanish government. Betances exiled himself to France, where he would continue to crusade for the island's independence until his death in 1898. He never returned to Puerto Rico and the Lares revolt was only a symbol.

El Grito de Yara. The third revolution was the *Grito de Yara* in Cuba, which signaled the beginning of the Ten Year War (1868–1878), Cuba's most serious attempt at independence to date. The leaders of the revolt cited the lack of liberties, corruption in government, unequal distribution of taxes, and inadequate public education, among others, as the reasons for revolt. In an effort to rally the support of the slaves they offered them emancipation. Ten years of bitter fighting elasped before peace was finally restored with the *Pacto del Zanjón* (Pact of Zanjón) on February 10, 1878.

Although the Lares revolt was short lived and Spanish authority over Puerto Rico secured, the Cuban revolution haunted the island's liberals in their quest for reform. Hereafter, the Cuban rebellion was an excuse for not granting Puerto Rico the modest reforms demanded by the liberals.

Reform under the Spanish Revolutionary Regimes

The various governments that ruled Spain from the *Gloriosa* to the restoration of the Bourbon dynasty under Alfonso XII proclaimed assimilation as their policy for the overseas provinces, thus forcing the island liberals to accommodate their position to it.

Some important changes for the island resulted from the political turmoil in the metropolis. One of the first acts of the provisional government headed by General Serrano was to send José Laureano Sanz to

Puerto Rico as governor and captain general. Sanz immediately restored the island's right to representation at the *Cortes,* allotting seven deputies to be elected. The press was granted freedom to discuss all matters related to political and economic conditions on the island; however, the discussion of slavery was expressly prohibited.

Requests for reforms during this period were not fruitful, and in spite of the provisions of a new constitution drafted in 1869, Sanz governed with unlimited power, favoring the conservative elements.

Luis R. Padial, one of the island's deputies to the *Cortes,* presented a petition at the session held November 13, 1869, requesting that the minister for overseas provinces state the government's position on a number of issues: slavery, political autonomy, the tax system, and the need to plan for the economic development of the island. Padial was highly critical of the despotism of many of the governors, which contrasted starkly with the loyalty of the islanders. Minister Becerra expressed the government's intent to grant the Spanish citizens of Puerto Rico the rights protected by the constitution. He also promised that the ministry would present a bill for a constitution for Puerto Rico based on the Spanish Constitution but with the necessary modifications for the island's conditions. Puerto Rico would become a Spanish province. The ministry proposed gradual abolition of slavery with proper indemnization to the slave owners.

Although Becerra kept his promises to present a bill on December 1, 1869, the reactions to his proposals were so critical that they forced his resignation. The Cuban rebellion became a stumbling block to the aspirations of Puerto Rico.

The island liberals had a respite under the governorship of General Gabriel Baldrich, who arrived on May 28, 1870 with precise instructions to pursue a liberal policy. The unlimited power of previous governors was abolished and the *Diputación Provincial* was reestablished. The new state of affairs ended on September 13, 1871, when Baldrich relinquished the governorship. For the next three years, until Sanz's return for a second term, the island saw a parade of four governors and one acting governor, reflecting the unstable political situation in Spain.

Social Reforms: The Abolition of Slavery

In Spain, meanwhile, the monarchy of Amadeo did not last long. Lack of support for his monarchy and the critical situation in Cuba forced Amadeo to abdicate. Out of the chaos surrounding this bizarre affair the

First Spanish Republic emerged in 1873. However, the republican camp was no more united than the monarchist and soon centralists were at odds with federalists. The outcome was easy to forsee. In 1874 the Spanish military intervened and restored the monarchy, opening the way for Alfonso XII's coronation in 1875.

For Puerto Rico, the most enduring action of the republican government was the abolition of slavery on March 22, 1873. This action, which freed 31,635 slaves, was the culmination of a process that had begun in the first half of the nineteenth century and involved several of the island's most prominent liberal minds. The Spanish government had hesitated to grant abolition, fearing its impact on the Cuban economy. In Puerto Rico the situation was totally different since the slave population was small in proportion to the overall population. By the 1860s, the main issue among the owners was not abolition *per se,* but adequate compensation for the loss of the slaves.

A view of San Juan in 1870 from the fortress San Cristóbal.

In Puerto Rico abolition was achieved without any major turmoil. Edward Conroy, the American consul in San Juan, wrote on March 31, 1873, "The Law has caused a good deal of excitement, still it is thought by most of the influential citizens, many of them slave owners, that there will be very little trouble in carrying it out." As to the impact of abolition on agriculture, the British Consul, Augustus Cowper, wrote that it would be negligible and that although commerce could be temporarily affected "confidence would soon be restored and things return[ed] to their normal state." Events showed the validity of both positions.

The Emergence of Island Political Parties

The eventful years following the Spanish revolution witnessed the formation of Puerto Rico's first political parties, which had not existed before 1870. The first party was the liberal *Partido Liberal Reformista* (Liberal Reformist Party). A few months later, the conservatives organized the *Partido Liberal Conservador* (Liberal Conservative Party). From then on, the two parties competed for an electorate of approximately 20,000. The Liberal party favored reforms and political assimilation, while the conservatives, who later were called *Incondicionales* (Unconditionals) defended the status quo.

Elections held up to 1874 were dominated by the liberals, who drew their support primarily from the professional and intellectual elites and the landed class. Liberals for the most part controlled municipal government and the *Diputación Provincial* and elected most of the island's representatives in the Spanish parliament. After the overthrow of the republic in 1874, the new Spanish regimes supported the conservative elements in Puerto Rico. Starting with Sanz's second administration, the *Incondicionales* dominated the political scene. They consistently obtained the support of the governors, who saw in them the staunchest defenders of national integrity. Electoral laws were modified restricting the electoral franchise to the advantage of the *Peninsulares* (Peninsulars) residing in the island. In 1880, when a new electoral law came into effect, only 2,004 out of an adult male population of 374,640 were eligible to vote. This restriction worked to the advantage of the conservatives.

In view of the political climate, the Liberal party abstained from participation in elections after 1874, leaving the field to the conservatives. This weakened the party, whose ranks included both assimilist and autonomist forces. In 1881 the assimilists gained the upper hand and proposed a program aimed at the complete assimilation of Puerto Rico with Spain. This did not end the crisis within the party. The autonomist wing began to challenge the leadership, promoting the Canadian model of autonomous government.

In February, 1886, a group of noted leaders from the southern part of the island, concerned with the increasingly precarious situation of the Liberal party, began reorganizing the liberal forces under the banner of autonomy with Román Baldorioty de Castro as their chief spokesman.

Baldorioty, since his return from exile in Santo Domingo in 1878, had campaigned in the liberal press for the autonomic ideal. The historian Lidio Cruz Monclova writes that Baldorioty "recommended the attainment of a type of self-government" within which most of the vital elements of Puerto Rico might develop with the greatest possible liberty. Politically, this gave highest priority to the individual rights of man, characteristic of the liberal era. Baldorioty's plans included extensive decentralization, a budget determined by the island, direct taxation, and complete freedom in commerce, industry, and education. The prevailing historical sense of national unity, according to Baldorioty, would effectively limit the abuse of such rights.

Baldorioty's campaign had an immediate impact on the liberals. Several leading liberal journalists followed his example and published articles favoring the autonomic ideal. Groups began to organize throughout the island to promote the adoption of his platform by the Liberal Reformist Party.

Their efforts were opposed from several quarters. Some liberal advocates of assimilation felt that there was no room for the partisans of autonomy in the party. The conservative elements interpreted autonomy as a grave peril for national unity, the gateway to independence. Most conspicuous among the latter was José Pérez Morris, editor of the *Boletín Mercantil* (Commercial Bulletin), a conservative newspaper.

The Ponce liberals, who had rallied around Baldorioty, drafted a plan for reorganization of the Liberal party. By mid-November of 1886, their program was completed. Its recommendations for the structure of government specified municipal autonomy, incorporating the greatest possible degree of political and administrative power within the framework of national unity. Baldorioty's formula had prevailed.

The autonomist movement was well established in Cuba and several Cuban deputies in the *Cortes* had recommended such a solution to the Antillean problem. Among Spanish figures who favored colonial reform were some, like Rafael María de Labra, who supported the autonomic formula. This support from abroad stimulated the local movement.

The date for the reorganization meeting of the Liberal party was set for March 7–9, 1887. From the meeting the *Partido Autonomista Puertorriqueño* emerged with a program inspired by Labra and the San Juan delegation. Its goals were political identity and administrative autonomy. This position meant a compromise on the part of Baldorioty and his followers to assure the existence and unity of the new party.

The *Compontes:* 1887

The conservative reaction to the new party was immediate. They accused the autonomists of covertly leading the island toward independence and searched for ways to nip the movement in the bud. A secret society, *La Boicotizadora* (The Boycotter) was organized almost simultaneously with the Autonomist party. With the aim of protecting Creole merchants from unfair competition from Spanish commercial firms, it provided an excuse to persecute the autonomists. However, the autonomists were suddenly paralyzed by the *compontes,* a systematic campaign of repression and torture upheld by the newly appointed governor, Romualdo Palacio González. The regime of terror instituted in 1887 by Palacio and his cohorts did damage to the nascent Autonomist party from which it did not recover for many years. The party was near collapse and several of its leading figures, Baldorioty included, were imprisoned at *El Morro.*

In Search of an Entente with a Metropolitan Party

The *compontes* did not do the only harm to the development of the Partido Autonomista. One of the most divisive issues the new party faced was the possibility of affiliation to one of the metropolitan parties. Some autonomists saw such a pact as the way to break conservative hold over the government of the island and the most expedient way to achieve an autonomous regime for Puerto Rico.

The idea of a pact with a metropolitan party that would support and execute the autonomist program was discussed at the Ponce meeting, but members were at odds in their choice of peninsular parties. Some favored an agreement with Republican parties and particularly with the Centralists, of which Labra was one of the most important leaders. Others favored an agreement with a monarchical party with better chances of actually governing, such as the Liberal Fusionists. The Ponce meeting compromised, leaving affiliation to metropolitan parties to the individual members.

It took four years for the idea of a pact to come to the forefront again. The leadership in this new drive fell upon Luis Muñoz Rivera, the editor of *La Democracia*. On February 11, 1891, Muñoz Rivera began to publish a series of articles in which he proposed a pact with the Spanish Liberal Fusionist Party of Práxedes Mateo Sagasta. This alliance, he argued, would increase the Partido Autonomista's chances of becoming the government party in the island, thus improving the outlook for autonomous rule for Puerto Rico.

The new campaign signaled the beginning of a bitter five-year struggle between the party's republican and the monarchical factions. Finally, in 1896, the party's governing body appointed a commission to go to Spain to secure an entente with one of the metropolitan parties which would formally proclaim its support of an autonomous regime for Puerto Rico.

The Autonomic Commission

The commission's four members, José Gómez Brioso, Rosendo Matienzo Cintrón, Federico Degetau, and Luis Muñoz Rivera, were led by Rafael María de Labra. The group arrived in Madrid on October 8, 1896, and remained until February 1897. At the end of their arduous efforts the commission agreed to a pact with Sagasta's Liberal Fusionist party.

The pact was ratified by the Autonomist party in Puerto Rico over some opposition. Led by Dr. José Celso Barbosa, the dissenters claimed that the commission went beyond its powers in accepting Sagasta's condition of transforming the local party into a provincial branch of the Liberal Fusionist party. Barbosa and his followers walked out of the meeting and subsequently established the *Partido Autonomista Histórico (Ortodoxo)* (Orthodox Historical Autonomist Party). The remaining delegates decreed the dissolution of the *Partido Autonomista Puertorriqueño* and constituted the *Partido Liberal Fusionista* under the presidency of Luis Muñoz Rivera.

Autonomy at Last

Conditions on the island were to be overtaken by a series of external events. On February 24, 1895, the Cubans, tired of waiting for promised

Above left, *Juan Ponce de León came to Santo Domingo with Columbus's second voyage, beginning the conquest and settlement of Puerto Rico in 1508;* right, *Ramón Emeterio Betances, a passionate abolitionist and separatist, was also an eminent doctor;* below left, *Luis Muñoz Rivera, a political leader and journalist credited with achieving autonomy from Spain shortly before the American occupation of Puerto Rico.*

reforms, rebelled once more and began the fighting that eventually led to the Spanish American War and Cuban independence. The bitter fighting that followed affected Puerto Rico in many ways. The island's separatists in exile, led by the venerable Dr. Ramón Emeterio Betances, joined the Cubans and organized a Puerto Rican Section of the Cuban Revolutionary party.

An appeal was made to prominent Puerto Rican political figures and Francisco Basora went on a secret mission to Puerto Rico to try to gain support for the Cuban cause. In 1896, plans were made for an invasion of Puerto Rico. General Juan Rius Rivera, a Puerto Rican at the service of the Cuban revolution, was chosen to lead the expedition. Rius came to the conclusion that such an endeavor could not succeed and returned to his post in the Cuban army. In spite of this setback, the Puerto Rican section and Betances continued to press their Cuban allies to demand the independence of Puerto Rico as a requisite to any settlement of the Cuban question.

Unexpected events in Spain were to bring about the fulfillment of the pact between Sagasta and the Liberal Fusionist Party of Puerto Rico. On August 8, 1897, Prime Minister Cánovas del Castillo was assassinated. The Queen Regent, María Cristina, entrusted the government in early October to a new cabinet headed by Sagasta, with Segismundo Moret Prendergast as Overseas Minister. The new government confronted the colonial issue without delay. Sagasta had promised that he would grant autonomy to the Antilles as soon as he came to power; this time he made good on his promise.

The international situation had now deteriorated so severely that swift action on the matter of reforms was essential. Sagasta decided to act immediately, and without waiting for the *Cortes,* gave Moret the task of drawing up the reform laws. On November 9, 1897, Governor Sabás Marín was informed of three decrees establishing an autonomous regime in Puerto Rico.

The first decree guaranteed political and civil rights to the Spanish citizens of the island. The second extended the electoral law of 1896 to Puerto Rico, with adjustments to the island's special conditions. The franchise was extended to all Spaniards 25 years of age and older who were in full enjoyment of their civil rights, and had been residents of the island for at least two years. The military were not allowed to vote while in active service. Voting would be by secret ballot. The third decree granted an autonomous regime to Puerto Rico. These acts provided the framework for the autonomic government soon to be established.

The Autonomic Charter

In accordance with the decrees the government of Puerto Rico was composed of the governor general; a bicameral parliament consisting of a house of representatives and an administrative council; a cabinet consisting of a president and five ministers appointed by the governor general: those of justice and state, of internal affairs, of education, of agriculture, industry and commerce, and of public works and communications; a provincial assembly; municipal governments; and a representation in the Spanish Parliament consisting of 16 deputies and 3 senators.

The governor general, appointed by the king on the recommendation of the council of ministers, represented the crown. He was responsible for the maintenance of law and order and for the overall security. All other insular authorities were subordinate to him. He enforced laws, decrees, treaties, and international agreements emanating from both the legislative and executive powers. He represented the ministries of state, war, navy, and overseas and was charged with carrying out their directives. He was empowered to suspend the publication and enforcement of any resolution of the Spanish government which he considered harmful to the general interest of the nation or the island, and required to inform the appropriate ministry of his reasons. In addition he was empowered to suspend capital punishment and constitutional guarantees, subject to the specific provisions in the constitution. The governor general was also responsible for the effective administration of justice. As the monarch's representative, he maintained direct contact with diplomatic agents and with consuls of Spain and America in matters related to external affairs.

As the principal colonial officer he had to see that the rights and privileges of the colonial administration were duly protected. He was required to publish the accords of the insular parliament submitted for his consideration. Whenever he felt that a decision of the insular parliament went beyond that body's authority, threatened the constitutional rights of the citizens, or jeopardized the interests of the colony or the state, he was to refer the measure to the council of ministers of the monarchy. If the council took no action within two months, the governor general was free to use his own judgment.

The governor general and his cabinet appointed the members of the judiciary and supervised the administration of justice. The governor general prepared the budget and presented it to the cabinet prior to

January of each year. The budget listed the income and expenditures related to colonial administration and the island's contributions to the national government.

Jurisdictional conflicts among the island's authorities which were not required to go to the central government, were to be brought before the courts of justice. The governor could appeal before the *Audiencia* all disputes between executive and legislative bodies.

Any jurisdictional matters between the insular parliament and the governor could, by petition of the parliament, be submitted to the high court. The court's decisions would then have the force of law.

The five cabinet secretaries acted as a corporation within the executive; they were appointed by the governor, who selected three of the five secretaries from among the members of the majority party in parliament. They were accountable to the parliament rather than to the executive. A member of either house of parliament could be appointed to the cabinet. As a cabinet member he could participate in the deliberations of both houses but could only vote in the house to which he was elected. The president dealt with matters affecting one or more departments and saw to it that cabinet agreements were enforced.

The administrative council, a kind of senate, consisted of fifteen members, seven designated by the governor general and eight elected. Qualifications for election required that: the candidate be a native Puerto Rican, or be a resident of the island for four consecutive years; meet the yearly income requirements, and have no contracts with either the national or the local governments.

While the council was in session its members could not legally hold any other position, although they could be given additional tasks by the local or national governments. The councillors appointed by the governor held their positions for life. Half the elected seats came up for re-election every two years.

The councillors were granted political immunity as a guarantee of their freedom of expression; they could not be arrested or indicted without a previous council resolution except when caught *in flagranti* or when the council was not in session. Any case involving a councillor was seen before the *Audiencia*. The immunity did not extend to attacks on the integrity of the nation, and authorship of books, articles, or pamphlets instigating military insurrection or of a slanderous nature.

The House of Representatives consisted of 32 elected members. Representatives were elected for five-year terms and could be reelected indefinitely. Except for those who became cabinet members, members of the

House of Representatives were barred from accepting any additional pensions, employment, or paid commissions.

The House of Representatives met annually, convened by the governor general. The governor was empowered to suspend or close its sessions, and could dissolve both the house and the administrative council at any time provided he reopened the session within three months.

Both houses met simultaneously except when the council was performing judicial functions. Legislative measures could originate in either chamber or with the governor, except for measures dealing with taxation and public credit, which had to come from the House. Members of the house enjoyed the same immunity as council members.

The Autonomic Charter granted the insular legislature power to legislate on matters related to the various cabinet departments; in addition, it had access to information on purely local affairs. It could legislate to change provincial, municipal, and judicial divisions; on sanitation, public credit, banks, and the monetary system. It could also regulate certain laws voted in the courts for the kingdom. It also had the right to determine electoral procedures; order a census; establish voting qualifications and regulate the voting system, provided it respected citizens' rights.

The insular parliament had a voice in some aspects of the local judicial system. It had exclusive authority over the local budget. However, neither house could consider the local budget until they had acted on the budget's contribution to the nation's finances.

It was before the parliament that the governor general took the oath of office; cabinet secretaries answered to the legislature for the performance of their duties, while the legislature proposed legislation to the central government through the governor and requested from him any executive resolutions needed on colonial matters. The legislature also set tariff duties and import-export taxes within certain limits.

The insular legislature had the power to negotiate commercial treaties with foreign nations, although the negotiations were to be arranged by the metropolitan government. The same procedure was followed on treaties that affected the island's interests. Treaties negotiated by the *Cortes* were to be submitted to the insular government for approval.

The provincial assembly was an elected body with exclusive authority over the island's educational system, welfare institutions, and transportation system. It provided for its own budget and appointed its own staff. Representation was based on population, with allowances for legitimate representation of minority groups.

Government at the local level was entrusted to the *Ayuntamientos,* with the power to legislate on matters of public education, transportation, health, and budget within their jurisdictions. The *Ayuntamiento* could also contract municipal loans; a recommendation by one third of the councilmen would result in a referendum, which then required a simple majority for passage.

Eligibility for the office of councilman varied with the size of the town. Special provisions for eligibility were granted to those having academic or professional degrees. The existing municipal laws continued in effect until parliament dealt with any given matter, except in areas specifically superseded by the new provisions or by the electoral law.

The charter itself could not be amended except at the request of the insular parliament. This provision guaranteed the permanency of Puerto Rico's form of government.

Sagasta's granting of autonomy without approval by the *Cortes* was a breach of the constitution. Nevertheless, with Spain still swept by war, the Spanish Parliament thought it wiser not to object to the decision. With Sagasta's action, the island's autonomists saw their expectations fulfilled and promptly plunged into the establishment of the new government. The task, however, was not devoid of thorny issues.

A Short-lived Experiment in Self-Government

Before the autonomic government could become a reality, the island's autonomists had to be united. The division brought about by the pact with Sagasta seemed insoluble. The Orthodox, under Barbosa and Fernández Juncos, considered themselves the true heirs of the program adopted in Ponce in 1887, while Muñoz and the Liberal Fusionist party were justifiably proud of having achieved the island's coveted autonomy.

However, the metropolitan government made it a condition that the factions come to terms and collaborate in establishing the regime. The *entente* between Barbosa and Muñoz was only attained after much pressure from Labra and the Spanish government. Eventually the governor, General Manuel Macías, achieved the needed reconciliation, after which the first autonomic cabinet was installed. The *Unión Autonomista Liberal* was the result of this effort of cooperation. The unity was shaky and short-lived.

The first elections soon divided the autonomist factions again; the Orthodox denounced the conciliation days before the elections. The elections were held without major incident; Muñoz Rivera emerged as the undisputed leader, with a wide margin of victory over the Orthodox.

The victory gave the Liberal Fusionists absolute control of the cabinet and of the legislature. The new government was scheduled to take office in May; however, the United States intervention in the war between Cuba and Spain forced a delay. The legislature did not convene until July 17. Eight days later the Americans landed and for all practical purposes the experiment in self-government ended.

Part Two

THE STRUGGLE
FOR IDENTITY

Arturo Morales Carrión

8
1898: The Hope and the Trauma

The Coming of the Americans

At daybreak on May 12, 1898, San Juan had its first taste of the war that on April 19 had broken out between the United States and Spain. A fleet of seven warships under the command of Rear Admiral William T. Sampson opened fire, without prior warning, on the centuries-old fortifications. The American men-of-war were searching for the Spanish fleet which had been sent to defend Puerto Rico, and had never reached the island, but found its graveyard in Santiago de Cuba. The clash soon became a show of poor marksmanship. The Spanish fire hardly touched the attacking ships. The American shells did little damage to the forts. Some hit the town, causing a number of casualties; others flew over the huddled population and landed harmlessly in the bay. Sampson had bombarded San Juan without instructions from Washington, hoping to capture it with a daring *coup de main*. Although he failed, the bombardment made it evident that Puerto Rico could not escape the war.[1]

The climax came two and a half months later. Early in the morning of July 25, the U.S.S. *Gloucester* sailed boldly into the bay of Guánica and landed a few troops who symbolically raised the Stars and Stripes for the first time on Puerto Rican soil. The *Gloucester* was soon followed by the *Massachusetts*, and by a convoy of ten transports with a total of 3,415 men. The invasion of Puerto Rico had started, and with it an American experiment in colonialism.[2]

The invaders knew little about Puerto Rico. A sympathetic American geologist, Robert T. Hill, who had finished a book on the West Indies just before the war, had observed that the island was less known to the United States "than even Japan or Madagascar. . . . The sum total of the scientific literature of the island since the days of Humboldt would hardly fill a page of this book."[3]

American interest in the West Indies had historically centered on Haiti and its dramatic revolution; on Cuba as the darling of U. S. expansionists; on Santo Domingo and its Samana Bay, desired by mid-century filibusteers; and even on the purchase of Saint Thomas as a strategic mart and coaling station. But little had been said or written about Puerto Rico. Some American leaders, like John Quincy Adams, Henry Clay, and James G. Blaine, had coveted the island; but the public knew almost

American troops land in Arroyo, located in southeastern Puerto Rico.

nothing about it. The best English source for information on Puerto Rico was a book published in 1834 by Colonel George Dawson Flinter, an Irish soldier of fortune. By 1898, Flinter's book was hopelessly out of date.[4]

It is interesting to note Hill's views on Puerto Rico, as yet unspoiled by war fervor or ardent jingoism. Delving into the island's history, Hill emphasized the profound changes brought about by the 1815 *Cédula de Gracias*—the decree which, in his opinion, started the prosperity of Puerto Rico "and from then until now the advance in wealth and population has been unexampled even in the West Indies." He observed that Puerto Rico had a "so-called system of autonomy with a premier and House of Representatives," that public instruction according to Spanish standards was flourishing, although poor from the American viewpoint.

He wrote:

Puerto Rico is essentially the land of the farmer, and the most highly cultivated of the West Indies. In fact, it is the only island where agriculture is so diversified that it produces sufficient food for the consumption of its inhabitants, in addition to vast plantation crops of sugar and coffee for exportation. Furthermore, the land is not monopolized by large plantations, but mostly divided into small independent holdings. Stock raising is also an extensive industry.

Hill also found the beginnings of a railroad system, many "excellent" roads and a growing telegraph and telephone network. The commercial, professional and planter classes were good-looking, happy, and prosperous, especially the women who were "sweet and flower-like." The peasants, though in his view indolent, were sagacious, skillful and hospitable. Most farmed; others lived from hand to mouth. Hill noted that as they spread over the island they prevented it from falling into the hands of the sugar monopolists. As to the black population, although race prejudice existed, it was different from the American. "I cannot tell," Hill concluded candidly, "why the Spanish man of color does not affect the prejudice against the negro which I feel in my own and other countries."[5]

Puerto Rico was, by Hill's testimony, neither a stagnant island nor a people living on the threshold of civilization. It could not be measured by the standards of the most advanced regions of the United States; but in many aspects, the social, economic and cultural development was ahead of many places in the Caribbean. Great illiteracy and poverty did exist, but the picture was not too different from the illiteracy and poverty in certain parts of the Deep South, at that time. Southern racism, indeed,

was more aggressive than the weakening ethnic barriers Hill found in
Puerto Rico.

But the eye of the geologist was not the eye of the military conqueror.
After Guánica, where Spanish resistance was weak, the invading fleet led
by General Nelson A. Miles landed in Ponce, Puerto Rico's main southern town, the center of a strong nativist spirit, and the bulwark of a
criollismo opposed to the proud military and bureaucratic power
entrenched in San Juan.

The surprise southern landing had been chosen on the advice of
Captain Henry H. Whitney, a sort of American 1898 James Bond who
had toured the area as a spy earlier in the year. He had observed much
dissatisfaction against Spain among the people as well as among several
of the landed interests, many of them of foreign ancestry.

Whitney was right; Ponce welcomed the invaders enthusiastically while
the Spaniards retreated into the hills. On July 28, 1898, Miles, as
commander-in-chief, issued a historic proclamation to justify the military
action. The first effect was the immediate end of Puerto Rico's political
relations with Spain, and, it was hoped, "the cheerful acceptance of the
Government of the United States." This was not simply a transitory military occupation. This was outright conquest. Miles said in part:

We have not come to make war upon the people of a country that for centuries
has been oppressed, but, on the contrary, to bring you protection, not only to
yourselves but to your property, to promote your prosperity, and to bestow upon
you the immunities and blessings of the liberal institutions of our government.
It is not our purpose to interfere with any existing laws and customs that are
wholesome and beneficial to your people as long as they conform to the rules of
military administration, of order and justice. This is not a war of devastation,
but one to give to all within the control of its military and naval forces the advantages and blessings of enlightened civilization.[6]

The proclamation was a model of psychological warfare. It thought
to detach the Puerto Ricans from Spain by promising them, not only
protection, but the "liberal institutions" of republican America. Offering
"the advantages and blessings of enlightened civilization," it stood for a
war against darkness and despotism and for freedom and light. It was a
proclamation to kindle instant allegiance with the hope of full and
immediate assimilation into the American political system and way of
life.

But there was quite a distance between promise and fact. A second
proclamation on July 29 told a different story. It instructed the com-

manders to see that the inhabitants obeyed the authority of the United States, "the power of the military occupant being absolute and supreme and immediately operating upon the political conditions of the inhabitants." If the inhabitants obeyed, their property and the municipal laws were to be respected. If crimes were committed, jurisdiction was vested on military commissions; taxes were paid to the military occupant; and private property was taken when needed, to be paid at a fair valuation. The rhetoric of freedom was one thing; the harsh realities of war were another.[7]

The conquest of Puerto Rico was, therefore, a peculiar offshoot of the Spanish-American War, a sideshow of the international crisis over Cuba, which had been brewing for years. Puerto Rico had caused the United States no political or economic concern. On the contrary, the last American consul, Philip C. Hanna, who watched the establishment of the autonomous government with great interest, reported on December 3, 1897, that "Porto Ricans are generally jubilant over the news received from Spain concerning the provincial autonomy and the natives generally believe that Spain will grant them such a form of Home rule as will be in every way satisfactory to them." The captain general, Manuel Salas Marín seemed to be popular, noted Hanna, "among all classes of people and there is every evidence of peace and contentment amongst the people of San Juan."[8] On January 8, 1898, just before the grave events that led to the war, Hanna observed: "Autonomy will, I believe, increase American trade with this Island. . . . The trade of Puerto Rico is of more value to the United States than is the trade of many of the South and Central American Republics."[9] Peaceful friendly relations thus existed between the American consul and Spanish officials during Puerto Rico's preparation for its fleeting era of autonomy.

Puerto Rico was, of course, less valuable to the United States than Cuba, yet it had an important position in the field of inter American commercial relations. In the 1880s, when the United States began to develop an aggressive policy in the rising Latin American trade, a report was prepared for Congress which throws some interesting light on the commercial role of Puerto Rico and fully supports Hanna's views. Imports from Puerto Rico, mostly sugar, totaled less than those of Brazil, Cuba, Mexico, the British West Indies, and Venezuela, but ahead of imports from the Caribbean and the rest of Latin American, including Colombia, Uruguay, Chile and Peru. In terms of exports, Puerto Rico was the tenth market for American goods in the hemisphere, with a favorable trade balance of nearly $2.5 million.[10]

But trade was not the only reason to invade. More important was the belief, on the part of a resolute imperialist elite, that the time had come to kick Spain out of the hemisphere, to establish American hegemony over the Caribbean, and to embark on the "large policy" leading to a prominent role in Asia, the penetration of the oriental market and a position of world power. In George F. Kennan's apt phrase, it was "the smell of empire."[11]

Naval supremacy was the key element, and in an age of steamships this implied coaling stations at strategic places. A new geopolitical conception was developing, based on the brilliant, persuasive writings of Captain Alfred T. Mahan. To Mahan, control of the isthmus and the Caribbean was essential for rapid communication between the Atlantic and the Pacific. If the United States was to look outward in the industrial competition of empires, the supremacy over the Caribbean was a must. Mahan's most prominent disciple was Theodore Roosevelt, who with his lifelong friend, Senator Henry Cabot Lodge, and other "jingoes," created most of the pressure to take Puerto Rico.

Roosevelt, then assistant secretary of the navy, wrote privately to Mahan on May 3, 1897, that "Until we definitely turn Spain out of those islands (and if I had my way that would be done tomorrow), we will always be menaced by trouble there."[12] In November 1897, he again wrote about interfering on behalf of the Cuban revolutionaries and "taking one more step toward the complete freeing of America from European dominions." His position was clear: "from my own standpoint, however, and speaking purely privately, I believe that war will have to, or at least ought to, come sooner or later; and I think we should prepare for it well in advance."[13]

By early March, 1898, Roosevelt had worked on war plans in close consultation with Mahan, who first advised not to do much with Puerto Rico in the beginning. When war broke out, Roosevelt took a strong position in favor of total expulsion of Spain from the hemisphere. As he left to join the Rough Riders, he wrote Cabot Lodge: "do not make peace until we get Porto Rico, while Cuba is made independent and the Philippines at any rate taken from Spain."[14] With regard to Cuba, he had observed that he did not want it to seem "that we are engaged merely in a land-grabbing war." But this scruple did not apply to Puerto Rico. As Lodge reassured Roosevelt on May 24, "Porto Rico is not forgotten and we mean to have it."[15]

In April, Admiral George Dewey's decisive naval victory over Spain in the Philippines gave boost to the annexionists. By the end of May,

McKinley, who had at first wavered, was rumored to favor establishing a permanent colonial government in Puerto Rico. In McKinley's view, this would be "ample salve to the imperialists."[16]

By the time Miles landed in Guánica and Ponce, the policy had been set. Puerto Rico was to be part of the war indemnity. Its acquisition was part of a new geopolitical vision of U. S. hegemony over the Caribbean and the isthmus. After the war, Mahan defined the military importance of Puerto Rico in the American effort at empire building, British-style:

Puerto Rico considered militarily, is to Cuba, to the future isthmian canal, and to our Pacific coast, what Malta is, or may be, to Egypt and the beyond; and there is for us the like necessity to hold and strengthen the one, in its entirety and in its immediate surroundings, that there is for Great Britain to hold the other for the security of her position in Egypt, for her use of the Suez Canal, and for the control of the route to India. It would be extremely difficult for a European state to sustain operations in the eastern Mediterranean with a British fleet at Malta. Similarly, it would be very difficult for a transatlantic state to maintain operations in the Western Caribbean with a United States fleet based upon Puerto Rico and the adjacent islands.[17]

Thus, Puerto Rico became a key pawn in the rising competition of the industrial empires. Its future development would be determined by its strategic imperative, the basic clue to American interest in the island. The events of two world wars would bear out Mahan's prediction.

As Miles' troops fanned out from Ponce, Spanish power came to an end. In Spain's suit for peace, the Spaniards were willing to abandon Cuba, but offered to trade other territory in return for Puerto Rico. The Spanish position was that Puerto Rico had never been an element of conflict between Spain and the United States, and its inhabitants had remained loyal to the crown. But McKinley was adamant on the immediate evacuation of Cuba and Puerto Rico. He did not care about the constitutional difficulties that the Spanish government would have with the *Cortes*. Spain had no choice and the Spanish representatives signed the peace protocol on August 13, 1898. It provided for a three man commission to arrange within thirty days for the evacuation of Spanish troops and the transfer of sovereign rights.[18]

On August 26, 1898, President McKinley issued confidential instructions to the commissioners for "the future control and government of [Puerto Rico] by the United States." Puerto Rico was "to become the territory of the United States. Therefore all things done by you in the discharge of your commission should be done with a view to the future welfare of the island and the improvement of the state and condition of their people as Dependencies of the United States."

The commissioners were asked "to facilitate the speedy re-establishment of trade, commerce, business and other peaceful pursuits of the inhabitants." They had to be prepared to advise the general in command on the means "to continue good order and the administration of the local laws and ordinances after the departure of the Spanish forces."

The president added an important instruction: "Where it can be done prudently, confer with the leading citizens of Porto Rico in an unofficial manner and endeavor to ascertain their sentiments of loyalty to the United States and their views as to such measures as they may deem necessary or important for the future welfare and good government of the island."[19]

For the invaders, the war in Puerto Rico was a marginal operation which Miles vainly hoped would give him enough glory to help what many thought were his presidential ambitions. His friend, the jingoist newsman Richard Harding Davis, fought the idea prevalent at that time in the United States, that the Puerto Rican campaign had been a successful military picnic, a sort of comic opera war. Compared to the fighting at Santiago, Davis called it nevertheless a *fête des fleurs,* and in his view, Miles had killed the Spanish bull with the thrust of a good *matador* and with hardly any blood shed. "The course of empire to-day," Davis wrote, "takes its way to all points of the compass—not only to the West. If is moves always as smoothly, as honorably, and as victoriously as it did in Porto Rico, our army and our people need ask for no higher measure of success."[20] But the path of empire was not to be that smooth; instead, it led into an era of sharp ambivalence and misunderstanding, into a clash of social psychologies and cultural values. If taking Puerto Rico had looked like a military picnic, ruling the island was quite another story, for there was more to Puerto Rico than the strategic imperative or the smell of empire.

A View of Puerto Rico

Puerto Rico in 1898 was not like any of the other territories which the United States acquired by treaty or by the force of arms. It did not resemble the American Southwest or Alaska with great expanses of uninhabited land. With nearly one million inhabitants, Puerto Rico was already densely populated, not an open frontier for human settlement. It could not be easily overcome like old California, by a tidal wave of enterprising pioneers. It had the characteristics of a small cultural nationality, of a people forged in a West Indian melting pot of Indian-Afro-Spanish extraction.

A census report published in 1900 confirmed several of Hill's observations. Total population was 953,243 with a population density seven times that of Cuba, twice that of Pennsylvania, and almost equal to the industrial state of New Jersey. But Puerto Rico was essentially a rural society. Its urban population constituted only 21.4 percent. This population was youthful with a median age of 18.1 years as compared with 20.7 for Cuba and 21.9 for the United States. Of the nearly 1,000,000 inhabitants, 61.8 percent were classified as whites (many with some mixed blood) and 38.2 percent as colored. The white population had a greater concentration in the mountainous interior (66.3 percent) than in the coast (58.8 percent).[21]

This mixed population, with a higher proportion of whites than in the rest of the West Indies and in the southern United States, lived in a land where latifundia had not taken over. Agriculture was by far the leading occupation. In 1897, it was estimated that there were 60,953 *fincas* (farms) with a total of over 2 million *cuerdas* (acres). Of this total, 61,556 acres were devoted to sugar cane and 122,358 to coffee which had become the leading crop. Its production reached over 51,000,000 pounds in 1897 with a value of over 12 million pesos, as compared with 126,000,000 pounds for sugar with a value of over 4 million pesos.[22]

The pattern of cultivation reveals that absentee ownership was limited. Fully 93 percent of the farms were occupied by their owners, while in Cuba the corresponding figure was 43.5 percent. Colored people already owned 9 percent of these lands; coffee farms leased by them rose to 31 percent. Their average farm had three *cuerdas* as compared with seven *cuerdas* for the whites. In the sugar lands, their ownership was negligable: only 1 percent. Sugar was the white man's almost exclusive realm as concerned land ownership, but coffee was more family-oriented, more ethnically diversified, with a trend towards minifundia in certain areas.[23]

In the last decade of the century, coffee had found a profitable market in Europe and had become the main export crop, while sugar, depending on export to the United States, was an essential source of customs revenues. The sugar interests longed for free access to the American market. By the early 1880s, the introduction of new machinery was changing sugar production and the island's producers feared the expansion of beet sugar in Louisiana and increased American investments elsewhere.[24] Puerto Rican sugar represented a frontier for expansion of American capital in 1898, if free trade was established with the American market, tariff protection was assured, and a government under control of elements was sympathetic to the sugar trusts. The tutor that would rule the island for the next half century would be, above all, the trusted partner of the sugar trusts. Politically, this was the hey-day of American colonialism; economically, the age when sugar became king.

The autonomous charter, granted in 1897, signified a peaceful revolution, the fulfillment of a century-old dream. It was government by a

The era of King Sugar: cutting sugar cane near Yauco.

native elite of variegated extraction. Some members represented the native *hacendados* who resented the Spanish trading interests entrenched in San Juan. Others belonged to the professional classes—lawyers and doctors well versed in the political trends of the day. Some had studied in Spain and been drawn to Spanish liberalism including the doctrines of federalism. Others had trained in the United States, like José Celso Barbosa, an able colored physician who absorbed in Michigan the tenets of the Republican party during reconstruction. And then, there were men like Luis Muñoz Rivera, a brilliant and realistic mind, largely self-taught, a man with a sharp pen and an imposing, charismatic figure.

Inexperienced in government, they tended to quarrel among themselves. Personal loyalties were deeply felt, and by 1898 the country was divided between *muñocistas* and *barbosistas*. The system had condemned these proud men to be outsiders until the system cracked, and at the last minute, they were called to join hands and save the motherland. They lacked the political savvy of the Tammany wards, but they were determined to be masters in their own house. Autonomy was the promise; before they had time to realize, however, the implications in practice, autonomy was dead and they had to deal with the U.S. military governors.

The Initial Contacts

In the last years of Spanish power, the United States had been a subject of debate in the Puerto Rican partisan press. Two trends emerged: one was highly critical of American life and mores. Articles stressed what they called the hypocrisy of American ideals, and the country's lack of culture. The sensationalism of the U.S. jingo press was regarded with misgivings. The scandals and fraud in American elections, especially at Tammany, were denounced. Puerto Ricans were warned of U.S. plans to dominate the Caribbean and Latin America. This was, indeed, the "Yankee peril."

Other writers disagreed sharply. They admired the freedom of expression in the U.S. press, and the change of parties as a result of elections. The United States was looked upon as an idealistic nation, willing to intervene in Cuba for moral reasons. While the McKinley policies on Cuba and protectionism gave cause for concern, these writers acknowledged the insular need for American markets. And writers like Barbosa dreamed of the day when Puerto Rico would be governed like

Michigan. The "Yankee peril" was, to many like him, the "Yankee model."[25]

While on the southern coast disaffection was rife because of the hated *Compontes* of 1887, in San Juan many rallied to the support of the government as war approached. The insular council, fully representative of the autonomist forces led by Muñoz Rivera, urged resistance to invasion as a show of gratitude to the Spanish government that had recognized the island's rights. Red Cross groups were organized, and a call for volunteers was issued while all kinds of rumors circulated on the impending demise of Yankee power. At one stage, as the political leader José de Diego later revealed, he and Muñoz Rivera asked General Macías for 9,000 rifles to organize popular resistance to the United States, a proposal the Captain General refused to consider.[26]

The news from the Philippines soon had a sobering effect and after the May bombardment, the facts of war led to the rapid evacuation of San Juan while the leaders remained to share the fate of the defenders. The formal inauguration of the Insular Parliament on July 17 could not hide the fact that things were going from bad to worse. The news from Guánica and Ponce shook the defenders. On August 13, further news came about the signing of the Peace Protocol. On September 6, General Brooke was already in San Juan paying a formal, protocolary call on the Spanish governor. The transfer of power was arranged in a polite atmosphere, devoid of rancour. On October 18, at noon, the city was officially delivered to Brooke at the old Fortaleza palace. In contrast to the rejoicing that had met the troops at Ponce and Mayaguez, the atmosphere was grave and restrained.[27] As Albert Gardiner Robinson of *The Evening Post* observed, there were not enough ardent supporters of the new government "to lead to any very effusive demonstrations on the part of the citizens." Of this solemn moment he wrote,

It was all a quiet affair. There was no excitement, and but little enthusiasm. An hour after its close, the streets had assumed their wanted appearance. There was little to show that anything important had taken place, that by this brief ceremony Spain's power on the island of Puerto Rico had ended forever. There was little to indicate a change, except that over the grim walls of the Morro, over the frowning heights of San Cristóbal, and over all the public buildings of the city, there shone the bright stars of the red, white and blue, instead of the red and yellow of Spain.[28]

Most of the liberal elite rejoiced at the coming of the Americans. The reaction covered a wide spectrum: there were those who offered their

services to Miles in the belief that the landing meant the coming of freedom to the island. Others along the southern coast, who had favored the
separation of Puerto Rico from Spain, joined the American troops as
interpreters or scouts. The mayor of Yauco, a southern town, ecstatically
hailed the invasion as a "miraculous intervention of a just God, who
returns us to the American matrix in whose waters Nature has put us."[29]
On August 27, the United States was highly praised by a representative
group of autonomists led by José Celso Barbosa. "We aspire," they said,
"to be another State within the Union in order to affirm the personality
of the Puerto Rican people, accepting in the meanwhile whatever transformations the Congress deem necessary in accordance with the civic
and cultural state of the country. . . ."[30]

On October 21, after the formal occupation had taken place, this
group, plus other well-known leaders, issued a manifesto with two basic
objectives: the extension of U.S. citizenship and full local self-government.
The aim was statehood, but the group insisted that Puerto Rico had to
demonstrate first that it had learned how to govern itself through a
preparatory period as a territory. Military government was incompatible with American freedoms and should end as soon as possible.[31]

There was a consensus that Spain had ill-prepared Puerto Rico for
democracy. Thus a period of tutelage was thought necessary. Even the
separatists in New York who had joined the Cuban Revolutionary party
were anxious to help the United States overthrow Spanish power. Only
in France did the old revolutionary, Ramón Emeterio Betances, urge
armed revolt to secure independence. José Julio Henna, a distinguished
physician highly respected in New York, had become the Puerto Rican
spokesman in the United States and had visited Theodore Roosevelt to
press for invasion. He was later joined in New York by Eugenio María
de Hostos, an outstanding social thinker and educator who had long
favored Puerto Rican independence from Spain under a West Indian
federation. A great admirer of republicanism and federalism, Hostos
felt that the United States should prepare Puerto Rico to choose, after a
20 year tutelage or *mentorado*, between statehood and independence, the
latter being his own preference.[32]

Hostos had reached the United States from Chile in the summer of
1898. He had found that the Cubans no longer cared about Puerto Rico
and that there was need for prompt action in Washington and Puerto
Rico to affirm the island's rights. A fruitless trip took him to the capital
precisely at the time when the U.S. troops were landing in Guánica. As
the cession took place, he left for Puerto Rico and launched his *Liga de*

Patriotas or Patriot's League, on the south coast. Hostos, an early fore-runner of the doctrine of self-determination, thought the cession was illegal. His view was essentially juridical: the United States should recognize Puerto Rico's legal personality and prepare the country for republican democracy and a plebiscite through a *mentorado* in the best U.S. constitutional tradition.

With the help of Matienzo Cintrón and other friends, he set up the *Liga* and joined Henna and Manuel Zeno Gandía in presenting their views to McKinley. It was an odd meeting. Hostos' halting English did not help, and McKinley was not a man to understand his brilliant but unrealistic scheme. A few years later, Hostos died in Santo Domingo, broken and disillusioned. The smell was of empire, not of populist and constitutional democracy.[33]

Some Puerto Ricans had high expectations, others faced the change with ambivalent feelings. One of them was Luis Muñoz Rivera. He had been an outspoken critic of Spanish rule or *caciquismo*. He had revived the autonomist movement and obtained a pact with a monarchical party in spite of his republican convictions. Autonomy with real power was his overriding consideration.[34]

But power slipped through his fingers in the turmoil of war. He and his colleagues felt honor bound to support the Spanish government in its last throes, hoping that the invaders would respect their hard-won freedoms. He had distrusted U.S. intentions before 1898. "Annexionism," Muñoz wrote in 1895, "had always seemed to me absurd, depressing and inconceivable."[35] In the brief armed struggle, the autonomist government, hardly organized, had been side-tracked. As Brooke prepared to take over the country, he had to decide what to do with these leaders who stood for freedoms granted under a charter no longer recognized by the United States.

In an interview for the U.S. press, Muñoz Rivera outlined his positions. He denounced the political clique that had ruled Puerto Rico before autonomy, and emphasized the charter's encouragement of native leadership. The American invasion had, however, stopped the process. "The island accepted the invading army with great rejoicing which I considered premature," he observed, "the most elementary discretion counseled a noble and sober reserve, until the thinking and action of the Washington legislature was manifested. . . ." Great things were expected from the United States by both the leadership and the people. But Muñoz warned that Puerto Rico already had its own personality as an autonomous state which should be respected. Only if Washington was aware of this fact would the strong current of admiration endure. The colonial had to be changed into a citizen.

His plan was succinctly stated: a brief military occupation; the declaration of Puerto Rico as a territory, but with the full powers of self-government and, soon thereafter, statehood. This political program should be complemented by an economic one: Tariffs should be lowered to help the laboring classes, who were greatly in need of higher wages. Public primary education was also indispensable.

Muñoz Rivera, like Hostos, defended Puerto Rico's personality, but he did not consider a 20 year span of Americanization necessary in order for Puerto Ricans to demonstrate their attachment to freedom before attaining self-government. In Muñoz Rivera's view, the process was the reverse: if self-government was maintained, statehood would be acceptable.[36]

General Brooke handled the transfer of powers tactfully. He invited the Autonomist Council to join him at the transfer ceremony and refused to accept its resignation. He chose not to change immediately the system of laws to avoid chaos and disorder. He explained to Washington the nature of the Council of Secretaries set up under the autonomous charter. "As far as I have been able to learn," he observed, "the selection of the Secretaries appointed at that time was through an expression of the will of the people. . . ." After making investigations and weighing all the information he could get, Brooke appointed the four secretaries who were still active, with Muñoz Rivera as president of the council.

In order to expedite government, Brooke decided to refer every question to the appropriate department reserving to himself the final decision. While in several instances he did not always follow the council's advice, he recognized that their recommendations had been based "on patriotic and unselfish motives and that they have at heart the best interest of the island."[37]

In spite of Brooke's good intentions and of his ad hoc arrangement with the autonomists, perplexing problems began to arise. A feud developed in the press. Growing resentment arose, punctuated by drunken brawls between soldiers and sailors, and constant clashes between troops and civilians. The sudden appearance of evangelizing Protestant ministers also led to sharp local criticism.[38]

On December 10, 1898, the Treaty of Paris was signed, in which Spain formally ceded Puerto Rico to the United States. According to Article IX, the civil rights and the political status of the inhabitants were to be determined by Congress. In the island, political lines began to be drawn.

Though statehood was the common objective, a subtle difference was manifested between the Republican party, founded by Barbosa and the signers of the October manifest, and the Federal party, organized in the same month by the followers of Muñoz Rivera. While both parties supported "identity," meaning full incorporation into the American system, the Federals emphasized that the United States was "a State of States and a Republic of Republics." Their aim was to be one of those states and republics. They did not insist on a *mentorado* to learn self-government. Provided autonomy was retained, they were willing to accept territorial status.

Other problems piled up in several places: *partidas* (bands) attacked Spaniards and sacked Spanish property. Old animosities revived, particularly in the northwest where the memory of the Lares revolt still lingered. In many cases, local judges protected the *partidas*. American troops stepped in, killing several of the leaders and arresting about sixty.[39] To the American commanders, the *partidas* were sheer banditry.

Fiscal matters went from bad to worse in the transition. The last Spanish budget, 1897–1898, had left a $483,157 surplus; Brooke, however, found an empty treasury. Most of the revenues came from customs duties, but the whole trading pattern was soon in disarray. As Puerto Rico fell within the United States tariff system, coffee and tobacco had to face new high tariffs abroad, while there was still no free trade with the United States. The exchange of American money for Spanish money also worked to the detriment of the people. Brooke fully realized the problem and urged the U.S. government not to ignore it.[40]

These perplexing questions taxed the ability of the military commanders. Brooke was honest enough to state that they were unprepared to handle them. Issues regarding tariffs, crop reports, and markets were beyond their expertise, not to mention the complexities of local politics. Military rule, Brooke thought, was only a temporary expedient requiring in due time a civil government with sufficient military force to preserve order.[41]

The End of Autonomy

Over a full year was to elapse, however, between the end of Brooke's mandate on December 9, 1898, and the coming of the first civilian governor appointed by the president on May 1, 1900. In this interim period, crucial decisions were made; many were to shape the role of the government, and the life and cultural mores of the people. The American colonial tutelage was established even before the full scope of U.S. authority was legislated by Congress under the Foraker Act of 1900. A tone, a style, was set ahead of the juridical framework.

The man who started the change was Brigadier General Guy V. Henry, described by a Puerto Rican Republican who knew him well as "thin and boney." Henry, he wrote, "admitted no discussion, nor that anyone contradict him; he commanded and wished to be obeyed."[42] He was blunt and honest; a law and order man, and a strict tutor. "I am getting in touch with the people," he wrote, "and trying to educate them to the idea that they must help govern themselves, giving them kindergarten instruction in controlling themselves without allowing them too much liberty." Notwithstanding their gentle and peaceful nature, he "thought they had acquired very liberally the Spanish habit of lying and cannot be trusted."[43] His cultural outlook and training as a strict disciplinarian colored Henry's approach to his job. He wanted to improve sanitation, revise election standards, speed Americanization through the teaching of English, establish an efficient policy system, and check freedom of the press. He reserved for himself the granting of public franchises to avoid dishonest contracts. He imposed a heavy tax on alcohol and tobacco, for in this land of rum and *aguardiente,* he viewed drinking as a vice that interfered with moral progress.[44] Henry brought the Puritan strain to Puerto Rico; but for too many Puerto Ricans he was not too different from some of the Spanish governors who had used their absolute powers, their *facultades omnímodas,* to impose their personal views on ethics and government. Many of the liberals had fought this dictatorial trend, this *mandonismo,* in Spanish times; faced with *mandonismo,* American style, a clash was unavoidable.

From the very beginning, Henry asserted his authority. His methods were tactless and strong-handed. He instituted many reforms but was unwilling to respect freedom of the press. He did not take kindly, particularly, to criticism by *La Democracia,* the organ of the Liberal Autonomists. And on February 6, 1899, he did away with the Insular Council which Brooke had retained judging it "incompatible with American methods and progress."[45]

Henry came to view Muñoz Rivera as the *bête-noire* of Puerto Rican politics. Muñoz's insistence on retaining native self-rule clashed with Henry's estimate of Puerto Rican abilities. On January 23, 1899, he wrote to McKinley: "I understand that these people are anxious for another form of government. My own opinion is that the form they now have is the one under which they should work for some time to come. . . ." Under any other arrangement, he felt politics would be brought into it and the people would not get what they were getting now. "They are still children, each one has a different idea and they don't really know what they do want. . . . Political parties at present seem smothered. With another form of government these jealousies would break out afresh. They take to politics as naturally as a duck takes to water. . . ."[46]

Henry replaced the Insular Council with three secretaries of his own choosing. These were his men, his "ducks," including a representative from the Republican party. He put General John Eaton in charge of public instruction, thus gaining direct control of a key area. In selecting Francisco de Paula Acuña, a Supreme Court judge, as secretary of state, he wrote the president: "He [Acuña] is head and shoulders above Rivera in ability and is independent in politics."[47]

Muñoz Rivera and his followers saw Henry's action as a deathblow to the remnants of home rule. They accused Henry of destroying representative democracy in Puerto Rico and prepared for battle. When criticisms continued in the press, La Democracia was brought to court; another newspaper, La Metralla, was suspended and a third, El Territorio, was also threatened.[48] The children had to be spanked.

But this was only the beginning. In his February 28 letter, Henry stated:

Muñoz Rivera has been beaten at his own game. He is, however, a political agitator and is bound to make trouble in the future. He is going to the United States to claim independence and failing in this, he will try to form what he calls a separatist party. The newspapers announce, whether true or not, I do not know, that [Máximo] Gómez has written saying he would join with this element in a movement to make all of these islands independent.[49]

On March 10, 1899, Henry wired the adjutant general that he had received reports of plans for an insurrection and that Muñoz Rivera was at the bottom of this, expecting aid from Máximo Gómez, the Cuban insurrectionist. He insisted he was prepared "to give them all the lead they need, thus furnishing American object lesson of progress—settling matter forever."[50] On the same date, he urged early approval of his recommendation for organizing a Puerto Rican regiment.

Henry's superiors in Washington felt, however, that he had gone too far and that it was time for more tact in Puerto Rican affairs. Under instructions from the president, the secretary of war wired that Henry's apprehensions were unfounded. There was nothing to the Gómez story.

"Be tactful and conciliatory," the telegram advised. "Wise counsels should prevent a conflict."[51]

Henry's problems, however, were not limited to the autonomists. He also faced criticism from the opposite side. Other army officers, led by General Grant, son of the Civil War commander, wanted the army to be in full charge. The small but influential American enclave urged the abolition of the Spanish courts. In their eyes, Henry was not strong enough to handle Puerto Ricans; the general felt that this group reflected little credit on the United States. By the end of his term, he was coming to the conclusion that Puerto Ricans would eventually be prepared for territorial government and should then run the island influenced as far as possible by American ideas. Concerning the American enclave, he could not care less.[52]

The Framing of Tutelage

In May, 1899, Henry was replaced by Brigadier General George W. Davis. Muñoz Rivera felt vindicated. He had brought his charges against Henry to American public opinion. His experience set a pattern. Puerto Ricans who did not side with the Washington governors would be considered anti-American; their political enemies and the American enclave of traders and bureaucrats in San Juan would attempt to discredit them while proclaiming the gospel of "Americanism," as immediate subservience, if not blind acceptance, of official policies. The dissatisfied groups would then complain to Washington of the misrule of their appointee. The federal government thus became more and more enmeshed in Puerto Rican politics. The American appointees felt that Puerto Ricans should stop their politicking, tinged with a high dose of *personalismo,* which they found distasteful. They embraced, therefore, a rather naive idea that the best way to promote the U.S. style of democracy was to teach that partisan activity, job-hunting and jockeying for power, so typical of U.S. politics, were somehow harmful to Puerto Rican development, and constituted an undesirable pressure disturbing the good role of the tutor. It was the application of a double standard.

Even before the island's territorial status had been determined by Congress, a peculiar set of colonial interrelationships came into being; an institutional structure was established; a form of political behavior developed; and power was centralized in such fields as justice, education and security. In this sense, the old tradition of the Spanish centralized government based on the authority to govern the island as a place under siege, was replaced by an emerging tradition of centralized power, which contradicted many American principles and values. The *mentorado* was, indeed, on its way, but over a rather bumpy road.

Davis, the fourth military governor in less than a year, was not a West Pointer; as professor Henry Wells has pointed out, Davis and his civil and military officers represented a cross section of American middle class values at the turn of the century.[53] He was more scholarly and tactful than Henry, but his very strong prejudices marred his good intentions. The different race and high illiteracy rate of Puerto Ricans were to him very strong arguments against home rule. He could well understand the economic crisis and became a champion of free trade with the mainland. But politically Henry perhaps more than anybody else, helped define the role of the vigilant tutor.

In fact, Davis was one of the two primary shapers of the McKinley administration's colonial policies towards Puerto Rico. The other was Elihu Root, secretary of war since July, 1899. A prominent New York lawyer with close ties to the eastern Republican establishment, Root was known as a man of keen intellect and as a flexible negotiator. A friend of Roosevelt, Root was a political conservative, who admired the British imperial system; hence, much suited to the tutorial role expected of him. On most matters he agreed with Davis and was influenced by his reports.

Davis continued the centralization of power with the executive. But in order to conform to American practices, somehow he had to take into account the people's wishes. Having considered the Puerto Ricans unfit for self-government, Davis relied on hand-picked advisory boards of what he called "distinguished citizens of Puerto Rico." The aim, he insisted in an August 15, 1900 circular, was to prepare for territorial government. To the actions undertaken by Brooke and Henry, he added significant legal measures: the institution of the writ of *habeas corpus* and the appointment of a United States provisional court, with trial by jury and reorganization of the judiciary on recommendation of the judicial board. In the August circular he outlined a colonial administration by a governor working with a cabinet which with little modification was to continue in Puerto Rico after civil government was established in 1900. He left the practice of self-government to the municipal area which he considered chaotic. To Davis, cooperation from the political parties was the first step of the learning process. Only when this lesson was mastered would the people be ready for an insular legislature. The political education of Puerto Rico was thus to proceed gradually under the watchful eyes of a hopeful tutor.[54]

With his August circulars and other acts, Davis had boldly entered into the area of legislative fiat. Root, too, was searching for an administrative diagram of what he called "The Principles of Colonial Policy." In his 1899 Report as Secretary of War he outlined his views: Since the United States was a nation endowed with the powers essential to national life, it had all the powers with respect to the territory which it had thus acquired. The people of the territories had no legal right whatsoever to assert against the United States, but had "a moral right to be treated by the United States in accordance with the underlying principles of justice and freedom which we have declared in our Constitution." The people of Puerto Rico, for instance, were entitled to demand not to be deprived of life, liberty, or property without due process of law, but when it came to the form of government, it was a different matter. Here, the most important fact to be considered was that the people had not been educated in the art of self-government or any really honest government. Since only 10 percent could read or write (the proportion was, indeed, higher), they did not have any real understanding of the way to conduct a popular government. In Root's view, Puerto Ricans were in the same rudimentary stage of political development as the rest of the West Indies and Central America. They had to learn the principles of self-control and respect for constitutional government. Root wrote:

This lesson will necessarily be slowly learned, because it is a matter not of intellectual apprehension, but of character and of acquired habits of thought and feeling. . . . They would inevitably fail without a course of tuition under a strong and guiding hand. With that tuition for a time their natural capacity will, it is hoped, make them a self-governing people.

This passage clearly presents the American theory of colonial tutelage in the first half of the twentieth century. Together with the doctrine of congressional supremacy as provided by the Treaty of Paris, this stance denied the people of Puerto Rico any natural rights to self-government. They would have only the rights that their tutors and Congress chose to give them. The Jeffersonian philosophy of government by consent, based on inalienable rights, as set forth in the Declaration of Independence, was conveniently shelved.[55]

While the new colonial policies were being shaped in Washington and Puerto Rico, the economic realities were adding unexpected new pressures. With the coffee market in sharp decline, the tobacco market closed, and the American sugar market still subject to a high tariff, Puerto

Rican agriculture was plummeting. Furthermore, money exchange was working to the disadvantage of the Spanish *peso*. The economy, like the political structure, was also going through a traumatic period. Then a natural disaster struck. On August 8, 1899, *San Ciriaco,* the worst hurricane within memory, cut through the island. More than 3,000 lives were lost; the coffee crop valued at more than $7 million was totally destroyed. Plantain trees were washed away and whole coffee *haciendas* were abandoned.[56]

American officials, new to the tropics, were appalled at the havoc wrought by the fierce storm. Davis' wires and dispatches told of the absolute helplessness of the population, the deaths, and the vast numbers of destitute. Davis asked for food, for a loan to help meet the financial losses, and especially recommended free trade with the United States, "a measure which I could not fully endorse until this calamity came upon the island."[57]

San Ciriaco was, then, a disaster that touched the nerve of moral duty. Root was already reaching the conclusion that the island had been bottled up by Cuban, Spanish, and American tariffs on tobacco, coffee, and sugar. He now viewed opening the U.S. market as "the only essential thing." *San Ciriaco* was a call to action: "The terrible destruction and impoverishment of the people by the recent hurricane," he wrote the president, "brings matters to a climax." He asked that imports of Puerto Rican products to the United States be declared free by executive decree, or by a special session of Congress. "The great burst of public beneficence," he concluded, "will not last long, and we will have a starving people in our hands very soon—starving, because this great, rich country, after inviting the Puerto Ricans to place themselves in our hands, refuses to permit them to send their products in our markets without the payment of a practically prohibitory duty."[58] While he mobilized with great effectiveness a nation-wide humanitarian effort, Root viewed free trade as a moral duty. He was also receptive to the requests from planters and businessmen for help to keep the economy going, provide work for their *peones* (field hands) and restore agricultural production. The economy had to be put on its feet if the colonial diagram was to work.

Basic questions arose from the first two crowded years of contacts and crisis. How were the Puerto Ricans to be governed? What types of economic relationships were to be established? What values were to preside over this change from a Spanish to an American system? The issues were debated in Congress in 1900. But before then, Davis and Root, following Brooke and Henry, had already established the theory, provided the administrative system, and set the tone for the American tutelage over the island. And they prepared themselves with key recommendations so that the transition to civil government would confirm the usefulness and propriety of what Root called "The Principles of Colonial Policy."

9

The Rise
of Colonial Tutelage

Between October, 1898, when the American flag was raised at *La Fortaleza* and November, 1948, when the Puerto Ricans chose their first elective governor, a full half century was to elapse. During this period, colonial tutelage was put to the test. The system called for the executive power to be controlled by Washington, especially in such key areas as justice, education, and security. Washington also controlled the legal system through presidential appointments to the Puerto Rican Supreme Court and the role of the U.S. District Court. Only in the legislative branch was the Puerto Rican voice fully heard. Obviously a clash between the legislative and the executive branches was inevitable. But power remained in Washington and in the hands of the presidential appointees, the key interpreters of U.S. tutelage.

The substance of colonialism was preserved, although the semantics changed. Puerto Rico was not called a "colony," but a "dependency" or "possession," juridically defined as an "unincorporated Territory." This era was, as previously noted, the era when sugar was king. It saw a profound economic transformation as American corporate capitalism, with huge investments, expanded and controlled the sugar industry. Modernized production turned Puerto Rico into a plantation economy, with emphasis on monoculture and deepening social and economic cleavages. When the burgeoning population and the 1929 depression combined, the situation became grave and explosive, a far cry from the hopes of the early tutors. Puerto Rico was not to be a happy, prosperous island, well-taught and well-behaved, but a poorhouse, and in the words of Rexford G. Tugwell, the last and brightest of the tutors, "a stricken land," foundering in despair.

The Foraker Act

When President McKinley gave Root responsibility for colonial policies as secretary of war, he wanted Puerto Rico to have "the best possible form of government." Root and Davis did their homework, but the Philippines, Cuba, and Puerto Rico posed different problems. As a result, their recommendations to Congress were a hybrid of American experience of territorial government and British imperial touches.

When in 1900 Davis drafted his recommendations on Puerto Rico's future civil government, he admitted that there were no U.S. precedents to help him and that it was necessary to turn to the experience of other nations. In searching "points of resemblance," he turned to the island of Trinidad, captured by the British in 1797. At that time, Trinidad had had Spanish laws and institutions, some slaves, no Indians, the Catholic religion, and sugar. Davis praised Trinidad's stability under the British: the rise in population, revenues, and production; the expansion of education; the presence of religious freedom; and the emphasis on road-building. Davis believed that the native population of Spanish, Negroes, and "maroons" would have reduced Trinidad to chaos. "Home rule," he pointed out, "was fortunately not accorded to this island, but instead it was governed at first by military officers directly. It is now a crown colony, having an executive council of five officials and three native appointed members, the governor presiding." Trinidad also had an elective council of twelve members. According to Davis, the island's population was content. This was, then, the model that influenced Davis. In Puerto Rico, he thought, there were men of learning and ability who would abuse power and take advantage of the profound illiteracy of the people. Since he considered both the people and the elite incompetent, he recommended withholding self-government unless there was "a plain demonstration of their competence to exercise it." In his view, only a few wanted it, the masses were stolid and the business class opposed it.

Davis also recommended that Puerto Rico be called a "dependency," with a governor, an executive council and later on a legislative assembly. The resemblance to a British crown colony model was obvious. The executive council would consist of a governor and seven chiefs of administrative offices plus four other members chosen from the legislative assembly. The legislative assembly would be composed of thirty-five assemblymen, with a town council for each municipality. All members of the Supreme Court and the United States Federal Court would be appointed by the president, who would also have the authority to disallow, repeal, alter, or annul any action of the governor or the assembly. Power was, therefore, firmly to remain in Washington.

But even this scheme, Davis insisted, should not be immediately enacted in its entirety. For the present, the governor and executive council should control legislation. "When experience shall have shown that the people comprehend the gravity of the duties and obligations of self-government will be soon enough to establish the lower house," he wrote. Only the tutor would judge when the time would come.[1]

Root agreed with Davis. He too recommended a form of insular government, but with the United States in complete control of the rights, property, and obligations of the people. He accepted elections for mayors and municipal councils, but specified that if they failed to perform their duties, the governor could remove them and order free elections.

Root considered the people too inexperienced to elect a legislature, and recommended that until they learned how to govern themselves at the municipal level, they should not have a legislature. He viewed elementary education as the key to success; if necessary, it should be defrayed by the United States. But the overriding consideration was economic: free trade should be established at the earliest possible moment.[2]

The president and the Congress had other advisers who viewed Puerto Rican abilities with more respect and less ethnic prejudice. McKinley's special commissioner, Henry K. Carroll, was one such observer. Carroll's report, based on first hand information from all classes, was complete and up-to-date. While supporting American sovereignty over Puerto Rico, Carroll came to like the people, tried to understand the culture, and had some profound insights into the problems of governance and intercultural relations.

Carroll often relied on Puerto Rican opinion; and he admitted the liberality of the system of autonomy, and some positive features of Spanish administration. He was particularly impressed with the human values of the poor: their system of mutual helpfulness, kindness, and hospitality. He did not equate extreme poverty and squalor with vice and unhappiness. He saw the Puerto Ricans as peace-loving, law-abiding, and deeply desirous of a civil government. Above all, Carroll insisted that illiteracy should not bar the people from self-government. He observed:

They may be poor but they are proud and sensitive, and could be bitterly disappointed if they found that they had been delivered from an oppressive yoke to be put under a tutelage which proclaimed their inferiority. . . .

"Education," he wrote, "is not the invariable line which separates good citizens from bad, but active moral sense." He argued that Puerto Ricans were better prepared to govern themselves than most Latin Americans, and reiterated that they could learn the art of government the only possible way: "by having its responsibilities laid upon them, by learning from their blunders."[3]

Early in January, 1900, legislation was introduced in the House and Senate, providing for civil government for Puerto Rico. Senator Joseph P. Foraker of Ohio led the debate in the Senate. Republican Congressman Sereno Payne, chairman of the Ways and Means Committee, was in charge on the House side. The hearings brought out the clash between the gradualist tutors and the partisans of autonomy. But economic issues were also prominent, especially free trade, which was opposed by the U.S. sugar and tobacco lobbies. The long Republican tradition of protectionism which had helped elect McKinley was now challenged by Puerto Rico's claim to free access to the American market. To some, like the New England Tobacco Growers' Association, this meant nothing less than the destruction of the American system of political economy. Lobbyists for the beet sugar industry invoked old prejudices: free trade meant that "the Latin race, after years of the rule of despotism, if suddenly given power, is a troublesome if not a dangerous power with which to deal."[4]

The two main questions in the debate were the extension of the constitution to the newly acquired territories and the question of free trade. Both issues were hotly debated.

The debate was held under the shadow of a larger issue: whether the people and products of the Philippines should have free entry into the United States. The fear that legislation for Puerto Rico would set a precedent for the Philippines influenced many positions and filled the debate with racist rhetoric. Senator Bate of Tennessee, an anti-imperialist, described the Philippines as "Pandora's box, full of ills, some of which are upon us, and others are to come. That is the real question. Puerto Rico is but its front shadow."[5] He talked disdainfully of the "mongrels of the East" and feared the omnipotence of Congress as asserted in the Puerto Rican bill. Here racism was an ally of anti-colonialism.

The question of citizenship further complicated these issues. Root, for instance, never wavered from his view that U.S. citizenship should not be extended to Puerto Rico. He did not favor the complete incorporation of the island into the United States. For strategic reasons, he wanted to keep Puerto Rico, but he thought Puerto Rico should eventually have self-government, increasing as the people grew more competent.[6]

McKinley's Special Commission, on the other hand, recommended both free trade and citizenship. This was the line originally taken by Senator Foraker. But the urgent need to raise customs revenues until tax legislation was enacted, together with the fear that granting citizenship implied statehood, led Foraker to reverse himself. American citizenship was denied in the final version which was approved by the House and Senate in April 1900.[7] In providing the congressional framework for tutelage, incorporation and citizenship were both discarded.

The result of this debate was an "Act temporarily to provide revenues and civil government" which was to last for seventeen years. It was based on compromise. Free trade was put off for two years and in the meantime a 15 percent tariff was imposed on all merchandise coming into the United States from Puerto Rico, and vice versa. These revenues would be used by the president to benefit Puerto Rico until the new civil government enacted and put into operation a local system of taxation. The President would then decree free trade.

The act created a body politic under the name of "The People of Puerto Rico," composed of citizens of Puerto Rico entitled to the protection of the United States, but with very limited rights—a real colonial anomaly.

In the political field the Root and Davis doctrines of a hybrid executive council and the omnipotence of Washington prevailed, but with a significant change. Puerto Rico was granted a House of Delegates, elected by the people. This was another compromise between believers in the American commitment to representative democracy and those who insisted on strict imperial tutelage. The act created a paternalistic government, dominated by Washington, and run primarily by an American bureaucracy with a smattering of Puerto Rican participation.[8]

Many Democrats bitterly opposed the bill, but few were as sharp and direct as Congressman William H. Jones of Virginia. He objected to the Republican tactics of railroading the bill through the House; he considered the executive council's power to grant franchises as "offensive and repugnant."[9] Jones' concern foreshadowed later events. In 1916–1917, he was to steer the question of political reform in Puerto Rico during the Wilson Administration.

Another aspect of this legislation was crucial for the future. A Joint Resolution (S.R. 116), introduced by Senator Foraker, passed the Senate after the passage of the act. It provided for the continuation of military government pending the establishment of the permanent civil government. In the House, Congressman Jones pressed for an amendment to protect Puerto Rico from corporate latifundia by prohibiting corporations from carrying the business of agriculture. Jones warned that unless the amendment was adopted, the condition of the population would be reduced "to one of absolute servitude." The Senate did not accept this drastic measure, but compromised by limiting corporate ownership not to exceed 500 acres of land. The joint resolution then passed the Senate; behind the limitation adopted were the interests of the American Beet Sugar Association, the tobacco interests, and some Congressional prejudice against the power of the trusts.[10] For almost half a century, however, the 500-acre restriction was a dead letter in the agrarian history of Puerto Rico.

The Problems of Implementation

The Foraker Act, with its strong colonial overtones, had to be tested in the courts. But judicial opinion was as influenced by the ardent expansionism of the age as was the political arena. The anti-imperialists, who had fought against the Treaty of Paris and had sharply criticized the Foraker Act, waged another losing battle in the so-called Insular Cases (1901). The majority of the Supreme Court was strongly nationalistic and ready to find legal rationalizations for empire-building. Their interpretation created a new political entity neither a state nor an incorporated territory. This was the "unincorporated territory," also known as a "possession" or "dependency," where constitutional uniformity would not fully apply. Puerto Rico, therefore, "belonged to but was not a part of" the United States, to be governed by Congress under the territorial clause of the Constitution. As Chief Justice Fuller wrote in a dissenting opinion in *Downes v. Bidwell,* Puerto Rico was left "like a disembodied shade in an intermediate state of ambiguous existence."[11]

The "unincorporated territory," however, offered a flexibility in economic and fiscal relationships which later was put to advantage. Since Puerto Rico was excluded from the federal internal revenue system, the island could shape its own taxation structure. Furthermore, federal customs and excise revenues were diverted into the insular treasury. This assistance, forced by the fiscal crisis, inadvertently became a cornerstone in the relationship between the island and the United States.

The Foraker Act was sharply criticized by American liberal opinion. The Democratic party, as a foe of Republican expansionism, included in its 1900 platform some very strong words against the act; "a flagrant breach of the national good faith," a "colonial policy, inconsistent with republican institutions," an act that doomed to "poverty and distress a people whose helplessness apeals with peculiar force to our justice and magnanimity."[12]

If American opposition was this strong, among many liberal Puerto Ricans the reaction was far stronger. When Henry gave way to Davis, this was seen as the prelude to autonomy under the American flag. Muñoz Rivera returned from the United States in September, 1899, with high expectations. He had, he thought, secured Henry's removal. He was impressed with what he had seen in the North and felt that Puerto Rico should struggle to attain the same civil and economic level as American life. He argued for equal rights and for support of the U.S. government, in the hope that direct representative democracy would soon be granted. "I bring," he said, "encouraging impressions. I see new hope in the horizon after my Washington meetings. Even before Congress meets, full justice will be done." His conviction led him to say that to be a good Puerto Rican you also had to be a good American.[13]

He found Davis experimenting with municipal democracy under the watchful eyes of the army. The elections were cumbersome since only those males over 21 years of age who knew how to read and write were allowed to vote. The elections started in July, 1898, and ended in January, 1900. They were a political marathon, popularly known in the island as the Election of the One Hundred Days. All the old passions and animosities flared up; not even *San Ciriaco* dampened the show. At the end, the Federals under Muñoz Rivera won 44 of the 66 municipalities. The tutor had served a heavy dose which left the people sharply divided in their traditional political groupings and Davis despaired about their passionate, partisan fervor.[14]

Many Puerto Ricans were sharply disappointed with the Congressional action. At the time of the hearings, the Republicans, represented by Dr. Henna, had accepted the Henry scheme if modified with a Lower House, elected by the people, and the election of representatives to the Executive Council. Henna's reasoning was typical: "I believe that the Americans should be the mentors of the Puerto Ricans for some time; but when a child goes to school he should be taught all the things that he can learn in the shortest possible space of time without injuring his health. . . ."[15] The Federal party held a different view: Puerto Rico should not have less than under the less liberal government of Spain, especially after Miles's proclamation. Nothing short of a territorial government with two popularly elected houses and a governor appointed by the president would satisfy the people.[16] They thus rejected wholly the concept of tutelage.

The Federals were sharply disappointed with the law as finally approved. They called the Executive Council an "exotic" arrangement; it would really be run by Americans. Some thought this attempt at "Americanization" was a joke, since it contradicted American principles. As the disillusioned Muñoz Rivera wrote McKinley, the Foraker Act was "unworthy of the United States which imposes it and of the Puerto Ricans who have to endure it. . . ."[17] The rosy dream he had brought in September vanished into thin air. Political lines were sharply drawn concerning the act. The Republicans would support it and enjoy the favor of the first American civil governors. The Federals would try to control the House and use every opportunity to oppose the *mentorado*. The dynamics of confrontation would soon begin.

On May 1, 1900, Charles H. Allen was inaugurated as the first civil governor of Puerto Rico. At his recommendation, the president appointed four Puerto Ricans as members of the council: José C. Barbosa and Rosendo Matienzo Cintrón for the Republicans; José De Diego and Manuel Camuñas for the Federals; and Andrés Crosas, an American, as an independent. The elected chairman was the Executive Secretary William H. Hunt.[18]

The fireworks soon started. Matienzo Cintrón made clear in his opening statement that Puerto Rico was ready to submit, "as an adolescent to the discreet lessons of the American people, while preserving its personality." De Diego, on the other hand, insisted that the United States and Puerto Rico should join in developing a free people under a free sovereignty. Under the prevailing system, Puerto Rico was condemned to an inferior status and deprived of its rights.[19]

One of the first duties of the Executive Council was to divide the island into electoral districts for the election of House delegates. The Republican and Federal members were deadlocked. A plan prepared by Crosas and adopted by the Republicans smacked of gerrymandering in one of the districts. The Federals, incensed, resigned from the council. This was certainly not the type of American political lesson they liked.

A turbulent period followed. *Personalismo* was rampant among the partisans of Muñoz and Barbosa. A cleavage began to develop between

San Juan, the seat of official power, where the *barbosistas* were strong, and inland Puerto Rico, heavily committed to the *muñocistas*. On September 18,1900, a climax was reached. Muñoz Rivera's paper, *El Diario*, which had sharply attacked the mayor of San Juan, was destroyed by a mob. Mob rule (the *turbas*) became a real threat to Puerto Rico's incipient democracy. The Federals took two steps to remedy the situation. They decided to affiliate with the Democratic party, sending Muñoz to the States as their spokesman, and, over Muñoz's opposition, they withdrew from the elections. The Republicans thus gained two places on the Executive Council and swept the island virtually unopposed at election time.[20]

The new House enacted legislation in several fields such as trial by jury, a revenue law based on U.S. assessments, education, and the establishment of a code commission. A law chartering foreign corporations helped investment in sugar. This pleased Governor Allen, who strongly felt that every acre of rich sugar land should be developed. As an apostle of King Sugar, in his first annual report he insisted that "when the American capitalist realizes that there is a surplus of labor accustomed to the Tropics, and that the return of capital is exceedingly profitable, it is my feeling that he will come here . . . to the immense and permanent prosperity of the island."[21]

The urge to create revenues led to the approval of a bill that would tax real property at 1 percent to provide the government with funds. But the Federals thought that further taxes on land, during this economic crisis, would force owners to sell to outside interests, to the benefit of the American trusts. They feared that the trusts would eventually own the country, forcing landless Puerto Ricans to migrate. This fear was a harbinger of things to come, for throughout the period of the Foraker Act a transfer of property rights took place leading to a growth in sugar latifundia. Allen's prediction was realized concerning the fat profits of the sugar companies, but the new wealth would not filter down to the peasantry.[22]

While Muñoz was campaigning in the States and publishing *The Puerto Rico Herald*, which circulated in New York and Washington, a tide of criticism rose in Puerto Rico against Republican rule. Municipal administration, especially tax collection, was a mess, while the hasty approval of laws, imported from the United States without much thought as to their suitability, spread deep concern. This was a period of *tabula rasa*, when the apostles of Americanization believed that the old culture could be easily legislated away. Hunt, who succeeded Allen in 1902, frankly favored the Republicans, who won the elections on November 4, 1902.

This time, however, the Federals participated, electing 10 of the 25 members of the House.[23]

The election's results did not reflect the true situation. Many Republicans were becoming disenchanted with the system. One of them, Rosendo Matienzo Cintrón, as a member of the Executive Council, had embraced wholeheartedly the theory of tutelage. But he found that the Puerto Rican council members were mere figure-heads. A social darwinist and spiritualist, Matienzo believed in the struggle for existence as the iron law of history. To him the United States and England represented civilization triumphant. At a meeting in February 1902, he held that Puerto Rico had to get rid of its moral weakness and accept Americanization. For Americanization was, above all, self-reliance. Therefore, Puerto Rico must rely on itself. It could not seek its regeneration if it was divided by sheer partisanship. The time had come for unity; for doing away with parties and personal squabbles in order to assert Puerto Rico's own personality.[24]

The sociological theories were less important than the plea for unity. Matienzo Cintrón, though brilliant, was not much of an organizer. His ardent rhetoric, however, paved the way for the founding of the *Unión de Puerto Rico* on February 19, 1904. Muñoz Rivera, back from New York, promptly took on its leadership with De Diego. The new political organization, based on the principle of government by consent, wanted self-government either as a federal state, an autonomous state, or as an independent nation under a U.S. protectorate. This last position—the fifth point in the program—was adopted after heated debate.[25] The three historical positions on status were, thus, enunciated at this meeting. The Foraker Act by failing to satisfy Puerto Rican aspirations and by imposing a narrow tutelage, had destroyed the consensus on statehood and deepened the split in the Puerto Rican political mind. The bourgeois leadership, as represented by the *Unión de Puerto Rico*, now rejected tutelage. While this group would from time to time make accommodations, it became the implacable foe of the colonial principles of the Foraker Act.

The Unionist Challenge

Many forces coalesced under the Unionist banner. The leaders came from the intellectual and professional groups; landowners and farmers from the interior provided financial support; the *muñocista* masses added their fervor; while an opening was made for the incipient labor movement. Samuel Gompers of the American Federation of Labor was visiting the island the day the new party adopted its program. At Muñoz Rivera's suggestion, a committee was appointed to visit him. The emblem of the Federation, two interlocking hands, became also the emblem of the Unionists and some Federation leaders were included on the slate for the 1904 elections.[26] The alliance with the labor groups was to be short-lived, as shall be noted later. But in 1904, the Unionists were marshalling strong sectors of public opinion. At election time, the new party swept the island. For the next quarter century, it was the dominant force in Puerto Rican politics.

Even before the elections, Hunt had resigned, President McKinley had been assassinated, and Roosevelt was in the White House. His plan was to develop a colonial service. His appointments were typical. Beckman Winthrop, the new governor, was a young official who had had experience with colonial rule in the Philippines. Regis H. Post, the executive secretary, was Roosevelt's personal friend, slated to be governor after Winthrop's stint.

The new men saw the need to reach an accommodation with the Unionists. They realized that the growing discontent, now touching both parties, had to be controlled without surrendering the rights and privileges of political tutelage. Both Winthrop and Post followed this policy to the great chagrin of the local Republicans. The Unionists hoped that Roosevelt would heed their political demands, but they were soon disappointed. In his 1905 Message to Congress, Roosevelt asked for American citizenship and for certain economic measures for Puerto Rico. In his view, the problems were essentially commercial and industrial. He found no fault whatever with the political and administrative structure "since it has inspired confidence in property owners and investors."[27]

The reaction was inevitable. Muñoz Rivera and his colleagues rejected the idea that citizenship should perpetuate a colonial regime. This would be a citizenship in name only; devoid of rights and freedoms, without voice and vote in the republic, a citizenship for pariahs. Puerto Rico was being treated as a factory, not as a free society.[28] Muñoz urged that the Puerto Rican should exercise the right of petition. If the president considered the Puerto Ricans prepared to be American citizens, why were they not prepared to govern themselves? In Muñoz's view, Puerto Rico should cease being governed by an executive council, several of whose members were mere *rara avis*. The fight was for self-government; the League of Municipalities, which represented the grass-roots, should lead the way in persuading Congress. Matienzo, who had fathered the new party, put it succinctly: "Citizenship is worthless without self-government."[29]

The Unionists did not reject American citizenship; they rejected the colonial tutelage that came with it. To the Congress, riding the crest of a proud nationalism, bestowal of American citizenship was the greatest blessing a person could receive. The clash of values and perceptions added fuel to a smoldering misunderstanding, especially at the congressional halls.

In July, 1906, Elihu Root, now secretary of state, visited Puerto Rico, in the course of developing a new Latin American policy for the Roosevelt Administration. At De Diego's request, the House of Delegates regiterated to Root the Puerto Rican petition for American citizenship with an elective Senate and asked Root, of all people, to speak for Puerto Rican aspirations before the President.[30]

But the Roosevelt Administration was firmly convinced that no changes were needed. Roosevelt himself believed in an enlightened tutelage with Puerto Ricans gradually appointed to secondary positions. He had once suggested to Hunt that a Puerto Rican be assistant commissioner in each department or that only native and naturalized citizens be allowed in the service.[31] Hunt, however, was cool to the idea.[32]

Roosevelt insisted on providing the best possible service for the islands. "The problem is far too grave and too delicate to admit of any other course being pursued," he wrote.[33] He was proud of his choices, and convinced that he had not only raised the standard of administration, but had it at a high pitch.[34]

Late in November, 1906, Roosevelt visited Puerto Rico on his way back from the Panama Canal. He was at the zenith of his power and fame, and was warmly received everywhere. He had much to say about the beauty of the land and, as a naturalist, he reveled in the splendid tropical flora. But he was less interested in the inhabitants. "There is something pathetic and childlike about the people," he wrote to a family member. "We are giving them a good government and the island is prospering. I never saw a finer set of young fellows than those engaged in administration."[35] On December 11, he sent a special message to Congress describing the island and suggesting improvements in the San Juan harbor. He was full of praise for the American administrators, the "excellent character" of the insular police and the Puerto Rican regiment. The people were loyal and glad to be under the American flag;

they deserved full citizenship, but it would be a very serious mistake to give more. "This scheme," he wrote, "is working well; no injustice of any kind results from it, and great benefit to the island, and it should certainly not be changed at this time."[36]

To this slap, the House of Delegates replied with a respectful message. It reminded Roosevelt of his cordial reception and the hope that he would do justice to the people. It quoted Winthrop on the fairness of the elections, the devotion to work, and the spread of education. It petitioned for an elective Senate and a cabinet appointed by the governor with the consent of the Senate. But again there was no reply.[37]

In June, 1907, the Unionists made a more direct approach. De Diego, as speaker, was invited to a conference in Virginia. He made the most of the opportunity to present the Unionist view. He visited officials in Washington and finally was received by Roosevelt at Sagamore Hill where he delivered the House message to the president, but Roosevelt remained extremely cool to any political reform. His indifference again begot profound disenchantment among the Unionists.[38]

Although their relations with the governor remained cordial, the Unionists saw that a showdown was approaching. Patience was running out and tension was building between the House and the Executive Council.

Roosevelt's indifference had incensed Muñoz who opened fire against what he called the six *caciques* or bosses in the council. Even the governor could not control them. Each one played his tune and there was no baton, no conductor. And yet they claimed that Puerto Ricans were unprepared for self-government! A *camarilla,* a clique, ruled Puerto Rico as in the Spanish era. Muñoz wanted action; he thought the House's very limited powers should be used to the hilt. This was the seed of the 1909 confrontation.[39]

Post was now governor. In spite of his goodwill, he was caught in a political maelstrom. The leading party was becoming more radical in reaction to Washington's indifference. The Roosevelt Administration was coming to a close, to be succeeded by William Howard Taft, a more conservative man. In the 1908 elections in Puerto Rico, the *Unión* defeated the Republicans two to one and brought into the political picture a new generation. This group wanted immediate action against the colonial statute and was ready to challenge Muñoz Rivera, if he did not share their hard-line approach. They leaned towards independence and socially they were especially concerned with the plight of the coffee areas and the working masses.

The Economic Backdrop

The political crisis was unfolding against a contradictory economic backdrop. Puerto Rico had certainly progressed in a decade of American rule. The era of flattering statistics had started, with the rapid influx of corporate capital and the establishment of free trade. In 1901, the total value of articles purchased from and sold in the United States and foreign countries amounted to $17,502,103; in the fiscal year 1910 the total rose to $68,595,326, a 400 percent gain. Eighty-five percent of the total trade represented shipments to and from the United States, as Puerto Rico made an excellent captive market for American goods.[40] Sugar exports had risen from 68,909 tons valued at $4,715,611 in 1901 to 244,257 tons valued at $18,432,446 in 1909. The death rate of 22 per 1,000 compared favorably with many similarly populated countries, and Dr. Bailey K. Ashford had distinguished himself by identifying the parasite *uncinaria* and conducting a brilliant campaign against anemia.[41] The rise in educational facilities was dramatic: in 1901–1902, there were 874 common schools, enrolling 42,070. In 1909, there were 1,912 common schools enrolling 114,367.[42]

On the other side of the ledger, the crisis in the coffee industry was worsening. While exports increased, the average price per pound in 1909 was a half cent less than 1905.[43] Many of the farmers had been unable to secure money to rehabilitate their farms after the hurricane, thus adding to a large army of unemployed. Wages on coffee plantations were 30 cents a day; compared to 35 cents on tobacco plantations and 55 cents on sugar plantations. This was practically a starvation level; and it signalled the rise of a landless proletariat as subsistence farming declined.[44] George Milton Fowles, in his book *Down in Puerto Rico* defended the Puerto Rican people: "The cause of the strong anti-American feeling that is found among some classes of Porto Ricans is due very largely to economic conditions which would influence the people of any other land in much the same way."[45]

A key factor in the ensuing confrontation was the pressure to create an Agricultural Credit Bank to help the coffee growers through their crisis. This legislation, which would later become common, was sharply opposed by the American members of the Executive Council. Their seeming indifference to the plight of the coffee growers, many of whom were Unionists, contrasted with their eagerness to help King Sugar. Other key issues contributed to the conflict. Native lawyers resented Federal judges who knew no Spanish and ignored the legal traditions of the country, thus invalidating the scope of local courts.[46]

The House of Delegates decided to strike in March when Governor Post refused to accept party recommendations for some judicial vacancies. The House countered by making judicial vacancies elective, establishing the agricultural bank, and taking other measures. The governor, who had already warned "that Armageddon was coming," decided to meet the threat head on. He set a deadline for the House to pass an appropriation bill. When the House refused to act, he cabled Washington urging that his complaints be included in President Taft's message to Congress. The Unionists sent a Commission to Washington; the governor did likewise. The gauntlet had been thrown.[47]

Post's official recommendation was that if an appropriations bill was not passed, the appropriation for the previous year would be repeated automatically. This controlling measure had been used in the Philippines, where Taft had learned colonial administration. As president, he pushed for an amendment to the Foraker Act in this regard, and used the occasion to punish publicly the rebellious pupils.

On May 10, 1909, Taft sent a special message to Congress about this situation, which he termed "of unusual gravity." He accused the House of Delegates of trying to subvert the government, and made it plain that he thought too much power had been vested in its members. Describing Puerto Rico as "the favored daughter of the United States," he enunciated gains in education, in road building, in sanitation, and in trade and prosperity. Since the House had the right to make laws, he said the Puerto Ricans should seek reform in an orderly way and not paralyze the existing government. Before any legislative reform was considered, Taft insisted that the absolute power of appropriation be taken away "from those who have shown themselves too irresponsible to enjoy it." To him, the United States had been too generous. Taft's message thus smacked of righteous indignation. The ungrateful colonials must be called to order.[48]

Taft was recommending less, not more, autonomy for the island. His public spanking found support in a segment of American opinion. Sharp criticisms of Puerto Rico appeared in several newspapers. Congressman John Kennedy of Oklahoma ranted against the Spanish race, which he said had never added anything to human knowledge but the thumbscrew! But others, like Congressman John Martin of Colorado, claimed that the president wanted "to point the way of Porto Rico's little craft into the harbor of carpet bag government."[49]

In the meantime, even the island's Republican party felt that Taft had gone too far and also sent a commission to Washington to see the president. They wanted to make clear they appreciated American benevolence and favors. They were the good pupils who did not deserve a presidential "roasting." They found Taft incensed with the Union party, and wondering how this serpent had been allowed in the garden. Post was not going to remain, but there had to be some face saving, he said.[50]

While Congress approved the Olmstead amendment, giving Taft what he wanted on appropriations, a change of governor became inevitable. The congressional debate revived the old divisions between imperialists and anti-imperialists. Both sides made charges, and Tulio Larrínaga, the Puerto Rican resident commissioner, took advantage of the controversy to urge a liberalized system. Although the Unionist commission had lost the appropriations battle, the seeds had been sown for revision of the Foraker Act. Some administrative measures followed. Puerto Rican affairs were now put under the Bureau of Insular Affairs of the War Department. The War Department would now be in charge of structuring policies with a firm hand.

Revision, however, did not come about for several years. The Taft Administration, deeply resentful of the Unionist challenge, wanted restrictive legislation instead. This was particularly true of the War Department. At the end of 1909, the secretary of war, J. M. Dickinson, accompanied by General Edwards, the bureau chief, visited the island. They found much sentiment for an elective Senate and the extension of American citizenship. However, influential Americans, such as Judge James H. Mac Leary, wanted to restrict the scope of elections even further.[51]

The Taft Administration now determined to break the Unionist hold. Dickinson recommended that judges be appointed, not elected, and that patronage and appointments be controlled by the governor. He wanted the Assembly of Delegates to meet biennially, thus limiting its power, and recommended an upper house composed of eight appointed and five elected members. The draft became the basis of the administration's proposal to Congress.[52]

In the meantime, Taft had picked Colonel George R. Colton to succeed Post. Colton had had wide experience in the Philippines and Santo Domingo and considered himself a civil servant, not a political appointee. In his inaugural address on November 6, 1909, he shrewdly identified himself with Puerto Rico without singing the usual praises of the United States. He emphasized his concern for the coffee industry, a subject close to the Unionist heart, but spoke cautiously about self-government. It would surely come, and he pleaded for individual responsibility and obligation to the body politic as essential features of safe popular government. This was his only criticism of the Unionists. He promised to govern as a civil servant and to put the more deserving men in public office. He extended an olive branch to the House and stated that "We of the Anglo-Saxon race, who come among you, have much to learn from the intellectual courtesy of the Latin people. . . ." This exercise in flattery was a far cry from the imperious tutor in the Henry mold. The serpent in the garden had to be tamed and Colton was resolved to tame it.[53]

It was important to start with some house cleaning. Not everything was well with the tutors that Roosevelt had praised. Colton cabled Washington that George C. Ward, the auditor, was despised and distrusted by both Americans and Puerto Ricans. Judge Bernard S. Rodey of the U.S. District Court had never made friends. Executive Secretary Graham was "a joke from business standpoint."[54] Among the several American officials there were some who, according to Fowles, "had disgraced both themselves and their country." There was an American judge who was said to have been in close relationship to one of the worst saloons and gambling dens on the island; a U.S. commissioner that was notoriously given to drink; an appointee who headed a department who got drunk on the boat going down and remained in that condition until he was recalled. This un-Puritan behaviour contradicted the tutor's preachings and did not make Puerto Ricans, in Fowles' words, "particularly anxious to have them as teachers in self-government."[55] To American officials the Puerto Rican attachment to *personalista* politics made them unfit for self-government; to the Puerto Ricans, Americans seemed more interested in bounties of carpetbagging and drinking than in the ideals they preached about democracy. An estrangement in values and perceptions was the result between the imported bureaucracy and the native elite.

In spite of his flattery, Colton was convinced that the United States should weaken the Unionist hold on the island. When, as expected, the Unionist party attacked the Olmstead Bill, Colton turned to what he called "the substantial people" of Puerto Rico for support. Muñoz Rivera had written to Colton that the new bill "will delay the Americanization of our Island and will leave in the spirit of the people of Puerto Rico, a germ of perpetual bitterness." To Colton, these were the feelings of the "radical politicians" and not "the substantial people." The conservatives were the U.S. friends and they were satisfied with the bill so long as it did not mean a return to government by military officers.[56]

Colton took other action against the Unionists. Since male universal suffrage was the basis of Unionist strength, Colton strongly urged that voting be limited to those who were literate and paid at least five dollars in annual taxes. He hoped this would break the Unionist hold; the party bosses, he claimed, handled "the ignorant class like sheep." Restricting the basis of suffrage was essential: The salvation of the country, he wrote in February, 1910, "depends upon the removal of despotic political power from the hands of a few political bosses."[57] Once the peasantry, the backbone of Unionist strength, was prevented from voting, the "substantial people" would take over and Muñoz Rivera would be removed from power.

A second key factor of the bill was the land provisions. The sugar corporations now saw their chance to remove the 500 acre limitation which they had ignored in their drive to control the economy from the books. The bill would increase the limit to 5000 acres. The sugar lobby, led by Guánica, pressured for 10,000 to 15,000 acres but would settle for 5000 if it meant only cultivated land.[58] Their aim was congressional approval of increasing latifundia as the basic U.S. economic policy.

The Olmstead Bill of 1910 was, for these reasons, more regressive than the Foraker Act. It strengthened colonial tutelage, and furthered the big sugar interests. A minority report called it "ungenerous, restrictive and reactionary." Despite a storm of protest in Puerto Rico, the administration continued to press its passage. The bill cleared the House but not the Senate. Colton's battle against the Unionists failed; they not only won the 1910 election, but sent Muñoz Rivera to Washington as resident commissioner.

By January, 1911, Muñoz Rivera was already making his case in the U.S. press. The *Washington Post* on January 30 printed an article by the new commissioner in which he stated that he preferred even the Foraker Act to the more restrictive Olmstead Bill, one objectionable feature being the permission to corporations to lease land in addition to the 5000 acre limit, "it being feared that moneyed interest will be placed in control of the entire country and make natives a labor tool."[59]

The elective Senate, the removal of the land limitation clause, and the granting of voluntary U.S. citizenship were the main issues in the Senate. The influential Henry Cabot Lodge opposed the elective Senate; others were reluctant to please the corporations; and Elihu Root, now a senator from New York, was dead set against granting U.S. citizenship. Time ran out for Puerto Rican legislation at the extra congressional session.[60]

Colton now found himself in a difficult spot. A rapprochement with the Unionists was in order. He had already assured Muñoz of his interest in a prosperous, self-governing Puerto Rico and reiterated his commitment to govern without partisan politics, and to follow a policy "in which personality counts less, and efficiency most." He ended by placing "the highest value upon the confidence and friendship you have accorded me."[61]

Colton took other measures to placate the Unionists. Unlike his predecessor, Colton showed great interest in developing an American market for coffee and was in close touch with one of the largest producers, William Mc Jones, who campaigned in the U.S. for the industry. He also put pressure on the State Department to consider Puerto Rican interest in its review of a commercial convention with Cuba.[62]

The Stimson Proposal

The rapport with the Unionists increased as a result of Henry L. Stimson's appointment as Secretary of War in 1911. Concerned for the security of the Panama Canal and for the U.S. role in the Caribbean, Stimson visited the area in July–August 1911. He soon found that American policies in Puerto Rico were a cause of friction in inter-American relations. For the first time, the U.S. role in Puerto Rico was reexamined in the context of the hemisphere. In his Annual Report, 1911, Stimson urged a redefinition of the relationships leading to the most complete local and fiscal autonomy with citizenship as a permanent link; an analogous relation, in his opinion, to that enjoyed by the British self-governing colonies.

When the Annual Report came out, Muñoz Rivera wrote Stimson to praise the secretary's stand as the first member of the executive who had been both pragmatic and liberal. But Stimson had also urged that Congress legislate on health matters, municipal courts, and other subjects which Muñoz considered purely local. He found an evident contradiction between the action recommended and Stimson's liberal blueprint, and objected to a proforma citizenship without self-government.[63]

Stimson, seeking an accommodation with the Unionist leader whose views seemed to parallel his own, had a cordial private meeting with Muñoz in January 1912. Stimson stated then his preference for a British type of autonomy, Canadian style. But he wanted the Puerto Rican House to concentrate all health matters in the Health Department to avoid congressional legislation.[64]

After the meeting, Muñoz Rivera urged action from his friends. He kept in touch with Stimson and with Jones, who as Democratic Chairman of the Committee of Insular Affairs, was already at work on a reform bill. On March 29, Stimson congratulated Muñoz Rivera on the progress of the insular legislature as the best evidence that the people of Peurto Rico were moving toward self-government.[65] In his reply, Muñoz urged movement toward an autonomic form of government.[66] The correspondence revealed that understanding could be achieved if both sides contributed. The emphasis was now in a *quid pro quo*.

On May 7, 1912, Stimson appeared before a Senate committee to support a citizenship bill for Puerto Rico. After praising Puerto Rican loyalty, he added:

Last summer I traveled through the West Indies and saw a good many Latin-American peoples, and I found that when they would speak to me frankly they regarded this attitude of the United States toward Porto Rico as an evidence that we regarded not only the people there, but Latin-American peoples in general, as of a different class from ourselves, and of an inferior class. And therefore not only in respect to our political relations with Porto Rico itself, but to our diplomatic relations with other countries of the same blood, it seems to be a deep-seated sore and irritation.

Stimson spoke of the need for obtaining "that sympathetic relation with the island which must be the foundation of a satisfactory government." The solution did not lie in ultimate statehood, which Stimson observed "would not be of benefit to either Porto Rico or the United States." A way had to be found to avoid a position of drifting and he favored a frank expression of views on the subject by the different branches of government.

Stimson's personal belief was that American citizenship and the ultimate ideal of independent local self-government were not inconsistent. In his opinion, most people in the U.S. would favor

a relation where they exercise supervision over their own fiscal and local self-government; with the link of American citizenship between the two countries as a tie, and in general such relations between the United States and Porto Rico as subsist, and as has been found perfectly workable in the case of the various self-governing portions of the territory of Great Britain—Australia, for instance, and Canada, to the mother country.[67]

This was the revival of the autonomist doctrine, American style. In the last third of the nineteenth century, a group of Spanish liberals had been attracted by the Canadian model after the British North American Act of 1867. Their *Autonomismo* wanted to preserve ties with the Spanish West Indies, while granting most of the essential features of sovereignty. This was the model favored by Baldorioty de Castro in 1887 and later by Muñoz Rivera in the dying days of the Spanish empire. It helped shape the short-lived autonomous charter of 1897, but was submerged in the American imperial adventure of 1898. Davis and Root, also fascinated by the British experience had turned, instead, to the political straight-jacket of the crown colony. But now Stimson was looking beyond, again stealing a leaf from the British knack for empire-building. The "unincorporated territory," in his view, could evolve into a modified dominion status, boldly based on the possibility for constitutional innovation. Even more than the Puerto Ricans, Stimson was defining the parameters of home rule.

That Stimson was intent on reshaping American policy, beyond the narrow limits set by the Republicans, there was no doubt. On December 6, 1912, Taft's Annual Message to Congress reflected Stimson's views: rejection of statehood as the ultimate link between the island the United States and a clear-cut endorsement of a relation "analogous to the present relation between Great Britain and such self-governing colonies as Canada and Australia." The Foraker Act would be left behind and Taft's earlier righteous tone was abandoned.[68] But by the time the message was sent, a series of events had taken place: Taft had lost the presidential election; Stimson, therefore, was on his way out, and a new man, Woodrow Wilson, was coming into the White House.

10
The Wilsonian Era in Puerto Rico

The Wilsonian era was a momentous, complex period in American history, a chapter finally forged in the fires of war. It was also a milestone in U.S. relations with Puerto Rico, involving political reform under a new shade of tutelage, the bonanza of the sugar barons, the emergence of labor trade unionism as a new political factor, and the stirrings of independence. American citizenship was granted in time to assure the island's loyalty in the new Armageddon. The strategic imperative turned Puerto Rico into a key defensive outpost with an armed contingent of 18,000 men. This era saw the passing of the old party leadership: Matienzo, Muñoz Rivera, De Diego, Barbosa. The cultural, social, economic, and political issues were to be sharpened by the time the Wilsonian dream of world moral regeneration faded into oblivion.

Statistically, everything was expanding. Population rose from 1,118,102 in 1910 to 1,299,809 in 1920. Trade with the United States continued to flourish as the American market took 85 percent of total exports. At the beginning of the war, sugar shipments fell because of a transitory decline in prices. But prices rose again, leading to a sugar bonanza between 1916 and 1919. By 1921, the price of sugar and tobacco had dropped and the Bureau of Insular Affairs observed "that there is now marked recession from the crest of prosperity."[1]

Harbor improvements, road building, and irrigation were diligently attended to during these years. They provided the economic infrastruc-

The Guanica Central during the reign of King Sugar.

ture for the expansion of sugar cultivation, led by the big absentee companies: the South Porto Rico Sugar Company, incorporated in 1900 in New Jersey; the Fajardo Sugar Company, incorporated in New York in 1905; and the Central Aguirre Sugar Companies, a voluntary trust organized in 1905 under the laws of Massachusetts.[2] King Sugar was more dominant than ever.

Education was heavily centralized, unlike the U.S. tradition, and the commissioners of education pushed for an intensive program based on Americanization to shape teachers' and students' minds with values, principles, and methods derived from the U.S. educational experience and the nationalist exultation of its historic role. As 80 percent of the population was still rural by 1910, rural schools were rapidly established. To reach the island's children, double sessions were used in 90 percent of the schools by 1920. Secondary and higher education also expanded; by 1920 there were eleven high schools and the University of Puerto Rico had been founded.[3] The numbers and organization were impres-

sive. But grave issues were in the making to haunt Puerto Rican education.[4] Among them were the zeal to make Puerto Ricans bilingual, even
at the expense of their vernacular Spanish; the unsuitability of many
American methods to the cultural environment; and the ill-concealed
disdain for traditional social values and the historical heritage. The cultural give and take with dynamic aspects of U.S. civilization was marred
by the implicit colonial assumption of the superiority of everything
American. While many Puerto Ricans accepted this assumption as part

Americanization in the schools.

of the island's new "manifest destiny," others reacted passionately against the stigma. Thus began a long cultural struggle embracing fundamental values, mores, perceptions, and attitudes. The great debate had started.

As tensions continued to accumulate in the political and cultural fields, the system was challenged from a new source: the field of labor. During the Wilson era Puerto Rican labor finally made itself felt politically, foreshadowing the coming clash with the absentee and native landlords of King Sugar.

The Rise of Labor

Although the labor movement was supported by American trade unionism, it was not truly a creation of the U.S. period. Even before 1898, labor radicalism had reached Puerto Rico, and a few devoted leaders, mainly artisans, were familiar with the theories and principles of anarchism and international socialism.[5] Into this narrow circle stepped a restless youth, a Spanish agitator of humble origins, self-taught and self-reliant, who had been forced to flee Cuba for Puerto Rico. His name was Santiago Iglesias.[6]

Iglesias galvanized the native radicals with a relentless, methodical campaign culminating in a historic meeting on December 28, 1896, where the bases were laid for a Regional Workers Federation and for the subsequent printing of *Ensayo Obrero,* a weekly paper devoted to socialist theories. At this time, the movement was linked to Spanish socialism and its great leader, Pablo Iglesias. The movement spread to the chagrin of the insular government. Persecution marked the pre-1898 years. The labor anarchists were considered dangerous; Iglesias, known as their leader, was jailed by the captain general when he tried to flee to New York, and was found to have American dollars in his possession. He never forgave Muñoz Rivera for his role as minister of government; and, although at some periods there was an ephemeral rapprochement between the two, Iglesias in later years seldom lost an opportunity to attack the Autonomist leader.[6]

Liberated by the Americans, Iglesias was befriended by Commander Scott of the Artillery Corps. He joined the army in the occupation of several municipalities as a stump speaker, preaching his doctrines of social justice and workers' liberation, to the amazement and wrath of many landlords.[7] Even if the army leaders little understood what he was saying, they obviously liked to have the youthful, passionate orator on their side as they took over the country.

The occupation was a profound experience for Iglesias and his friends. Their ideological attachment had not been to Spain but to the socialist idea of the brotherhood of the oppressed. The generals and the Stars and Stripes afforded them a golden opportunity to agitate and proselytize. When accused of conspiracy at the time of General Brooke, they knew exactly what to do: they went to Brooke and pledged allegiance to the American flag.[8]

A tacit alliance thus developed between the incipient labor leadership and the first military tutors. In October, 1898, the labor leaders regrouped forces and founded the Regional Federation of Puerto Rican Workers. Their first objectives were transnational: solidarity until the complete liberation of the proletariat. But they later proclaimed themselves annexionists, relying on the justice of the American republic. Their main social goals were the eight-hour day, a minimum wage, the prohibition of child labor, and the establishment of school churches. The program had shifted from the revolutionary rhetoric of the European *Internationales* to concrete, pragmatic objectives.[9]

Contacts were now established with the American Socialist party and May 1, 1899, was celebrated, for the first time, with great rejoicing. General Henry was so impressed by the show of discipline that he ordered the observance of the eight-hour day throughout the island. This workers' victory sealed the alliance with the governing military.[10]

The Republican party obviously wanted the workers' organization for an ally. Thus began a great issue for the labor movement: whether to enter politics or stick to their objectives of social justice. In July, 1899, the Free Federation of Workers and the Socialist Workers' party were created. The Free Federation was for activism; the party, for political proselytizing. Of the two, the first was able to sail the stormy seas of the social struggle; the second foundered badly at first. When the U.S. Socialist party invited Iglesias to its national convention in January, 1900, Iglesias first took the workers' case before the American public opinion.

At this time, Iglesias espoused socialist ideals. Relations were established with the Spanish-American tobacco unions, which, led by Cuban workers, had pioneered in the cause of labor radicalism. Iglesias and his group sharply condemned Davis' municipal elections because of their restricted suffrage. In spite of the protection which he had received from the generals, Iglesias demanded an end to a system where a colony was run by a few army men and capitalist politicians, bent upon turning the Puerto Rican workers into political slaves of the new rulers.[11] This was, indeed, very strong language which Iglesias' military protectors would hardly have approved.

The labor leaders returned determined to challenge the economic system. They opposed the exchange of *pesos* for dollars, which worked to the disadvantage of the workers' wages, and insisted on the observance of an eight-hour day. A general strike followed in August, 1900. But the system had hardened. Repression and strike-breaking were the order of the day. The local Republicans revived the charges of anarchism against Iglesias, and sent the experienced *turbas* after the strikers. Jailed more than once and fearing for his life, Iglesias left for New York in September, 1900. The labor movement desperately needed new, external allies.[12]

Just as Muñoz Rivera had left the island to seek support among the American liberals, so Iglesias now looked for a job and friends in the labor movement. The Federal newspaper had supported the workers' challenge of the system. In New York, Muñoz's paper, *The Puerto Rico Herald,* praised Iglesias's efforts. It was a brief, fleeting rapprochement between two men who shared a talent for dealing with American public opinion, but were estranged from each other by temperament and conviction. However, Iglesias soon found the powerful allies and protectors he needed in Samuel Gompers and the American Federation of Labor.[13]

There was, however, a price for this protection. Iglesias had been a socialist of Marxist leanings. Gompers, on the other hand, was antisocialist. His trade union movement worked within the system, eschewing revolution and direct political activity. Its aim was to create unity among the workers and to use every opportunity to wrest all possible concessions from the industrial capitalists. It preferred to avoid strikes, although strikers were supported if necessary. The thrust was pragmatic, unlike the idealistic, revolutionary language of the pioneers of Puerto Rican socialism.

Iglesias became Gompers's faithful disciple. Invited to Washington in December, 1900, he underwent a profound conversion. He learned the principles and methods of American trade unionism, the doctrines of U.S. constitutionalism, the intricacies of U.S. politics, and the propaganda system the A.F. of L. used to spread its gospel. He became Gompers's man in Puerto Rico, and eventually, in the Caribbean and Latin America.

Gompers had been an anti-imperialist, but once Puerto Rico had been annexed, he felt that Puerto Rico was irrevocably part of the American union and that its working people should have the full cooperation and sympathy of the working people of the United States. In his several trips to the island he developed warm feelings for the inhabitants, and eventually was drawn into the political struggle for full rights and self-government. He was a benign, eager tutor in the labor field; but still a tutor who wanted to Americanize labor attitudes, structures, and methods in Puerto Rico. "You are now more united to the United States than ever before, to all intents and purposes we are one country, so we must have one common interest and one common destiny," he said in a San Juan speech on February 22, 1904.[14] At heart, Gompers was a U.S. nationalist, proud of the Declaration of Independence, the founding fathers, and the U.S. constitutional tradition. He wanted American citizenship for Puerto Rico and promised "to help secure the Porto Rican rights under the banner of our starry flag . . . done cordially, heartily and promptly." Thus Puerto Ricans would be "one of the children of the great fatherhood of the American Republic."[15] This proud, nationalistic ideal of the great American fatherhood was preached to a labor leadership reared in the view that the old concept of *patria,* or motherland, which many Puerto Ricans felt so strongly, was a capitalist conspiracy against the brotherhood of the oppressed, a remnant of the old, hated Spanish system. So with Iglesias at the helm, many of the leaders were willing to answer Gompers's call to action and to embrace the new strong fatherland and its promised freedom. But this labor *mentorado* was also bound to find a bumpy road; for the new fatherland had become the staunch ally of King Sugar.

Gompers's helping hand was soon evident. In October, 1901, he took Iglesias to see President Roosevelt. Iglesias's mission was outlined and Roosevelt dictated a letter to Governor Hunt asking that Iglesias not be bothered by insular officials. Gompers followed with another letter: Iglesias was to organize the wage earners "upon the national and progressive basis of trade unions . . ."[16] In other words, Iglesias was no longer the anarchist, but a man with presidential support who should be protected against harrassment.

Gompers instructed Iglesias to tread softly, to report to American Federation of Labor headquarters at least once a week in English, and to work within the organization's guidelines. But as soon as Iglesias landed in Puerto Rico in November he was jailed for failure to appear in court and involvement in a conspiracy to raise the price of labor. *The San Juan News* highlighted the case, describing Iglesias as an "agitator" and "incendiary." In the quiet of his cell, Iglesias wrote to the *News,* emphasizing his peaceful intent. "My mission is eminently American," he added. From Washington, Gompers sent Iglesias money and moral support, and got in touch with the president. Iglesias was released on bail, *The San Juan News* then sang his praises, and one by one the crafts voted to affiliate with the American Federation of Labor.

But Iglesias had not counted on the *Federación Regional* (Regional Federation), the *de facto* labor wing of the local Republican Party. Sensing the emergence of a powerful rival, the group called upon the *turbas,* which shot at Iglesias's headquarters. The District Court of San Juan added to his woes by sentencing him to three years in prison. When the A.F. of L. learned the news, all hell broke loose. Gompers's indignation was shared by the powerful union. Angry protests and appeals in Washington and San Juan led to Iglesias's absolution. Iglesias had, at last, triumphed. But Gompers's influence was behind the *denouément* of the local drama. The euphoric leaders of the *Federación Libre* (Free Federation) assured Governor Hunt "that they had adopted American customs and principles and that they are Americans at heart."[17] From now on, American trade-unionist philosophy would prevail over Spanish labor radicalism. Americanization, evident in the schools, the army, and the courts, shaped the course of the labor movement.

One aspect of American trade-unionism was not adopted. While the *Federación Libre* continued its successful organizing campaign against its rival, the pull of political participation was too strong. In 1902 and 1904 the *Federación* was willing to run its candidates under the Federals's insignia. This was not to Hunt's liking, and the labor group faced government hostility. Hoping to mend the rift, Gompers visited Puerto Rico early in 1904.

He received VIP treatment as someone who had the president's ear. He met with the Executive Council to discuss an eight-hour day bill for government employees and an employers' liability bill. The Regional Federation (Iglesias's archrival) placed itself at Gompers's disposal, enabling Gompers to promote unity between the two organizations. At Muñoz Rivera's request, a committee of the newly formed Union party called on him to secure his support. Gompers saw at first glance the sharp social and economic cleavages, the contradictions between increasing wealth and spreading social misery. Everywhere he went, he preached his American labor philosophy: social justice within the context of American nationalism.[18] And he did not mince his words upon his return to the mainland. Replying to the political tutors, he insisted that conditions on the island were not a credit to the United States. From then on, he remained a courageous critic of the social inequities of King Sugar.[19]

During the Foraker period, the labor movement was caught between its commitment to non-partisan trade-unionism and the lure of political power which promised quick results through legislation. The first test

Women tobacco strippers at work exemplify life in the era of King Sugar.

within the Unionist party did not fare well; the Unionists represented many elements and classes. Although men like Muñoz Rivera and Matienzo had shown their concern with labor, the party as a whole had deep roots among the coffee growers, the mountain peasantry, and the professional groups. Its influential *hacendados* were not exactly pro-labor nor did the labor leaders share the party's interest in the defense of Puerto Rico's personality and its sense of cultural regionalism. They rather preferred to wed the class struggle to the rights identified with American citizenship.

During the Foraker period, the Free Federation was concerned with the social injustices and the increasingly uneven distribution of wealth;

the question of political rights for Puerto Rico was secondary. The Unionists, on the other hand, opposed the Foraker Act for its colonialism and the inferior status it imposed on Puerto Rico. The more restless elements denounced the plight of the coffee areas and the possibility of absentee ownership dominating the land. To them, American citizenship would only be welcome if it brought political rights and wiped out carpetbagging, however well disguised as altruistic tutelage. At this historic stage, a political convergence of the two forces was an impossibility. They drifted apart, and in the 1909 confrontation between the House and the colonial tutors, the Free Federation labor leadership sided with the latter.

By 1908, the Free Federation had two roles: to promote the cause of trade-unionism and to Americanize Puerto Rico. Iglesias wrote to Gompers in that year:

The labor movement in Porto Rico has no doubt been, and is, the most efficient and safest way of conveying the sentiments and feelings of the American people to the hearts of the people of Porto Rico. If the people of Porto Rico should really become Americans, the A.F. of L. would be the only institution to be held responsible for it. . . .[20]

To the labor movement, the 1909 confrontation was the result of an anti-American reactionary wave. Despite its small numbers, the labor movement saw itself as a most powerful influence in preventing public deviation to what Iglesias called "the reactionary and monarchical cause." He claimed the legislature had refused to enact a group of labor bills because they were American. When the Unionists sent their leaders to Washington to ask for more political power, "our A.F. of L.," Iglesias observed, "started another campaign against the anti-Americans with a magnificent success for the honor and dignity of American institutions." The present government, he claimed, while not democratic in form, should continue under the control of honest and true Americans and Porto Ricans, and prevent the reaction of the monarchical elements, supported by the majority of the ignorant masses.[21]

In a parallel document handed to President Taft on November 27, 1909, the Free Federation leadership again presented itself as the shining knight in armor of true Americanization in Puerto Rico. It opposed self-government on the grounds that it would bring "slavery, ignorance and disgrace to 90 per cent of the population." It strongly defended the continuation of an Executive Council appointed by the president until a much larger portion of the people of Puerto Rico knew how to read or write. Thus, the Free Federation supported limited suffrage, a key objective of Taft's policies in 1910. Politically, the document preached complete subservience to a more strict tutelage under federal governmental authority.

The document had a *quid pro quo.* In return for his espousal of outright colonialism, Iglesias wanted action from Washington, including U.S. citizenship, the expansion of education, legislation for an eight-hour day and employers' liability protection to the sugar workers, establishment of health inspection of factories and of a branch of the U.S. Labor Bureau, and prohibition of child labor below 14 years of age.[22]

The petition was a shrewd bid for Taft's political support. Iglesias realized that the Free Federation, with 11,000 members, lacked political power to defeat the Unionists. Iglesias's support of the anti-democratic trend in administration thinking was a tacit admission that the labor movement had not reached the great mass of illiterate peasants or *jíbaros.* Therefore, he abandoned the early positions labor had taken in defense of universal suffrage during the Davis period, and joined the move to check and destroy the Unionists, in the belief that Taft's social and economic concessions would politically strengthen the Federation as the best tool for promoting Americanization.

By 1910, Iglesias and his group were ready to try their political luck again. With Gompers's friendly support, Iglesias's reputation as a leader in the Americanization program enabled the Free Federation to challenge the Unionists and Republicans who had dominated island politics since 1900. Two local labor parties in Aguadilla and Arecibo gained some votes in 1910. The results were especially hopeful in Arecibo, a sugar area, where the labor propaganda was particularly effective.[23] In 1912, Arecibo yielded 2,359 votes to a new *Partido Obrero Insular;* in 1914, the party received 2,871, and wrested the local government away from the Unionists.[24] It began to seem that an insular labor party, with an economic and social program following the A.F. of L. trade-unionist philosophy and fully committed to Americanization, could now become a third rising political force. Created in 1915 in the town of Cayey, and rooted in the old traditional social conscience of the tobacco workers, the new Socialist party now undertook island-wide political organization.[25]

Parallel with this drive was the aggressive campaign to improve working conditions for cigar workers and cane cutters. The cigar strike of 1914 and the cane strike of 1915 were landmarks in the rise of trade unionism and the backdrop of the political effort. They highlighted the contrast between high sugar and tobacco prices and deplorable working

conditions. In his last trip to Puerto Rico in 1914, Gompers saw the
strength of the labor movement in Arecibo, the political center. But he
was deeply disturbed by the increasing unemployment in the sugar fields
and the deteriorated conditions in which the workers lived in contrast
with the industry workers. Their poverty and misery he considered "a
stigma upon the record, the history and the honor of our country."[26]

In challenging King Sugar, Iglesias had been careful to identify himself with American ideals and to involve powerful American friends. He

Ox carts in a sugar cane field were a common sight during the years of King Sugar.

was clearly on the political road. In the elections of July 16, 1917, he was elected to the Senate while the party got 24,468 votes.[27]

By that time, reform had taken place, thanks largely to the Unionists' long and stubborn campaign, which Iglesias had tried to sidetrack seven years before. Now that an elective Senate existed, the erstwhile European anarchist, turned into a shrewd politician in the A.F. of L. mold, could pursue his aims in the Senate without having to wait for an electorate who could fully read and write.

Tutelage Modified: The Jones Act

The Jones Act, signed on March 4, 1917, by President Wilson, was the culmination of the drive for congressional revision of Puerto Rico's status. The drive had had its ups and downs, its sporadic debates, its shifting emphasis. To study this process from printed congressional sources is not enough because it may lead to a narrow interpretation of the many forces that shaped congressional indecision and, at last, congressional action.[28] Several external factors influenced Congress: presidential interest or indifference, the coming to power of the Democratic party, the changing pressures from the Bureau of Insular Affairs, the complex political picture in Puerto Rico, and the rumblings of war which finally accelerated the process.

The legislative effort went through three main periods. First came the Olmstead Bill of 1910, already discussed, which embodied a restrictive reactionary policy aimed at hurting the Unionists politically, the putting in power what Colton had called the "substantial and conservative" elements. This bill linked American citizenship with political regression; it passed the House but failed the Senate. The Jones and Shafroth Bills of 1914 provided for individual or collective citizenship and an elective Senate. These bills were more responsive to a revision of the Foraker Act, but were bogged down by complicating factors. The new Jones Bill of 1916, which was able to run the gauntlet of both inquiry and indecision with strong presidential support, finally became law shortly before the United States went to war with Germany.

The personal intervention of the president was crucial in the final resolution of the Puerto Rican issue. More than McKinley, Roosevelt, or Taft, Wilson embodied the conscientious tutor. Since his professorial days at Johns Hopkins and Princeton, he had given considerable thought to the U.S. role vis-à-vis Cuba, the Philippines, and Puerto Rico. Like many of his generation, he was deeply influenced by British example and thought, particularly Edmund Burke's emphasis on freedom as a product of English history and his view that liberty requires discipline and self-control. Self-control, therefore, must precede self-government. Regarding the countries the United States had taken over in trust, particularly the Philippines, Wilson had written in 1901: ". . . They must first take the discipline of law, must first love order and instructively yield to it. . . . We are old in this learning and must be their tutors."[29] And he had added: "We must govern as those who learn; and they must obey as those who are in tutelage. . . . They are children and we are men in these deep matters of government and justice."[30]

These views, however self-righteous they may sound, did not preclude Wilson from acknowledging what he called "the schooling of action." People cannot always remain as children. Only from contact with the polity itself can they make good citizens. "Life," he concluded, "is their real master and tutor in affairs."[31] So there was in him a disposition to relent. "In developing liberty," he also wrote, "we have to learn how to hold certain persons in check without choking them to death."[32] He, therefore, would not favor the repressive Olmstead solution, but would prefer the pupil to learn more from "the schooling of action." However, it would take time and the coming thunder of war to get real results.

Wilson's election was well received in Puerto Rico, particularly among the Unionists who since 1909 had hoped for a Democratic return to power. The House of Delegates immediately cabled the new president, through Muñoz Rivera, with congratulations and a petition:

Our people request a new constitution providing for two elective houses, ample legislative powers in all local matters, an executive cabinet composed of *bona fide* residents of Porto Rico and other measures worthy of the high sense of justice of the American people and of the demonstrated capacity and natural rights of the people of Porto Rico.

Muñoz added his conviction that Puerto Rico's only hope rested with the Democratic party; the Republican party, on the other hand, had refused to recognize the island's right to self-government for fourteen years. He asked the president to mention Puerto Rico in his message to Congress and reaffirmed his hope that the coming Administration would grant Puerto Ricans "the home rule to which they aspire with the same right as other countries in the world."[33]

The Citizenship Question

But for many reasons the new administration was not ready for immediate action. The powerful Bureau of Insular Affairs, under General Edwards, had been checkmated in Congress when the Olmstead Bill failed to pass the Senate. When the Democrats came to power in 1911, the Bureau had been in close touch with Jones, who was committed to a revision of the Foraker Act. The twin questions of citizenship and self-government were crucial. Jones had opposed individual elective citizenship which Olmstead had favored. But the problem was how to reconcile the granting of citizenship when many Puerto Ricans preferred to retain their Puerto Rican citizenship or opposed compulsory action by Congress. The solution came from a bright young law officer of the bureau, Felix Frankfurter: American citizenship should be given to all Puerto Rican citizens except those who, by registering in some form to be provided for, declined to become American citizens. The bureau approved this idea and Jones used it in his many legislative proposals. It finally was embodied in the 1917 law.[34]

Spurred by the bureau, Jones had introduced legislation early in 1912, granting collective citizenship. This action had greatly concerned the Unionists. Muñoz Rivera had explained to Jones that the people of Puerto Rico considered the elective Senate and other issues more important than citizenship.[35] When he knew about the introduction, Muñoz cabled De Diego. After heated discussions, the House cabled the resident commissioner requesting that no action be taken unless it included an ample measure of self-government. At this stage, Colton, after discussions with De Diego, wired the Bureau that some further participation in self-government should be granted to avoid a difficult situation.[36]

Jones then introduced another bill including an elective Senate, a Department of Labor, and other features.[37] Congress did not act on either Jones bills although the citizenship bill passed the House. This was the situation when Wilson took over. No action was taken on Puerto Rico in 1913, as the president was feeling his way in Washington. The advice Wilson got on Puerto Rico was mainly negative. As judge of the U.S. District Court he had appointed his close friend, Peter J. Hamilton, who had gone to Puerto Rico eager to familiarize the island with American judicial ideals.[38] Hamilton, unfortunately, showed a stereotyped racism. He counseled the president to proceed cautiously. The Puerto Ricans, he wrote, "have the Latin-American excitability, and I think America

should go slow in granting them anything like autonomy. Their civilization is not at all like ours yet." And a few months later, he added this
racist gem: "the mixture of black and white in Porto Rico threatens to
create a race of mongrels of no use to anyone, a race of Spanish American talkers. A governor of the South, or with knowledge of Southern
remedies for that trouble, could, if a wise man, do much. . . ."[39] This
was certainly colonial tutelage at its worst.

Wilson's Secretary of War, Lindley M. Garrison, also urged caution.
On October 6, 1913, he sent a memorandum to the president, which
had been prepared by General Frank McIntyre, now head of the Bureau
of Insular Affairs. His recommendations included individual rather than
collective citizenship, the latter course being "fraught with danger." He
saw no need to change the structure of the Foraker Act, but suggested
more Puerto Rican appointments to the Executive Council, as a means
of increasing participation in government. His views were a throwback
to the narrow colonialism of the Olmstead formula.[40]

No wonder, then, that disappointment hit political opinion in Puerto
Rico and deepened the partisan divisions. The Republicans grew more
convinced that a new effort should be made to link citizenship to the
declaration of an incorporated territory. This dual objective now became
their goal.[41] Among Unionists, disruptive tensions appeared. It was
becoming obvious that extension of citizenship was the only action Congress was ready to take. Time and again the Unionist leadership had
insisted that citizenship without self-government was worthless and did
no honor to American democracy. The Olmstead debate had left deep
scars; Stimson's promise had come to naught, and now Wilson was showing signs of neglect and inaction.

In an extraordinary assembly in November, 1913, the party adopted
a new program, denouncing the injustice done to Puerto Rico in depriving the people of their political rights; and attacking the "oligarchy" that
had ruled the island. The Unionists came out for full independence or
independence under a protectorate. But under the influence of Muñoz
Rivera and others, they added home rule or autonomy as a transitory
goal. Statehood was then eliminated as a third option.[42]

Muñoz Rivera now had to deal with De Diego's turn towards independence. In a speech to the Lake Mohonk conferences of 1913, which
had become a U.S. sounding board for political trends in Puerto Rico,
De Diego had forcefully rejected the Stimson view of Puerto Rico as a
tropical Canada, judging it inapplicable to American federalist principles. Statehood or independence were the only options, and neither the

United States nor Puerto Rico really believed in statehood. The only solution left was a republic under a protectorate after the Cuban model.[43]

The Union party was, therefore, divided into the *muñocista* and *dieguista* wings. But there were other elements in the internal struggle. Two new generational groups had emerged: one was deeply attached to independence and was stressing, with such distinguished intellectuals as Luis Lloréns Torres and Nemesio Canales, a new concern for socio-economic questions. Another group, under Martín Travieso, represented a professional elite, educated in the United States and anxious to challenge the hold of the older generation.

It was an extremely difficult situation for Muñoz Rivera who had developed a remarkable prescience regarding American politics. He had predicted the Democratic victory in 1912; and had come to realize that Congress was more inclined to grant American citizenship and that it would be extremely difficult to obtain any measure of home rule without it. But he felt that party cohesion was essential to Puerto Rico's political evolution. He now relied on trusted lieutenants such as Antonio R. Barceló, a man of integrity and moderation who took the chairmanship of the party. And, always the master politician, Muñoz Rivera urged the party to take action to help the urban workers and the rural *jíbaros*.[44]

By the end of the year, Wilson had at last appointed a new governor, Arthur Yager, one of his fellow students at Johns Hopkins, and president of Georgetown College in Kentucky. Yager was well-intentioned, but inexperienced in Puerto Rican matters.[45] He soon saw the unpopularity of the Foraker Act and began urging Washington to revise it.[46]

President Wilson's message to Congress in December, 1913, mentioned Puerto Rico in the context of a new American concept of tutelage. The new overseas territories were not to be exploited; they were part of an "enlightened statesmanship," and he hoped to bind Puerto Rico and Hawaii to the United States "by ties of justice and interest and affection." He promised the "ample and familiar rights and privileges accorded our own citizens in our territories" to Puerto Rico.[47] As Muñoz Rivera was quick to point out, the language was lofty but vague and enigmatic. If Wilson wanted reform he should establish home rule and later consider the advisability of national independence.[48]

By the end of the year, McIntyre, always the efficient bureaucrat, had prepared a plan for the new situation. The main issues were whether Puerto Ricans should continue as citizens of Puerto Rico or become American citizens, and whether the island should become a state of the union or be given autonomy; separation not to be seriously considered.

McIntyre's policy recommendations included making U.S. citizenship accessible and free of cost; as complete autonomy as compatible with the interests of Puerto Rico, with no committment to statehood; and a constitution with an elective Senate and an executive council appointed by the president, including four members to be selected by the governor from elected members of the majority party in the legislature.[49]

Before the new policy could be developed and announced, Senator Shafroth decided to visit the island and see for himself what should be done.[50] The stirrings of independence within the Union party were creating new pressure on bureaucrats and congressmen.

On January 18, Shafroth announced that he would introduce a bill providing for individual citizenship and civil government. Jones followed suit and by late February both legislators had introduced bills including citizenship, an elective Senate, and an absolute veto for the governor to counteract the measure of home rule. Though Jones's bill advocated collective citizenship, both bills were largely influenced by Yager and the Bureau. Wilson found the drafts satisfactory, and suggested the bills be considered by committees, but not pressed for passage.[51]

In the light of these moves, Muñoz Rivera developed his own strategy. First, on February 27, he introduced his own bill in Congress, providing for home rule, an elective Senate, and Puerto Rican citizenship. This put his moderate position on the record. Secondly, he urged Barceló and De Diego to come to Washington, while Muñoz supported a House of Delegates's *Memorial,* written by De Diego, maintaining its opposition to American citizenship. The *Memorial* reiterated in clear, emphatic terms the Union's 1913 platform. Then, on March 3, 1914, the Congressional Record printed a letter from Muñoz expressing the House of Delegates's position that the bill should not be considered without a general modification of the Foraker Act.[52]

At the Senate committee hearings Muñoz Rivera pressed for a postponement of the citizenship question until Puerto Ricans had demonstrated their capacity for self-government under home rule. In this sensitive situation, he wanted assurance that American citizenship did not rule out future independence. At this and other hearings, he had expressed a preference for independence, but he was quite convinced that Congress would not consider it. Jones himself had called independence "an idle dream." What to do then? Rejection of American citizenship if imposed, and as a result face exclusion from public life? Revolution? Proscription? Muñoz's realistic mind found revolution impossible. If the struggle for reform did not continue, the Unionist party would collapse, the Republicans would take over, and servilism could then triumph as in 1900 and 1902. This was unbearable to him.[53] He had once told a Congressional committee that if statehood was immediately offered, he would immediately accept it. But this was simply a tactic to counteract what he called "the terrible distrust of Congress."[54] More than ever he felt committed to a patient course while seized with dark, anguished forebodings.

If there was zig-zagging in Puerto Rico, there was also zig-zagging in Washington. The House committee favored collective citizenship; the Senate was for individual options. The House of Delegates's protest discouraged the administration and led to doubts about the passage of the bills.[55]

To complicate matters further, Jones, the sparkplug of revision, fell ill by the end of the spring. The Republican party in Puerto Rico sent a delegation to Washington to promote a declaration of territorial government with collective citizenship. They found a ready ally in Senator Saulsberry who introduced a bill providing for territorial government for the island and placed it under the jurisdiction of the Interior Department.[56] In San Juan, Barbosa's *El Tiempo* asked Yager to support the Saulsberry bill, considering anything better than being a ward of the War Department![57] The Congress was being swamped with Puerto Rican bills and the War Department tutors were satisfying hardly anyone.

The year dragged on and nothing happened. Governor Yager could not spur the administration to new efforts. Jones, not being physically well, was unable to push the bill through the House. Wilson was not too much involved in the bill's fate. "I wish with all my heart it might be brought up and passed, but other things are for the present apparently crowding it to the wall," he wrote.[58] Tutorial discouragement was visible. The only action was the appointment, on the bureau's recommendation, of Travieso and Domenech to the Executive Council—a move that Judge Hamilton promptly hailed as lessening the influence of "such extremists as Muñoz and De Diego—the little islanders."[59] Preparing for the elections, the Unionists ratified the 1913 stand amid open discord between Muñoz and De Diego. Rules of political conduct were adopted to the effect that while independence should be defended, nothing should be done to impede the effort for a transitory autonomy. The Republican party, in turn, favored territorial government as a transition to statehood—the position it was defending in Washington.

The election results showed new straws in the political wind. The

Republicans won three of the seven electoral districts; the workers' party won Arecibo and showed strength in the eastern part of the island. The Unionists were still dominant and Muñoz Rivera was reelected, but the internal dissent was beginning to take a toll.[60]

Muñoz was more apprehensive than ever. He had professed a warm friendship for De Diego but wanted him to see the realities of the situation. The independence propaganda was hurting the Union in Washington and weakening its political hold on Puerto Rico. More than ever, Muñoz feared that the Republicans would return to power.

By early 1915, Muñoz had lost a lot of faith in the Wilson Administration because of its inaction and indifference. Muñoz was convinced that there was no desire to liberalize the political system, no long-range plan, no far-sighted policy. The Democrats were, he wrote, a failure, a very sad failure.[61]

De Diego, on the other hand, had definitely embarked on a campaign for independence and was looking beyond Puerto Rico for moral support. With good friends in the Dominican Republic, where he was greatly admired for his writings, he founded *Hermandad Antillana* (Antillean Brotherhood), and committed himself to the old Hostos dream of closer relations between the islands. From June to August, 1915, De Diego visited Santo Domingo and Cuba, laying the basis for the Antillean Union (*Unión Antillana*), which promoted cultural interchange between the islands as a prelude to political confederation.[62]

These cultural contacts broadened the perspective of writers and intellectuals in Puerto Rico, but added fuel to the Republican propaganda. Muñoz Rivera, while willing to support cultural exchanges with the other Antilles, felt very strongly that his first duty as resident commissioner was to strive for home rule. He told this to De Diego, but privately he was alarmed at the negative impact in Washington.

In October, 1915, the crisis in the Unionist party came to the surface. Muñoz Rivera decided to face the two opposing groups. One was headed by Travieso, who had become an ambitious administration man; the other by De Diego, with his passionate nationalist yearning. The resident commissioner stood by the 1914 platform: home rule as a necessary stage toward independence. He won the day, but the party faced rough weather. Relations were never the same with De Diego, who now devoted himself to cultural propaganda for Puerto Rican independence. And Muñoz Rivera had to face the machinations of Travieso who became acting governor and used his position to undermine Muñoz's leadership.[63]

Having defeated De Diego's wing by a vote of 106 against 35, Muñoz Rivera easily stopped Travieso's bid for party control. Upon his return to Washington, the resident commissioner asked Wilson to recommend action in the president's message. Wilson's reply was heartening: "I shall certainly not forget Porto Rico. . . . My interest in it is deep and sincere."[64]

The atmosphere then began to change. More was involved than the relations between the United States and Puerto Rico or the vagaries of colonial tutelage. Much of the world was at war, and defense considerations now impinged on many decisions of the Administration. Beyond the moral duties of the self-imposed tutor, there was the strategic imperative, the great basic consideration which had led to the 1898 landing.

On December 7, 1915, Wilson delivered his Third Annual Message to Congress. It was a long message devoted to a continent at peace in a world of hostile, armed rivalries. It preached a hemispheric unity, very much like the unity Franklin Delano Roosevelt was to invoke a generation later. It also emphasized the need for defense, for what Wilson described as "disciplined might." The president asked for an increase in the standing force, a force which should be adequate not only to perform upon the continental coasts, but also in the Philippines, in the Hawaiian islands, and in Puerto Rico. He asked likewise for a great naval expansion, both in men of war and in the merchant marine which could help link the two Americas together.

Wilson also emphasized another matter which, to him, was "very intimately associated with the question of national safety and preparation for defense." That was the policy toward the Philippines and Puerto Rico. He stated: "Our treatment of them and their attitude towards us are manifestly of the first consequence in the development of our duties in the world and in getting a free hand to perform those duties." The Puerto Rican question now became part of a world-wide defense strategy. It was essential for the United States to be free "from any unnecessary burden or embarrassment" and there was no better way "but to fulfill our promises and promote the interests of those dependent on us to the utmost." Bills for the Philippines and Puerto Rico were submitted to Congress. But now there was a note of urgency, since these bills would clear the way for what Wilson called the "great policies" by which the United States would make good its right to leadership. Justice to Puerto Rico, therefore, was mainly a question of national security.[65] In this international crisis the Jones Bill came to life again.

On January 20, 1916, Congressman Jones introduced the new measure dealing with collective citizenship and other features. Support for the bill cut across party lines, especially since the minority committee leader, Horace M. Towner of Iowa, wanted to hurry its passage. The bill was reported without dissent to the House five days after its introduction.[66] There was general expectation that now things would go smoothly and that Shafroth would be able to expedite matters in the Senate.

But conflicting opinions from Puerto Rico created new problems as the island's Republicans pressed for the Saulsberry bill and a new controversy developed on the jurisdiction of the federal court. Its abolition had been requested by the Puerto Rico Bar Association. Its defenders felt that the court protected American residents and its removal could create profound discouragement and operate against the inflow of American capital.[67]

On March 5, 1916, Muñoz Rivera spoke in the House. The speech was an eloquent reminder of Puerto Rico's struggles for self-government and the Democratic party's obligation to do justice to the island. Puerto Rico wanted full home rule and the Jones Bill failed to provide it. But it was a step forward and Puerto Rico was ready to show Congress that it was able to govern itself. One by one, Muñoz demolished the traditional arguments used to deny the islands rights. Illiteracy? In the early days of the American republic, 80 percent of the people did not know how to read and write. Color? More than ten states had a higher colored population than Puerto Rico. Population? Eighteen states had less than the island. Only one thing had prevented self-government: the host of office seekers who descended on the island as they had on the South after the Civil War.

Muñoz called attention to the international situation and to the U.S. responsibilities toward Latin America. If Puerto Rico was treated fairly, and not subject to an imperialistic tutelage, the United States could assert a moral hegemony; if the United States failed, Puerto Rico might turn elsewhere to Paris, London, even Berlin.

He reemphasized the Unionist defense of Puerto Rican citizenship. If Puerto Rico were offered statehood, it would gladly accept American citizenship. Without statehood Puerto Rico would prefer its own citizenship. A plebiscite should decide the matter and American citizenship should not be imposed.

He took another strong stand against the restriction of suffrage provided by the bill, a hangover from the 1909 Olmstead Bill. One hundred sixty-five thousand Puerto Ricans would be deprived of a right they had exercised. If there had been accusations of vote-buying, so had there been in the United States, including the state of Massachusetts.

At the end, Muñoz stated the Unionist commitment: to prove to the Congress that Puerto Rico, under the new act, could be a field of experimentation, and in due time Congress would decree its independence, as it had done in Cuba and would do with the Philippines.

But before the debate was over, Muñoz Rivera had to reply to "Uncle Joe" Cannon of Illinois, who firmly believed that Caucasian civilization was not exportable to the tropics. The stale prejudices reappeared, with their pseudo-Darwinian arrogance. Muñoz had been trying to raise the debate to basic issues related to American democratic principles; Cannon debased it to the level of racial slurs. Muñoz countered that it was not the island's fault if it had to demand legislation that, according to American principles, would be the island's inalienable right to adopt for itself.[68]

On May 23, the Jones Bill passed in the House, but complications arose in the Senate which had nothing to do with the basic issues. One was a prohibition amendment. The implication was clear: if Puerto Rico wanted a larger dose of self-government, the price was to do away with rum-drinking. Rum and home rule could not go together. Rum, it seemed, was the enemy of Caucasian constitutionalism! Governor Yager was greatly distressed, for prohibition meant losing the rum revenues. The War Department lent its support to the governor's frantic objections. They were able to stop the prohibition move on the House, but not in the Senate.[69]

Time was running short in the election year of 1916. President Wilson himself went to the Capitol to press for passage of several administration measures, including the Jones Bill. Despite his efforts, without the prohibition amendment, the Senate bill would go nowhere. To avoid embarrassment, Shafroth attached a last rider to an appropriation bill, suspending the Puerto Rican elections indefinitely. The promise was implicit: Congress would pass the bill in December.

The Passage of the Act

Muñoz Rivera had worked backstage to add some basic amendments to the bills. He obtained the conditional rather than the absolute veto of the governor; universal suffrage in ten years (on the assumption that by 1928 illiteracy would have largely disappeared); and the Senate's right of approval for school curriculum. Always a realist, he was less optimistic than the administration about passage of the bill in 1916, and he was proved right.

He was gradually overwhelmed by a sharp sense of frustration. In his opinion, the status question would come to a choice between statehood and independence, if the new generation did not accept evolution towards the Canadian model. He professed a faith in independence but insisted that reform would come gradually: the next step would be an elective governor and full legislative powers. He wrote those thoughts to Ramón Siaca Pacheco, under secretary of Puerto Rico, on August 11, 1916.[70]

By the end of the summer, he felt he had done his duty and that his labors in Washington had come to an end. He wrote Barceló about his irrevocable decision not to run again. To others, he mentioned that this was his last campaign. His thoughts were now on a return to Puerto Rico. A deep pessimism seized him, in spite of the fact that at no time since 1899 had he been so carefully heard or respected in administration circles.

His clashes with De Diego and Travieso had left a deep mark. He regretted the estrangement from De Diego, his friend and confidant of many years, and he felt bitter toward Travieso, whom he had promoted and supported. But he especially feared for the Union party, rocked by dissension, and attacked from without. All perspectives—he wrote—are full of shadows.[71]

Physically he was very sick, weakened by the long fight. On September 19 he was welcomed by a large crowd in San Juan. His charismatic leadership reasserted itself. But two days later he felt indisposed. At first, the doctors thought that the high temperature that gripped him was malaria. But it was a ruptured gall bladder and the infection spread until it became septicemia and there was little else that could be done except the pain of a useless surgical operation and the long, long wait. Finally, on November 15, 1916, he passed away not without reinstating his guiding principles: the fight for home rule, for good relations with the United States; and for deep attachment to Puerto Rico.[72] Indeed, he was a man severely tried by history.

A tremendous outpouring of grief accompanied him to Barranquitas, his native town. The country was deeply shaken and the emotions of bereavement brought a brief political convergence between the Unionists and the Republicans which helped create a favorable climate in the States for the last lap. A bipartisan commission, headed by Barceló, left for Washington early in December to press for passage of the Jones Bill. It carried a letter from Governor Yager praising them as excellent men who would unanimously support, in the name of both large political parties, the Jones Bill and would aid in adjusting amendments in the best possible manner.[73] Muñoz Rivera had favored the bill as a whole, Yager wrote to McIntyre, and his approval should help reconcile the people to all the bill's provisions, thus making the present moment the right one for its passage.[74]

On December 20, the commission appeared before the Senate committee, and all members united in a statement read by Barceló, advocating passage of the bill with certain amendments. Although the bill could not be acted upon before the holidays, a promise was made to push the measure in the new year.[75]

But action not only came because of the long political shadow now cast by the man whom Judge Hamilton had disparagingly called "the little islander." The international situation was worsening and the War Department and the White House felt an urgent need to clear the way for political reform in Puerto Rico. Sharpening this concern was the awareness that inaction would fan the flames of independence in the island. Since July, 1916, McIntyre had insisted that passage of the bill would put an end to the agitation for independence, which had been due to the failure to give Puerto Rico a government responsive to the Puerto Rican people as was the Spanish autonomous government of 1897. He had been, at that time, impressed by De Diego's propaganda.[76] On November 28, 1916, he sent a letter to the Secretary from Coll y Cuchi, outlining the "formidable dimensions" attained by the independence movement—a factor which was another plea for haste in passing the bill.[77] So, to the Americans, adoption of the Jones Bill was to a considerable extent a response to the separatist feelings which had been growing since the 1909 crisis.

Defense, however, became the uppermost consideration within the Wilson Administration during 1916. Some defense initiatives directly or indirectly touched legislative revision concerning Puerto Rico. One was the purchase of the Danish West Indies, which the United States had wanted since 1867. After the outbreak of World War I, there was great fear that the Germans would secure a coaling station in Haiti and would take advantage of the European upheaval to absorb Denmark and obtain legal title to the Danish West Indies. When pressure was put upon the Danes, they at first resisted, but were advised that if the Germans compelled Denmark to cede the island, the United States would seize them.

The naval general board had advised in December, 1915, that while the harbors of Puerto Rico were adequate, it was advisable to forestall a possible enemy by bringing the islands under the U.S. flag.[78]

Twenty-five million dollars were offered in exchange, as the president became convinced of the inevitability of war with Germany. A hitch developed in the negotiations. The United States proposed a clause in the treaty patterned after the Treaty of Paris, leaving Congress the right to determine civil rights and political status of the native inhabitants. But the Danes insisted on a provision of American citizenship. Secretary of State Lansing pointed out in June, 1916, that it was impossible to do so, because full citizenship had not been accorded to Puerto Ricans, though the matter was being considered by Congress. When the Danes demurred, President Wilson personally decided to waive American objections. The treaty was signed on August 4, 1916, and presented to Congress as a way of thwarting German ambitions in the Caribbean. Under Article VI, the inhabitants who did not declare within a year their intention to preserve their citizenship in Denmark were held to have renounced it and to have accepted American citizenship.[79]

The pressure to grant American citizenship to Puerto Ricans now became a matter of high priority for the administration.

Wilson's Message to Congress on December 5, 1916, highlighted this point. He placed the bill amending the organic law of Puerto Rico among three matters of capital importance awaiting Senate action. The argument, he said, was "brief and conclusive." The present laws were not just. Expectations had been created and not satisfied. "There is uneasiness among the people of the island and even a suspicious doubt with regard to our intentions concerning them which the adoption of the pending measure would happily remove. . . . We ought to do it at once," he added.[80]

On February 16, 1917, when the bill still awaited Senate action, the secretary of war summarized the administration's viewpoint. The whole moral dominance of the United States in the American Mediterranean was involved in the treatment of the Puerto Rican people, and the delays in Congress gave agitators the chance to claim U.S. neglect of the people's real interests. The contentment of the Puerto Rican people was "of the utmost importance if we are to soon face an international crisis. . . ." The delay filled him with apprehension.[81]

On February 20, the Senate finally passed the bill, with a modified prohibition amendment; on March 2, Wilson signed the new organic law of Puerto Rico expressing deep gratification. In just a few weeks war would be declared against Germany. Puerto Ricans could now join the regular army as American citizens and through legislation which paralleled the Jones Bill, the Puerto Rican Regiment was raised to full strength.[82] On March 9, 1917, Yager was already discussing the regiment's probable departure for Panama, while a start was made on forming the Puerto Rican militia.[83] Well could General McIntyre state in his 1917 bureau report:

The wisdom of these acts has been vindicated as measures of preparation for the present emergency. They have been accepted by the people most concerned as a timely recognition of their rights to self-government and as an additional evidence of the unselfishness of the American people in their relations with their newest territory.[84]

In 1897, the Puerto Rican liberals, led by Luis Muñoz Rivera, had made a pact in Spain to obtain autonomy for the island. But it was the imminence of war which finally impelled the Spanish government to grant the charter of November 1897. From 1910 to 1916, Muñoz Rivera had battled to extract home rule from a reluctant Congress. But it was the certainty of war with Germany that finally led the administration to insist on congressional action. A fact was emerging in the long and patient Puerto Rican struggle to achieve self-determination. The administration and the Congress could only pay real attention when the issues ceased to be internal and were related to the U.S. national security and its Caribbean hegemony.

It would take another 35 years and another world war to shake Congress from its lethargy and indifference to Puerto Rico's inalienable right to govern itself. By then both King Sugar and the proud claims of colonial tutelage were in deep trouble.

11

The Aftermath
of the Jones Act

The Jones Act, while liberalizing certain provisions of the Foraker Act, retained the substance of colonial tutelage. It granted Puerto Ricans American citizenship, which helped assuage many a guilty conscience among the tutors. An elective Senate enlarged the area of legislative self-government; it could now exercise some influence on the selection of certain cabinet officials. But presidential power remained paramount in the executive and judicial branches. The president still appointed the governor, the commissioner of education, the attorney general, the auditor, and the Supreme Court judges. Basic decisions on economics, education, justice, and security were still made in Washington. Furthermore, the Jones Act was no constitution; it was an act of Congress, which Congress could amend at will. "Congress," as Antonio Fernós Isern, a distinguished Puerto Rican political leader, once wrote, "continued to be an absolute sovereign, albeit a benevolent sovereign."[1] In this period, it was also an absent-minded sovereign, facing too many other issues to allow it to concentrate on the complexities of Puerto Rican life and politics, and with too few congressmen willing or able to understand their Caribbean wards.

The War Effort and Prohibition

The approval of the Jones Act, however, brought a period of good will. A few weeks after its passage, the United States declared war on

Germany. The people of Puerto Rico supported the war effort in many ways. Barceló, the first president of the new Senate, cabled President Wilson to apply the selective draft to Puerto Rico. Over 236,000 men were registered and nearly 18,000 selected. The Puerto Rican regiment became part of the regular army in May, 1917, and was sent to Panama with an enlistment of 4,000 men. The troops remaining in the island continued with their training in preparation for overseas service when armistice came. They also learned what racial segregation meant, as whites and blacks were separated. A national guard was also authorized. The citizenship granted by the Jones Act paved the way for these measures.

Puerto Rico also contributed to the war effort with generous support for the American Red Cross. A war fund of $112,000 was subscribed, and as the American writer, Knowlton Mixer, pointed out, two pounds of White House wool "were auctioned and sold at the highest price paid at any point in the United States." Not even New York could match that! In its army quota and in the purchase of over $10 million in Liberty Bonds the island ranked higher than many of the states and territories.[2] With great satisfaction, General McIntyre informed the secretary of war on June 30, 1918, "The outstanding feature in Insular affairs for the past year was the heartfelt display of patriotism of the people of our islands and their determined support of our war policies."[3]

There was especially a touch of pathos in the support from other sectors. De Diego, the spokesman for independence, which caused so much worry in Washington, had left for Spain after his clash with Muñoz Rivera to continue his cultural campaign for Antillean political unity based on Hispanic values. He had joined the Hispanicist wave of sympathy which in many places of the Caribbean and Latin America had developed due in a large measure to Spain's overwhelming defeat in 1898. In Madrid the leading intellectuals welcomed him as a modern prophet.

Despite his grief over Muñoz's death, De Diego returned to Puerto Rico intent on pursuing his cherished nationalist goal. He campaigned in 1917 for a plebiscite to be held in 1920 with the options of statehood or independence under a U.S. protectorate. He was encouraged by the plebiscite just held in the Danish West Indies in connection with the cession, and even more so by Wilson's moral preachings as the democratic leader of a nation at war.

Nothing in De Diego's writings expressed hate or rancor against the United States. In fact, De Diego, as Hostos before him, was a Caribbean forerunner of Wilson's international doctrine of self-determination. But neither Puerto Rico nor Washington was ready to understand him. Already a sick man, De Diego on November 6, 1917, appeared before the new House of Representatives to move that the resolution which embodied his plebiscite proposal be tabled. In a memorable speech he warmly defended his own ideas, while praising American democratic principles. It was the time, he said, to support the United States and the Puerto Rican soldiers who were ready to die on behalf of freedom. Rather than create any disturbance with his proposal, he would wait and support the United States in its epic struggle. Even at this critical hour, another of the "little islanders" was willing to rise above his own predilections to look with a Wilsonian view at the larger issues of war and peace. This was De Diego's political testament. On July 16, 1918, he died in New York after a cruel sickness; in the coming rough and tumble of Puerto Rican history, he would become the vivid symbol of the independence idea.[4]

During these years the Puerto Ricans never had a chance to express their status preferences in a plebiscite on the Wilsonian model, a subject of keen internal concern. But in a referendum in 1917, they were asked to do so on the external issue of prohibition. It was the promise of this referendum that removed the last obstacles to the approval of the bill. Prohibition was tied to American citizenship in the public mind, or to identification with the United States in an hour of crisis. The voters were asked to choose between the symbol of a bottle for legal liquor and a coconut for prohibition. The coconuts had it, 102,413 to 64,227. Voters, it was reported, were provided with coconut milk before casting their ballots. Thus rum was expelled from the island, despite its historical link with the Caribbean since the early eighteenth century trade with the Thirteen Colonies, and its contemporary revenues for the insular government.[5]

It was a pyrrhic victory for prohibition. Hard liquor now helped revive a time-honored Caribbean tradition: smuggling. The man of means could buy his bottles from a clandestine traffic that grew to great proportions. The poor man used molasses to ferment his *ron cañita,* a strong brew from a homemade still or *alambique.* The rum revenues were lost, but not the taste for rum or whisky. Prohibition became more than a social farce; it became a cultural aberration. It also left its imprint on local folklore. When someone had been fooled, it used to be said that he had been given coconut milk!

The administration's hopes that the Jones Act would still the troubled waters of the status question proved premature. To the Republicans, the attainment of American citizenship was a great victory. But they made it clear in their general assembly of May 14, 1917, that they wanted Congress to state explicitly that Puerto Rico was an incorporated territory, headed for statehood. They also demanded an elective governor and the suppression of the U.S. district court.[6]

The redoubtable Barbosa, now in the twilight of his life, reaffirmed his commitment to statehood as a senator and journalist. He was a strong partisan of what in the United States would be called the doctrine of states' rights. He understood the American federal system as a system in which the states were sovereign, and left only a fraction of their sovereignty in federal hands. He was convinced that the United States had ignored the principle of government by consent in Puerto Rico. In his debate with the independentists, Barbosa insisted that he too wanted independence, but real independence within the United States system. Independence under a protectorate, as De Diego suggested, meant intervention by the U.S. government, as was happening in Haiti and Santo Domingo, and had happened in Cuba. Barbosa preferred an elective Puerto Rican governor to the authority of a United States admiral and his marines. He had preached statehood in Puerto Rico, but seldom carried the fight personally to the United States and never became directly involved in the arena of prejudice, disdain, neglect, and misunderstanding which had been Muñoz Rivera's lot.

From the distance of Barbosa's beloved Caribbean island, the United States looked like an ideal blueprint for freedom which would not fail the Puerto Rican people. He preferred to play down the overpowering U.S. cultural nationalism and ethnocentric prejudices which were so influential in the relations with the island.[7] El Viejo de la Torre, the old man from the tower, as he was affectionately called, died on September 21, 1921. He had emerged from Puerto Rico's nineteenth century society, where a proud elite of generals, merchants, and hacendados had ruled over an illiterate mass of agregados (squatters) and peons; a colonial society little used to political democracy, yet flexible enough to allow a talented black man to lead a white man's party, something which in many sections of the American Union would have been totally unthinkable.

Throughout these years, the Unionist party maintained its position of preponderance. But it won the elections of 1917 and 1920 by smaller margins. In 1917, its majority over the combined votes of Republicans and Socialists was only 4,787 votes; in 1920, it was reduced to 3,461. Of the three parties, the Socialists were the rising star. They polled 24,468 votes in 1917 and 67,306 in 1920. Iglesia's constant hammering at social and economic issues was having its effect, particularly in the sugar cane areas, where conditions remained depressed despite the price bonanza of the war years. Attacked as "radical" and "subversive" by the Unionists, the Socialists kept growing under A.F. of L. protection while openly opposing the pro-independence stand of many Unionists.[8]

The new leadership of the Unionist party lacked Muñoz's powerful hold on the masses. The party now favored liberalization of the Jones Act through an elective governor, a measure which the new resident commissioner, Félix Córdova Dávila, promoted in Congress in 1919. Yager, who was very friendly with the Unionists, increased the number of Puerto Ricans in government and in 1919 could claim that of the 5,953 civil servants only 208, mostly teachers, were not natives of the country. He exulted in the progress he saw, which in his view, could "not be equalled by any people anywhere in the world in the same length of time." Carried away by his rhetoric, he assured both Puerto Ricans and Americans "that the next two decades will see even more wonderful progress and development."[9] "Marvelous," "wonderful," "remarkable," those were the glowing terms with which American presidential appointees were prophesying Puerto Rico's future.

But a change in the tutorial guard was coming. Warren S. Harding won the 1920 Presidential election to the great satisfaction of the local Republicans, and Yager, the pro-Unionist man, was out. After eight years in office, the longest term ever served by an American governor, Yager had some realistic advice for the Administration: Do not believe the Republicans' claim to be the only American loyal party; do not take too seriously the Unionist pro-independence rhetoric. Avoid selecting a superpatriot as governor who might drive the Unionists into an anti-American position. Be careful about the Puerto Ricans' feelings for their one-star flag.

These were wasted words. Harding saw the Puerto Rican governorship as a good tropical, political plum for a loyal friend. So on May 6, 1921, the plum went to a new tutor called Emmet Montgomery Reily.[10]

The Reily Nightmare

In American history, the Harding Administration is an embarrassment, an age of mediocrity and scandal. In Puerto Rican history the Emmet Montgomery Reily Administration is a nightmare, a throwback to the worst aspects of tutelage, canceling many of the gains made under Wilson. Reily in Puerto Rico, like many Harding men nationwide, tried to preach 100 percent Americanism and, in the name of a mythical, harmonious past, to persecute all forms of dissension. "America," the evangelist Billy Sunday proudly declared, "is not a country for a dissenter to live in."[11] To Montgomery Reily and to Harding, the Puerto Ricans' longings for independence and love for their flag were akin to treason.

Montgomery Reily came from Kansas City. He was a mortgage broker who knew little about government. About Puerto Rico, he knew nothing. Even before leaving Kansas City, he informed the Bureau of Insular Affairs that he would not work with any organization that was opposed to the president. At Harding's request, his Puerto Rican tutor was the old local Republican, Roberto H. Todd. In his memoirs, Todd claims that Harding himself asked him to be sure that Montgomery Reily followed the right path. Todd had already met the new governor and had seen for himself what an experienced Washington hand had told him, that Montgomery Reily was a "damn fool."[12]

As historian Truman R. Clark has pointed out, Reily had two outstanding characteristics: tactlessness and superpatriotism. His inaugural address keynoted both traits. His enemy was Puerto Rican separatism. He reminded the audience that there was no hope for Puerto Rican independence, no room for its supporters in Puerto Rico, and no room for other flags than Old Glory. Americanism also meant the supremacy of English in the schools. Reily came out strongly for statehood and also made clear that he despised any labor leader who professed socialism and created social strife. The speech was a blunt declaration of war on Puerto Rican dissenters from Harding's brand of 100 percent Americanism.[13]

The local Republicans, delighted at what seemed to be the "liquidation" of the Unionist party, eagerly supported Montgomery Reily. The Unionists took it as a bombshell. Barceló offered to resign rather than submit to what he called "a German-type colonial policy." The party refused and insisted that Barceló make clear to the governor the authority of the legislature by the people. When Barceló proposed some candidates, Montgomery Reily refused to accept the recommendation and sent the Unionist leader a tough letter. He would not be controlled by the local politicians. "Sever your connection with the independence party and become a loyal Porto Rican American, or we cannot have any friendly political relations," he wrote.

The Unionist's reply was to open a campaign against Montgomery Reily in Puerto Rico and the United States. The governor was supported by the Republicans and a group of continental Americans. A newspaper war ensued in which Reily would be praised by the Republicans but called "Darling Caesar," by the Unionists. In due time, however, Montgomery Reily alienated almost everybody. He communicated directly with the president, bypassing the Bureau of Insular Affairs, to the utter disgust of that old fox, General McIntyre. Reily's sweeping removal of Unionists from office and his attacks on Puerto Rican courts worried Secretary of War John W. Weeks. Reily hated Córdova Dávila, the resident commissioner, and warned the president not to see him alone since "every Porto Rican politician carried a pistol." To Reily, Ruerto Ricans were unsteady, unprincipled children. Not even Todd escaped his scorn. "Mr. Todd," Reily wrote Harding, "is a half-blooded Negro, and sometime ago deserted his wife and is living with a woman of the streets. Personally, I am quite friendly with him, but you can see that he is the kind of man I cannot associate with or consult with much."[14]

This was E. Montgomery Reily, whom the Puerto Ricans nicknamed *Moncho Reyes*, "Monty, the Superking." He embarrassed the administration, spent hardly any time in the island, and was criticized in Congress for his carpetbagging proclivities. Finally, a grand jury in San Juan charged him formally with the misuse of public funds. Harding defended Reily, but his days were numbered. Early in 1923, he resigned, and Harding, under pressure from Republicans in Congress, chose Horace Mann Towner who had helped steer the Jones Bill and had a reputation for tact, ability, and integrity, as the next governor.[15]

The Reily governorship was brief, but its ripples went far. It dramatized the clash between the elective Legislative Assembly and the executive, which was an instrument of American colonial tutelage. It emphasized the importance of the new Insular Senate and the political power of its president, who stood as the highest voice of Puerto Rican political leadership. It became a key position of partisan power, not to be lightly pushed aside by the Washington governors.

For the system to work, the appointed governors had to be willing to negotiate and cajole in the matter of appointments, to share power in certain limited areas. Paramount authority over key policies remained in federal hands, but a resolute Legislative Assembly could make life difficult for a tactless incumbent. The name of the game was mutual accommodation.

There were other ripples. Yager had predicted that an American superpatriot would stir the independence flame. Reily's tirade against independence and his persecution of the Puerto Rican flag had done just that. Under De Diego, independence did not entail anti-Americanism. After Reily, certain groups came to feel that Puerto Rico had to fight "Americanism" tooth and nail. For "Americanism" was not seen as a movement to stress democratic principles in government or as a drive to assert individual freedoms, but as a crude imposition of extreme American nationalism, with no room for dissent. The birth of the Nationalist party in Puerto Rico was a result.

In the face of unrelenting United States hostility to independence, the autonomist wing of the Unionists began looking for new forms of home rule. Influenced by the recently established Irish Free State and by the thoughts of Stimson and Frankfurter, as well as Puerto Rican jurists such as Luis Muñoz Morales. The concept was advanced of an *Estado Libre Asociado* (Free Associated State) a free, not an incorporated state, in association with the United States. A Unionist party delegation sent to Washington in 1922 persuaded Representative Philip Campbell, chairman of the Rules Committee, to introduce H.R. 9995, known as the Campbell Bill.

The bill provided for an elective legislature that would in turn elect the governor, who would choose his cabinet and appoint the Supreme Court judges with the advice of the Senate. It suggested two Resident Commissioners instead of one, and the appointment of a United States Commissioner to Puerto Rico. As Barceló wrote to Towner, the aim was to establish "a noble association of a permanent and indestructible character with the United States."[16]

Without administration support nothing came of this effort, except a breakthrough in the formulation of a theory of home rule that thirty years later would rise again under different historical circumstances.

Governor Towner came to Puerto Rico to pour oil on the troubled waters. He opposed independence and personally favored statehood, but he had learned from Reily's mistakes and realized that he needed to work with the Unionists in order to govern. His was the touch of the diplomat, not of the bully.

He had been on good terms with Córdova Dávila in Washington and accepted advice on cabinet appointments. He created much good will by replacing American-born officials with capable Puerto Ricans. Men like Guillermo Esteves in Interior, Carlos Chardón in Agriculture, Pedro N. Ortíz in Health, and Juan Gallardo in Treasury were outstanding public servants during the Towner period.[17]

Furthermore, Towner worked toward building up a political consensus on behalf of an elective governor. In 1923 a legislative commission, including Towner, visited Washington to lobby for an elective governor and for the extension to Puerto Rico of federal laws pertaining to vocational education, agriculture, and other matters of public welfare. Calvin Coolidge, the new president, was cool to the idea. The island was prosperous, he said, and the attitude should be one of contentment.[18] He did not support the elective governorship nor was he sympathetic to statehood. Inside Congress there was, as usual, a wide divergence of views, while in the Bureau of Insular Affairs, General McIntyre, still opposed to statehood, favored an elective governor by 1932, contingent upon a rise in the percentage of literacy in the electorate.[19] Reflecting the bureau's viewpoint, the bill actually passed the Senate and an elective governor bill was later sent to the House. There, a single representative, Guinn Williams of Texas, refused to give his unanimous consent to place the bill on the calendar. The measure, therefore, was sent back to committee where it lingered and died. A single arbitrary vote in Congress delayed a right for nearly a quarter of a century.

This narrow defeat shook some of the top political leadership in Puerto Rico, including Barceló and the new chairman of the Republican party, José Tous Soto. Both feared the growing strength of the Socialists; both came to think that neither statehood nor independence was a viable formula in Congress. Self-government, with an elective governor and broadened powers as suggested in the Associated Free State, seemed a more realistic goal. So on the way home, both leaders drafted a manifest on March 2, 1924.

The manifest called for an alliance or *Alianza* between the two parties. The formula was rather vague: "self-government to attain full Puerto Rican sovereignty within American sovereignty." Since status would not be an issue, the country's energies could turn to pressing social and economic problems. There were, among others, the agrarian problem, which required the control of latifundia and the redistribution of rural farms; the expansion of education and rural communications; protection of the coffee industry through tariff control; a full revision of the tax system to finance new schools, irrigation projects, industries, etc.[20]

The manifest led to a realignment of parties. Many Republicans refused to follow Tous Soto. Under Rafael Martínez Nadal, they promptly reached an understanding with the Socialists, and so the *Coalición* (Coalition) was born, based on their common adherence to statehood. In November, 1924, the *Alianza* triumphed over the Socialists and dissident Republicans combined, 163,041 to 90,479; but the Socialists again showed their strength by pulling 56,103 votes.

The Kaleidoscopic Era

Politics in Puerto Rico now entered a kaleidoscopic era. The shift to self-government and the shelving of independence did not please the ardent, young leadership emerging in the Unionist party. On the other hand, the rapprochement between the Socialists and Republicans would gradually dampen the old social fervor of the labor leaders as they became more absorbed in power squabbles than in labor proselytizing. Beneath these complex, shifting political loyalties, was the social question, the contradiction between dynamic progress in certain areas, in urban and professional growth; and the deepening crisis in the rural proletariat, especially in the coffee districts.

Towner was far from a progressive, populist governor. But under his governorship, awareness of the increasing social dislocation grew. His official reports began to present a more restrained view of Puerto Rican development. His concern for the uneven distribution of wealth led to a revamping of tax legislation. Conditions in the coffee areas and the price fluctuations of sugar were troubling.

Income tax reform took place with the help of a U.S. expert, Robert Murray Haig, a Columbia University professor. The principle was the higher the profit, the higher the tax; with a surtax on earnings over $10,000.[21] The near collapse of the industry was frankly discussed, with stress on the benefits of the federal land bank loans, which the Executive Council had blocked under the Foraker Act. During the Towner period, coffee cooperatives were greatly encouraged.[22]

Concern also prevailed about the sugar industry. By 1925, it was producing a record crop of 660,000 tons; three corporations alone controlled 43.6 percent of total production; large profits were assured and there had been wage increases, but they did not keep up with the rise in living costs. Obviously the conditions of farm labor had not improved in the last decade.[23] The situation called for strong remedies, but these were not forthcoming and the crisis was mainly attributed to population growth.

Even though Towner was no social reformer, his stiffer tax laws with *Alianza* support were firmly opposed by U.S. corporate interests and by many Republicans and local federal appointees. A joint effort was made to undermine the governor in Washington. The effort failed. Towner's tact and self-effacement kept him in the good graces of his superiors.[24] As a representative of a conservative, *laissez-faire* U.S. administration, he was not willing to change much. But neither would he preach strident 100 percent Americanism. No Ugly American like Reily, he was the Quiet American, a respectful and respected tutor.

His term did not end without a highly embarrassing episode that highlighted the deep chasm in understanding between official Washington and the Puerto Rican majority leadership. In 1928, Charles Lindbergh, fresh from his amazing feat, visited Puerto Rico. He was warmly received by the people in a joint ceremonial session of the Puerto Rican legislature. Barceló and Tous Soto decided to send a message to President Coolidge through the good offices of the Lone Eagle, as Lindbergh was called. In florid language they condemned Puerto Rico's colonial position and asked Coolidge to "grant us the freedom that you enjoy, for which you struggled, which you worship, which we deserve, and you have promised us." They also asked the president to grant Puerto Rico the advocacy of justice and self-determination which he had made at the Sixth Inter-American Conference in Havana.

This was waving a red rag before the Republican bull. The president had been quite cool to Puerto Rican requests. In his view, the islanders were inhabiting the best of all worlds, thanks to American generosity. In a letter to Towner on February 28, 1928, Coolidge made this clear. The status of Puerto Rico was far more liberal than any status in its entire history; he argued that Puerto Rico had more internal sovereignty than any state of the Union. The Treaty of Paris had promised nothing to Puerto Rico that had not been received. Coolidge pointedly reminded the Puerto Rican leadership that giving Puerto Rico greater liberty and powers of government "for the exercise of which its people are barely prepared can not, with propriety, be said to be establishing therein a mere subjected colony." After a long recital of all that in his view the American government had done for the island, the President advised those who spoke for Puerto Rico to limit "their petitions to those things which may be granted without a denial of such hope." Coolidge's letter glorified the *status quo*. He slammed the door shut on further reforms asked by the *Aliancista* leaders.[25]

Coolidge's reply incensed many sectors of public opinion in Puerto Rico. The so-called Pure Republicans under Todd, however, rallied to his support; many in the American business and corporate enclave were delighted. This public spanking, however, irritated the *Alianza*. In Washington, Córdova Dávila refuted the president's allegations in a long speech. In San Juan, Tous Soto and Barceló wrote another long statement, claiming the right to petition for political reform and followed it with a concurrent resolution asking for a congressional investigating committee.[26]

Coolidge's letter, aside from its blatant, self-righteous paternalism, was blind to the socioeconomic factors that were eroding the island's economic structure in spite of the impressive rise of statistics. The letter was written in February 1928. In less than two years Puerto Rico would be hit by two devastating hurricanes: one, *San Felipe,* a natural phenomenon; the other, the 1929 depression, a manmade disaster. The glaring social irregularities of the King Sugar era would tell more about the situation than the presidential rebukes.

12
The Plight of the 1930s

On September 13, 1928, Puerto Rico was hit by a devastating hurricane, *San Felipe*, with winds that may have reached 200 miles per hour. Its diagonal path across the island left no area unharmed. It was even stronger than *San Ciriaco*, although alert action by the authorities kept loss of life to only 300. But there was havoc everywhere. Over 250,000 homes were totally destroyed, one-third of the cane crop was lost, and fully half of the coffee trees were uprooted. Five hundred thousand people were left destitute and losses amounted to over $85 million.[1] The efforts to improve the coffee industry and reduce the plight of the upland areas received a grievous blow. More than ever, there was gloom and hopelessness among the *jíbaros* of Puerto Rico.

San Felipe marked the end of the era of flattering statistics. The era of dismal statistics then began. No longer would American officials talk, as Yager did, about the "marvelous" progress of Puerto Rico. Stark socioeconomic realities began to creep into the picture. What to do with Puerto Rico gradually became a puzzle to policy makers in Washington, bringing about a stream of studies and plans throughout the 1930s.

The Roosevelt Program

The turnaround came when the new president, Herbert Hoover, appointed Theodore Roosevelt, Jr., as governor to succeed Towner. This was the first governor known nationwide with a name and influential political connections. Hoover probably felt that the relationship between

Puerto Rico and the United States involved the Caribbean and Latin America, and that a man of Roosevelt's caliber would be a good listening post for Latin American reactions to American policies.[2] After Theodore Roosevelt, Jr., it took another Roosevelt, Franklin Delano Roosevelt, several years of trying experiences to learn that a governor for Puerto Rico should be a man of caliber and vision.

Roosevelt tackled his job with great zeal and gusto. Even before he arrived, he read voraciously about Puerto Rico and its problems and tried to learn instant Spanish. By the time of his inauguration, he was convinced that the island's chief troubles were economic and that great overpopulation in an agricultural community was the root of the trouble. While he was determined to try new policies, Roosevelt saw the outlook as gloomy. He also felt that the United States had been too complacent and resolved to tell the truth as he saw it.

With strong support from Hoover, Roosevelt was very much his own man in Puerto Rico. To understand his policies, we must understand his thinking. Like his illustrious father, he carried the "white man's burden." But he believed that white domination had reached a peak and that it would be impossible indefinitely to control and administer large alien populations. Either the home country changed its policies or the colony became independent. To him, as the writer Walter Lippman pointed out, the imperialistic dream of 1898 had proved to be unrealizable and the management of an empire by a democracy like the American democracy was impossible.[3]

Like his father, Roosevelt admired the British imperial system. But the crown colony model favored by Davis and Root did not attract him. Like Stimson, he found a model in the British dominions. The question was whether it could be applied to the relations between Puerto Rico and the United States.

In his book, *Colonial Policies of the United States* (*1937*), Roosevelt defended American policies toward Puerto Rico and the successes in administration, health, education, roadbuilding, and economic development. But he saw the shortcomings of the traditional policy to Americanize Puerto Rico: the refusal of American officials to speak Spanish, the assumption of cultural and racial superiority, and the domination of American capital. He found the rich coastal plain largely in the hands of big sugar companies, and the farmers forced back into the rugged interior. "Poverty," he claimed, "was widespread and hunger, almost to the verge of starvation, common."

Roosevelt surrounded himself with very able Puerto Ricans. He wanted action on the economic front and on the cultural front as well. He saw no reason in continuing what he called "the hopeless drive to remodel Puerto Ricans so that they should become similar in language, habits and thoughts to continental Americans." He felt that statehood implied an unbearable economic burden, if the island was to contribute to the federal treasury. A dominion status was the best, with the island realizing self-government within its borders.[4]

His program involved the promotion of vocational schools and rural

Kitchen in a rural household.

The plight of the 1930s: a barefoot child in school.

agricultural centers to help establish small farmers on land of their own; the creation of an independent Department of Labor, which he put under a respected Socialist, Prudencio Rivera Martínez; the enforcement of tax laws on wealthy citizens and absentee corporations; and the promotion of new manufacturing enterprises.[5]

Roosevelt's reliance on Puerto Rican abilities was significant in the education field. The Department of Education was headed by a liberal-minded educator, José Padín, who combined a solid U.S. educational background with deep attachments to the land and the people. Padín stated boldly that the *jíbaros,* anemic, needy, and sad, were three-fourths of the Puerto Rican *patria.* Their social and economic redemption was an educational problem, and, taking a page from the Mexican Revolution, he believed that the revolution had to be accomplished in the school. He pleaded for an industrialization program which should be based on an educational effort, for rural schools as centers of social rehabilitation, and for Puerto Rico to appoint its own commissioner of education and chart its educational policies. He defended the vernacular as basic to Puerto Rican cultural growth, but insisted on the acquisition of English as essential to relations with the United States. Padín's educational philosophy brought him sharp criticism from the Republicans and the partisans of assimilation, who labeled him anti-American. His identification with the American ideals of social liberalism, on the other hand, brought him under attack from the emerging anti-American sectors.[6]

Under Roosevelt, the achievements and failures of colonial tutelage were coming under more realistic appraisal. Some of the programs initiated or proposed pointed to the future. But, in the end, the effort foundered badly.

When the 1929 depression hit the island, the conditions of the masses were already deplorable, according to a 1930 Brookings Institution Report which was, if anything, politically conservative. The average income of rural workers was barely $150 a year. Earnings of the town workers were slightly better, but prices were not responsive to wages, particularly since much food and clothing were imported from the United States. The report stated that the population "had outrun the capacity of the present economic resources and organization to furnish full employment and satisfactory living conditions." Four out of five rural workers were landless and there was appalling poverty and disease, particularly after the hurricane.[7]

On the other hand, the 500-acre limitation imposed in 1900 was a myth. By 1917, 477 individuals, partnerships, and corporations pos-

The slums called El Fanguito *characterized the hard times of the 1930s.*

sessed more than 500 acres with an aggregate of 537,193 acres or over 26 percent of all rural lands.[8] These were among the best lowlands in the country; the cane area increase at the expense of pasture lands and minor crops was estimated at 262 percent since 1896! Surplus labor in Puerto Rico had little bargaining power with these voracious latifundia. But profits soared for the sugar trusts, especially for the absentee companies which controlled 59 percent of the wealth. South Porto Rico's steady dividends were estimated on preferred stock from 4 to 115 percent; Central Aguirre's were 35 percent in 1929. These profits, as Professor Bailey W. Diffie pointed out, were "a veritable Drake's treasure."[9]

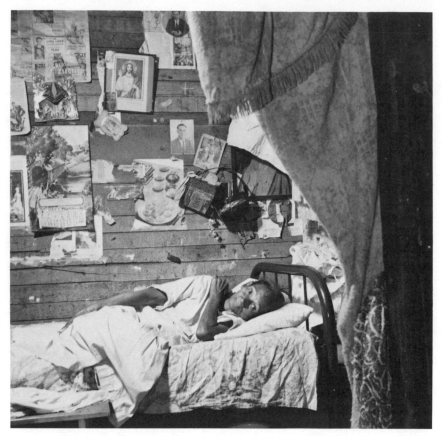

Illness at home during the 1930s.

Conditions in Puerto Rico could not improve without a profound structural change. This was impossible in a system of colonial tutelage based on a conservative *laissez-faire* philosophy. Furthermore, change required a coherent political drive from Puerto Rico itself, and this was lacking. Instead, political confusion and disintegration were the rule, leading to sharpening polarizations.

The *Alianza* had won the 1928 elections, but only by 9,410 votes. The coalition's power was growing. But the union envisaged by Tous Soto and Barceló never materialized. The hard core of Republicans, under Martínez Nadal, strengthened their pact with the Socialists. The cement was their commitment to statehood and their opposition to independence. Within the Alliance, two trends appeared. The old pro-independence wing now had the support of a fervent generation of leaders who deeply resented all aspects of colonial tutelage. The moderates preferred autonomy. A showdown with the independence wing was inevitable. If keeping both wings under control had been extremely difficult for Muñoz Rivera, it was impossible for Barceló, a sincere, vibrant man of rugged honesty, but too given to emotional shifts.

By the end of 1929, the Alliance was in shambles, a marriage of convenience that had failed. Most of its Republican members now returned to the old party, along with some of the more conservative Unionists. There was a resurgence of the Unionist party, this time under the spell

A child's funeral during the 1930s.

of independence. This trend towards polarization produced chaos in the Legislative Assembly.

Roosevelt found it difficult to reach an accommodation with such shifting political leadership, more than ever dominated by *personalismo*. He gradually lost interest in the intricacies of Puerto Rican politics and began to look towards his next goal: the governorship of the Philippine Islands. By the time he obtained it in 1931, he had grown sick and tired of the politicians and the people themselves.

Roosevelt left an able man, James R. Beverley, as acting governor. Years afterwards, in a private exchange of letters discussing the Puerto Rican celebration of the *Día de la Raza* (or Columbus Day), Beverley claimed it was common for Puerto Ricans to say, "*Somos nobles por naci-miento*," (We are noble by birth). Roosevelt supposedly snorted: "*Nobles por nacimiento? Sinverguenzas por nacimiento*" (shameless by birth), "that is what it should be. . . . I don't know anything more comic and irritating than Puerto Rico."[10] Thus exited the man who had been the most philanthropic and most dynamic of the tutors. After a third of a century of dominant tutelage, little was being achieved in interpersonal, intercultural understanding. The economy made it crucial to formulate policies to free Puerto Rico from want and exploitation. But it was also crucial to free Puerto Rico from degrading cultural stereotypes. The United States had the capacity to plan an economic and social strategy, but the second need required an insight into the distinctive worth of each human society, and respect and tolerance for social diversity, traits that could hardly be learned in the self-gratifying climate of Manifest Destiny and the messianic conviction of the superiority of the American gospel.

If any one factor galled many Puerto Ricans, it was this implicit notion of the proud superiority of everything American. The old generation had begun to fight this assumption which permeated education as well as politics. The generation of the 1930s was much more aggressive and critical. Its protest would be sharper, and in its more uncompromising elements, it would turn to revolutionary tactics.

The Critique of Tutelage

Certain factors helped shape the critique of American colonial tutelage during this period. The immediate, overriding one was the economic depression and the near starvation in many areas. Another was the success of one of the most important U.S. tutorial initiatives: the founding and development of the University of Puerto Rico. In 1925, under Towner, it had been finally organized as a university, not a normal school, under the direction of Thomas C. Benner, a distinguished American educator, and one of the ablest tutors.

At the university, students could read John Dewey on educational philosophy; keep abreast of the U.S. social sciences; come in contact with the brilliant writers of Spain, such as Miguel Unamuno and José Ortega y Gasset, who were transforming Spanish thought; or they could read the deeds of the Mexican Revolution and meet one of its intellectual mentors, José Vasconcelos. Few U.S. colleges and universities of the size, scant resources, and great limitations of the University of Puerto Rico could provide such diverse offerings. The contrast with the platitudes of the pervading colonial reality fanned the flames of protest and dissension among many of the upcoming young leaders.

Another influence was exerted by Puerto Ricans, largely trained in the United States, who had returned to the island. Like Barbosa in the late nineteenth century, other Puerto Ricans became familiar with U.S. history and society. Two of them brought the rationale for independence. One was Pedro Albizu Campos; the other, Luis Muñoz Marín. Their influence would loom large for the rest of the century.

Pedro Albizu Campos was born in Ponce in 1893 of a mixed marriage. A Masonic lodge gave him a scholarship to the University of Vermont in 1912, and for the next nine years he studied in the United States, including six years at Harvard studying engineering, chemistry, letters, and law. His education was interrupted by the war. Drafted at Cambridge in 1918, he was transferred to Puerto Rico for training and emerged a first lieutenant at the end of the conflict. He went back to Harvard, where he received his law degree in 1923.[11]

At Harvard, Albizu distinguished himself as a bright, intense student who gradually shifted to law and international relations and became very interested in world liberation trends. Boston was the place to study, particularly the Irish Republican movement, the *Sinn Fein*. The intransigence of the Irish in fighting British rule must have impressed him deeply. He also saw and perhaps experienced American racial prejudice. Unlike Barbosa, he did not absorb an undying faith in American political institutions; In time, his reaction was the very opposite and the United States and its institutions were the object of a fiery, uncompromising attack.

The revolutionary came into full bloom gradually. Upon his return to Puerto Rico, Albizu gravitated towards the *Alianza*. His early lectures and writings in 1923 were skilled, well-documented attacks on the Barbosa notion, so strongly held by the Republicans, that the American states had full sovereignty with only a fraction of it left to the federal government. Albizu refuted this idea, emphasizing the dominant role of the federal government in American history. Each state, he claimed, was dominated by Anglo-Saxon views and traditions, and no state had been admitted into the Union until this domination had been established. Puerto Rico with its long history, peculiar civilization, and high population density did not fit the system.[12]

What to do, then? His answer was that Puerto Ricans should meet in a constitutional convention. They could then petition for statehood because it was their inalienable right, but it would be suicide for Puerto Rico's personality and Congress would refuse because of ethnic and cultural differences. Albizu was inclined towards dominion status based on the Canadian or Irish model. He wrote:

American citizenship makes permanent the harmonious relationship between both countries and is no obstacle to complete sovereignty for Puerto Rico. The British Empire has just put to an end the conflict between local sovereignty in its dominion and the necessary imperial cohesion. The solution has surprised the world, because it admits local sovereignty in spite of British citizenship. Canada, Australia, South Africa, and Ireland have joined the League of Nations as equals among the peoples of the world, by virtue of the most perfect recognition granted by England, the mother country. . . .[13]

He praised Tous Soto and Barceló for their joint initiative and asked them to include the Socialists in what he felt was a breakthrough in the island's collective inertia.

Albizu probably hoped to be an Alliance candidate in the coming elections. If so, he was soon disappointed because something happened between April and May 1924. He suddenly turned against the *Alianza* when he realized that the selections of candidates was tightly controlled and that the idea of a constitutional convention was put aside. He felt that Washington was committed to a do-nothing policy on the status question while the political leaders had shelved independence.[14]

Other Puerto Ricans had felt like Albizu and had established the Nationalist party in 1922 to keep the old flame burning. But Albizu was, in his intensity and background, a different man. To him, nationalism became a mystique, a religion, a way to justify one's existence. It could not thrive in the narrow confines of local political squabbles, but must look for friends and allies beyond Puerto Rico in the anti-imperialistic circles of the Caribbean and Latin America.

So Albizu joined the Nationalist party and went on a cultural pilgrimage in 1927, as De Diego had done ten years before. He visited Santo Domingo, Haiti, Cuba, Mexico, Panama, Peru, and Venezuela, returning to Puerto Rico in 1930. Everywhere he went, he looked for anti-imperialist groups critical of Dollar Diplomacy and American interventionist policies. At this stage, he was influenced by José Vasconcelos with his defense of Latin America as *la raza cósmica* (the cosmic race), the Indian revival, and his stern opposition to the United States. Albizu returned convinced that there should be no compromise with Washington and that the creation of a vigorous national conscience was the first priority.

His first task was to consolidate the party. He did this by completely dominating its General Assembly and becoming the new president in May 1930. Then he began a strenuous campaign of lectures and speeches in which independence for Puerto Rico was only part of a movement toward an Antillean Confederation and the eventual creation of what he called the Ibero-American Union. He did not abandon his idea of a constitutional convention, but now it would proclaim a free, sovereign republic which he felt could be done through the electoral process. The ideology became more and more defined: the fight was against annexionism and there was no nationalism outside the Nationalist party. The party was the fatherland's shield; it was the nation organized to recover its sovereignty. This was not rhetoric. The Yankee was the enemy.

Throughout 1930, people went to hear Albizu, particularly the professional groups, the students, and the critics of the system. His sharp, staccato phrases; his terse sentences; his clear, merciless logic; and biting tongue enraptured his audiences. It was a new type of thought, with no stilted language and no flowery endings.

But it was still within the bounds of democratic persuasion. Albizu wanted to destroy the system by working from within, no matter how hard-hitting and shocking the propaganda. His listeners came from many parts of the political spectrum. He drew attentive crowds, but when it came to voting, they shied away from his vehemence and deserted him. At the 1932 elections, he received slightly over 11,000 votes and the party 5,257 votes out of 383,722 votes cast. From thereon, Albizu lost all hope in the democratic process. He now saw his party, not as a mere political organization, but as an army of patriots with 5,000 soldiers. This militancy required an iron-handed control of party affairs, an authoritarian command, and unquestioned obedience.

With Albizu Campos, a revolutionary style aimed at violent confrontation emerged in Puerto Rican politics. With Luis Muñoz Marín, another revolutionary style came into its own, more akin to a social democratic upsurge, based on mass electoral action through vigorous personal effort. For both movements, the 1930s were the breeding ground for their claims to leadership. Both worked against a backdrop of decaying colonialism and economic crisis. Both were the prophets of doom for King Sugar.

Luis Muñoz Marín was the son of Luis Muñoz Rivera. Born on February 18, 1898, a few days before the Spanish-American War broke out, he inherited a great name and a distinguished political tradition. He was, therefore, born into the world of public life and influenced by the long Puerto Rican struggle to achieve self-government and self-dignity. But he was not to play the dutiful role of a successor, reaping the advantages of a political inheritance. He was a man in search of his own answers, his own style, and his own personality. A powerful bond linked him to his father's times; but he also felt the need to go out into the world and carve a name for himself.

Muñoz Marín spent much of his first thirty years in the United States as a student and as a struggling writer and concerned intellectual. In contrast with Albizu, he was never an academic man nor did he achieve a professional education. A gifted poet and journalist he committed himself early to the social question. Like many of his generation in the United States, he was attracted by populism, socialism, and the fight against big business. But his heart was in Puerto Rico, and the social issue most troubling to him was the plight of the *jíbaro*. His closest friends were in the island and there was also, in the background, the memory of those brief adolescent years which he spent with his father in Washington when he learned so much about the anguish of that man in the cold halls of Congress.[15]

By 1920, Muñoz Marín was a socialist of the Fabian type, influenced by the traditions of social democracy. Returning to Puerto Rico, he joined Iglesias and the Socialist party in the campaign, scandalizing the Unionists. He brought to the Socialists an intellectual dimension that was lacking among the tough leaders of a movement which was challenging the economic *status quo*. But Muñoz Marín could not accept Iglesias's deal with the Republicans and broke with him, returning to the States. He lived as a creative writer with works in leading publications like *The Nation* and *The American Mercury*. In a style full of Shavian wit and humor he would occasionally pound away good-naturedly at Puerto Rican foibles and the pretentious tutelage of the United States.

In 1925, he wrote:

You cannot consider the most articulate portion of the Porto Rican soul without getting the suggestion that it is afflicted with an inferiority complex. In an island where nothing grand ever happened, everything happens in the grand manner. . . . Street-corner meetings are grandiose, the applause at the end of a well-turned paragraph is invariably "delirious," any American Congressman is "the great statesman," verbose political spellbinders are always called great "orators" and frequently "nightingales!" I have been called sublime for donating two dollars to a worthy cause.[16]

But there was a keener edge in his writings by 1929:

By now the development of large absentee-owned sugar estates, the rapid curtailment in the planting of coffee. . . . and the concentration of cigar manufacturing in the hands of the American trust, have combined to make Puerto Rico a land of beggars and millionaires, of flattering statistics and distressing realities. . . . It is now Uncle Sam's second largest sweat-shop.[17]

In 1931, Muñoz Marín returned to Puerto Rico, this time to stay. He arrived in the middle of the political crisis when the Unionist party, having split from the *Alianza,* found itself without a legal name and had to register again as the Liberal party. It was the time when the depression was adding its own burdens to the woes of *San Felipe.* Muñoz Marín was now a definite asset to the party. He was also a friend of Roosevelt, Jr., and had praised his official policies in the American press. He was no longer a fiery young Socialist, but a mature leader, committed to a fight against absentee ownership and colonial tutelage. He was also a nationalist who believed that the Unionist shift toward independence was the solution. But he wanted mass action through democratic means, with the new Liberal party as the spearhead of the effort. He criticized American policies, but did not see the United States as the enemy. These were his views as he began to lead the new progressive forces in Puerto Rico.

The Arrival of the New Deal

In November 1932, Herbert Hoover was utterly repudiated by the American electorate. Hoover had taken more interest in the island than most other Presidents. He had appointed Roosevelt, Jr., a national figure, and supported his unorthodox ways. When Roosevelt left, he appointed Beverley, a quiet, efficient, dedicated man who knew Spanish and was the only American governor to make Puerto Rico his home. He had appointed the brightest and most committed commissioner of the whole tutelage period, Padín, who happened to be a Puerto Rican. Furthermore, Hoover was the first president to visit the island since Theodore Roosevelt. In his four troubled years in office, Hoover had shown a surer hand in selecting governors than almost all of his predecessors; it would take Franklin Delano Roosevelt many years to match Hoover's experience.

As Roosevelt was defeating Hoover in 1932, the Coalition was winning a close fight in Puerto Rico. The *Union Republicana* (Republican Union) obtained 110,794 votes; the Socialists received 97,438; the Liberal party got 170,168; and the Nationalists only 5,257. The electorate grew as women who could read and write were enfranchised. The Liberals were the main party, but the combined forces of the Coalition gave them a 38,000 majority.[18] Just before the elections, on September 26, 1932, another hurricane, *San Ciprián,* wrought great destruction, adding to the island's economic adversity.

The return of the Democrats to power was seen as good news. Many still hoped that a Puerto Rican would be chosen as governor; others considered an American who knew Spanish and had good connections an acceptable second best. But the governor, as a federal appointee, was supposed to be free from political influences. Could such a Puerto Rican be found? Certainly Dr. Padín would have qualified, but he had been attacked by the Coalition which was linked with the stateside Republicans.

While speculation ran wild in the island, Robert Hayes Gore of Fort Lauderdale, Florida, was appointed governor on April 27, 1933. As the historian Thomas G. Mathews has pointed out, the nomination "arrived on the unsuspecting Puerto Rican scene like the announcement of a visit of a Tibetan Lama."[19] Gore had been a newspaper editor in Terre Haute, Indiana; had later prospered in the insurance business, had retired to Florida, was a devout Roman Catholic, and had written a 1920 editorial predicting that FDR would someday be president. He may have been qualified to run his local Chamber of Commerce but running Puerto Rico was a different matter. To him, and to the island, it became "Gore's hell."

Even before his arrival, Gore had promised a dynamic program matching Roosevelt's Hundred Days. He favored more trade with Florida, cockfighting, and statehood. This last brought rejoicing to the Coalition leaders, while the Liberals dissented. The Bureau of Insular Affairs, always the vigilant tutor, had to tell the governor that Puerto Rico was not prepared for that status.

But these were just a few clouds on the horizon. Things began to warm up when it became known that Jim Farley, the king maker, was recommending two women for posts in Puerto Rico: Mrs. Jean Whittemore and Mrs. Henry Dooley, who had been active in the small Democratic state committee that had supported Roosevelt. Mrs. Whittemore was to be commissioner of Education; Mrs. Dooley, to head Immigration. The idea that the unqualified Mrs. Whittemore would supplant Padín sounded preposterous.

La Democracia protested and the War Department objected, but Gore and Farley supported Mrs. Whittemore. Like Riley before him, Gore was dead set against Puerto Rican independence. He refused to deal with the Liberals, and even thought of promoting a Democratic party in Puerto Rico to simplify the tangled disputes.[20] Furthermore, misinterpreting a letter from the Bureau, Gore announced that for all his appointments he would require an undated resignation to control the position at any moment he might believe convenient, in line with the President's policy. When this became known in Washington, Ruby Black, the alert reporter for *La Democracia,* wired that the president denied such a policy, and that it sounded to him "like a fairy tale."[21]

Thus patronage, that hallowed goal of partisan politics, was the first step of Gore's downfall. The Coalition praised him, especially since he not only spanked the Liberals, but promoted cockfights to attract tourists, and cockfighting was Martínez Nadal's favorite sport.

A succession of minor issues rapidly created a negative atmosphere for Gore. *La Democracia* was now headed by Luis Muñoz Marín, with his Washington and stateside connections. The paper's attacks turned vitriolic. Gore, fresh from his initial *faux pas,* now turned to a favorite subject: dropping Padín before his term expired and imposing a new version of "100 percent Americanism" by recommending the appointment of José Gallardo, a Puerto Rican professor at Charleston College, who was supported by the mayor of Charleston and the Chamber of Commerce, but was completely unknown in the island.

Picking a fight with Padín proved a false move. Padín was good friends with Mr. and Mrs. James Bourne, who were close to Mrs. Eleanor Roosevelt, and Mrs. Roosevelt, of course, had the ear of the president.

Gore also tried to strengthen the Coalition's hold on the university by appointing a socialist, Rafael Alonso Torres, to the board of trustees. Perhaps, under other circumstances, a Socialist trustee would have been considered a good idea. There were several socialists who were respected for their intellectual attainments. Alonso was a tough, hard-working party leader. He was a good organizer and deeply concerned with the deplorable conditions of the masses. But he had an ax to grind about the university. It was rumored that he was intent on removing the Liberals from the institution. When the students objected to his appointment, he derided them and wrote a piece satirizing them. The answer was a students' strike. The Liberal party used this opportunity to the hilt.

When a student delegation called on the governor to present their viewpoints, he first refused. Until then, the students had opposed Alonso, not Gore. But Gore's reaction was so negative and his handling of the situation so inept that the students rapidly turned against him too.

What happened next was unusual. Until now, the university's occasional strikes or students' protests had hardly concerned the general public. But the strike against Alonso and Gore galvanized people all over the island. Meetings were held in every important town, and a mass meeting at Río Piedras, the university town, that brought together nearly 10,000 people. The students' strike released all the pent-up frustrations of this period. Alonso finally had to resign, almost a nervous wreck.[22]

Gore continued to defend Alonso in Washington and to attack Padín, actually issuing an ultimatum: Padín's stay was incompatible with his own position. But Roosevelt refused to replace the commissioner, and wanted Padín to finish his term. Mrs. Roosevelt, who now took an intense personal interest in Puerto Rico, came to the conclusion that Gore had neither the personality nor the tact for his post. Gore had lost the Washington battle. His parting was only a matter of time. A way had to be found to remove him without loss of face. Dr. Ernest Hopkins, president of Dartmouth College, was sent to find this way.

A liberal and independent educator, Hopkins heard everybody, including the students, the politicians, and the civic groups. He concluded that Gore was honest, but "probably the worst blunderer that ever came along . . ." He cautioned Washington not to identify too much with the Coalition which was dominated by "sordidly acquisitive groups." Early in 1934, Gore, having heard of this report, resigned. To the secretary of War he suggested that the only governor who could be successful would be one who had a long association with the people of Puerto Rico, who knew them well, and could assimilate their "moods and mysteries."[23] This sound, sincere advice was probably Gore's best service to both Puerto Rico and the United States.

But the administration cared more about saving face and establishing order. Rather than choosing a candidate sensitive to the "moods and mysteries" of Puerto Ricans, their choice was the adjutant general of the War Department, Blanton Winship of Georgia.

The New Deal: Relief, Rehabilitation, and Reaction

The story of the New Deal in Puerto Rico (1933–1938) is complex, involving a large-scale relief and rehabilitation effort for a people in desperate straits, an effort which foundered in a human morass of misunderstandings, violence, and recriminations. Most of the characters in this historic drama ended up bitterly attacking each other, while the great socioeconomic issues remained largely unresolved. And yet the ideas, methods, and techniques proposed or tested then had a profound effect on the future development of the island.

The American government was aware of the plight of Puerto Rico before the Roosevelt Administration. Teddy Roosevelt, Jr., had forcefully brought the matter before official and public attention. But the federal government was hardly responsive to his pleas. Under Franklin Delano Roosevelt, the situation was different, for helping Puerto Rico to its feet was but one more aspect of the commitment to use government action to get the nation out of the doldrums of the depression.

Devising a socioeconomic program would take time; but more was needed: a clear perception of the ticklish political picture, a willingness to face the status issue fairly and realistically, and wisdom in the choice of presidential appointees. These were sadly lacking at first. The governors FDR chose during the 1930s were among the worst ever appointed. Gore was a political misfit; Blanton Winship was characterized as the wrong man at the wrong time in the wrong place; Admiral William D. Leahy had professional merits, but was a wartime appointment; and Guy Swope (1941) was an obscure and undistinguished politician, a "nice guy," at most.

This gallery of mediocre men with no special training or background in dealing with a people of Latin American extraction, with no knowledge of the culture and the language, had to face a Puerto Rican political scenario in which the Socialist party, by allying itself with conservative Republicans, had lost much of its zest for economic reform. Its founder, Iglesias, now resident commissioner in Washington, could hardly lead a forceful fight for his old program in the island. But the Socialist votes had put a Coalition in power, and the Republican Union leader, Rafael Martínez Nadal, was the island's real *cacique*. Martínez Nadal was a contradiction; born in Puerto Rico and reared in Spain, he spoke very little English, yet he supported a return to 100 percent Americanism. He was particularly ill suited, by training and temperament, to face the New Dealers. His political counterpart was Barceló, who had seen the *Alianza* collapse and was haunted by his failure to preserve Muñoz Rivera's political inheritance. If Martínez Nadal was swayed by the conservative forces, fundamentally opposed to the New Deal, Barceló was rocked by the surge for independence and the challenges of Muñoz Marín and Albizu Campos.

From 1933 to 1936, Muñoz Marín, through his contacts in Washington, was the New Deal's golden boy. He had friends and knew his way around; the spirit of innovation and experimentation in Washington suited him nicely. Eloquent, witty, and articulate, he could hold his own with the New Deal intellectuals who dreamed of reshaping the American republic. Unlike Barceló, Martínez Nadal, and Iglesias, Muñoz was not a quaint Latin, but one of the boys. This relationship was not to last, and by 1936 the honeymoon was over.

The first phase of the New Deal in Puerto Rico encompassed relief of unemployment through public works, the Federal Emergency Relief Administration (FERA), and the National Recovery Act (NRA). A problem immediately arose, particularly in industry, of whether Puerto Rico should pay the U.S. federal wages or should instigate a wage differential. It was a simple problem. Prices were going up on what the poor people bought, but the wages, especially in the needlework industry, were at sweat-shop levels. Wages had to go up as a matter of social justice, but if they rose to mainland levels, factories would close and more people would be out of work. This wage dilemma haunted many federal initiatives in Puerto Rico.

In Puerto Rico, FERA—locally known as PRERA—was headed by James Bourne. He and his wife Dorothy had been neighbors of the Roosevelts, and were deeply committed to the New Deal. From 1933 to 1936, Bourne directed the relief side, the PRERA, with great devotion, in spite of political storms. PRERA was designed to alleviate the grave economic ills under the rules formulated in Washington.

The need for relief was greatly increased in 1934 when the Costigan-Jones Act put sugar production on a quota basis and paid bonuses to land owners for not growing cane. But the act made no provision for agricultural workers who lost their jobs. Though the Bournes selected and trained Puerto Ricans in several aspects of social welfare, established free maternal health clinics, investigated some of the incredible poverty

Waiting in line for free food distribution during the Puerto Rican relief (PRERA) period.

of the countryside, promoted public works, fostered home truck gardens, and encouraged canning centers and rural cooperatives, they merely scratched the surface. Because he employed Liberals, Bourne was declared a public enemy of Puerto Rico by the Legislative Assembly in 1935.[24]

With the cutback in sugar production came the opportunity to find new sources of wealth and employment to break the domination of King Sugar. Muñoz Marín had been pressing for this goal, and a new generation of Puerto Rican technocrats had new answers to the economic and colonial blight of the island. As Muñoz wrote Mrs. Roosevelt:

It was a generation educated in the United States, wanting to fight hunger with social justice and to break the stronghold of land monopoly, restore the soil to the people who work it, diversify crops, and foster industrial development to help support the relatively enormous population. It wants to give dignity and purpose to political action.[25]

Muñoz thought of formulating a general economic plan for the island based on these ideas. A key element was to enforce the 500-acre limitation and set up a land distributing agency. Agrarian reform—the old Latin American dream, the heritage of the Mexican revolution—became a desired goal. Muñoz found an ally in Mrs. Roosevelt, who visited the island in March 1934. Turning her back on the governor's palace, she went into the slums and the impoverished areas and, as Ruby Black later wrote, was astounded to find cleanliness in the people and "a sense of self-reliance and worth of the individual" among the most poverty-stricken. The assistant secretary of Agriculture, Rexford Guy Tugwell, who accompanied her, was also shocked, but his impressions were not so positive. He wrote to Henry Wallace:

I rather dislike to think that our falling fertility must be supplemented by these people. But that will probably happen. Our control of the tropics seems to me certain to increase immigration from here and the next wave of the lowly . . . succeeding the Irish, Italians, and Slavs . . . will be these mulatto, Indian, Spanish people from the south of us. They make poor material for social organization but you are going to have to reckon with them.

In a few years, Tugwell would be in a position to revise this derogatory judgment and do something about its implications.[26]

The visitors left with the realization that Puerto Rico needed rehabilitation, not relief, and a profound structural change, not palliatives. The collapse of one of the sugar companies, United Porto Rico Sugar Company, offered a possible opening for socializing the industry. Truck farming, diversified agriculture, the beginning of a real manufacturing program, and birth control were also advocated. A Puerto Rican Commission was created, headed by Chancellor Carlos Chardón who gave his name to the plan which finally evolved in 1934.

A series of complex moves followed, including the transfer of Puerto Rican affairs from the War Department to Interior in 1934, and the establishment of an Inter-Departmental Committee. It was the first determined effort to reshape a colonial economy that had been left to itself for a third of a century; an economy largely based on absentee ownership with a landless proletariat, swelling slums, and rising unemployment.

Though a public corporation was needed, there were bureaucratic delays in Washington and political opposition in Puerto Rico. The Coalition saw that this program would be run according to Washington directives with federal funds, and with the enthusiastic participation of the Liberals. To them, it was an intolerable intrusion by the federal government that denied them patronage and a significant role in reconstruction. Their conservative elements feared the innovative proposals. Governor Winship was a reactionary army man, unhappy with the dreams of social reformers. His solution was to make Puerto Rico a tourist paradise. Within the Liberals there was jealousy of Muñoz Marín, too rapidly becoming the charismatic new leader with the blessings of his Washington friends.[27]

Action began when Secretary Harold Ickes appointed Dr. Ernest H. Gruening, the managing editor of *The Nation* and a well-known Latin Americanist, to head the new division of Territories. Gruening knew Muñoz and turned to him for advice on Puerto Rico. Other leaders concerned with the island showed their support for the young Liberal leader. Even the president used Muñoz to communicate his firm determination to promote the Chardón Plan to the Puerto Rican people. To the dismay of the Coalition, Chardón, Muñoz's friend, was named regional administrator. The appointment of Benigno Fernández García as attorney general signified that legal action would be taken to break up the landholdings of the great absentee companies.

But this social and economic revolution was to fail. Running a program with Washington directives was not an easy matter. Gruening clashed with Bourne and disagreed with Winship. Bourne was removed, but Winship held his ground. Gruening next engaged in a battle of mutual accusations with the Coalition. By early 1936, however, the Puerto Rican Reconstruction Administration, the PRRA, was moving under Chardón. Then the Nationalists struck.

Between 1933 and 1935, Albizu's campaign had gained stridency and revolutionary purpose. His nationalist creed was not based simply on the cultural and historic values he had praised in his 1930 political crusade. His rhetorical fury now turned against all *"yankis."* He considered Roosevelt a dictator with a despotic hold over Puerto Rico. He claimed he had a revolutionary army of 5,000 men to oppose the hated invader.[28] When Roosevelt made a short visit to the islands in 1934, the Nationalists called him *persona non grata.* For a while, Albizu seemed to rely on the workers, warmly supporting strikes of cab drivers and sugar cane workers in 1934. But his favorite instrument was his closely knit, fervent group of black-shirted Nationalists who idolized him.

Some of these came from the University, but the students, as a whole, were not drawn to Albizu. When he bitterly assailed them in a speech in October, 1935, the students felt insulted and held a protest meeting. Tempers ran high and bloodshed was feared. At the entrance to the university, a car full of Nationalists was intercepted by the police and a gun battle occurred leaving a policeman wounded and three Nationalists dead. At their burial, Albizu accused the governor and the chief of police, Francis E. Riggs, of planning the murder of the Nationalists and promised to avenge them. On February 23, 1936, Riggs was shot by two young Nationalists, Hiram Rosado and Elías Beauchamp. At police headquarters, both were immediately killed by the police. These double murders started a fateful string of events.[29]

Those events stirred strong feelings in the American government. Governor Winship resolved to get Albizu behind bars; Dr. Gruening supported Winship and asked Muñoz Marín in Washington to condemn Riggs's shooting. An influential senator, Millard Tydings of Maryland, who was Riggs's friend, decided to push a bill for independence. In Puerto Rico, there was shock at the killing of the chief of police, but also profound concern at the way the police had taken the law into their own hands. Sensing these mixed feelings, Muñoz Marín wrote a letter to the Washington Post expressing his "unqualified condemnation" of the murder of Riggs, but refusing to take a one-sided view, considering the highhanded methods of the police.[30]

This was the beginning of the end of Muñoz's brief period of glory in Washington. While committed to independence, he had come to realize that economic reconstruction was more urgently needed. But the

Nationalist violence had driven a wedge of distrust and bitterness in the New Deal political establishment. While the FBI was collecting evidence to accuse Albizu of conspiring to overthrow the federal government in Puerto Rico, Gruening and Tydings were working on a bill to offer Puerto Rico its independence in a referendum. At a cabinet meeting on March 18, 1936, the bill's introduction was approved, but not as an administration measure. Secretary Ickes expected the bill to have a quieting effect on the island and he pretended not to know about it.[31]

As well as the emotional reaction against Puerto Rico, there were other motives behind the bill. It was in line with the Tydings-McDuffie Bill, which had given independence to the Philippines; with the abrogation of the Platt amendment in Cuba; and with the general objectives of the Good Neighbor Policy. And, of course, it was framed "to call the bluff of those that were arguing for independence." It offered a referendum on whether Puerto Rico should be sovereign and independent. If the vote was affirmative, a constitutional convention would be called and the people—and the president—would approve or reject the document. A four-year transition period would follow, then a tariff would be imposed with a 25 percent yearly increase, and other U.S. grants would be terminated. The implications were clear: Puerto Rico would not be eased out, but kicked out of its political relationship with the United States, with as short a transition as possible. This was clearly a punitive action not against a fanatical group, but against a whole people.[32]

Meanwhile, Albizu and some followers were accused on March 5, 1936, of conspiring to overthrow the federal government in Puerto Rico. They were to be tried in a Federal court, and the governor practically forced the U.S. attorney in San Juan, A. Cecil Snyder to prosecute. According to an FBI report of March 31, 1936, searches made on the homes of known Nationalists elicited no evidence of value, and the U.S. attorney believed that Albizu and his associates, if tried, would be acquitted "as all things said and done by them appear to have been said and done in the open." Snyder thought they could be convicted if the government could prove they had acquired arms, had made arrangements to acquire some, or had committed terrorist acts. Such information was very difficult to obtain.[33]

The first trial ended with a hung jury composed of seven Puerto Ricans and five North Americans. The second jury, carefully chosen, had only two Puerto Ricans. It brought a speedy guilty verdict and Albizu and his companions were sentenced to jail for two to ten years. Albizu had shrewdly conducted the defense in the first trial, denying that the

arms shown were used for insurrection. He had argued his point forcefully, but many Puerto Ricans were disappointed in his legalistic approach
so unlike his erstwhile fiery denunciations.[34] Later revelations by the
painter Rockwell Kent and one of the jurors, Elmer Ellsworth, indicated
that an effort was indeed made to have a complaisant jury for the second
trial.[35]

These events created great tension in the island and marked the
beginning of the end for the PRRA. The Puerto Rican reaction to the
Tydings Bill surprised Ickes and his friends. Instead of quieting the people, it had the opposite effect. The administration, as Earl P. Hanson
wrote, "seemed now to be showing its hand by ill-naturedly telling the
island that it could damn well starve, too, if it did happen to want it."[36]
Even ardent advocates of statehood were shaken. The Republican Union
stated that if statehood was unattainable they would vote for independence. Barceló was ready for independence, even if it meant starvation.

Muñoz Marín, deeply shocked by the administration's move, decided
to fight the bill and to marshal opinion in favor of a more equitable
measure. But he had lost ground as a political leader and could no longer
count on a united party. He rightly felt that the introduction of the Tydings Bill would not only split the Liberal party, but would strengthen the
forces of reaction in Puerto Rico at the expense of the helpless, downtrodden masses. Since 1936 was an election year, the defeat of the Liberals would be the defeat of independence and of social democracy. So
he argued for electoral abstention, to many a questionable way to face
the issue. The party rejected abstention by only one vote. Barceló out-
maneuvered Muñoz Marín, but the price was high. In November, 1936,
the Coalition won the election by 44,566 votes.[37] Muñoz Marín's days as
a Liberal leader were numbered; so were the days of Chardón, the PRRA,
and economic reconstruction.

The period from 1936 to 1940 was one of the most critical in Puerto
Rican history. The crisis reached beyond politics and the economy into
every aspect of social life and organization. It was a crisis of the whole
system of tutelage. For nearly half a century the United States had ruled
Puerto Rico as a colony, as a possession, with powers retained in Washington and its insular appointees. There had been modernization: roads,
schools, bridges, and dams were built; business and banking developed;
new programs were begun; political institutions associated with democratic republicanism were introduced. But the policy had overlooked the
Puerto Rican drive for self-government, and the people's desire to have
their own personality, their own sense of belonging respected and

understood. Americanization meant more than an affirmation of the worth of the individual and the protection of his freedoms. Americanization meant the supremacy and superiority of everything American, and blind loyalty to the symbols of American cultural and political nationalism. With Americanization had come the rise of absentee ownership, the collapse of the coffee culture, and the migration to the growing slums; the shocking poverty in the rural areas; and, finally, confusion and fatalism settling as a dark psychological fog on the society. To many Americans, with little grasp of the complex and pathetic experience, Puerto Ricans were ungrateful emotional children who must be taught a lesson or cast adrift as Tydings wanted. It was difficult for them to understand that the United States had taken the island as war booty and had ruled it with a mixture of paternalism and neglect, with self-righteousness and condescension. Primary responsibility for the crisis thus devolved on those who had asserted primary rights. For absolute power also implies absolute responsibility.

From 1936 to 1940 the tutors and the pupils were in sharp disarray. Albizu was now in Atlanta, but his movement had split the New Deal and the progressive leaders of the Liberal party. Gruening and Winship started a reactionary head hunt and prominent Liberals who had worked for the PRRA were forced out. Chardón's authority was reduced until he had to resign in November, 1936, accusing Gruening of mistrusting native ability, undercutting the Puerto Rican employees by favoring continentals, and evidencing a "sly and insincere conduct." Earl P. Hanson, a professional geographer who had helped direct PRRA planning, was accused of having organized a conspiracy as a "renegade American." Hanson's prophetic retort was that a "blow up" would occur if present policies continued.[38]

Another prominent Puerto Rican was on his way out: Dr. Padín. His sin was that Puerto Rican children had not learned English to the satisfaction of Senator William H. King of Utah, who had toured the island and discovered, much to his chagrin, that rural children knew very little English. Padín's successor was Gore's man, José Gallardo. President Roosevelt himself instructed Gallardo in a letter dated April 8, 1937: "It is an indispensable part of American policy that the coming generation of American citizens in Puerto Rico grow up with complete facility in the English tongue." To achieve this bilingualism the teaching of English must proceed "with vigor, purposefulness and devotion, and with the understanding that English is the official language of our country."[39] Padín's handling of English as a subject and a second language was to be shelved. The implication was that Spanish was to be downgraded as a medium of instruction. Once again language teaching became a political football in Puerto Rico.

As progressive Puerto Rican leaders were removed from the scene, Gruening turned to the Republicans and became embroiled in the 1936 elections.[40] Secretary Ickes, resenting Gruening's Puerto Rico, ordered a confidential investigation of Gruening's rule. So Ickes turned against Gruening and forced him out as PRRA's top administrator. Still director of the division of Territories and Island Possessions, Gruening then joined forces with Winship and decided, in Ickes's words, "that the mailed fist is the proper policy in dealing with these subject peoples. . . ."[41]

Winship considered it his duty to destroy the Nationalist party. But this was a fanatical, dedicated group; deeply resentful of Albizu's conviction. No longer interested in electoral politics or the status debate, the Nationalists wanted vengeance. Attempts were made on the lives of Federal Judge Cooper and Iglesias.[42] An anti-American campaign was kept alive in Puerto Rico and Albizu was presented as a martyr of U.S. imperialism in Latin America.

When a parade request was denied to the Nationalists in San Juan they decided to parade in Ponce, on the southern coast, on Palm Sunday, March 21, 1937. The permit was first turned down, but the mayor finally consented, with the understanding that the march would be peaceful. Winship ordered the chief of police, Colonel Orbeta, to tell the mayor to rescind the permit. The Nationalists refused the mayor's last minute appeal not to march. The marchers did not carry arms; but the police were heavily armed. It is not clear who fired the first shot; the photographic record, however, shows that the police had surrounded the marchers and had fired into the crowd after the first undetermined shot. Nineteen people were killed, including two policemen. A later inquiry by the American Civil Liberties Union recognized the dogmatic, fanatical frame of mind of the Nationalists but concluded that there had been "a gross violation of civil rights and incredible police brutality."[43] The event is known in the history of Puerto Rico as the "Ponce Massacre."

The governor was sharply criticized in Puerto Rico and in the United States. Ickes sent a special adviser, Walter F. McColeb, who reported that in his opinion Winship had lacked judgment and may have been criminally negligent. But President Roosevelt chose to support the general.[44] The violence continued. On July 25, 1938, Winship decided to show the mailed fist with a grand military parade in Ponce, to celebrate the U.S. landing in 1898. A Nationalist student fired almost point-blank at the governor and killed the National Guard colonel, Luis Irizarry, before being killed by the police.[45]

As Ickes admitted, "a vicious round" was gripping Puerto Rico. The general's mailed fist provoked more fanatical determination. Ickes could not topple the governor at this time, but he was able at last to remove Gruening. Finally, in June, 1939, Winship resigned, to be succeeded by Admiral William D. Leahy.[46] As Tugwell was to point out, Winship had been the president's free choice after his sad experience with Gore. Roosevelt "always felt a confidence in elderly naval and military gentlemen not shared by his liberal friends." In Tugwell's views, Winship ruled Puerto Rico like a southern plantation "with the sugar men as his foremen and the people as good or bad folk as they did their work and accepted their livings without or with complaint."[47] Winship's emphasis on law and order would have delighted Henry. The New Deal left him cold, although he was diligent in bringing funds to the island. Tourist development was his economic panacea, and Colonel Orbeta became his Puerto Rican hero. In retrospect, Winship resembled an antebellum character, who would have marched proudly with Robert E. Lee, or danced in Savannah with a southern belle. In Puerto Rico, he was not simply gone with the political wind as so many of his predecessors; he became permanently associated with the Ponce Massacre and with the policy of the mailed fist—the symbol of a sad, disturbing time of violence, reaction, and great human poverty.

If there was bitter infighting among the U.S. policy makers, there were now deep and sharp divisions among the island's leaders. The Coalition, which had beaten the Liberals in the 1936 elections, would split apart in the next four years. The Socialists had shown electoral strength and had their man in Washington. But gradually the party was emphasizing its political interests at the expense of its commitment to the working class. Between 1938 and 1940, its close ties with the business and industrial elements in the Republican Union party led to great dissatisfaction among the rank and file. Open political warfare developed between Senator Bolívar Pagán, Iglesias's son-in-law, and Prudencio Rivera Martinez, an old and respected leader.[48] Iglesias could not control the situation from Washington. Then, late in 1939, he suddenly fell ill with malaria, and by the time the Washington doctors diagnosed the disease, Iglesias was beyond cure.[49] The persistent Galician who more than anyone else had been responsible for the rise of tradeunionism in Puerto Rico, died just as the party he had founded was falling apart. The Socialists were coming to a political dead end; but Iglesias's socioeconomic creed was very much alive and would be continued by other men.

The other side of the Coalition fared no better. Martínez Nadal's *caciquismo* was challenged by Speaker Miguel Angel García Méndez, who aspired to create a new version of the Alliance. By 1939–1940, the differences were so deep that García Méndez left the party in search of new political combinations.[50]

But the most dramatic and significant split took place within the Liberal party. Barceló and a group of party leaders deeply resented Muñoz Marín's refusal of an elective post. The more conservative elements were also very much opposed to his independence campaign, which they thought contributed to the party's defeat. In May, 1937, a showdown took place. With 50 petitions from the local boards, Muñoz requested a general assembly to resolve internal differences. The motion was not only defeated, but a general reorganization of local boards was ordered. For Muñoz, this was the massacre of the Liberal party. He left the assembly. The rupture was complete when the board decreed his expulsion.

This was a fateful step in Puerto Rican political history. What seemed at the time the eclipse of a promising career, the pilfering by a political bohemian of his father's name and illustrious tradition, was really the beginning of a peaceful revolution of far-reaching consequences. For Muñoz, with his great talent and political insights, had to search for power not in Congress, or in the White House, but among the vast majority of Puerto Ricans who lived in great poverty and squalor. The old guard forced him into a period of grass-roots maturation, into what Wilson would have called "the schooling of action."

By himself, in spite of his extraordinary gifts, Muñoz would have done little. But the tides were with him. There was a new generation of leaders ready to help him fight the political battles; an elite group of highly educated Puerto Ricans who could provide the administrative cadres; a people anxious to her a new message of hope, without the strident call to violence; and an opposition that was splintering in a frantic struggle for patronage and power. Furthermore, the tutors were divided as well as sick and tired of the Puerto Rican hornet's nest. They did not think much anymore about the "café poet," but had no more attractive option. When Muñoz went into the hills, Winship had already left and Leahy was the new governor, trying to reach an understanding with the Coalition leaders, whom he despised, and watching over the defense of the Caribbean. In a few years the strategic imperative, which had brought the United States to Puerto Rico, would be uppermost in thought and consideration as the coming of World War II made Puerto Rico a key base for repelling the Nazi submarine challenge. From the hills, the café poet and his followers would bring a message promising loyal support in the war against totalitarianism but would also pose a clear challenge to the proud claims of colonial tutelage. By 1940, a new era had begun.

13
The Forging of Consensus

During the next quarter century (1940–1965) Puerto Rico underwent a profound social and economic transformation. This period saw the collapse of King Sugar and the ushering in of the industrial age. It was a time of bold experimentation and intense social and geographic mobility. Population grew from 1,869,000 in 1940 to 2,350,000 in 1960. Migration to the United States, which had begun slowly in the first half of the century, now became a powerful wave, creating the large Puerto Rican *barrio* in New York, but also spreading in the eastern and midwestern states. Most migrants came from rural areas. With little education and often speaking little English, they faced tough conditions; many suffered from discrimination, prejudice, and cultural deprivation. Many others returned to Puerto Rico with new experiences and skills. If there was an outgoing migration, there was also a return migration, which added to the complex human mobility.

By 1965, there were two distinct Puerto Rican communities: the inner community, in the island itself, close to the core of the historic, cultural nationality; and the outer community which, with the Hispanic minority in the United States, struggled painfully for social betterment and identity. The quaint tropical people that Miles's soldiers had found in 1898 no longer inhabited only their remote West Indian island. Now they staffed the New York service industries; running elevators, working in hotels and restaurants, or if they were women adept at needlework, earning more money in the garment industry. A few Puerto Ricans were already leaving their imprint on sports, the trades, the arts, and the professions. Tugwell's prophecy had come true: they were the new "lowly" wave and they had to be reckoned with.

But this story focuses on the inner community, on the change from an intensely rural to a highly urbanized society, with the emergence of new middle sectors.

The Framework of Adversity

Some vital statistics of the late 1930s and early 1940s provide a needed framework of reference. The 1940 population was 1,869,000, a sign of an increasing high density. Nearly 70 percent of this population was rural; 44.7 percent were engaged in agriculture. It was a young population: fully 40 percent were less than 15 years old as compared with 25.1 percent in the United States. It was also appallingly poor: 80 percent of the rural folk were landless. Sugar cane workers could have seasonal employment for the planting and harvest but King Sugar had its dead season, its *tiempo muerto,* when enforced idleness added to human poverty.[1]

In 1930 the estimated net per capita income in Puerto Rico was $122, less than one-fifth of the net per capita in the United States. The depression lowered it to $85 in 1933. The 1930 level was not reached again until 1940. Defense expenditures improved income, although prices increased correspondingly.[2]

A very small middle class had developed. At the narrow top were the great landowners, the bankers, merchants, and high government officials with their spacious homes and fashionable clubs. The small American enclave of businessmen and bureaucrats had their own clubs, which would accept few of the native inhabitants. This was particularly true in the great sugar estates like Guánica or the well-known Union Club of San Juan.

Puerto Rico was a place of great contrasts; it could be the land of the hibiscus; it could also be the land of the hookworm. The Brethren Service Committee published a report in 1945 describing life for the overwhelming majority:

More than 85 percent of the people are without real property, and 75 percent of them never had more than the barest necessities of life. The average Puerto Rican lives a life of want from the cradle to the grave; he is born of parents who are afflicted with hookworm or malaria, suffers from malnutrition in childhood, and spends his entire life in a crowded shack with no sanitary facilities whatsoever.[3]

This large landless population, indeed the whole economy, depended to a very considerable extent on King Sugar, and matters were going from bad to worse within its realm. The industry was beset by world depression, government restrictions, and foreign competition. Puerto Rican sugar could not compete in the world market with Java, Cuba, or the Dominican Republic, which had better soils and more land. Insular costs were higher and relied on the U.S. tariffs for protection. The tariff wall which had ruined coffee was enabling sugar to survive. But the social cost had been great, and the reaction against the big sugar estates and their absentee owners would shake the system to its foundations.

This background must be kept in mind to understand the course of Puerto Rican politics and its interplay with colonial tutelage. There was fertile ground for a populist movement under the banner of agrarian reform. This was the task assumed by the *Partido Popular Democrático* (Popular Democratic Party or PPD) which Muñoz founded in 1938. The time was ripe for its meteoric rise to power.

The Rise of the PPD

On July 22, 1938, the PPD announced its registration in the voting precincts of Luquillo and Barranquitas; the former a seashore village, the latter the interior town where Muñoz Rivera had been born. The party emblem, the profile of a *jíbaro* in a typical straw hat, clearly identified the party with the long-suffering rural population, the backbone of Puerto Rico's society. Under the emblem, Muñoz Marín wrote *Pan, Tierra y Libertad* (Bread, Land, and Liberty), an echo of the Mexican Revolution cry for agrarian reform.

The political roots of the new party were in the pro-independence wing of the Liberal party. To this were added fervent social and economic reformers. The new party had battle-tested legislative leaders like Ernesto Ramos Antonini; pro-independence intellectuals like Samuel R. Quiñones and Vicente Géigel Polanco; farmers representing the small sugar grower or *colono* like Jesús T. Piñero; men of wide government experience like Antonio Fernós Isern; and able organizers like Felisa Rincón de Gautier. The party's leadership was drawn from the middle or lower middle class, the university intelligentsia, and the small farmers or landowners. In contrast with the Socialists, it was not a worker's party, though the social and economic objectives were similar to those held by Iglesias and his companions. There was an important difference: while the new political group was not anti-American and had many ideological affinities with the New Deal, it was not committed, as the Socialists were, to Americanization. The PPD did not favor an outspoken political nationalism, but rather a strong sense of regionalism, a feeling of belonging to a distinct cultural nationality, committed primarily to social justice for the *jíbaro* and the downtrodden. Their anticolonialism ran deep.[4]

To the rest of the partisan leadership in Puerto Rico, Muñoz Marín and his friends had gone into the political wilderness. Without money, without a strong political base in the legislature, they seemed destined to be another splinter group in a severely splintered political spectrum. Their tactics, however, were highly unorthodox as they crisscrossed the island, setting up grassroots organizations in the 75 municipalities and the 786 rural *barrios*.

Several signs of the party's power went unnoticed. Very soon the party was able to file all the required petitions for eligibility to participate in the 1940 elections. Its rural meetings sometimes attracted 5,000 people and its biweekly propaganda organ, *El Batey*, had a circulation of 100,000. Muñoz Marín saw *El Batey* as the main weapon. It was read to the illiterates in all the *barrios*.[5] In clear, simple language, it explained the party program, its fight against the absentee corporations (the real *bête noire*), and its philosophy of land distribution. It preached against vote buying and appealed to the voters' sense of dignity with the battle cry: *Verguenza contra Dinero!* (Dignity against Money). The campaign was largely based on democratic ethics.

There was, however, the ticklish question of political status. In their grassroots contacts, the PPD discovered that most of the people were deeply concerned about immediate independence and its economic impact on the island. The campaign against the potentially disastrous consequences of the Tydings Bill, which Muñoz himself had conducted, had impressed the average voter. Making status the overriding consideration would alienate votes that a social economic reform program would attract. So Muñoz hit upon a pragmatic, effective formula: "the political status is not in issue." Several years later he wrote:

The votes in favor of the Popular Democratic Party would not be counted either for separate independence or for federated statehood; they would be votes in favor of an economic and social program. Our political status would be decided by the people on another occasion—wholly apart from the regular election—presumably in a plebiscite.[6]

The backbone of the program was breaking the corporate strangle-hold on Puerto Rico through land distribution, assistance to small farmers through credits and rural cooperatives, the treatment of the sugar industry as a public utility, and the protection of coffee and tobacco through the establishment of a People's Bank. It promised to help squatters (*agregados*) obtain land, and to establish social security, slum clearance, educational scholarships, as well as the right to collective bargaining and picketing. It promised to provide special incentives to industry through tax exemption. Many of these measures were not new. They had found their way at different times into party platforms or resolutions. Some could be traced to Socialist or Unionist programs. Many others came from the Chardón Plan and the Puerto Rico Reconstruction Administration's rehabilitation efforts. But there was a new sense of resolve and commitment, and a joining of forces against King Sugar. By separating the status question from a strictly partisan election, the PPD was able to coalesce the will of many voters searching for an alternative to the foundering politics of the 1930s.[7]

The *Populares*, as they were called, went to the 1940 elections with a bold platform, a mystique, an unorthodox campaign, and an imaginative leadership. Even so, it would have been difficult for them to succeed if the Coalition had held firm as in 1932 and 1936. But the Coalition was in grave disarray. García Méndez had feuded with Martínez Nadal among the Republicans; Rivera Martínez with Pagán among the Socialists. Dissensions were the order of the day. And the Liberals were further weakened when Barceló died on October 15, 1938. He was the last leader of the Muñoz Rivera era: honest, deeply patriotic, with much of the civic *caudillo* in him, but swayed by the complex, disturbing trends of a critical decade he could not understand.

So the PPD ran against both the Coalition, and the splinter groups, which joined in the *Unificación Puertorriqueña Tripartita,* a tripartite organization that vainly hoped to resurrect the old *Alianza.* The new party was also aided by the fact that universal suffrage had been extended to all and by a new electoral law providing full representation to all parties and a system of closed polls to avoid the fraud of multiple voting. It was a fair system, established under the vigilance of Governor Leahy, and was to serve the island's electoral system well for forty years while giving the political process a reputation for fairness and honesty.

Over 568,000 voters participated in the close 1940 election. The results were highly surprising to traditional analysts. The Coalition polled 223,423 votes; the Popular Democratic Party, 214,857; and the *Unifica-*

ción, 130, 299. The Coalition won three districts, including San Juan, the seat of their traditional strength, and also elected Pagán as resident commissioner, but the Popular party won four other districts. The PPD won the Senate by one vote and tied the House 18 to 18, with 3 votes going to the *Unificación.* At first glance, it looked like a stalemate, with the *Unificación* holding the balance of power in the legislature. But by winning the Senate by one vote, the PPD had conquered the traditional bastion of native leadership. The moral victory against great odds was tremendous. It shook many members of the Liberal party, as well as some of the dissenting Socialists, whose program was not too different from the PPD's. Muñoz Marín's great talent was the ability to forge these other elements into a powerful legislative consensus supporting the PPD's platform.[8] However, there was still Washington to deal with. The ultimate powers of government still resided in the governors and cabinet officials appointed by the president. Status could be postponed, but it was a primary consideration in basic long-range policies. For if the legislature had to face a hostile governor and federal establishment, the party's energies would have to be employed, as in 1909, in debating the question of respect for the people's will. Colonialism always lurked in the background.

The Caribbean Malta

External circumstances would help the social democratic revolution in Puerto Rico. As in 1916–1917, Puerto Rico was emerging from its obscurity because it was again involved in U.S. national security. By early 1939, Roosevelt was convinced that war in Europe was almost certain and that Adolf Hitler, if successful, would turn to the world sphere. If the Germans captured the British and French navies, they could well menace the Western Hemisphere. Defense plans were urgently needed.[9]

A Joint Planning Committee turned in a report on April 21, 1939, embodying the RAINBOW plans. The plans contemplated the rapid development or completion of defense installations in Hawaii, the Canal Zone, Alaska, and Puerto Rico, and devised alternate strategies. A key element was the acquisition of new base facilities in the Western Hemisphere. By that time, there were congressional proposals to annex European possessions in return for the cancellation of World War I debts. The proposals were not supported by the administration but congressional discussion made clear that in the face of the Nazi challenge, the United States wanted to extend its power and influence, particularly in the Caribbean. The development of an air base in Puerto Rico was considered essential for the defense of the eastern approaches to the area.[10] In the imperial struggles of the first centuries of colonization, the Spaniards had described Puerto Rico's position as the "Christian Rhodes," the "Key to the Indies." Mahan had seen it as the Caribbean Malta; so the strategic imperative in 1939 dwarfed all other considerations.

In July, 1939, a new Army Department was activated in Puerto Rico. Winship, during his term as governor, had urged "the paramount importance of Puerto Rico as a strategic point for the defense of the Panama Canal, the South Atlantic and Gulf States, and the trade routes of the Caribbean."[11] Puerto Rico's conversion into a new military department involved the immediate reclamation of land in San Juan for naval purposes, the construction of a runway and large graving docks, the strengthening of the National Guard, and the beginning of construction of armories.[12]

Puerto Rico became a key element in a defense triangle including Mac Dill Field, near Tampa, Florida, and Panama.[13] Since the United States was forecasting the need for an Army air base at Natal, Brazil, the Puerto Rican base was a fundamental link in the chain of hemisphere security when the European war broke out.

When the Nazis unleashed their successful attack in May, 1940, there was great alarm in Washington. If both England and France caved in, if their navies were lost to the Germans, Nazi intervention in Brazil could be a fact. Plans were hurriedly made for an expeditionary force to the Brazilian coast, as well as for the occupation of key British, French, Dutch, and Danish possessions in the Western Hemisphere.[14]

In the fall of 1940, President Roosevelt had sent an Investigation Commission into the Caribbean. The commission was led by Charles Taussig and included Tugwell, who was concerned with the squalor he saw and thought little of European rule. He concluded that drastic reform was needed along with defense measures. He suggested a general Caribbean government, dominated by the United States, which would permit Federal welfare agencies to act, even if it took a generation.[15] This implied a welfare-oriented U.S. imperialism to follow the soldiers as they established their protective ramparts in the Caribbean.

The Department of State had other plans. It favored a Pan-American trust scheme, to be used in case of need, approved at Havana in 1940. The most delicate problem involved the French islands, particularly Martinique, where several warships took cover. Plans were made for an expeditionary force but two factors helped in reorienting defense. One was the British attack on French warships in Algeria and the second was the destroyer base agreement of September, 1940, by which the United States obtained key bases in the British possessions for the transfer of fifty destroyers. Roosevelt turned aside the suggestion that the islands be sold to the United States.[16]

Under these circumstances, the American governors of Puerto Rico became deeply concerned with the relationship between internal problems and U.S. security. As in 1917, the question of loyalty was crucial. It was also essential not to run against the tide of public opinion, which in Puerto Rico was mobilizing for social and economic reform. The Popular party opposed the inequalities of the economic system, but its thrust was more toward reform than radicalism. By postponing the status question, it had toned down the ticklish issue of independence. World conditions had made the Tydings policy of punitive independence for Puerto Rico highly unrealistic.

Furthermore, the PPD had approved a platform eloquently supporting the democratic cause in the hemisphere. It asserted that neither independence nor statehood nor social justice could be achieved if democracy perished in the American continent.[17] Puerto Rico was not insulated; its fate depended on the events that were shaking the world. These words, which reflected Muñoz's thinking, put the PPD on the side of the anti-Nazi forces.

The American governors, therefore, were willing to listen to Muñoz and to support the party's objective. Leahy's successor, Guy C. Swope, had few credentials to govern Puerto Rico at this crucial stage. He accepted Muñoz, but he feared his followers. According to Tugwell, he felt they were anti-American communists who could force Muñoz to extreme measures, and suggested that they had the tacit support of the Franco *falangistas!* And Swope believed that the press, out of malice, had one dominant policy: "to harrass and to foment dissatisfaction with any and all continental men and measures. . . ."[18] Obviously Swope, like so many of his predecessors, had little grasp of the intricacies of the situation. He was another wrong man in the wrong place.

The Last of the Tutors

At this moment Tugwell reappeared. On his visit to Puerto Rico in 1934, he had sympathized with the island's plight, although he had disdained the island's politicos and ruling classes. On his return in 1937, he was again appalled by the conditions he saw. These experiences led him to feel that the United States had a great responsibility in the Caribbean, especially to Puerto Rico. When Ickes offered him the position of head of the division of Territories in 1941, Tugwell felt that the United States needed a colonial office with enlightened leaders, but that Congress would not support it.[19] In the same year, he was offered the position of chancellor of the University of Puerto Rico. At the same time he was pressing Washington for an appointment as governor. Roosevelt and Ickes finally chose him, thinking that a man like him, with his views on the area and his concern for defense, would be the right United States representative. So on September 19, 1941, Tugwell became governor of Puerto Rico—the last, probably the brightest, and certainly one of the most controversial tutors.

Socioeconomic reform became a shared goal of the new political leadership of Puerto Rico, bent on removing the afflictions and injustices of the King Sugar era, and the federal policy makers, who wanted to give the New Deal another try in the island. Correcting economic exploitation was not only a social goal; it was of the utmost importance in securing Puerto Rican support and participation in the war effort. In Tugwell, Roosevelt had at last found a man who could add administrative experience to the strategic concern, but it had taken the president eight long years to learn the lesson.

In his long background of public service, Tugwell had demonstrated an inventive mind and a flair for administration. He was particularly adept at planning, bringing rationality and purpose to a *laissez-faire* society. His forte was devising blueprints for action, but he would tend to look down on politicians and legislative assemblies. He would feel very much at home with the technocrats, but was impatient with partisan wranglings. He had a certain intellectual arrogance that set him apart from the give and take of public life. Although government attracted him, he was not a practitioner of the art of politics. He was a great help in developing teamwork at a crucial time in Puerto Rico's relationship with the United States. Tugwell inspired great devotion among his close collaborators, but never attained real, spontaneous popularity. At the end there was an estrangement between him and Muñoz; between the planner, with his demanding parameters, and the forceful political leader, with his intuitive insights.

From the beginning of his administration, Tugwell made two things crystal clear. As a fervent New Dealer, he would command every resource of government to better the condition of the poor. If this attitude created conflict, he was ready for it. "I will be the friend of every man and woman who helps; I will be the opponent of every man or woman who hinders," he said in his inaugural message. His second point was a call for Puerto Rican collaboration, as the strategic center of the Caribbean area, in what he called the "great struggle for freedom and decency."[20]

When Tugwell became governor, Muñoz had already moved quickly in the legislative arena. At the first session, he made it clear that campaign promises would be kept. First and foremost was the Land Law, creating a Land Authority empowered to purchase, for just compensation, lands held in excess of the 500-acre limitation. Farm wages would include proportionate shares of the profit. Homestead or subsistence farms would be parceled out to landless peasants. Small farms, clustered in villages, would be supplied with water, electricity, and other facilities.[21] These measures started a whirlwind of legislative activity destined to change the role of government in Puerto Rico. Other basic reforms included setting up the Water Resources Authority (1941); the enactment of a minimum wage law (1941); the Transportation Authority (1942); the University Reform Law (1942); and other social measures.[22]

As Tugwell assumed the governorship, Puerto Rico was entering a period of great tension and complexity. The first factor was the crippling effect of the war, soon to be sharpened by the submarine blockade, the drastic fall in shipping tonnage, and the food and petroleum crisis. Second was inflation and the rise of unemployment from 99,100 in July, 1941, to 237,000 in September, 1942. On June 12, 1942, Tugwell presented the situation forcefully to the Washington authorities. Lights had been shut off in 37 communities; gasoline had been restricted to the army and navy and to some essential services. Economic life was paralyzed and unemployment was growing.[23]

The third factor was the dynamic urge for reform leading to a statutory revolution. Besides the PPD goals which Muñoz had been pushing, the bases were laid for a new public administration system with a Tugwellian accent: a powerful planning agency; a modern budget organization; and two economic development agencies of great future import, the Puerto Rico Development Company and the Development Bank of Puerto Rico.

This sudden rush of public initiative and power created deep resentment in the conservative elements. The Coalition, still powerful, could not stop the legislation. Ignored by Tugwell, it accused him of trying to establish a corporate state. Others called him a socialist or a communist. He became the target of great resentment and was accused of being more radical than the radicals. His anti-New Deal enemies in the United States joined the chorus, and in 1943, congressional committees sent subcommittees to the island to find out what was happening.

In February, 1943, Tugwell stated his case before the Senate Sub-committee on Territories and Insular Affairs, headed by Senator Dennis Chavez of New Mexico. He minced no words in describing U.S. responsibilities. If there were no humanitarian reasons for taking immediate action on the economic situation, there were strictly military ones. "American policy in Puerto Rico," he argued, "has the choice of economic assistance with a rather hopeful prospect or of suppressing an angry people who would feel very deeply that somehow they had been wronged."[24]

If his support of the Puerto Rican urge for reconstruction indicated "an imperfect understanding of a colonial governor's duties," Congress had also been at fault; for the Jones Act assigned duties "in controlling this possession to others than the governor." This act, he held, had the inherent quality of all older approaches to colonialism in that the home government reserves the right to prescribe what a people cannot do, because if they were free, they would do something unwise. Since the act had been in force for twenty-six years, why had the United States failed to move decisively? "Two million people" he stated, "cannot permanently be kept in the twilight of colonialism."

The legislature of Puerto Rico, in his opinion, was under the tutelage of Congress, and Congress had to decide whether to move towards independence or to grant greater autonomy. In either case, the United States was responsible for creating conditions for its success. The same held true if the policy decision was for statehood. With unusual frankness, Tugwell concluded that no one could guess what U.S. intentions were for Puerto Rico—a situation ideally calculated to create dissension and agitation, with Puerto Ricans being continuously at each other's throats.

As a colonial governor, Tugwell considered himself the target of accumulated grievances, for he exercised a control "which is a constant affront to their dignity as a people." No governor could be really effective, in his opinion, until the act was rewritten to provide for an elective governor who was a citizen of Puerto Rico as well as of the United States. This would reduce the power of political parties and put a stop to executive strangulation.

But these observations had to be related to the war crisis after Pearl Harbor and the threat of a Nazi attack. Puerto Rico, he observed, was the only center of real resistance in the ring of Canal defenses. In outlining the measures taken in Puerto Rico, "where everything had to be done at once," he insisted on the need for agricultural improvement, for industrialization, and for a policy to supersede the old colonialism. An elective governor was the beginning, as he had suggested to the president since 1942. The long period of indecision should come to an end after a few years of a deliberate policy of assistance, and the Puerto Rican electorate must be allowed to express itself.[25]

In this crucial statement, Tugwell vented his own views and feelings. Without realizing it, in his own words and from his New Deal perspective, he also summarized all the old arguments that Puerto Rican leaders had used since the establishment of colonial tutelage under the Foraker Act. There were, in his words, many echoes of old pleas and representations, going back almost half a century. He was answering Root and Davis, and explaining the failures of Riley, Gore, and Winship. In siding with Muñoz and his social democratic revolution, he was tacitly accepting the principle of government by consent, which the early tutors had spurned. Now more was involved than a colonial squabble. The United States was at war, and Puerto Rico was one of the exposed outposts, and its people were flocking to join in the defense of the hemisphere against totalitarian aggression.

But there were compensations for the adversity and danger of the times. There was a drive for reform and reconstruction, with a new sense of purpose; the wranglings between the executive and the legislative branches were reduced to a minimum; and federal expenditures were helping the economy. The rum industry benefited from the absence of competition from Europe in the U.S. liquor market. In five years, its net income rose from $1.6 million to $14.3 million.[26] Income directly traceable to war activities of the federal government rose from $8.1 million in 1940 to $106.4 million in 1944.[27] By the end of the war, manufacturing was becoming relatively more important than in the war years.

Puerto Rico's economic development was not taking off, but neither was it stagnant. Federal expenditures brought capital in and the new governmental set-up provided the needed infrastructure. The conditions for a postwar drive were being established. A significant factor was the improved use of human resources. The University of Puerto Rico, under a young dynamic chancellor, Jaime Benítez, was committed to providing the needed administrative cadres. A whole new group of Puerto Ricans with impressive professional training was given wide public responsibilities. Men like Rafael Picó in planning, Teodoro Moscoso in industrial promotion, and Roberto Sánchez Vilella in administration, together with many others of the same generation, brought public service new viewpoints as well as a drive and dedication Puerto Rico had

Luis Muñoz Marín (1898–1980), campaigning among the jíbaros (*peasants*).

rarely seen. As technocrats, they clustered around Tugwell, but their political commitments were with the Popular Democratic party, and their real tutor for Puerto Rico's future was Muñoz Marín.

As the social and economic program began to move, tension grew in the political sphere. As noted, Tugwell had been pressing for an elective

governor since March, 1942, when he suggested to Roosevelt that Puerto
Ricans should choose their own officials. With Ickes's support the idea
found its way in a presidential message to Congress, dated March 9,
1943, which called for amending the Jones Act to permit an elective
governor and a revision of federal-insular relations. It also provided for
a President's Advisory Committee with joint U.S.-Puerto Rican participation, including the minority leaders. There was heated discussion on
the powers of the governor; and finally a strong executive was recommended. But in Congress, it was the old story as the powers were sharply
curtailed and nothing happened.[28]

While these fruitless efforts were being made in Washington, the 1944
elections approached. The dynamics of change were affecting voting
patterns and developing new political loyalties throughout the island.
The PPD maintained that status was not an issue in the general elections,
but committed itself to a direct consultation at the end of the war, as to
the preferred choice of the popular will. It forcefully defended its recent
accomplishments and promised a wide social welfare program, as well
as increased productivity.[29]

The Republican Union reiterated its preference for statehood and
adopted a long list of social and economic measures. The Liberals asked
for a joint front against the PPD, a front which was finally forged with
the support of the Socialists. There was a strong feeling against Tugwell
and his immediate removal was requested. Liberals and Republicans
merged as the Progressive Republican Union. But this hurriedly assembled Coalition could not stop the PPD steamroller led by Muñoz's char-
isma. Out of 591,978 voters, the PPD obtained 383,280 votes, with a
174,764 majority over the combined votes of the opposition. The party
took the seven senatorial districts, 34 of the 35 representative districts,
and every municipality except four. It was a historic sweep which established the democratic hegemony of a party committed to social and economic reform for a quarter of a century.[30] And Tugwell, the last of the
tutors, felt fully vindicated.

14

The PPD Democratic Hegemony (1944–1969)

Under the dynamic leadership of Luis Muñoz Marín, the PPD in 1944 moved decisively to the center of Puerto Rico's political stage, a position it would occupy for a quarter of a century. During these years there was a great leap forward; a profound mutation in the society and the economy, in the political experience, in the Puerto Rican's view of himself and the world. No other period in the island's history saw such a dramatic transformation or such an alteration in the social horizon. The hard crust of an agrarian economy was permanently broken, and the rural character of the culture was changed by new population shifts and distribution. Puerto Rico became urbanized and increasingly industrialized, with new social classes of fluid mobility, an expanding mass education, new patterns in government and private organizations, and developing networks of external contacts. Old problems were put aside and new problems emerged. There was hope and drive, but there was also searching criticism and premonition. A victory over colonialism and the iron ring of poverty was attempted, and much was realized through popular consensus. But the shining goals of final achievement eluded the efforts. By 1969, the consensus began to dissolve, giving way to increasing confrontation about status, sharpened internal divisions, and acute perplexity. The economic momentum was maintained for a while until it led into a period of acute federal dependence. The contemporary Puerto Rican crisis then emerged, quite distinct from the hope and trauma of 1898 or the plight of the 1930s.

The Emergence from War

By early 1945, at the time when the PPD was establishing its domination of Puerto Rican politics, the war had entered into its final stage. The Axis troops were receding before the Allied onslaught and the submarine menace was fading. Puerto Rico was a busy, vital hub of armed activity. It had played its role as a Caribbean Malta by serving as a staging area, as a crucial base in the air bridge from the United States to Natal to Dakar to Northern Africa and beyond, and as a key defender of the Atlantic approaches to the Panama Canal and the "soft underbelly" of the United States, its unprotected Gulf coast.

The island's human resources had also contributed to the war effort. The great majority of Puerto Rican units in service were stationed in the Canal Zone and throughout the Caribbean, guarding the vital U.S. installations. Others went beyond the Western Hemisphere. The 65th Infantry Regiment, a descendant of the Puerto Rico Regiment of Volunteers established in 1899 by General Henry, went first to Panama, then to New Orleans, and then to North Africa on March 7, 1944. Some of its elements moved to Italy and Corsica as a security unit. The regiment finally joined the Seventh Army, fought in the Maritime Alps, and also participated in the march that swept into Germany.

The Puerto Rican National Guard, created in 1919 as a result of World War I, was federalized and brought into active duty on October 15, 1940, as the 295th Infantry Regiment. Its troops saw service in Curaçao, Aruba, Surinam, Trinidad, Cuba, and Jamaica. Another regiment, the 296th, after performing training missions in Panama, went to Hawaii as a regimental combat team and was ready to participate in the war operations gainst Japan when the war ended.[1]

A total of 65,000 Puerto Ricans served in the U.S. armed forces during World War II, compared with 18,000 in World War I. Over 36,000 men were drafted, but a very high proportion—23,000—were volunteers. Service in the armed forces attracted many unemployed youth in the island, but a number of problems arose in connection with the draftees. First, their English was inadequate to permit effective training and integration into regular units. Special orientation training programs were set up, but they were only moderately successful. Since a very high percentage of officers spoke only English, the lack of Puerto Rican motivation to learn the language, or their poor accent, added to the complications. Tests used for enlisted men were not designed for people of their language and culture, and many of them did poorly. In some cases, where mechanical skills were tested and the test was only given in English, only a limited number of Puerto Ricans were expected to meet the needed qualifications. Eventually, the army became more aware of these problems, and found that Puerto Rican soldiers could be as alert and capable as any other group. If the army was a school experience for Puerto Ricans, the drafting of Puerto Ricans also taught the military hierarchy some lessons on cultural diversity.[2]

The proportion of Puerto Rican officers was rather low: of over 45,000 enlisted men in the army, only 1,101 were officers. The great majority of officers were continentals, *americanos*. Although the troops had fought in Europe, MacArthur, according to Tugwell, had refused to include them in his operations, reflecting an official distrust.[3] Yet many Puerto Ricans came back with pride in their contribution to the defeat of Nazi power. The 69th Regiment had its heroes, and its march became a popular military tune. Their casualties were relatively low, only 368 dead in World War II, but they had dutifully defended not only their island but a vital area for United States hemispheric security and had fought a common enemy overseas.

These troops were drafted according to laws passed by a Congress that for nearly half a century had been quite indifferent to Puerto Rican pleas for self-government. Many of the soldiers, and certainly many of the civilians who supported them, firmly believed that they were fighting for the freedoms mentioned in the Atlantic Charter which Roosevelt and Winston Churchill had signed. The charter stated: "They [the United States and Great Britain] respect the right of all people to choose the form of government under which they will live; and they wish to see sovereign rights and self-government restored to those who have been forcibly deprived of them." But as Tugwell pointedly observed: "Puerto Ricans thought this applied to them; but they tended to forget that it was a Roosevelt-Churchill declaration and not a congressional one."[4] In the coming battles for self-determination in Puerto Rico, the armed forces would think mostly in terms of the U.S.'s new status as a superpower. The Navy, for instance, would for a time oppose an elective governor for Puerto Rico. To Secretary Frank Knox, the strategic imperative was all Puerto Rico was really about. If U.S. leaders were not thinking of a "Christian Rhodes," as Spain had in the sixteenth century, they were thinking as heirs of the British naval empire in terms of a Caribbean Malta in the American Mediterranean.

The war ended, with an inventory of problems and possibilities. The American military, now aiming at strategic globalism, saw Puerto Rico

The beginnings of industrialization in 1945 brought about an economic and social transformation to Puerto Rico.

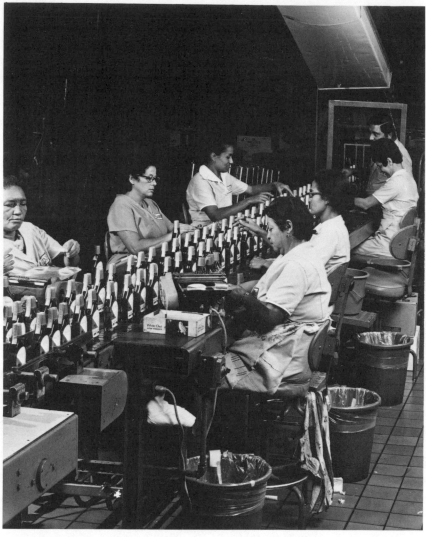

Bottling line inspection at a rum plant.

as a key link in a long chain. The Congress, dominated in no small measure by anti-New Deal forces, regarded Tugwell as a dangerous radical. The administration was torn by a desire to improve the colonial relationship and its mistrust of too much autonomy. The well-meaning new president, Harry S. Truman, needed time to achieve control. And in Puerto Rico, two crucial events took place: the readjustment to a peacetime economy and the renewed independentist drive to realize the war promises of self-determination.

As Tugwell wrote in his 1946 report, "the end of the war did not catch Puerto Rico napping." A marked advance in industrialization began in 1945–1946 when the Puerto Rico Industrial Development Company began operation of a paper board and a glass container factory, started the construction of a heavy ceramic plant and a shoe factory, and began a cotton textile mill.[5] This modest postwar development program led Puerto Rico into the industrial era. Tugwell's pet project at this time was the Puerto Rico Agricultural Company, which foundered badly. The Land Authority, on the other hand, was highly successful. Its Cambalache Sugar Mill paid the highest wages in the sugar industry and its proportional profit farms—one of the keys to agrarian reform—showed a net profit of over $191,000. Furthermore, nearly 15,650 *cuerdas* (acres) were distributed as homestead plots to *agregados* and 25 new rural communities were established.[6] The increase in the government's general fund revenue receipts from over $37.5 million in 1941–1942 to $82.2 million in 1945–1946 revealed the fast pace of progress in Puerto Rico.[7]

For Tugwell, 1945 marked the approaching end of his role. He had been gratified by the great outpouring of support for the PPD and its program which he, as governor, had tried to beef up with administrative knowhow. His advice for the postwar years was for the island to enlarge its sources of income and to promote productive enterprises, even if it meant making hard choices with respect to increasing social services. Now he began to consider status, searching for a new relationship that would avoid the old statehood / independence dichotomy. In his legislative message of February 13, 1945, he said:

The sacrifices inherent in complete separation seem to me to exclude that as a solution; statehood would involve a very long and distressing struggle; some formula for association as a more completely self-governing people within the framework of the United States seems to me one which would be agreeable to both Puerto Ricans and members of the States. It is possible to find a union in which Puerto Ricans can keep the citizenship and much of the economic relationship they have had now for three decades, and in which their right to self-government will be recognized.[8]

He strongly felt the times were propitious, since Washington was committed to freedom for all peoples, consistent with permanent peace in the world, as proposed in the Atlantic Charter. "It is time, past time, for Puerto Ricans to choose the form of government under which they desire to live. . . ." he said. It would be unfair to propose a plebiscite not authorized or defined by Congress. In fairness to everyone, Congress should offer the choices it was willing to accept rather than require the Puerto Ricans to petition for status with the risk of rejection.

The problem that Tugwell posed in this message was the crucial issue regarding status for the rest of the century. When the United States

New low-cost housing in 1946.

embarked on its imperialistic venture in 1898 and took Puerto Rico, its tutorial role was framed in the context of a new international policy. Congress willingly accepted this view and decreed a status somewhat similar to the British Crown colony model. Then Congress entered a period of "benign neglect." Galvanized by the coming World War I, Congress was willing to grant citizenship and make some adjustments, but firmly retained basic control of the island's destiny. And then it sank again into lethargy and indifference. World War II brought the strategic imperative and the cry for self-determination to the fore. But was Congress to be bound by the Atlantic Charter or by the principle of congressional supremacy over territories and dependent areas in the tradition of nineteenth century expansionism? Was Congress, innately conservative and jealous of its constitutional prerogatives, willing to accept that Puerto Rico, as any other dependent people under the United States trust, had inalienable rights above and beyond the dictates of a constitutional provision?

Tugwell thought that Puerto Rico could not be "abstracted" from the hazards of the nation and the world. He had the insight to realize that the old tutorial role had come to an end. His experience showed that an appointed governor whose power came from Washington could no longer function unless he was subservient to a Puerto Rican legislative majority. He could not serve two masters, particularly if they happened to be at odds. As the old tutorial scheme was collapsing, King Sugar was also challenged by the thrust toward industrialization. In proposing a free association based on common citizenship, Tugwell was not breaking new ground. Stimson, Frankfurter, Towner, and Roosevelt, Jr., under different circumstances, had come to the same conclusion. But the context had changed. The war had unleased all kinds of liberation movements and a profound change in the relationships of peoples all over the world.

The Piñero Appointment

In December, 1945, Tugwell announced his decision to resign. The Truman Administration now considered two possibilities: appointing a native Puerto Rican; or favoring an elective governor and a referendum on independence, statehood, or dominion. The new director of the Division of Territories, Edwin G. Arnold, prepared a list of possible nominees with Jesús T. Piñero as the first and best choice. Piñero had been elected resident commissioner in 1944; was very close to Muñoz; knew the economic problems of the island; and was an affable, modest man who got along well with his congressional colleagues. With little effort, he had become "one of the boys." Other candidates included a Puerto Rican general, Pedro del Valle, who had distinguished himself at Guadalcanal; Justice Cecil Snyder of the Puerto Rican Supreme Court; the perennial candidate, Martín Travieso; and José Gallardo, Gore's old choice. The list was not impressive.

Muñoz, naturally, preferred a candidate closely associated with or sympathetic to the PPD. The Republican-Socialist coalition, on the other hand, favored del Valle, who at one time was interviewed by Truman. It was politically preposterous for this general, who was completely out of touch with the island, to replace Tugwell in the complex Puerto Rican situation. The PPD legislature reacted promptly. On February 21, 1946, a joint resolution and two bills were passed. The joint resolution recommended that a candidate with popular approval, an elected representative, or a cabinet member should be appointed if the governorship became vacant. One bill provided that, if this was not possible, the people should express their preference at a special election. Another bill authorized a plebiscite. The people of Puerto Rico, Muñoz sardonically wrote, also had the right to make recommendations. "We are interested in the democratic significance of a policy," he added. "We would rather have, if it came to that, a liberal Chinaman than a reactionary Puerto Rican."[9]

Tugwell had to veto both bills on constitutional grounds. He would have preferred to avoid this confrontation with Muñoz and the PPD. Secretary of the Interior, Julius A. Krug, who had succeeded Ickes in February, 1946, was reluctant to support Piñero in view of his close association with Muñoz. But the PPD legislature forced his hand. It recommended Piñero by a vote of 54 to 3. The implicit message was clear: a governor not approved by the new reform forces dominating the island would have all kinds of trouble. Krug wisely decided to overcome his scruples and avoid an unnecessary confrontation; on his recommendation, Truman announced Piñero's appointment on July 25, 1946, an appointment confirmed by the Senate six days later.[10] The Jones Act, of course, was legally in force, but the spirit of the act had drastically changed, as Piñero's appointment demonstrated. It was not a stopgap measure, but the beginning of a real drive for the long overdue elective governor.

But as Muñoz fought bad judgment and misunderstanding in Washington, he had to brace himself for a much more difficult and heartrending struggle in Puerto Rico. There was dissension in the party on the delicate question of ideology. The restlessness, long brewing in the pro-independence wing, came to the surface. In spite of all efforts to avoid it, a deep schism developed which finally led to a parting of the ways.

Advent of the PIP

Since its beginnings, the PPD had had two wings: those who favored independence and those who favored autonomy or dominion status. The pro-independence wing was made up of two groups. One was fervently convinced that independence was the ultimate status and was willing to go along with Muñoz's removal of the status issue from the general elections, but insisted on a firm position in the days ahead. The other pro-independence group also believed in separation, but was *muñocista*, with absolute faith in Muñoz's political instincts and his deep sense of justice. They were willing to follow his leadership.

Supreme ability was required to orchestrate these divergent views. Moving from victory to victory, with the increasing devotion of the masses, Muñoz preserved unity, but by 1945–1946, the crisis finally broke. A brief recapitulation is in order. During the war, Senator Tydings again introduced an independence bill on April 2, 1943. It was less punitive than his 1936 bill, and gave the island twenty years to regulate its trade relations by a 5 percent yearly increase of the U.S. tariff. Secretary Ickes opposed the bill on behalf of the administration because it came at an inopportune time. The bill, however, led to the establishment of a Puerto Rican Commission on Status by the Legislature.[11]

In spite of meager support for the measure, Tydings doggedly insisted on holding hearings and asked for a report from the United States Tariff Commission on the implications of independence. The bill got nowhere, and only showed that Tydings had not forgotten the events of 1936. But it stirred the independence groups in Puerto Rico, and the Tariff Commission Report had a profound influence on the search for viable formulas.

Throughout 1943, various pro-independence groups promoted the idea of a general congress. Some were connected with the Nationalists and some were members of the PPD. Several members of the legislature had sent messages to Tydings in support of the bill. In April, 1943, a General Independentist Assembly was held in San Juan. It cabled Tydings, urging economic amendments to make independence viable under the Atlantic Charter.[12] In August of that year, the First Pro-Independence Congress (CPI) was held with the collaboration of several PPD members, including the Senate floor leader, Vicente Géigel Polanco, who had drafted many of the social measures adopted by the PPD. The position of the CPI was clear: it proclaimed Puerto Rico's right to independence, reaffirmed its friendship with the United States, and asked Congress to recognize Puerto Rico's independence.[13]

With the 1944 victory, the CPI decided to press Muñoz for a constitutional convention. Muñoz insisted that the party would hold a popular referendum by the time peace was achieved. But he declined to encourage the movement. At the CPI's second meeting in December, 1944, there was a new momentum. The leader now was Gilberto Concepción de Gracia, a staunch believer in independence, who had been close to Albizu. A new friend for the movement was Congressman Vito Marcantonio from New York, who was ready to introduce his own independence bill. Muñoz saw that the trend was toward the founding of another party; he stated that he would not object but asked that it be done openly. The Executive Committee of the Congress reaffirmed its nonpartisan character; it did not want to break with Muñoz, but would not follow his leadership.[14]

In January, 1945, Tydings reintroduced his bill. Again the administration stated its opposition. The Interior Department thought that both "quick statehood" and "quick independence" would be disastrous for the island, while Tugwell was espousing his idea of a special relationship. Muñoz felt that the Congress should offer several alternatives, with the economic guarantees spelled out. Under pressure from a Puerto Rico Legislative Commission, Tydings finally agreed and a new bill was drafted, with the help of the resident commissioner, known as the Tydings-Piñero bill.[15] In a special message of October 16, 1945, Truman suggested that Puerto Rico's right to select its own governor with a larger measure of self-government should be added to the three formulas.[16] Though Congress did not approve the Tydings-Piñero bill, in Puerto Rico it precipitated the rift between Muñoz and the CPI. By September, a sharp polemic between Concepción de Gracia and Muñoz made the break complete.

In February, 1946, Muñoz accused the CPI of sabotaging the PPD program. He insisted that true *populares* should not be fooled and defied the CPI to go before the voters rather than resort to infiltration tactics. He wanted, he said, an open democratic fight. Puerto Rico should solve its status problem realistically. He was still unwilling to discard independence, but was tending to other solutions, and many party leaders were ready to go along with him.

Concepción de Gracia and his friends took up the gauntlet. On October 27, 1946, the Congress dissolved and became the *Partido Independentista Puertorriqueño* or PIP. Its goal was the attainment of immediate sovereignty, but it was willing to enter the electoral struggle. Its first act, if successful, would be a Joint Resolution demanding the independence of Puerto Rico and appointing a Commission to negotiate the terms.[17] In contrast to the Nationalist Party, the PIP opposed revolutionary action. It entered the fray as a democratic party and while critical of U.S. colonialism it was not, like the Nationalists, violently anti-American. Its leaders came from the professionals and the middle class, with a sprinkling of labor activists. It drew strength from intellectual circles, and favored the rhetoric of constitutional liberty and national sovereignty.

So, as the postwar world emerged, Puerto Rico had a native governor appointed by the president; an administration promise to search for different formulas; a very divided, confused, and conservative Congress to deal with; and a new pro-independence party. The events that soon followed put relations between the island and the United States in a new perspective.

Towards the Associated State: the Elective Governor

A crucial element in this changing picture was the PPD's shift on the status question. The shift was related to the economic realities of the period; several of which were analyzed in the U.S. Tariff Commission Report prepared at Senator Tydings's request. This document profoundly influenced Muñoz and the status controversy.

The report, prepared largely by the economist Ben Dorfman, considered the present basis of the Puerto Rican economy; the economic provisions of the Tydings and Tydings-Piñero Bills; and the prospects of economic betterment for the island through changes in political status, including the specific requirements for economic development. With careful, persuasive logic, it tried to justify the *status-quo*. It was dominated by a neo-Malthusian view; the real problem of Puerto Rico, it argued, was its growing population. The 1943 Tydings Bill, by placing Puerto Rico outside the U.S. tariff system, would do little to promote the island's economic welfare. The Tydings-Piñero Bill would seriously compromise the island's sovereignty by keeping it practically a U.S. dependency, but if the United States granted free trade to Puerto Rico, it would have to modify its reciprocal most-favored nation commitment to many countries. Since the United States had not granted free trade to the Philippines, Congress would probably not change the policy. The report acknowledged that the economic relationship of dominion status would be more favorable, but insisted that dominion would not solve the basic economic problems of Puerto Rico. If Puerto Rico became a state, it would have to be treated like any other state, and therefore would lose the customs collection, the federal excise taxes, and its privileged position *vis-a-vis* federal income taxes. No additional benefits that the island could reasonably expect to receive as a state would outweigh the loss of present benefits.

The commission found no ready made solutions, and predicted that even under the most favorable political circumstances, such economic progress as the island could achieve with its own resources and its own initiative was bound to be slow. "The immensity of the task," it dogmatically concluded, "should not deter the island's leaders from shouldering it and continuing to make whatever progress is possible." The report was, essentially, a "no-exit" document. Puerto Rico would remain a stricken island, as long as its population grew. Neo-Malthusian factors were blamed for what was the implicit acknowledgment of the shortcomings of tutelage. There was little else the United States could do and Puerto Rico was destined to a gloomy future, according to the iron logic of Dorfman's dismal science. After nearly half a century of dependency, this was Puerto Rico's balance sheet.

The commission's report and the experience of the Philippines deeply impressed Muñoz and his associates. It was becoming clear that Congress was unwilling to make any special concessions that would help Puerto Rico find a way out of its predicament, while affirming the principle of self-government. The commission report was telling Puerto Rico that political colonialism was its only reality. Muñoz could not accept this position; thus the search for an alternative began.

Several years later on July 17, 1951, in one of his most revealing speeches, Muñoz acknowledged that his 1945–1946 experience with the Tydings-Piñero Bill was a turning point in his thinking. The hearings on Philippine independence made it obvious that the United States would not continue granting free trade to Puerto Rico under a separate status. The most-favored nation policy was an insurmountable obstacle.

Muñoz decided to make his views known in articles published on June 28–29 in the newspaper *El Mundo*. He stated his conviction that no more energy should be spent on solutions to the status issue that were impracticable for Puerto Rico, but that a creative formula should be found that would not hinder the solution of the island's difficult problems, and would protect with dignity its association with the United States. Some members of the PPD's governing board still felt that the older policy should be continued, but Muñoz was authorized to judge when the time had come to chart a new course.[18]

Dr. Fernós-Isern also made a statement to *El Mundo* on July 4, 1946. With cogent logic, he insisted that no democratic solution of the status problem could be achieved until Congress expressed itself on Puerto Rico's right to sovereignty and reached an agreement with Puerto Rico where the terms would be defined bilaterally. He also proposed that, at the request of Congress, the people of Puerto Rico should adopt a democratic constitution which would contain the basic economic and political terms of association, leaving the future open. When Piñero became governor in September, 1946, Dr. Fernós succeeded him as resident commissioner. The PPD now had a man of unusual ability and political acumen in Washington.[19]

Behind this political reorientation, there was a socioeconomic purpose: the drive for industrialization and the need for the U.S. market. Not only had the status controversy reached a dead end; the King Sugar era was dying. Puerto Rico needed a new developmental model that could create more and better paid jobs, promote social mobility, and expand the business and entrepreneurial base of the economy. A shift was taking place in the economic promotion program, which now saw industrial capitalism as a way to turn the island's economy around. For the next quarter century, Operation Commonwealth and Operation Bootstrap would be the point and counterpoint of Puerto Rican development.

In 1947, Congress passed the elective governor's law. In the same year, developmental thought in Puerto Rico took another course. Both changes were influenced by one fact: Tugwell was no longer governor. Thus violent opposition to his New Deal views would subside in Congress; a climate of cooperation with Interior and the Puerto Rican leadership followed in preparation for the elective governorship. In Puerto Rico, the Development Company began a new strategy that was distasteful to Tugwell: the offer of special inducements to private capital and enterprise in order to multiply industrial concerns and job opportunities. Borrowing a leaf from the Mississippi Industrial Commission, the Development Company, under Moscoso, had begun an advertising campaign in the United States; but a special lure for the industrialists was

necessary. This was the exemption from income tax that became law in
1947. Tax exemption, free access to the American market, and the wage
differential became keys to Puerto Rico's industrialization effort. Under
these conditions, the rapid industrial development known as Operation
Bootstrap occurred. But the implication was obvious: the advantages
could not occur under independence or statehood, given the parameters
described in the Dorfman report.[20]

Early in 1947, both Muñoz and Governor Piñero visited Washington.
Their conferences with Interior officials and congressional leaders showed
that the most Puerto Rico could get out of Congress was an elective governor. Interior was willing to push for the measure, with Fernós laying
the groundwork in Congress. Although a pro-statehood bill and Tydings's independence bill were introduced, both were opposed by the
administration. Instead, full support was given to the Butler-Crawford
bills which stated a gradualist policy. Puerto Rico would get self-government "little by little." This policy clearly did not satisfy Puerto Rican
aspirations. To many, it meant undue delay, or "colonial reform." For
the PPD leadership, however, it was a step forward. With the governorship in Puerto Rican hands, new efforts could then be made.

The Butler-Crawford bills faced relatively smooth sailing in Congress.
The bills provided for an elective governor who would appoint his cabinet members. Congressional conservatism and distrust of Puerto Rican
financial responsibility was evident in the retention of the auditor as a
presidential appointee; and Senator Robert A. Taft forced a last minute
amendment keeping the Supreme Court judges as federal appointees.
The strategic imperative remained unaffected, especially since the navy
reclaimed half of Vieques Island in 1947, on the assumption that the
eastern area of Puerto Rico would assume great strategic importance in
the postwar era.[21]

In its other territories, the United States had appointed residents as
governors. This policy was not extended to Puerto Rico until Piñero was
appointed by Truman. The island had characteristically lagged behind
Hawaii, where governors were required to have three years of residence.
But in permitting an elective governor for the island, a change was made
in the colonial pattern which added to the uniqueness of Puerto Rico
within the American orbit.[22] It paved the way for the next step: the
Commonwealth relationship.

As Puerto Rico primed itself to elect its first governor in over four
centuries, it was obvious that the PPD was headed for another resounding victory. Its political platform was now committed to ask Congress for

a solution to Puerto Rico's political status based on a constitutional convention to draft a democratic constitution; an authorization for the Legislative Assembly to request a plebiscite at the appropriate time, to determine whether Puerto Rico should be an independent republic or petition to become a state; and an expression of congressional willingness to act in accordance with the Puerto Rican determination. The PPD was facing a coalition committed to statehood and the PIP, with its clear preference for independence.

The PPD with Muñoz for governor swept the country with 393, 386 votes to 182,977 for the pro-statehood coalition and 65,351 for the PIP.[23] It was not merely status that persuaded the voters, but the dynamic social and economic program that the PPD had set in motion and which was creating a broad political consensus across the island, including the traditional pro-Republican San Juan area.

Legally, the elective governorship was an amendment to the Jones Act and thus a unilateral concession which Congress could theoretically withdraw if it was not satisfied with Puerto Rico's future political behavior. In that sense, it was still a vestige of colonialism. But in practice, it signified a profound change in the way Puerto Rico was governed. The island's governors had been responsible to the president or had worked with instructions from Washington. Their source of power was not the people. They had had, however, to accommodate their policies to the pressures of the Puerto Rican legislature which, particularly in the area of appointments, was not an obedient tool of the imported executive. But the governors remained visible symbols of American tutelage.

All this changed when Muñoz became governor. He made it clear that his mandate came from the people, not Washington. He used his powers of appointment to make government responsive to the PPD program which had been strongly supported at the polls. He appointed Géigel Polanco as attorney general, emphasizing the ties with the legislature, while two of his closest associates, Ernesto Ramos Antonini and Samuel R. Quiñones, were elected speaker of the House and president of the Senate. Now close collaboration would supersede the traditional adversary relationships.

Muñoz further exercised his autonomous power by appointing a respected educator, Mariano Villaronga, as commissioner of education. Villaronga stood for teaching in the vernacular Spanish, with English as a second language. He had been nominated by Piñero, but Congress had not confirmed him. The language policy had been a crucial issue in U.S.-Puerto Rican relations, second only to the status question. Late in Tugwell's term, the PPD legislature had approved a law providing for the teaching of Spanish as the vernacular and English as a second language, but Tugwell had vetoed it. Now that the governor had the right to appoint the commissioner of education, Puerto Rico could determine its own language policy. This was an important gain for self-government in a very sensitive area, involving cultural values and feelings.

Since the governorship had been the visible symbol of American domination, Muñoz tried to make it a symbol of Puerto Rican popular democracy. He used it to carry out the party's program, and as a spring-board for new ideas, a political pulpit for his teachings. The governor's messages now dealt with recommendations for legislative action with the principles and objectives of democracy in Puerto Rico. They expressed Muñoz's public philosophy and the aims of the movement he had founded.

Muñoz called his economic objective "the Battle of Production," but he was also concerned with establishing clear priorities between invest-ment and social service. Though willing to promote private enterprise to increase production and multiply jobs, he was not preaching a *laissez-faire* philosophy, but rather the need to do away with extreme poverty and social insecurity as soon as possible. In 1950, he dreamed of greatly decreasing unemployment by 1960, of eliminating the adverse balance of trade, and of reducing economic dependence on federal expendi-tures. He was encouraged by the fact that between 1940 and 1950, the labor force had increased from 624,000 to 786,000, and that unemploy-ment had been reduced from 18 to 13 percent. He was especially grati-fied that Puerto Rico's per capita income in 1950 was already higher than most New World countries, except for the United States, Canada, Argentina, Uruguay, and Venezuela.[24]

Muñoz was highly optimistic in his projections. They contrasted sharply with the gloomy determinism of the Dorfman Report. Puerto Rico was ready to move away from the monoculture of the King Sugar era and the domination of American political tutelage. There was a cor-relation between greater self-government and the new determination to overcome the heritage of adversity. Some of Muñoz's rosy projections would be realized; others would not. But for those engaged in the devel-opmental effort, those were exciting years, when everything seemed possible.

There was an inherent contradiction in this public philosophy which would also be typical of many developing nations. The contradiction was between the values of the acquisitive society rapid industrialization would bring about and the ideal of the "good life" that Muñoz was preaching. The "good life," in his view, could never be the mere multiplication of gadgets induced by consumerism, but rather "the creative ideal of abolishing extreme poverty and enriching freedom and personal security."[25] By overcoming the heritage of adversity, he firmly believed that the people would hold fast to a value system and a life style that would enhance compassion, solidarity, a sense of collective worth, and a feeling of belonging to what he called *"la patria-pueblo"*—the people-fatherland— as distinct from the fatherland as an abstraction. He believed that creative diversity enriched the world, and that this creativity could lead to an understanding between Puerto Rico and the United States that would be revolutionary.

The new era in Puerto Rico would certainly go a long way in achieving and even surpassing some of the economic objectives. It would do much to reduce extreme poverty and provide vertical social mobility. Institutions like the Institute of Puerto Rican Culture would be created to affirm the heritage of *la patria-pueblo*. Muñoz himself would have the opportunity of going beyond Operation Bootstrap and Operation Commonwealth to define the ideal world of Operation Serenity. But the acquisitive society fathered by industrialism would be too strong for the deeply humanistic values of the PPD's public philosophy. The weakening of these values would give rise to a new period of perplexity, polarization, and confusion. But in 1950, Puerto Rico had a visible momentum: the status, the economy, the society were in a state of flux.

The search for a third political solution finally took shape. The old notion of dominion status began to influence PPD thinking led by Muñoz and Fernós-Isern. The resounding electoral victory gave weight to this solution. Three ideas were gradually intertwined: first, that Puerto Rico should determine the shape of its internal government by framing and adopting a constitution, republican in form and compatible with the U.S. Constitution; second, that the relationships between Puerto Rico and the federal government, as distinct from local matters, should basically continue under a statute regulating them; and third, that this process should involve agreement by Puerto Rico and Congress, with people expressing their endorsement in a referendum and Congress recognizing the principle of government by consent in the needed statutory enactments.

A complex series of moves followed. The first move, from March to July, 1950, involved initial congressional action; the second, from August, 1950, to February, 1952, covered the Puerto Rican response of debate, referendum, and constitutional convention. The third move, from April to July, 1952, involved Congressional legislation which was signed by the president on July 3, 1952. The final event took place in Puerto Rico: the constitutional convention adopted the terms set forth by the Congress on July 9, 1952, and on July 25, 1952, the new status—the Commonwealth of Puerto Rico—was officially proclaimed in a solemn ceremony, attended by visitors from the United States and the hemisphere.

During this period, there was intense debate in Puerto Rico and in Congress about the meaning and scope of the new relationship. The complexity of the move was such that, in retrospect, it is surprising that the change was made so quickly. Certain factors obviously helped. Congress now realized that the United States had to comply with the decolonization precepts in the United Nations Charter. The Truman Administration respected Muñoz as a political leader and Fernós for the wise ways in which he handled himself in Congress. Furthermore, a bipartisan spirit dominated congressional discussions. Even so, the establishment of commonwealth fell considerably short of the dominion model, and some areas were inadequately defined or were later open to diverse and critical interpretations. It was a significant step forward, but it did not put the status controversy to rest.

The manifold aspects of this political and constitutional process are beyond the scope of this book. Some of the highlights, however, will be emphasized. The commonwealth was proposed by the Puerto Rican leadership, bearing in mind the innate political conservatism of Congress. In contrast with previous legislation, which clearly bore a Washington imprint, the drafts were framed by the Puerto Ricans themselves. In a "Brief Personal Statement on How I See the Political Status Issue," delivered to U.S. officials at the end of 1949, Muñoz insisted that Puerto Rico was seeking "a new kind of statehood" of interest to the United States and the hemisphere; that it was growing, not as a theory, but rather as a political mutation, "more like phonetics develop than like Esperanto is constructed." The process should soon become the object of deliberate policy, he continued, with the people able to draft a constitution, subject to final congressional approval. To perfect the democratic relationship, provision should be made for Puerto Rican consent. Puerto Rico would continue to be exempted from U.S. tax laws, but Muñoz hoped that eventually productivity would increase to such an extent that Puerto Rico could pay federal taxes without harm to the population. At that time there could be no objection to the island becoming another federated state. But Muñoz was unsure if this was the desirable thing to do, for maintaining this new political mutation would serve the mutual interests of the United States and the rest of the hemisphere. He ended with the key concept which he was to repeat time and again: "The mutation may be worth preserving as a model for a world federating more and more dissimilar cultures into less and less great fraternal units."[26]

On February 27, 1950, Muñoz arrived in Washington to meet with President Truman, Interior Department officials, and congressional leaders. A draft of the proposed legislation was sent to Senators O'Mahoney and Butler; and Muñoz presented his views before the Senate Committee on Interior and Insular Affairs. On March 13, 1950, Fernós introduced the constitution bill (H.R. 7674) in the House. The bill recognized the principle of government by consent, stating that the proposed act would be "adopted in the nature of a compact so that the people of Puerto Rico may organize a government pursuant to a constitution of their own adoption."[27]

The administration provided support. In Congress, where the bill was carefully scrutinized, Fernós's insistence on the "compact" idea was accepted and a precedent was found in the Enabling Act of the Northwestern Territory; its roots, therefore, went deep into U.S. constitutional development. In hearings by the House Public Lands Committee, an impressive battery of administrative representatives pressed for passage. Edward G. Miller, Jr., of the State Department endorsed the bill by putting it within a wider context. In view of the importance of "colonialism" and "imperialism" in anti-American propaganda, the department felt that H.R. 7674 "would have great value as a symbol of the basic freedom enjoyed by Puerto Rico, within the larger framework of the United States of America."[28] As in 1916–1917, action on Puerto Rican status was related to U.S. international commitments and to its role in the New World.

Naturally, the bill was opposed by those who preferred statehood or independence. The Republicans wanted to be sure that the bill did not preclude statehood. Concepción de Gracia, particularly, objected strongly to any constitution subject to congressional amendment or suspension as violating Puerto Rico's inherent rights to sovereignty. In the House, Vito Marcantonio called the bill a "snare" and a "delusion"; only sovereign rights would solve the island's problems. But Congress felt that the referendum would let Puerto Ricans accept or reject the act, and that the bill followed the principle of extending self-government embodied in the U.N. Charter. Between May and June, strong bipartisan support developed. By July 1, 1950, the bill had cleared both houses and on July 3, 1950, Truman signed Public Law 600, setting the Puerto Rican constitutional phase in motion.[29]

In August, the Puerto Rican Legislative Assembly approved a law to schedule the referendum on June 4, 1951, to be preceded by the registration of new voters early in November, 1950. The public debate began in earnest in October; but it was not limited to verbal fireworks. This time the Nationalists were ready to strike and a brief, bloody interval ensued.

Albizu Campos, having served his term in Atlanta and refused to ask for pardon, had returned to Puerto Rico. More than ever he favored direct, revolutionary action in the face of the electoral strategy of the PIP. As soon as he arrived in Puerto Rico, he let it be known that Muñoz had to be stopped. His small band of Nationalists had been inconspicuous during his years in jail, but they had built considerable sympathy for their cause in Latin America. The Cold War had also helped their propaganda and many anti-American forces throughout the world, led by the Communists, were willing to accept *prima facie* the claims that Puerto Rico was occupied by U.S. troops and ruled by U.S. puppets.

For Albizu, independence could only be achieved through revolutionary action, spurred by resolute personal sacrifice. Stopping Muñoz was one phase; but the overall objective was to challenge U.S. power dramatically enough to command world attention. The Nationalists built up a cache of arms throughout 1950. As the debate unfolded and the new status seemed to be in sight, they decided to strike. Following a prison break, they began revolutionary action in two inland towns, Jayuya and Utuado, that were ill-protected by the police. Their most dramatic tactic involved a daring attack on the governor's palace. With guns blazing, two cars moved down the narrow street in an effort to penetrate the palace. They nearly succeeded. From behind the thick walls of the old building, a handful of defenders fired on the leading car and stopped it. Five Nationalists were killed and two policemen wounded. The attack was repulsed, and the governor's life was spared. The National Guard was immediately ordered to retake the two towns, which it did with machine guns, bazookas, and tanks. The uprising was soon quelled and arrests were made throughout Puerto Rico. Thirty-three persons were killed, and Albizu was jailed, after his house was surrounded by police.[30]

Puerto Rico had barely recovered from this brief, violent upheaval when other news stunned the country. Two Puerto Rican Nationalists, Oscar Collazo and Griselio Torresola, dramatized the revolt before world opinion through an assault on Blair House, Truman's residence while the White House underwent repairs. They exchanged shots with the police but failed to penetrate the building. Collazo and one policeman were killed, but Torresola survived. The attack on the president received world attention, and few people later remembered that Muñoz had been the first target.

The Nationalists failed, however, in their local objectives. They did not stop Muñoz, they got no revolutionary help from the independentist sectors, they did not prevent massive registration for the referendum, and they actually inspired a great surge of sympathy and support for the governor. But internationally, they succeeded in giving the impression in many places that theirs had been a popular revolt. The Cuban House of Representatives, for instance, cabled Truman lamenting events in Puerto Rico and requesting his intervention to prevent bloodshed and safeguard Albizu's life. They proposed to send a commission to investigate, which Muñoz strongly refused to accept, even though pressed at first by the State Department.[31]

Deeply concerned about the effects of the Blair House attack on American opinion, Muñoz wired Truman his condemnation of what he called the "dastardly attempt . . . against your person." He assured the president that the Nationalists had failed both in their primary objectives and in breaking the bonds of friendship, association, and trust between Puerto Rico and the United States. Truman replied in the same manner: "I am sure that the American public understands the irrational and insignificant background of the disorders and does not in the least hold the Puerto Rican Government or people responsible for them. . . ."[32]

After this short, bloody pause, the status debate continued its course. The vote on P.L. 600 demonstrated the PPD's strong popular following. There were 387,016 votes in favor; 119,169 against. In August, 1951, the PPD elected seventy delegates to the convention; the statehoooders elected twenty-two, an active minority group which included their new leader, the industrialist Luis A. Ferré.

The convention met from September 17, 1951, to February 6, 1952, under the chairmanship of Fernós Isern. Long and searching debates took place in a responsible atmosphere. Leading constitutional scholars were consulted and constitutional precedents were carefully studied. The result was a very progressive and widely praised document which asserted Puerto Rico's natural rights and its commitment to the democratic system and human rights, as well as its loyalty to the principles of the federal Constitution and the idea of a compact. The Constitution created the *Estado Libre Asociado* (Associated Free State), later translated as Commonwealth to allay fears that Puerto Rico was asking for statehood. In later years, this duality of terms would create ambiguity and misunderstanding.

A final resolution of the Constitutional Convention adopted on February 4, 1952, asked the governor to submit the constitution to the people in another referendum. It insisted that its adoption meant the attainment of complete self-government and that the "last vestiges of colonialism" had disappeared in the principle of compact. But the convention left the possibility open that Puerto Rico could develop in other ways "by modifications of the Compact through mutual consent" and reserved the people's right to propose and accept modifications in Puerto Rico's relations with the United States. Underneath the convention's pride was the feeling that the new status could grow in different directions, that it was not really a frozen framework for the relationship.[33]

The people went to the polls on March 3, 1952, giving the Constitution 373,594 votes to 82,877. Delivered to Truman early in April, it was transmitted by the president to Congress on April 22, 1952. After reviewing the steps taken, Truman stated that with the document's approval "full authority and responsibility for local self-government will be vested on the people of Puerto Rico. . . ." and added "No government can be invested with a higher dignity and greater worth than one based upon the principle of consent."

In Congress, the supporters of P.L. 600 promptly got to work to secure approval. In the House, some reservations were expressed about Section 20 of the Constitution which recognized the rights of every person to receive free elementary and secondary education and to obtain work and an adequate standard of living. These provisions led to heavy attacks in the House. To some congressmen, the section smacked of "totalitarian government"; to others, it was a "socialistic bill of rights" dooming the islanders to economic destruction. In the Senate, this section also aroused misgivings; questions were raised regarding the meaning of the compact and the authority of Congress. Senator O'Mahoney stated that Congress was reserving to itself the powers under the Jones Act which were set forth on P.L. 600 as the Federal Relations Act. If the people of Puerto Rico "should step outside," the authority of Congress would not be impaired.

Two efforts to amend the proposed legislation suddenly revealed that there were opponents within Congress. In the House, Congressman Meader of Michigan introduced an amendment to the effect that Congress had not made an irrevocable delegation, transfer, or release of its powers under Article IV of the U.S. Constitution, the territorial clause. But the House refused to go along with an amendment that would have been a very serious setback to the intent of the legislation. As Congressman Fernández observed, the amendment would have broken faith with the people of Puerto Rico. Finally, the House approved the Constitution.

In the Senate, the debate was even sharper. One of the opponents was Senator Olin Johnston of South Carolina who believed that Puerto Rico was a "gigantic incubator of peoples who often do not understand American traditions and ideals." Johnston sharply opposed Muñoz and believed that Section 20 implied that "socialism, or facism unwanted by the great majority of Americans will have crawled in at our back door." The senator not only wanted to limit the governor to one four-year term, but insisted that no amendment to the Constitution could be effective until approved by Congress. His intention, derived from what many thought was a racist bias against Puerto Ricans, was to assert clear and distinct congressional authority over the island. When he got the amendment approved, Muñoz responded with a cable insisting that the Johnston amendment would destroy "the whole spirit of the constitutional process." Reaction was highly negative in the island and the whole process hung in the balance. Fortunately, when the amendment was considered in conference, wiser counsels prevailed and a substitute amendment, proposed by Fernós, carried the day. Now any amendment or revision of the Constitution would have to be consistent with the applicable provisions of the U.S. Constitution; with the Puerto Rican Federal Relations Act; and with P.L. 600, "adopted in the nature of a compact." This brilliant maneuver shrewdly removed the dangerous monkey wrench thrown into the complex situation. The joint resolution finally passed as Public Law 447 on July 7, 1952. A few days later, the constitutional convention accepted the amendments on the understanding that the people would vote on them at the general election. The climax was reached on July 25, 1952, fifty-six years after Miles's landing, when the commonwealth was proclaimed and Muñoz raised the Puerto Rican flag, officially and symbolically side by side with the American flag at the old fortress of *El Morro*. In a gesture of good will, Truman, on that date, commuted Collazo's death sentence to life imprisonment.[34]

The establishment of the commonwealth relationship, the *Estado Libre Asociado* Associated Free State (or ELA) pointed to new ways and possibilities, but left crucial questions unresolved. To the PPD, P.L. 600, adopted "in the nature of a compact," could mean no less than a "compact," an agreement between the Puerto Rican people and Congress, subject to the principle of mutual consent. It could not be revoked unilaterally, which meant that limitations had been placed on the full authority given to Congress, under the Treaty of Paris, to legislate for Puerto Rico. In this view, the Constitution, the compact, and the principle of government by the consent of the governed ended the colonial relationship and the concept of "possession." Commonwealth, therefore, was a new form of federal relationship: an association with a union of states, capable of change and growth. The PPD insisted that this association was "permanent." While the terms of the specific relationships could vary at any given time—Puerto Ricans could, for instance, contribute to the federal treasury or participate more directly in the framing of commercial treaties affecting them—the link of a common citizenship would maintain Puerto Rico within the American political system. This link would be the "permanent bond" that Stimson once talked about.

In the process, Puerto Rico would retain its distinct personality, its historical identity in the West Indies, its cultural ties with the Spanish and Spanish-American world. It would not be lost or assimilated within the broad, powerful current of American life but would thrive on its diversity while helping the cause of hemispheric understanding. In Muñoz's quaint expression, it would be the olive in the martini.

At the time of the creation of the commonwealth, a strong popular consensus in Puerto Rico supported this interpretation, and many sectors in the United States looked with great favor on this creative, positive way out of a most difficult dilemma. High hopes and expectations were based on the visible evidence that the island was moving forward, with improvement in the standard of living and an increasingly good record in democratic government and public service.

But there were also many skeptics. The proponents of statehood either rejected the relationship or saw it as a stop on the way to political assimilation. The advocates of independence considered it a deceptive colonial status: nothing but separation would satisfy them. Even friendly supporters of the commonwealth felt that Congress had been too conservative or feared that the consent given by the people of Puerto Rico had been too broad and too generic with regard to congressional authority. In what was obviously the most thoughtful defense of the commonwealth, the great expert on federalism, Carl J. Friedrich, pointed out some failures of the framework in 1959. These included the lack of Puerto Rican participation in the federal legislative process and in foreign affairs and defense, as well as the failure to contribute to the federal treasury. With remarkable prescience, he wrote: "There may be some serious danger ahead, should the present party fall apart or be replaced by another as the island's outlook and viewpoint change."[35]

These were prophetic words, but in 1952 the outlook was rosy. After over fifty years of a colonial tutelage with its mixture of good intentions and self-righteousness, altruism and ethnocentric claims to moral superiority, the Puerto Ricans had achieved a breakthrough. They were electing one of their own as governor to head a centralized state. Moreover, their other top officials were no longer chosen in Washington; their judicial system was now to be run by Puerto Ricans, except, of course, the U.S. District Court. No American auditor would check their public expenditures. No appointed commissioner of education would impose an imported philosophy on the system. And the powers of the commonwealth government in local matters stemmed from a Constitution, framed and devised in Puerto Rico itself, and not in Congress.

Future generations would have trouble understanding the profound psychological change that took place in 1952 when Puerto Ricans established a right to their own anthem and flag. It was a great emotional experience when Muñoz symbolically raised the Puerto Rican flag at *El Morro*. The sight would have brought ulcers to men like Henry, Reily, and Judge Hamilton; but would have been hailed by Carroll, Stimson, and Roosevelt, Jr.

Events in Puerto Rico attracted considerable attention. The island had become a haven for many democratic exiles from totalitarian governments in Latin America and Spain. By the late 1940s, such distinguished Spanish intellectuals as the poets Pedro Salinas and Juan Ramón Jiménez (later a Nobel Prize winner) had made Puerto Rico their home. The world renowned cellist and freedom lover, Pablo Casals, whose presence made the creation of the Casals Festival possible, a yearly international event in classical music, also made Puerto Rico his home. The University of Puerto Rico offered its academic hospitality to outstanding Latin American professors who had to leave their countries: Risieri Frondizi of Argentina, Mariano Picón Salas of Venezuela, and Luis Alberto Sánchez of Peru, among others. In the 1950s one of the architects of the democratic revival of the Caribbean, Rómulo Betancourt, exiled himself in Puerto Rico and developed a lifelong friendship with Muñoz Marín. Visited by men like President José Figueres of Costa Rica and Alberto Lleras Camargo of Colombia, Puerto Rico became a hub of what later was called the Latin American "democratic left": a loose movement of parties committed to social and economic change, profoundly opposed to totalitarian governments, and critical of U.S. support of the prevailing dictatorships of Santo Domingo, Venezuela, and Argentina. A host of sympathetic U.S. public figures also visited the island, among them Roger Baldwin, Norman Thomas, Frances Grant, Archibald MacLeish, Adolf Berle, and such academics as John Galbraith, Sidney Mintz, Julian Steward, Daniel Boorstin, Henry Wells, and many others. Literature in the social sciences presented a new vision of Puerto Rico as a land beset by difficult problems, but no longer condemned to poverty and despair.

If in 1940–1945 Puerto Rico had played the role of a Caribbean Malta, from 1952 onwards it became a bastion of democratic thought and action in the Caribbean. Many in the Caribbean and in Latin America traditionally favored independence; but others admired the way Muñoz and his associates were transforming a heritage of poverty and want while progressively achieving growing powers vis-a-vis the most powerful nation in the world. This role would be enhanced during the 1950s. But first, it gained international attention at the United Nations.

Puerto Rico at the United Nations

The colonial question had caused much concern and debate at the United Nations since its inception. The promise made with regard to self-government in the Atlantic Charter and later reaffirmed in the declaration adopted by the United Nations appealed as a principle applicable to both the peoples under colonial rule and the metropolitan powers. Article 73 of the charter approved at San Francisco in 1945 stated a general obligation of the member states which administered non-self-governing territories—a euphemism for colonies. This obligation recognized that the interests of the inhabitants of these territories were paramount and included their political, social, economic, and educational advancement. Article 73 (2) obligated the member states not only to develop "self-government" but also "to take due account of the political aspirations of the peoples, and to assist them in the progressive development of their free political institutions." The San Francisco conference did not precisely define the term "non-self-governing territories," nor did it specify criteria for determining when a territory is, or ceases to be, "non-self-governing."[36] This lack of definition later posed very difficult problems which affected the international status of Puerto Rico under the United Nations charter.

In 1947, the United Nations General Assembly created the Committee on Information from Non-Self Governing Territories, usually referred to as the Committee on Information. Its function was to examine the information transmitted by the metropolitan powers and make reports and recommendations to the General Assembly; these included the examination of the factors to be taken into account in determining whether a territory was non-self-governing. This committee became the watchdog of the commitments made under the charter. In 1952, it was composed of an equal number of administering and non-administering members elected by the United Nations Fourth Committee. It was the Committee on Information that examined United States reports on its dependencies, including Puerto Rico.

With the achievement of the commonwealth relationship, the Puerto Rican government felt that the United States should cease communicating information about the island to the United Nations. Dr. Fernós, with Muñoz's support, made this proposal. A draft letter prepared for the president encountered, however, some unexpected objections to Muñoz's insistence that Puerto Rico should no longer be referred to as a "territory," as well as legal reluctance in Washington to accept the implications of the compact. It took strong pressure from the governor to overcome this resistance, but finally an agreement was reached on the communication the governor would send to Truman, as well as on the president's memorandum accompanying this document. Muñoz's letter clearly described the compact theory as "the precise formula that the people, through their elected representatives had requested." The laws enacted by the commonwealth government pursuant to the compact, it said, "cannot be repealed or modified by external authority." The president's memorandum dwelt at great length on Puerto Rican political development, and pointed out that Puerto Rico had entered into "voluntary association with the United States" on the basis of "mutual consent" and that Puerto Rico had attained a "full measure of self-government." These documents were to be the basis for the forthcoming debates at the United Nations.[37]

To explain the Puerto Rican position, Dr. Fernós was made a member of the U.S. delegation. But the governor felt that foreign delegations at the United Nations, especially sympathetic Latin American delegations, should be approached informally, that the developing world should hear the story of Puerto Rico's hard road to self-government and social and economic development. Furthermore, invitations should be extended to any United Nations member who wished to see the Puerto Rican realities for himself. To this effect an *ad hoc* group was appointed to develop close contacts and hold conversations with United Nations delegates. The group included the speaker, Ernesto Ramos Antonini; secretary of justice, José Trías Monge; and the under secretary of state, Arturo Morales Carrión. From time to time other officials participated in these efforts, including Senator Víctor Gutiérrez Franqui, Secretary of the Treasury Sol L. Descartes, and public relations specialist Rafael Torres Mazzorana.

A systematic round of informal meetings took place and visits to Puerto Rico were arranged for representatives of United Nations member states, including Israel, Uruguay, and Ecuador. President elect Figueres, who was touring Latin America, helped in this effort after he was provided with a memorandum. Eventually, a strong core of Latin American governments not only participated in the U.N. debates but sponsored a resolution asking for the cessation of information. This group included Brazil, Colombia, Ecuador, Peru, Costa Rica, Panama, and Chile and represented several of the democratic governments in the area.

While the pro-commonwealth group was active, the PIP and the Nationalists also approached U.N. members to acquaint them with the case for independence. Although they could not obtain a formal hearing, they discussed the Puerto Rican case with several delegations and circulated abundant material. Delegations from Guatemala, Honduras, India, Indonesia, and Mexico were particularly receptive to their viewpoints.

A procedural matter almost defeated the resolution on Puerto Rico sponsored by the seven Latin American nations in the General Assembly. A clause was added to the effect that the General Assembly was competent to decide whether a non-self-governing territory had or had not attained a full measure of self-government. A number of administering powers and other states which favored the resolution then decided to abstain. Finally the assembly adopted the Latin American resolution by a vote of 26 to 16 with 18 abstentions. The vote came after the U.S. delegate read a message from President Dwight D. Eisenhower to the effect that if at any time the insular legislature requested "more complete and even absolute independence" the president would recommend that Congress grant it. The U.N. resolution asserted, therefore, the competence of the General Assembly to decide whether a territory is self-governing or not; recognized that Puerto Rico had achieved a new constitutional status, had established a mutually agreed association with the United States and had in fact become an autonomous political entity. In favoring cessation of information, it added a significant clause: the assembly expressed the assurance that due regard would be paid to the will of both the Puerto Rican and the American peoples in the event either of the parties might desire any change in the terms of Association.[38] This clause, drafted by the Peruvian delegate, Víctor A. Belaúnde, was included to bring Latin American support and protect Puerto Rico's right to further development of its status. The commonwealth, the Peruvian delegate affirmed in the debate, had "the momentum of freedom" on its side.[39]

The United Nations resolution was a victory for the Puerto Rican government's interpretation of the new status. Since Muñoz, as elected governor, was not the U.S. representative in Puerto Rico, he did not have to report to Washington on his administration in Puerto Rico. His duty was to report in an annual message to the people who had elected him. A point was also scored when the American delegate, Congresswoman Frances B. Bolton, affirmed in the debate that Puerto Rico had a compact with the United States, and that mutual consent was necessary to make any changes. The fact that the resolution had been sponsored by seven Latin American nations, many of which were recognized democracies, strengthened the democratic role of Puerto Rico in the Caribbean. But the resolution was adopted by an assembly which was just beginning to include Third World countries. Eventually, as their numbers grew, the concept of self-government was to be identified with independence and the basis of the Puerto Rican arrangement with the United States came to be questioned in the 1960s and 1970s.

Another event affirmed Puerto Rican ties with the United States. In June, 1950, the United States became involved in what was technically called "a U.N. police action" in Korea, but was really a bloody war in support of South Korea. Although the United States was not prepared for this action, the Truman administration was ready to act in support of its "containment policy," designed to stop Communist expansionism on a global scale.

The U.S. Army was short of troops and had to turn to its National Guard regiments. On August 11, 1950, the 65th Infantry Regiment of Puerto Rico was alerted and brought to full strength. On August 25, the troops left Puerto Rico under the command of Colonel William W. Harris, a West Pointer from St. Louis, Missouri, and on September 23, they were already in Pusan, Korea, ready for battle.

At first the regiment protected the main supply routes and engaged North Korean guerrilla units. But more serious duties followed. In pushing towards the north, General MacArthur ignored intelligence reports and recklessly overstretched his lines. The Chinese came down in great strength and surrounded the First Marine Division in the vicinity of the Chozin Reservoir. The 65th Regiment went to the rescue and formed a corridor to relieve the besieged forces. When the north was evacuated, the regiment was among the last troops to abandon the beach. It was an outstanding performance of the Korean War and the whole regiment was commended for its heroic action.

Many individual feats were carried out by Puerto Rican soldiers during the war. The regiment, nicknamed "The Borinqueneers," fought with great determination and valor but paid a high price in casualties. Puerto Rican casualties added up to 3,540, of which 743 were soldiers killed in action. One out of every 42 U.S. casualties was a Puerto Rican; and the island had one casualty for every 660 inhabitants, compared to one casualty for every 1,125 inhabitants of the United States.[40] The troops, which General MacArthur had despised in World War II, had given a good account of themselves, and the island had sustained proportionally more losses than most states. The "gigantic incubator of peoples" so disparaged by Senator Johnston had strongly helped the proud General MacArthur extricate U.S. troops from his ill-advised military move.

The Economic Take-off

As commonwealth status began to develop, its economic underpinning—Operation Bootstrap or *Jalda Arriba!*—started to show amazing results. The concerted attack on extreme poverty, the emphasis on productivity, and the reliance on planning increased the tempo of development. In 1950, an expert planner, Harvey S. Perloff, studied the Puerto Rican experience, and observed that in contrast to many other areas of the world which had been subject to frequent political upheavals and whose economic plans were largely wishful thinking, "The Puerto Rican people have displayed a noteworthy political maturity as characterized by their ability to evolve an essentially sound and balanced development program in the face of inordinately difficult circumstances."[41] The 1950s, as an economic historian would note, were the "exuberant years." More and more factories came into the island. By the end of 1955, they were pouring more than half a million dollars in wages alone into the economy every week and employing 28,000 workers, the goal Perloff had recommended. Private investment increased at 36 percent per year from

1950 to 1954; and at about 46 percent from 1955 to 1959. Industrial employment brought unemployment to a low unparalleled in the history of Puerto Rico's labor statistics: 12.4 percent in the last quarter of 1959.[42] It was, again, an era of flattering statistics.

But if the establishment of commonwealth status had left several question marks in its wake so it was with the march into industrialization, known as the *Fomento* effort. It was true that new, higher paid wages were available; that income from manufacturing with its multiplier effect was now supplanting sugar as the leading source of insular revenues, and that the construction industry was in full bloom. But underneath. the *elan* there were nagging problems to cope with. An unexpected variable was post-war migration to the States. The two-way flow left a "net

The new working class.

migration" of people who left the island: over 500,000 between 1947 and 1961. The bulk of these migrants were unskilled or semi-skilled workers, with little formal schooling, or with unstable or seasonal employment.[43] They were highly motivated by the search for employment opportunities. As American citizens, they could move freely between the island and the mainland in an unplanned, unpromoted wave. *Fomento* was reducing unemployment, but could not provide jobs for the Puerto Ricans who left in search of new horizons and had to face their *Jalda Arriba*, their uphill fight, in a more tense, prejudice-prone, racially divided society. In 1957, Governor Muñoz frankly acknowledged the problem. It was still extremely difficult to create good, abundant jobs and abolish unemployment. Migration had stabilized population growth, but even the new economic energy had not created the necessary employment opportunities and people were leaving the island. "We should not agree with this continuing situation," he observed. "Our productivity should also overcome this problem."[44] But unemployment and migration persisted in spite of the great effort.

In the meantime, the political hegemony of the PPD was assured. The 1952 elections, following in the wake of the constitutional process, reaffirmed the PPD majorities. The old Coalition was crushed at the polls. The erstwhile Republicans had changed their name to the Statehood Republican party or PER, with a clear-cut ideological stance against commonwealth. The Socialists were simply a shadow of themselves and the PPD had taken their program. Only the pro-independence groups were aggressive opponents. When the votes were counted, the PPD had 431,409, the pro-statehood party, 85,591, and the Socialists only 21,719. But the PIP doubled its 1948 vote and polled 126,228. It became the second party in Puerto Rico and promised to be a driving force in insular politics.[45] The Socialists, as a result of the elections, decided to dissolve and join the PPD.

Within the PIP, however, there were ideological contradictions. It openly respected the Nationalists, but wanted to dissociate itself from their tactics. It sharply criticized commonwealth status as a farce and a hoax, and claimed that in accepting P.L. 600 the people had consented to remain a colony. But the PIP's elected representatives swore loyalty to the constitution as a juridical reality within which they would struggle to realize their objectives. Furthermore, they had difficulty in balancing their two extreme wings: on the left, they were supported by the Communist groups, with their Marxist orientation; on the right, by militant Catholics. Only a common devotion to independence brought the disparate factions together. It was not enough. Concepción de Gracia was a true believer in the cause, a man of firm democratic convictions, and a lawyer and parliamentarian of unquestioned ability. But the party failed to penetrate the great bulk of the masses. Furthermore, it was rent by internal dissension. Factional disputes brought disenchantment to many of its supporters, particularly to those who had given the PIP their protest vote. By 1956, the PIP's attack on the PPD and Commonwealth foundered badly. In 1956, it obtained only 86,386 votes; in 1960, it went down to 24,103.[46]

The Republican Statehood party, or PER, on the other hand, began to recuperate during this period. The leadership after 1952 was assumed by two brothers-in-law, Miguel A. García Méndez and Luis A. Ferré. Both were rich men with long experience in politics. Of the two, García Méndez had been more politically voluble, more involved in internal squabbles. Ferré, on the other hand, was more oriented towards American politics and to a moderate conservatism found in certain U.S. Republicans. He strongly believed in a dynamic capitalism in which capital would perform "an exalted mission of high moral character and in which the worker will have satisfied his thirst for justice without having surrendered an atom of his right to freedom." Statehood to him was the redeeming force that would do away with want and make Puerto Ricans participants "of the grandeur of the United States, the nation of which we are loyal and honorable citizens."[47] To achieve these aims, which he turned into a mystique, it was not enough to campaign in Puerto Rico. Fruitful connections with the mainland Republican party would be useful, particularly in matters of patronage and attitudes towards Puerto Rico in Congress. The wheels of fortune would help Ferré as the Eisenhower era began in the United States in 1952.

If the PIP accused Muñoz and the PPD of having hoaxed Puerto Rico into accepting colonialism and fiercely denounced the governor as a United States puppet, the PER, under Ferré, accused Muñoz as wanting, through devious means, to bring about independence. Any act of the commonwealth government that differed from what the PER considered the correct behavior of a federal state would be denounced as proof that the PPD really wanted separation. Ferré began to emerge as the man who was regrouping the old pro-statehood, Republican forces. He was personally a symbol of industrial success at a time when industrialism was changing Puerto Rico. His commitment to developing a new capitalist ethic for the island as a businessman-politician, combined with his philanthropy and his links with U.S. moderate Republicans, gave him

Above left, *Pedro Albizu Campos, a Harvard educated lawyer and the leader of the Nationalist party;* right, *Luis Muñoz Marín, the first governor elected by the people of Puerto Rico in 1948 and founder of the Commonwealth of Puerto Rico;* below left, *Luis A. Ferré, leader of the Republican pro-statehood party, was elected governor in 1968.*

the image of a Puerto Rican Nelson Rockefeller, and gradually brought him a mass following. He and his associates, more than the PIP lawyers, became an important force in the 1960s.

For Muñoz and the PPD, trouble came from both ends of the political spectrum. The social and economic changes were bringing great relief and new opportunities to many Puerto Ricans, but were creating new problems and tensions and changing many social values as a new middle class emerged. Muñoz was guiding the ship of state through the Scylla and Carybdis of political polarization. The consensus his movement had built depended not only on its social and economic success, but on a full understanding of his ideal of the *patria-pueblo,* his mid-way philosophy, not only in Puerto Rico but in the United States. The consensus certainly needed further growth of the commonwealth status and further definition by the Congress of its key concepts as a form of creative federalism. Personally, Muñoz would continue to gain in stature as a visionary statesman, but he would fail in his political objective. The whirling success of 1948–1952 would not be repeated in his lifetime.

With Eisenhower's election as president, the PPD, for the first time, was faced with the problem of dealing with a Republican administration. The social awakening in Puerto Rico and the PPD's drive towards reform and self-government had taken place under the Democrats. While some Republicans in Congress and in the party were sympathetic to Muñoz and his objectives, it was not expected that Eisenhower would be as receptive as Truman. The Eisenhower administration, on the other hand, was concerned with Caribbean affairs and Puerto Rico had become a focal point for democratic and technical exchanges as well as a key strategic area in this important region.

When President Truman had launched his celebrated Point Four program in 1949 to make U.S. technical know-how available to what were then described as underdeveloped areas, Muñoz had offered Puerto Rico as a training center, particularly for Latin Americans, and as a demonstration area for new techniques in planning, education, public health, and economic development. Truman had accepted and the program began under the Puerto Rico Planning Board.

With the establishment of commonwealth, a Puerto Rican State Department was created. Special legislation promptly entrusted this department with the responsibility for initiating programs to make Puerto Rico better known abroad. This agency was ready to assume wide responsibilities for coordinating technical and cultural exchanges in close collaboration with United States and international agencies. The facilities of the commonwealth government were at its disposal, including the manifold educational programs of the University of Puerto Rico.

When Muñoz first visited Eisenhower in 1953, he told the new president that the new commonwealth was ready to make a contribution in an area vital to new international policies. He had come to offer and not to ask, he said. A formal collaboration was planned with the new International Cooperation Administration (ICA), headed by Harold Stassen. In this agreement the Technical Assistance Program would encompass the Caribbean and Latin America. Thus, an increasing stream of visitors came to Puerto Rico, while Puerto Rican technicians went abroad. A host of Puerto Ricans participated as delegates in inter-American and international conferences even beyond the Western Hemisphere.

The program gradually expanded at Puerto Rico's initiative to include cooperation with international organizations, such as the United Nations and the Organization of American States and their specialized agencies. By 1959, 6,500 trainees had come to Puerto Rico from 118 different countries, over half from the Caribbean and Latin America. Fully one-third had been sponsored by non-U.S. programs, indicating a growing international interest in the Puerto Rican experience.

But the program did not limit itself to technicians. During this same period, over 1,400 leaders of opinion and specialists from 79 countries came for short visits to get a general view of Puerto Rico and its development programs. A program of international conferences in varied fields was also carried out, bringing over 2,200 people from 56 countries to discuss a wide range of subjects from public health to economic planning, history, social theories, medical sciences, and more. The results were hailed in the United States and in much of Latin America. The program turned Puerto Rico into a hemispheric meeting ground and added to the Puerto Rican sense of pride and accomplishment. The uniqueness of the program corresponded, in Muñoz's view, with the uniqueness of the commonwealth relationship with the United States. Aside from its political connotations, it went beyond Puerto Rican insularity, opening up a window to the world.[48]

This growth, it was thought, would help to create better understanding for a clearer congressional definition of Puerto Rico's status. There was a general feeling within the PPD that movement had to take place, to face critics from all sides of the spectrum and preserve the strong political consensus. By 1954, Muñoz was laying the groundwork in an article in *Foreign Affairs,* in which he argued that the time would come for an evaluation of the commonwealth experience, with the basic points of association spelled out in an act of Congress, agreed to by the Puerto Rican electorate. He felt that the area of federal functions which could not be left to specific consent included minimum wages, quota arrangements, common defense, and political treaties; but other functions and legislation could be extended to Puerto Rico at the commonwealth's own request or with its specific consent. The long-range U.S. interest in the relationship was not only military but also commercial. In addition, he wrote, Puerto Rico had become "a small but effective engine of understanding of and goodwill for the United States." His proof was the international programs that the commonwealth was developing.[49]

Muñoz had suggested to the new administration that a commission be created, at the executive level, to study the ways in which further clarification of the status could take place. But nothing came of the idea and eventually it was decided to go to Congress, where there were still friends and a dominant Democratic party.

The Governor had many challenges, and one of them involved the Nationalists. Jailed after the events of 1950, Albizu was in failing health. He claimed he was being tortured by death rays and kept himself wrapped up in wet towels blaming the United States government for what he called "burning emanations" against his person. Albizu's incarceration created a dilemma for Muñoz: his imprisonment made him a political martyr in the Nationalist campaign abroad. If he were freed, Muñoz was convinced that Nationalist agitation and violence would result, disturbing Puerto Rico's development. But Muñoz, weighing both ends of the dilemma, decided to pardon Albizu in September, 1953, after doctors had declared the revolutionary leader a paranoid.

The predicted reaction took place. Less than a year later four Nationalists led by a young woman, Lolita Lebrón, entered the Visitors Gallery of the U.S. House of Representatives and began shooting wildly at the legislative chamber, shouting "Puerto Rico is not freed!" The attack had been planned in New York to coincide with the opening of the Inter-American Conference at Caracas on March 1, 1954, to draw world attention. It was a suicidal attempt, in line with the Nationalists' fervent conviction that only revolutionary action could bring independence to Puerto Rico. The planning showed that the revolutionary nucleus was now found mainly in the Puerto Rican communities in the United States. In the island itself, there was no reaction except the government's determination to send Albizu back to jail, which was done after forcing his surrender with tear gas.[50] Miss Lebrón and her companions were condemned to life imprisonment by a U.S. court; years later they were pardoned by the Carter administration.

Soon after his return to jail, Albizu suffered a stroke in 1956. He was taken to the Presbyterian Hospital in San Juan and put under the expert care of a group of well-known Puerto Rican doctors. On November 15, 1964, Muñoz again pardoned him. A few months later, on April 21, 1965, the fiery leader of Puerto Rican revolutionary nationalism passed away. He had stood, until the end, for open, hostile confrontation with the United States. Although supported in his last years by the Communists, his ideology was influenced by his profound attachment to Hispanicism and Catholicism—a far cry from the positions prevalent in Latin American Marxism. To his followers, he remained an exalted and romantic symbol, but his heritage of hatred and hostility to the United States and his use of violence would later be continued by groups committed to a Marxist-Leninist revolutionary view of history.

Five Congressmen were wounded in the Nationalists' attack on the House. Congress, however, did not react angrily against Puerto Rico. When Fernós deplored the attack in a speech to the House, he received a standing ovation. Governor Muñoz flew to Washington to meet with congressional leaders, and called on those who had been wounded. The shooting apparently had left no official ill feelings, but it certainly did not promote the cause of revision. On April 12, 1954, Representative Alvin Bentley, who had been wounded, said that Puerto Rican migration to the United States should be controlled. Two days later, Republican Congressman Frank T. Bow of Ohio, under the influence of Ferré and the Puerto Rican Statehood party, introduced a joint resolution requesting a special committee to study all phases of the Puerto Rican relationship with the United States, especially migration.[51] Nothing came of this resolution, except the evidence that the statehood forces in Puerto Rico, through their friends in Washington, would do everything possible to discredit commonwealth and prevent any further congressional action.

But the pro-statehood forces in Puerto Rico could not check Muñoz and the PPD at the polls. In 1956 the PER's program made a pitch for the support of the workers and the emerging middle class by insisting on applying the federal minimum wage to Puerto Rico and assuring full integration with the American economy. Puerto Rico's destiny, it insisted, "by the design of Providence as well as by historical determinism is to be a State of Union."[52] Ferré, as the candidate for governor, challenged Muñoz, but the results confirmed the strong political consensus on behalf of the PPD, which obtained 433,010 votes to 172,838 votes for the PER and 86,386 for the PIP.[53] If it was a clear-cut victory for Muñoz and the PPD leadership, it was also an encouraging sign for Ferré. His party had regrouped and doubled its poor 1952 performance and it was showing new strength in the urban areas, including metropolitan San Juan, where the new middle class was beginning to appear in the sprawling suburbs.

The restructuring of the economy and the society with more and more dependence on American capital, as well as the emergence of a new urban lifestyle heavily influenced by consumerism, created a new arena for political competition, unlike the rural Puerto Rico of the 1930s and 1940s. The expansion of the postwar U.S. industrial economy was benefiting Operation Bootstrap. Under this new industrial development, more wealth was reaching the middle and low sectors of the economy. But heavy unemployment and pockets of distressing poverty persisted.

To Muñoz, it was necessary to create more productive wealth through savings; to invest more in education as the great economic multiplier; to prevent superfluous and conspicuous consumption; and to get more people, including the workers, to own stock in corporations.[54] A note of urgency began to creep in, a feeling that the commonwealth status had to grow in answer to its critics. This need for action was increased as Congress prepared to admit Alaska and Hawaii into the Union. In his message to the Legislative Assembly and in his speeches in the United States, including the Godkin Lectures Muñoz gave at Harvard in 1958, he insisted on the concepts outlined in his *Foreign Affairs* article. Within the government a working group was quietly analyzing the alternatives and in 1959 a new effort was made with the introduction of the Fernós-Murray Bill, in response to a request from the commonwealth legislature.

The Fernós-Murray Bill sought to replace the Federal Relations Act with the "Articles of Permanent Association of the People of Puerto Rico with the United States." Its aim was to clarify the concept of a compact, which had been under fire since 1953. Some important powers held by the federal government were to be transferred to Puerto Rico, such as the right to fix its own duty on coffee and the right to petition Congress for reductions on specific imports such as codfish, a staple of the Puerto Rican diet. On the other hand, while Puerto Rico would continue to be exempted from the payment of federal revenue taxes, the bill did provide for the island to share in the expenses of federal functions in Puerto Rico. In introducing the bill to Congress, Fernós made clear that Puerto

Rico was not going the way of Alaska or Hawaii, nor was it asking for a dissolution of ties. It wanted to strengthen the commonwealth as a sensible, dynamic concept which could preserve all its contemporary achievements.[55]

In essence, the Fernós-Murray Bill presented no far-reaching proposals. There was nothing in it that was not based on some precedent in the relations of Puerto Rico with the United States. But in spite of strong support from some influential members of Congress, it got nowhere. In the hearings held in Puerto Rico and San Juan, there was great praise for many of the accomplishments of the commonwealth government. The Puerto Rican view on the compact, however, was sharply questioned by Senator Henry Jackson. Both Fernós and Muñoz made their views crystal clear: P.L. 600 was a compact. Their position was supported by the opinion of the great U.S. constitutionalist Edward S. Corwin, who affirmed that Congress, by using its inherent sovereign powers, could enter into a compact with the people of Puerto Rico. A somewhat similar opinion was expressed by the U.S. Department of Justice. But there was much pressure from the pro-statehood movement in Puerto Rico against the Fernós-Murray Bill. The question dragged into 1960, an election year, and finally died in committee. By that time, the PPD had to face another challenge: the intervention of the Catholic church led by the bishop of Ponce, James McManus, and of San Juan, James P. Davis, in the island's politics.

The Church Question

The intervention of the church in electoral politics was an aberration in Puerto Rico. In the nineteenth century, the church had been closely linked with and supported by the Spanish government. Church and state were separated after 1898. A shift took place in the higher clergy, as American-born bishops replaced the Spaniards. Generally, the church collaborated with the new rulers, and learned to live in a society in which Protestantism became an active religious force. No Puerto Rican attained the rank of bishop. Views and attitudes of the U.S. Catholic clergy began to dominate the church's social behavior. But the church, knowing that it served the faith of Puerto Ricans of all ideological persuasions, from Albizu to Ferré, was careful not to embroil itself in politics.

This changed in 1960. The bishops were pushing for legislation to provide for religious education in the schools, a practice the majority of legislators opposed. The clergy also wanted to stop the dissemination of information on birth control practices. Bishop McManus had an additional motivation: he was dead set against the commonwealth relationship. In 1959, and during the hearings on the Fernós-Murray Bill he had written to the chairman of the congressional committee urging that the committee make it clear that Puerto Rico was just a territory of the United States.[56] Behind the opposition to the PPD lurked other motives which were not religious.

A mass rally took place on May 22, 1960. Bishop Davis used the occasion to censure the PPD and urge the organization of a Catholic political party. This was followed by a well-orchestrated campaign, including a pastoral letter issued on June 30, to help the registration of the Christian Action Party (PAC). At the same time, press articles asked Catholics not to vote for Muñoz, the real political target of the bishop's move. On October 4, McManus made his personal objective clear: destroy the PPD and attain statehood.[57]

The church's intervention became a boomerang for those responsible. Muñoz and the PPD were restrained in their reply, eschewed all anticlericalism, and appealed to the historic role of a church above parties. At election time, no dent was made in the PPD's political strength: in November, 1960, the party obtained 457,880 votes to 252,364 for the pro statehood PER and only 52,096 for the PAC. The PIP was a distant fourth with only 24,103.

The PAC proved to be a *rara avis* in Puerto Rican politics. In 1964, it polled only 26,867 votes and was on the way to extinction.[58] The Catholics who supported it returned to their traditional loyalties. PPD Catholics took their complaint discreetly to the Vatican, and a change of church policy became evident over the next years. Without much fanfare, McManus and Davis left the island, and Puerto Ricans, for the first time in the century, now headed the higher clergy. Under Pope John XXIII, in Puerto Rico as in many other places, there were changes in the church's social role. Neither clericalism nor anticlericalism found a significant place in the complex, heated issues of the island's politics.

Muñoz and the Kennedy Interlude

In November, 1960, as the PPD was sweeping Puerto Rico, John F. Kennedy was elected president of the United States by a very thin margin. His years coincided with the high water mark of the Muñoz era in Puerto Rican history. The period also saw the closest relationship ever established between a Puerto Rican political leader and a U.S. president.

Kennedy had a genuine liking for the people of Puerto Rico and great admiration for Muñoz and his achievements. There was another reason for the prominence of Puerto Rico during those years. Kennedy, as no U.S. president before him, was deeply concerned with Latin America. He thought that a new hemispheric partnership was in order and that Latin America needed as much support and encouragement from the United States as Europe had received under the Marshall Plan.

It was natural that Kennedy should turn to Muñoz for advice and help. By 1960, Muñoz was already a strong voice of the "democratic left." His views now encompassed not only the Puerto Rican realities, but the problems besetting the hemisphere and, indeed, the developing world. Between 1956 and 1960, as the commonwealth relationship was attracting attention, Muñoz used every opportunity to set forth his ideas. In offering the Puerto Rican experience, he was not asking for a mere aping of the so-called Puerto Rican model. Unfortunately, in later years, a distorted view of the Muñoz position would be expressed. Muñoz was trying to emphasize that to attain economic security and democracy Puerto Rico had been "healthily undoctrinaire, with no fixed taboos, no immutable sacred cows. . . ." He staunchly believed that democratic peoples had to be constantly creative and that "the Commonwealth of Puerto Rico, the people of it, are naturally by no means pretending to offer a pattern of political union." He reiterated the need for a people to be fired "by a vision of what human energies can do to overcome man-created or nature-created misery." He proposed a plan for the hemisphere with the abolition of extreme poverty as a basic goal to be attained within the lifetime of children already born. "Let us not be doctrinaire either as to socialism or capitalism, but only as to freedom and human dignity," he argued. In his opinion, political democracy could not be permanently rooted until there was an effort at productivity and distributive justice.[59]

Muñoz had been active in promoting these views among leaders in the hemisphere. When Richard M. Nixon had stopped overnight in San Juan, after his ill-starred trip to Latin America in 1958, Muñoz had counseled him that the United States should reserve its embrace for its truly democratic friends, and keep the dictators at an arm's length. When Milton Eisenhower was sent on a fact-finding mission to the area, Muñoz had gathered a distinguished group of Latin American democrats and experts in economic and social development, and at an impromptu meeting in San Juan had urged the president's brother to recommend a more farsighted policy in support of planning and aid through an Inter-

American Development Bank. He was, furthermore, in touch with the Latin American democratic leadership and gave his moral support to movements engaged in promoting free governments and social and economic reform.

Attracted by Puerto Rico and Muñoz's views, Kennedy selected the island for his first major speech on Latin America as a presidential candidate. On December 15, 1958, at a Democratic dinner, Kennedy put forth the gist of a program of basic concern for human rights and democracy, of recognizing Latin America as a vital force in world economic and diplomatic affairs, and of closer economic cooperation. For that, he claimed, there was need for leadership, "leadership such as that which you have achieved here in Puerto Rico. . . . which our nation needs today in both domestic and foreign affairs. . . ."[60]

This was neither rhetoric nor self-serving flattery. As soon as he was elected president, Kennedy appointed a task force for Latin America which included two close associates of Governor Muñoz: Teodoro Moscoso and Arturo Morales Carrión. The task force, chaired by another close friend and admirer of Muñoz, Adolf Berle, prepared a basic set of recommendations which became the starting point of the Alliance for Progress, Kennedy's key Latin American policy. Before the task force members submitted their report, they attended Muñoz's inaugural on January 2, 1960, and discussed the highlights of their recommendations with him.

Puerto Rican input during the Kennedy administration was further assured when, upon the advice of Senator Mike Mansfield and others, Morales Carrión was appointed deputy assistant secretary of state for Latin American and Moscoso was named ambassador to Venezuela, where Rómulo Betancourt had been elected president. Moscoso was later called to direct the U.S. economic contribution to the alliance, which had been adopted in August, 1961, at a hemispheric meeting at Punta del Este, Uruguay.

There were great hopes during those years that two countries close to Puerto Rico, Cuba and the Dominican Republic, would march along the path of democratic and economic reform. Together with Venezuela, they were linked with the historical experience of Puerto Rico. When Fulgencio Batista was overthrown by Fidel Castro, there was rejoicing in the island, where Castro's movement had great support. In his trips to the United States, Muñoz argued on behalf of the Cuban revolution and hoped to develop a close personal relationship with Castro. But Castro was going in a different direction and soon Puerto Rico began receiving disenchanted supporters of the Cuban revolution who told Muñoz a different story. The ill-conceived Bay of Pigs invasion, planned under Eisenhower, but supported by Kennedy early in his administration, contributed to the estrangement.

Castro's way was the way of a Communist and the democratic left soon found in him an implacable opponent, much to Muñoz's disappointment. Castro made clear his complete backing of the Puerto Rican Nationalists and soon began a campaign at the United Nations to question the validity of commonwealth status.

More promising was the situation in Santo Domingo after Trujillo was killed by personal enemies. For Kennedy and Muñoz, as well as for Betancourt and other Latin American democrats, this was an acid test of what they had been preaching. They joined hands to support an attempt to provide democratic government in a country torn by grave dissensions, with externally difficult economic problems and little training in electoral practices. To emphasize his concern, Kennedy sent Morales Carrión as special emissary to Santo Domingo at the end of 1961 to assure all democratic groups of his personal interest in returning democracy to the country.

On December 15, 1961, the president paid a special visit to Puerto Rico. In contrast to Eisenhower, who had come to address an educational meeting and play golf and had limited his contact to a brief interview with Muñoz at the airport, Kennedy came to see the people themselves. He received the greatest reception ever accorded a visitor. Nearly 700,000 Puerto Ricans lined the streets and the avenue leading to the airport to cheer him. This tremendous outpouring of support moved him deeply.

To stress his admiration and respect, Kennedy hosted a dinner in honor of Muñoz at the White House on November 12, 1961, followed by a concert in which Pablo Casals, the great cellist, performed for the president and his friend. In 1963, Kennedy awarded Muñoz the Presidential Medal of Freedom, an award for those "whose life can be graced with the fullness with which it can be lived."[61] This was probably Muñoz's finest moment. No Puerto Rican had been so honored before; no United States president had ever shown such real affection and respect for the people of the island. The partnership created in 1952, after the long era of tutelage, seemed to be bearing the best of fruits. But it still needed revision and redefinition to strengthen the popular consensus. Yet when the effort was tried, it failed again.

No further action was attempted on the Fernós-Murray Bill in Congress. Muñoz had begun to press the executive branch, where he counted on Kennedy's support and understanding. On February 10, 1961, he had asked the president to clarify the unique position of the commonwealth before all executive departments and agencies. He especially wanted to avoid the notion that Puerto Rico was a U.S. territory or possession. Kennedy obliged, after careful consideration, with an Executive Order issued July 25, 1961. The order, printed in the Federal Register, became established U.S. policy. It was issued because "of the importance and significance of Puerto Rico in the relations of the United States with Latin America and other nations. . . ." The order summarized the 1952 legislative action and the 1953 U.N. resolution and instructed all departments, agencies, and officials of the executive branch to "faithfully and carefully observe and respect this arrangement in relation to all matters affecting the Commonwealth of Puerto Rico."[62] Furthermore, a presidential assistant, Lee White, was now the White House liaison for Puerto Rico, and an informal group of Kennedy aides, including Arthur Schlesinger, Jr., the noted historian, met from time to time with Muñoz to advise action on the commonwealth status.

But basic progress had to be made in Congress. Fernós had succeeded in obtaining approval of an amendment of the Federal Judicial Code to provide for direct appeals to decisions from the Commonwealth Supreme Court to the U.S. Supreme Court and not to the Boston Circuit Court. It was another step to remove the territorial or possession stigma.[63]

In preparation for new congressional action, an exchange of letters between Kennedy and Muñoz took place in 1962. In his letter, the governor suggested that it was high time for the relationship to grow and suggested the recognition of the basic principle of self-government for Puerto Rico "in permanent association with the United States on the basis of common loyalty, common citizenship, mutual dedication to democracy and mutual commitment to freedom." He insisted on the need to clarify the moral and juridical basis of commonwealth and the maximization of its powers and authority by devising ways for the people of Puerto Rico to participate in the federal functions that affected them. His final suggestion was that the people of Puerto Rico should have an opportunity to vote on the arrangements, but also to indicate their preferences for any other form of relationship.[64] In sum, he wanted action through a plebiscite to decide the status issue.

Kennedy replied by stating his full sympathy. He saw no reason why the commonwealth concept should not be fully developed "as a permanent institution in its association with the United States," if that was what the people desired, and agreed that in fairness to all concerned, the people should be consulted "so that they may express any other preference, including independence, if that should be their wish."[65] Legislation approved in 1960 already made a plebiscite possible in Puerto Rico, whenever 10 percent of the electorate so desired. The way was open for another expression of the people's will. On December 3, 1962, a joint resolution of the commonwealth legislature formally proposed a procedure to Congress to solve the status issue. It comprised a consultation based on the three formulas: statehood, independence, or commonwealth, including that formula which Congress would agree with respect to the new terms of association under the commonwealth relationship.[66]

As Fernós later wrote, it was a rocky road to travel. The PER had already demanded that the term "permanent union" in the resolution be substituted for "permanent association." It was more than a semantic question, for the PER thought "permanent union" meant the direct road to statehood. Any return to the original concepts of association, debated in 1952 and included in the United Nations resolution and the Muñoz-Kennedy exchange, would be denounced from now on as a devious way to promote separation. The aim of the PER was to destroy the concept of association as a viable, permanent alternative in Congress.

In April, 1963, H.R. 5945 was introduced in Congress. The bill would have established a twelve-man United States-Puerto Rico Commission to draft a proposed "compact of permanent union" between the U.S. government and the people of Puerto Rico which would be submitted to the Puerto Rican electorate, along with proposals for statehood and independence. If the majority voted for either statehood or independence, the alternative would be referred to further congressional action.

For the PER, this was a crucial challenge and they used all their partisan connections to stop the bill. Unlike 1917 and 1952, there was no political solidarity, but a bitter fight and sharp disagreement both in Puerto Rico and in Congress. The status divisions created at the time of the Foraker Act resurfaced now, in different men and different circumstances. Puerto Rico had gone a long way in achieving self-government. But the principle of congressional supremacy, rooted in the Treaty of Paris, still made negotiations extremely difficult; especially with a core of congressmen who were jealous of their prerogatives, had a narrow, restrictive, constitutional outlook, and were ready to side with any Puerto Rican opposition that might be mustered against the bill.

The leadership that handled the bill in Congress was utterly confused, and the administration failed to give it strong overall support.

Even Muñoz's powers of persuasion failed and he was grilled by Republican Congressman John Saylor of Pennsylvania, a close friend of the PER leaders. Saylor was disrespectful and inconsiderate, with an arrogance that was deeply resented by the PPD followers.

The Twilight of Muñoz's Governorship

The legislation Muñoz favored did not pass. In 1964 Congress only agreed to create a United States-Puerto Rico Commission on the Status of Puerto Rico, known as the Status Commission, whose function was to "study all factors . . . which may have a bearing on the present and future relationship between the United States and Puerto Rico."[67] The findings had to be submitted to the president, but there was no mandate for Congress to act and no provision made for a plebiscite. The commission had a chairman and two persons appointed by the president; four members of Congress; and six Puerto Ricans, of whom three were pro-commonwealth, two pro-statehood, and one pro-independence.

The commission worked from June, 1964, to August, 1966, under the chairmanship of James H. Rowe, an experienced Washington attorney. Its executive secretary was Ben S. Stephansky, who had brilliantly served as Kennedy's ambassador to Bolivia, knew Spanish well, and was sensitive to Puerto Rico's cultural ties with the Caribbean and Latin America.

The commission conducted hearings and published excellent studies on the U.S.-Puerto Rico relationship. In August, 1966, it recommended to Congress that the relationship should be based on the principle of mutual consent and self-determination, that each status alternative conferred equal dignity and equality (a point hotly contested by statehooders and independentists), and that any immediate changes in political status would involve serious economic dislocation. These changes could only be offset by special economic and financial arrangements, especially regarding statehood and independence. The commission further recommended that a plebiscite on status be held and that an *ad hoc* advisory group be created to recommend appropriate transition measures to the president, Congress, and the governor.[68]

Late in 1964, pressure grew in Puerto Rico for a plebiscite, although Congress was uncommitted as to its results. Muñoz then faced a difficult task. He was greatly respected in the United States and Puerto Rico, with powerful friends in Latin America, but his bright star had begun to set. He had hoped that the Kennedy administration could provide the legislative muscle he wanted to settle the meaning of commonwealth once and for all, but this was not forthcoming. In the Caribbean, his hopes that the presidency of Juan Bosch in the Dominican Republic would strengthen the ideals of social democracy were badly shaken when Bosch was deposed by a coup. In the legislature his old friend Ramos Antonini, a bulwark in the political defense of commonwealth before the masses, died. And on November 22, John F. Kennedy was killed by an assassin in Dallas. To Muñoz, the bullet that killed Kennedy was also aimed at Puerto Rico. For the governor, 1963 was a year of tragedy and adversity.

In 1964, near the end of his term, he became convinced that the time had come to surrender the helm of state. In his last State of the Commonwealth Message, he could point to the great strides Puerto Rico had taken. Both agricultural and industrial production were moving ahead. Cattle raising had become a most promising economic activity, while in industry nearly 24 percent of the new capital invested came from inside Puerto Rico. Net income was estimated to reach between $4.5 and $5 billion in 1975, a tremendous surge forward.

The time had come to ask what the "Purpose of Puerto Rico" was, the overall objective of the people of the island. It could not be, Muñoz argued, sheer economic progress. He considered the following six points crucial priorities: quality education for all, the best of health care, a home for every family, an orderly balance between rural and urban life, increased economic activity in the hands of Puerto Ricans, and the abolition of extreme poverty. Education topped the list because it was through education that a "civilization of excellence" could be achieved. This was not simply formal education; it was education for a lifetime, the constant inner enrichment of life, in cities that should be civilized above all, with neighborhoods where good human relationships would flourish. Muñoz called attention to social progress, in the terms defined by Pope John XXIII in his encyclical *Mater et Magistra,* and took his concept of the "family salary" as an objective. By the end of this last message, Muñoz was transcending the status question in search of a non-Utopian but achievable vision, not only by parties, but by generations joining hands together. There was great nobility in this vision, transcending the murky sea of politics. It could only be practical if the consensus held, if government was stable, if polarization was avoided, if generations learned to work together, if there was an understanding Congress, and if there was real feeling for *la patria-pueblo.*

The practical politician had returned to the basic beliefs and commitments that started his long and remarkable career. He was again a visionary, as a torrent of affluence engulfed the island with values, attitudes, conflicting views, and passions which were the negation of what was to remain, historically, the expression of a Platonic ideal. A different Puerto Rico was in the making, more inclined to social strife, dissension, urban violence, drugs, class animosities, sharp polarizations, and a decay in the political dialogue. A social crisis was coming but it still needed a few years to show its true dimensions.

Toward the Plebiscite

In the summer of 1964, convinced that it was time for a new generation to take over the daily tasks of government and for the party to institutionalize itself while he devoted his energies to resolving the status issue, Muñoz handpicked his most trusted lieutenant, Secretary of State Robert Sánchez Vilella, as the next candidate for governor.

The decision would eventually show how difficult it is to transfer the mantle of leadership in a democracy by an act of personal imposition. Sánchez had many assets: he knew Muñoz's thinking in every aspect of government, was thoroughly familiar with the administrative machinery, and was well known for his rugged honesty and integrity. On the other hand, he had never run for elective office, had opposition within the party, and lacked Muñoz's knack for dealing with divergent views and Muñoz's profound knowledge of the political world. To many *Populares*, who saw difficult days ahead, Sánchez's nomination was a serious mistake. An undercurrent of resentment remained.

With Muñoz's help, Sánchez carried the island: 487,280 to 284,627 for Ferré, 22,201 for the PIP, and 26,867 for the Catholic Party (PAC). Everything pointed to one more term of government action for the PPD, with Sánchez as governor while Muñoz dealt with the status question and Washington. It did not work. Sánchez felt he had to be his own man, with his own program and his own power base. Beginning with his inaugural address, he let it be known that Puerto Rico was entering a new era; and he started immediately to build up a power structure by turning to the younger party members for support. A psychological split developed, with growing strains in his relationship with the old guard. At a time when maximum cohesion was needed to face the plebiscite challenge, a rapid erosion took place within the government party. The situation was highlighted by Sánchez's divorce and remarriage—a matter which under different circumstances would hardly have had profound political effects but now became a delicate issue.

The 1967 plebiscite was held with the PPD already showing signs of internal dissension. Sánchez's role was muted and Muñoz carried the ball. The pro-independence groups, except for a splinter organization, refused to participate. The statehooders, however, rallied to Ferré's call, although the party officially was not involved. With good political instinct, Ferré headed the largest group, *Estadistas Unidos* (United Statehooders), with new people behind him, such as Carlos Romero Barceló and Hernán Padilla, destined to be the new Republican leaders of the 1970s. The admission of Alaska and Hawaii as states of the Union added to the momentum, but other factors helped the statehooders: the growing influx of federal funds from President Johnson's Great Society leading to increased dependency; the growing disenchantment of middle class elements, particularly in the metropolitan area, with the Sánchez governorship and the PPD predicament; and, especially, the fear of independence cleverly exploited by the statehood movement.

But Muñoz, in one of his hardest battles, held the party together. Nearly 66 percent of the registered voters went to the polls—a high percentage considering the efforts of those who opposed the plebiscite and wanted it to fail.

Of 702,512 voters, 425,079 or 60.5 percent favored commonwealth and 273,315 or 38.9 percent voted for statehood. In spite of the drive for abstention, it was obvious that commonwealth under Muñoz could still rally the country. The statehooders, on the other hand, were jubilant. They showed growing strength in the main urban areas of San Juan and Ponce. To them, the plebiscite was just the opening battle of the 1968 campaign. After the plebiscite, they registered a new party, the *Partido Nuevo Progresista*, or PNP. The palm tree now became the symbol for statehood—a regrouping of forces that was ready to challenge the PPD's historic role.

"Only the Popular Party will defeat the Popular Party," Muñoz once said as a warning on the dangers of political bickering and dissension. In 1967–1968, the disruptive forces were active. Sánchez became so estranged from the party's ruling machinery that he was denied the nomination.

Spurred by close followers, such as Luis A. Camacho and José Arsenio Torres, Sánchez left the PPD and arranged to lead a splinter party called the *Partido del Pueblo* or People's party. He was determined, he said, to revive the old ideals of the PPD which he claimed had "abandoned the people." His motto was: "Let the people decide."

Muñoz's admonition proved prophetic at election time. It was really a three-party contest among Ferré; Sánchez; and the PPD candidate, Senator Luis Negrón López, a devoted legislator and public servant who was close to Muñoz and the party machinery, but had no strong popular appeal. A new leadership had emerged in the PIP after Concepción de Gracia's death in 1967. Divided between moderates and radicals with a new wing influenced by *Castrimo,* the PIP failed to make a significant showing.

In November, 1968, Ferré squeezed through with a 23,000 plurality. His party obtained 390,922 votes, carried by the momentum developed by the plebiscite; the PPD received 367,901 and was strong enough to dominate the Senate; the People's party, as the spoiler, got 87,832 votes, enough to deny the PPD the governorship; and the PIP received only 24,729 votes, again showing its lack of mass support.[69]

Clearly, there was no majority for statehood, but it was also obvious that the Ferré brand of republicanism had a firm hold on the two leading urban centers, San Juan and Ponce. An electoral dichotomy was sharply visible between the metropolitan area and the rest of the country, where the PPD retained its traditional strength.

It was, in many ways, a momentous election, for the campaign had been extremely bitter and full of personal attacks, especially against Negrón López. For the first time, television made an impact on the voters and modern techniques of image-making were widely used. The PNP, with strong financial backers, had become a powerful political rival to the PPD. But while many observers read the results in terms of their effect on the status question, it was evident that the role of personalities, the unity or disunity of parties, the strength of electoral organizations, and the platform promises on social and economic issues were crucial to the voters' response. The consensus developed in a quarter of a century was gone and Puerto Rico was now entering a confusing, confrontational era.

15

A Postscriptum:
The End of Consensus

After 1968, a new period emerged in the island's history. The contours are still blurred and it would be presumptuous for the historian to delve into events with the certainty that a perspective of time usually affords. This is especially difficult when sharp and bitter divisions affect the body politic as is the case with contemporary Puerto Rico. Yet certain trends can be observed.

The Political Outlook

First and foremost, we have witnessed the end of political consensus. During the Muñoz era, the voters consistently provided huge majorities to Muñoz and the PPD. Since 1968, however, the situation has changed. The PNP and the PPD have been locked in close, hard-fought electoral battles. The PNP was in power from 1968 to 1972; then the PPD won by a comfortable majority, 609,680 votes to 524,039 for the PNP. The PPD lost again in 1976 by over 40,000 votes out of 1,464,600 voters. In 1980 the PPD came back with undeniable strength, missing the governorship by a little over 3,000 votes and winning the Senate and 52 out of 77 municipalities. A recent decision of the Commonwealth Supreme Court also awarded it a deciding district in the House, so in both houses the PPD now has a narrow majority. The Washington representation was won by the PNP by a clear margin. The PIP, on the other hand, remained a very distant third with a little over 5 percent of the vote, while the more radical *Partido Socialista Puertorriqueño* or PSP, with strong Cuban connections, failed to attract enough voters to remain as a registered party.[1]

Now Puerto Rico has, besides the core of the party faithful, a large floating vote with tenuous partisan allegiances, a vote less sensitive to the status issue and more concerned with personalities, programs, and performance. This vote is also affected by the chronic economic problems, and particularly by the backlash of the world recession. Bread-and-butter issues, therefore, play a very important role in the Puerto Rican political picture, largely overshadowing the thorny status question.

There is also an end of consensus around the political personalities involved. Ferré wanted to follow in Muñoz's footsteps as a charismatic figure who would attract the masses and lead them to statehood. But he failed to create a great coalition and was voted out of office in 1972, remaining as the PNP's elder statesman, the Mr. Republican of Puerto Rico, the friend of Nixon, Ford, and Reagan.

He was succeeded as governor by Rafael Hernández Colón of the PPD, a young, capable lawyer thoroughly devoted to commonwealth status. Operating from the Senate as a power base and with Muñoz's strong personal support, Hernández Colón was able to topple Ferré in 1972 and restore the PPD to power. But the world recession hit his government badly and, like Ferré, he failed to unite the great majorities of yesteryear. He was defeated in 1976, and, attempting a comeback, narrowly missed the governorship in 1980.

Hernández Colón was succeeded by Carlos Romero Barceló, the PNP mayor from San Juan. An uncompromising foe of the commonwealth and the PPD, Romero, although elected on the old platform that status was not at issue, promptly used every governmental resource to push for statehood and weed out most of the PPD's officeholders. Confident of an overwhelming victory in 1980, Romero started laying the groundwork for a 1981 plebiscite in Puerto Rico and the United States. His highly politicized administration failed, however, to obtain the solid, decisive majority he wanted. In November, 1980, he hardly managed to squeeze through, largely aided by the PNP strength in the metropolitan area and Romero's control of the party and the electoral machinery. In the metropolitan area, Romero lagged behind the mayor of San Juan, Hernán Padilla, a rising star in the PNP, with close connections to the U.S. Republican party.

In these elections, as stated, the pro-independence groups failed to make any significant showing. In part, this was due to their internal divisions and ideological cleavages. The PIP saw the emergence of a new leader, Rubén Berríos, a bright young lawyer, educated in the United States and Europe, with political affinities to European socialism. In spite of his rhetorical abilities, he has been unable to make much headway, merely retaining the party as a registered organization. The PSP, under the leadership of Juan Mari Brás, a forceful defender of Marxism-Leninism, has not fared better. The Castro connection has appealed to some intellectual and student groups and Mari Brás himself has evidenced a single-minded devotion to his cause reminiscent of Pedro Albizu Campos. But the partisan spectrum so far has demonstrated that there is little room for the extreme left. The battle is really for the control of a massive center of political opinion.

Puerto Rico is, therefore, divided as to political power, with the two main parties locking horns at every turn. Thus there is no clear mandate for any particular status, and the main immediate concern is the future of the economy, whose growing dependence on federal funds is now seriously threatened by the sharp reductions in federal expenditures under the Reagan administration and by uncontrollable inflation.

The confusing political picture also involves relations with the main U.S. parties. The PNP has shrewdly managed to establish close contact with both the Republican and the Democratic parties. A segment of the PNP, led by Ferré and Padilla, is affiliated with the GOP; while Governor Romero, the Resident Commissioner Baltasar Corrada del Río, and the House Speaker Angel Viera Martínez, are officially the Democratic leaders in Puerto Rico. The party has thus been assured of federal patronage under Ford and Carter, and now under Reagan. The PPD, on the other hand, maintains its traditional ties with the liberal wing of the Democratic party, especially with Senator Edward M. Kennedy. It was this wing that greatly favored commonwealth in its early years.

Under present conditions, it is highly improbable that any effective concerted action could take place on the status issue. The 1967 plebiscite consensus got nowhere. Under Ferré, the Ad Hoc Advisory Group simply explored the desirability of extending the presidential vote to Puerto Rico, an issue of great importance to statehooders but one on which commonwealth partisans were sharply divided. The advisory group recommended that the presidential vote be accorded to the people of Puerto Rico, and that the recommendation be submitted to a referendum. The Ferré gubernatorial debacle stopped the process.

Then, under Hernández Colón, a new Ad Hoc Advisory Group was appointed jointly by President Nixon and the commonwealth governor, pursuant to the 1976 status plebiscite. The group was co-chaired by former Governor Muñoz Marín and Senator Marlow W. Cook. It was asked to submit recommendations on how to further "develop the maximum of self-government and self-determination within the framework of Commonwealth."

After two years of studies, inquiries, public hearings, reports, and discussions, the advisory group concluded that a new compact of permanent union should be adopted to replace the Puerto Rican Federal Relations Act included in Public Law 600.[2]

The draft proposal went a considerable way toward meeting some of the traditional objections to commonwealth as approved in 1950–1952. It reaffirmed the permanent union through the principle of compact, founded upon common citizenship, common currency, common defense, and common market, with the U.S. Supreme Court as the final arbiter. It recommended that Puerto Rico be renamed the Free Associated State. It further recommended that Puerto Rico have a representative in each House, but suggested that unless Congress expressly extends a law to Puerto Rico by specifically mentioning its applicability there, Puerto Rico should not be covered. It also suggested that procedures be established under which the U.S. president and the governor could limit the number of aliens entering Puerto Rico in order to help alleviate its overpopulation and employment problems. These and other provisions contemplated a broadening of commonwealth authority and responsibility in areas that had traditionally been of federal concern.

The Nixon-Ford administration took little interest in the report. The same held true for an indifferent Congress. Resident Commissioner Jaime Benítez introduced a bill for the new compact in 1975, but it never received serious consideration. The Ad Hoc Committee's draft proved to be another exercise in futility. President Ford totally disregarded it. His interest was in promoting statehood. Before leaving office, and while skiing at Vail, Colorado, he made a proposal to Congress on January 1, 1977, in favor of statehood, even though Puerto Rico had not requested it and the United States was committed officially to respect the principle of self-determination internationally. The Carter administration, while ostensibly abiding by this principle in a declaration, actually favored statehooders in matters of patronage, and worked out a deal with Governor Romero to obtain his support at the first presidential primary held under local law in 1980.

Before becoming president, Ronald Reagan came out in favor of statehood to counteract Castro's influence in the Caribbean—a return to the dominance of the strategic imperative in United States-Puerto Rican relations. But in spite of these presidential expressions, backed by heavy patronage to the PNP leadership, there was no majority vote for statehood in the 1980 general elections.

If an important segment of the political establishment in Washington has seemed, during these years, to push Puerto Rico towards statehood, the international community at the United Nations, prodded by the Castro government, has pushed Puerto Rico in the opposite direction, towards separatism and independence.

Since 1953, when the United Nations Resolution on Puerto Rico was adopted, the assembly's complexion has changed greatly. Most of the 75 colonies which had become independent have supported the view expressed by the December, 1960, resolution, that in territories which still have not won their independence, "immediate measures should be taken to transfer all power to the people. . . ."

The Cuban government has taken the initiative in assailing the commonwealth at the United Nations Decolonization Committee, also known as the Committee of 24. Working with the leadership of the Puerto Rican Socialist party, particularly with its main exponent, Juan Mari Bras, the Cubans' repeated thrusts at the United Nations have been a thorn in the side of the United States. Of late, the Cuban attack on commonwealth has somewhat toned down, and the possibility of acceptance of the free association principle has found its way into the United Nations, provided there is a transfer of sovereign rights to Puerto Rico. This principle was adopted by the Decolonization Committee, and it now has been put before the assembly. Free association, as distinct from independence, maintains a political bond between the metropolitan power and the former colony; this was a basic consideration at the United Nations discussions in 1953. The commonwealth relationship obviously remains distasteful to Castroism, but the statehood movement with its connotations of cultural absorption has become more distasteful.

Under these circumstances, the Puerto Rican political mind is the subject of a tug of war among outside interests while internally the sharp, partisan squabbles make the road to consensus very rocky.[3]

The Economic Outlook

The end of political consensus must be considered against an economic backdrop in which the prevailing consensus on a developmental strategy has also vanished. The 1970s saw the weakening of Operation

Bootstrap and an increasing dependence on federal funds. The decade also witnessed the severe effects of the world recession on a fragile though dynamic economy. In the meantime, population pressure continued unabated and grew from 2.7 million in 1970 to over 3.1 million in 1980. A search started for new strategies to cope with growing unemployment, inflation, and a deterioration in the quality of life, punctuated by an increase in crime and violence, drug abuse, environmental pollution, and a decay in public service.

Industrial promotion faced increasing competition from new areas in the world that were offering low wages as economic inducement, while more and more industries in Puerto Rico were paying the federal minimum and even higher wage levels. But manufacturing persisted as the backbone of the economy. While the per capita gross national product increased significantly between 1947 and 1973, there was a decline of more than 2 percent after 1973, in response to the oil crisis and the subsequent recession. As unemployment intensified during this period, a sizable percentage of the population came to rely on increased federal transfer payments to bolster the family income. A few statistics tell the story. Net federal disbursements rose almost fourfold, from $608 million in fiscal 1970 to $2,381 million in fiscal 1977.[4]

The very large increases in federal disbursements were primarily due to the inclusion of Puerto Rico in the food stamp program and several other major federal assistance programs. These disbursements were useful in meeting social needs and, as an interagency report observed in 1979, they spurred consumption and demand. They maintained Puerto Rican purchasing power in the United States market. But they were not geared to a well-thought-out national plan for economic development, and reflected federal rather than commonwealth priorities.[5] There was little comprehensive long-range planning behind this aid.

Perhaps the two most effective programs in the long run were those directed toward the younger elements of the population: the CETA (Comprehensive Employment and Training Act) and the Basic Educational Opportunities Grants. These programs respond to a crying need in Puerto Rico to develop human resources, and increase occupational proficiency and labor productivity. The sudden entrance into the industrial age has hardly prepared the island for intense technological demands. When Muñoz put forth his concept of a "Puerto Rican Purpose," he emphasized education as a key objective; education to meet market demands and to shape the mores of a society with greater self-fulfillment. At present, the two ideals seem distant: the ideal of self-sustaining economic growth based on internal capital formation and greater and more effective productivity (the real economic takeoff), coupled with the ideal of a society in harmony with itself and with nature.

Income distribution aggravated the situation. From 1959 to 1969 there was a trend towards more equitable income distribution, but even so, in 1969, the poorer half of the economy received only 15 percent of gross domestic income while the upper 20 percent obtained 55 percent. In the meantime, personal per capita consumption increased considerably under the pressure of consumerism at the expense of savings. In short, a social and economic imbalance fueled by inflationary pressures was accentuated.[6]

A debate emerged *vis-a-vis* the socio-economic crisis. Recent studies have emphasized the need for new strategies or proposed conflicting economic remedies. Typical of these studies was the Tobin Report of 1975, submitted to Governor Hernández Colón and basically concerned with the grave financial backlash of the world recession. It contrasted the rapid transformation of Puerto Rico into an export industrial economy with the decline in productivity and insufficient internal savings. It recommended some strong and unpalatable remedies, with a freeze on wages and a reduction of the burgeoning public debt by curtailing expenditures and increasing taxation. This last measure, adopted by the Hernández Colón administration to avoid a grave financial crisis, was a contributing factor in his political defeat in 1976.[7] The voters refused to follow the prescribed path to austerity.

Taking a different line, a commonwealth interagency report emphasized the opening up of new areas by encouraging food production, the promotion of industries for the local market, and the creation of a complementary occupational system for young people. This inner-oriented strategy hardly had a chance as it was swept aside by the PNP victory of 1976.[8]

With the new government emerged a new economic philosophy, emphasizing greater—not lesser—dependence on federal funds and more integration of the local economy into the U.S. economy. Changes were made in the industrial incentives program to prepare industry for what the government felt was an irreversible tide towards statehood. Governor Romero Barceló proposed a joint U.S.-Puerto Rican committee to design a common strategy to President Carter, but instead Carter appointed a unilateral U.S. federal inter-agency task force which produced still another report, known as the Kreps Report of 1979. The office of the comptroller general worked on an additional report on Puerto Rico's political future, which it termed "a divisive issue with many dimensions."[9] There is no question that these "many dimensions" have been studied *ad nauseam,* but with the Reagan administration yet another interagency task force has been set up, mainly composed of people who are dutifully learning their ABCs on Puerto Rico. They plan to do what no other task force has been able to achieve since the *Gloucester* sailed boldly into Guánica Bay: solve the Puerto Rican riddle. But the more options accumulate the more evident it is that in the economic as in the political arena there is a lack of consensus. With the changing of the political palace guard every four years in the United States as well as in Puerto Rico, the laborious reports usually appear when there is little time for the federal or commonwealth administrations to implement them—a true case of love's labours lost. They form a log of dashed expectations, making Puerto Rico probably the most studied, scrutinized, and dissected area this side of the Greenwich Meridian.

The Houses Divided

In recent years, there has been only one moment of very fleeting unity. It was a unity of sorrow. On April 30, 1980, Muñoz Marín passed away after several years of failing health. To the very end, he preached the need to strengthen commonwealth as the most effective and realistic bond with the United States, while still preserving Puerto Rico's historic personality. He had labored hard to persuade his colleagues on the Ad Hoc Committee of the advisability of perfecting the relationship by clarifying the principle of compact. To his party, he had stressed the need for unity and dedication to the ideal of public service. He had urged the political establishment to put a stop to rampant *personalismo* and the debasement of partisan debate. At the end, he embodied the ideals he had espoused under what he had called Operation Serenity: a vision of a society less attracted by the acquisition of material goods and more in harmony with itself and with nature. He ended as an elder statesman whom everybody respected, but whose voice was that of a solitary prophet, preaching a life style largely at odds with the surrounding world.

There was great sadness in Puerto Rico as an estimated million people passed by Muñoz's bier or lined streets and roads to see the slow funeral procession winding its way to the mountain top of Barranquitas, where his remains were laid next to those of his embattled father. After this collective catharsis, this pause to honor the fallen democratic warrior, the people went back to their passionate, bitter, political bickering. In the United States, Muñoz's death was hardly noticed except by a handful of faithful friends.

Muñoz left a Puerto Rico which, in spite of its problems and perplexities, is quite alive, with a distinctive ethnic and cultural profile. But it is a house very much divided, buffeted by the contrasting pull of external interests—a unique island of people little understood by outsiders, facing a difficult destiny at the crossroads of the New World.

As a people, they are caught in a centuries-old dilemma, the dilemma between the fortress and the city, between the strategic imperative and the pull towards the emergence of a cultural nationality. The relationship with the United States is crucial. But it involves more than a set of juridical or economic questions. From the U.S. view, it poses the basic issues confronting American nationalism. Can the United States admit a special form of relationship with a Caribbean cultural nationality, a different *patria-pueblo*, with its own language, its ethos, its sense of identity? Although Puerto Ricans may learn English and be influenced by many American ways, the basic ties cannot be a common vernacular language or common historical and ethnic traditions. The ties have to be found elsewhere in the common belief and loyalty to democratic values or in the common hope that there are meeting grounds for understanding, mutual interest, and respect, beyond the frontiers of absorbing nationalism.

What is crystal clear is that the principle espoused in the 1901 insular cases, that Puerto Rico "belongs to but is not a part of" the United States, constitutes an offensive anachronism. No people "belong" to any other nation; they only belong to themselves, and no rights are given to others except those rights that are freely delegated.

In Puerto Rico, the United States is subject to a difficult test. It is a test of both its altruism and its national egoism; its capacity to understand and its proclivity to misunderstand, its mature world view and its self-centered parochialism.

Thus, Puerto Rican contradictions are matched by American contradictions. Regarding Puerto Rico, the United States has also been a house divided against itself, the basic tenets of its libertarian social and political philosophy clashing with the exacting demands of its military-industrial complex and its claims to moral superiority and Caribbean political hegemony.

So the Puerto Rican odyssey is closely related to the American perception of its role in a world of diversity and to its ability to transcend its ardent, inner-oriented nationalism. For both, this is the challenge of the future.

Part Three

EPILOGUE

María Teresa Babín

16
A Special Voice:
The Cultural Expression

Primary Factors

Through a history dating back to the pre-Hispanic Indian migrations, the arrival of Spanish power in the fifteenth century, and the early African presence in the growing colony, Puerto Rico was settled with human beings whose roots became entwined in a rich cultural pattern. From the late sixteenth century until 1897, traditions and customs carried the imprint of the Catholic religion with traces of Taíno and African elements. Country folklore, municipal festivities, and the plantation became the focus of attention for the artist, the poet, the storyteller, and the anonymous bard, while the intellectual began to challenge colonialism in its different expressions.

The culture of the land embodied the literary and artistic works of painters, poets, and singers, but also the precious legacy of oral legends, graffiti, and a wealth of ideas and proverbs full of the wisdom of the *jíbaro* and the poor rural population.

The creative effort of the people within the historical framework of the civilization is the main concern of the student of Puerto Rican folklore, as well as the sociologist or literary critic who must study all the ways in which the creative artist has given form and voice to the inner feelings and desires of man. Although these manifestations are inseparable from the political, economic, and social events of its history, the cultural manifestations of Puerto Rico have a place within the wider framework of Spanish American civilization, without disregarding the influences of the non-Hispanic Caribbean and the United States.

In the cultural evolution of the island, the following factors are of primary importance:

1. The island was a colony of the vast Spanish empire in the New World from 1493, when it was discovered by Columbus, until 1898, when it became a possession of the United States.

2. Puerto Rico lived under the influence of Spain for four centuries. The imprint of Spanish literary and artistic trends is evident in the literature, the music, the dances, and the rituals of life and death, love and patriotism.

3. The mixture of Indian, Black, and Spanish elements in the early days of the conquest and colonization enriched the ethnic and the spiritual structure of the population. The evidence is in the creative modalities of the folklore and the oral *décimas* (10-stanza couplets) of the anonymous popular poets, who still improvise their chants and play the traditional instruments: the *güiro,* the *cuatro,* the *tiple,* and the *guitar.*

4. The language of the people of Puerto Rico is Spanish, and the literature of Puerto Rico is written in Spanish, although many educated Puerto Ricans have learned English and some have written in English, mainly in newspapers and general magazines dealing with political and social problems.

5. English has been taught in the schools of Puerto Rico since the United States came to exert political power over the island, but English has never been the language of Puerto Rico in daily life, in literature, or in education, notwithstanding the efforts to promote English and the policy of bilingual education that has caused a chain of pedagogical changes in the school curriculum.

6. To study in depth the cultural spectrum of Puerto Rican life, it is essential to learn Spanish since the main sources available and the scholarly bibliography, the creative literature, and the oral testimony are, with very few exceptions, in Spanish.

7. The musical compositions, the songs, the plastic arts, and the folklore have in common the perception of the artist whose senses are tuned to the color, the movement, and the shape of the land, the fidelity to a patriotic ideal, and the beauty of the language. Even the most daring modern musicians and painters reflect the romantic and nostalgic traditional way of seeing and feeling the objects of their inspiration. This trend dates back to the beginning of cultural self-expression.

8. There is absolute freedom of worship in Puerto Rico. Although the Catholic religion predominates, Protestant Christian churches of all denominations and synagogues are established in the island. *Espiritismo* (spiritualism) is widespread, especially among low-income families in small towns, and some educated and prominent citizens also practice its rituals.

9. Before 1898 Puerto Rico dealt directly with Spain, called the *Madre Patria* (motherland), and all educational, social, economic, and political matters were brought to the attention of the Spanish Cortes and of the monarchs of the two powerful families that reigned from the time of colonization until 1898: the Hapsburgs and the Bourbons.

10. Although Puerto Rico did not become a republic, as did other colonial Latin American nations in the nineteenth century, Puerto Rico was granted autonomy in 1897. Puerto Rican patriots fought for the freedom of Cuba and Venezuela and defended the ideal of Antillean unity sponsored by Eugenio María de Hostos and his followers. The Treaty of Paris determined the fate of Puerto Rico, thereby changing the whole structure of the country from 1898 until the present (1980).

11. The abolition of slavery dates back to 1873. The fight for the freedom of slaves was a legal struggle without bloodshed, related in ideology to the quest for independence.

12. The *Ateneo Puertorriqueño,* an important cultural institution, was founded in 1876. Although centers of higher education at different levels existed in Spanish colonial days, not until 1903 was the University of Puerto Rico at the Río Piedras campus first established as a Normal school.

13. The educational system since 1898 has been guided by two objectives: to eradicate illiteracy and to establish a bilingual curriculum in order to teach English while preserving the vernacular Spanish and the heritage of the people. The language policy has been the core of the cultural struggle throughout the twentieth century.

14. American citizenship was extended to Puerto Ricans during World War I, in 1917. Before then, they were citizens of Puerto Rico under the protection of the United States.

15. The traditional political ideals since 1898 have been independence and statehood, but in 1952 a new form of autonomy, supported by the Popular Democratic party, was established under the *Estado Libre Asociado* or commonwealth, the creation of Luis Muñoz Marín (1898–1980).

16. The migration of thousands of Puerto Rican families to the United States, especially after World War I (1914–1918), has continued un-

abated, with variations according to conditions in the United States and in Puerto Rico, and at present many continental Americans (about 50,000 in 1960) have come to live in Puerto Rico. This demographic reality is beginning to be felt deeply in the culture.

17. The love of the people of Puerto Rico for their native land is expressed in poetry, in fiction, in music and art, and in everyday life, not only in the island but also in the United States, where the Puerto Rican communities are extremely active in social, political, and artistic endeavors.

The Early Manifestations

America became a reality in western civilization during the early period of the Golden Age in the Iberian Peninsula. By the seventeenth century the works of a few outstanding personalities already born in America had been added to European bibliography. Puerto Rico has also had its place in the literature of the Caribbean islands since the era of conquest and colonization. Letters and chronicles, epic poems and annals of the first governors, settlers, and missionaries, besides the accounts by early visitors who described the inhabitants and the landscape, provide a rich chronicle of the pre-Columbian existence of the island of Borinquen. They dwell on the encounter of the Spanish *conquistadores* with the brave Taínos who then inhabited the land. The letters of Juan Ponce de León, written from Puerto Rico to the Spanish monarchs and to church officials, describe the condition of the first settlements and the problems of the first captain and governor. Information of literary and linguistic interest appears in these memoirs and in documents dealing with the affairs of state and church. In these sources, the first mention of the island's tropical fauna and flora and the magic force of nature give the Spanish language of the *conquistadores* a touch of Indian color and a new vision of man and life in a setting unknown to the European before the discovery of America.

A legendary vein flows from that perennial fountain of Borinquen ancestry. It can be tasted in the subtle *achiote* (annato) coloring of the native foods as well as in the vibrant notes of a *güiro* or a *cuatro* or in the steps and figures of a *bomba* (typical dance with strong African influence) in the palm forests around remote small towns. From the heart of the Río de la Plata or the Río Grande, through mountains such as the Asomante and the Tres Picachos (Three Peaks), the written testimony of Puerto Rican creativity seems to be dictated by the echo of millions of

Students learn to play the traditional cuatro.

voices whose sound has been made part of the wind, the waves, the air, and the earth. Puerto Rican literature is only a partial proof of the existence of a much vaster and deeper creativity. The *jíbaro* and the slum dweller continue to tell stories orally, in which daily life and nightmares and dreams become legends that beautify the reality of the island's past and present. This trait seems to gain momentum instead of waning as the centuries pass, as if a secret pact had been made to communicate to others this search for an image in all the sources of the inner self. The intellectual and the ignorant, the city dweller and the mountain dweller, the university student and the sophisticated poet, are one in this respect. Puerto Rico is a most homogeneous and congenial country in terms of spiritual and emotional communication among its people. The poor and the rich, the well educated and the humble peasants understand the same signs and respond to the same silent motions, like and dislike the same flavors, and speak the same language of love, of despair, of hope, and of rage.

The writers of Puerto Rico have succeeded in expressing their oneness as a people, sometimes with the strong colors and lines of romantic and realistic expression, and at other times merely suggesting a shade of grief and melancholy. In these infinite litanies in prose and verse in which the absence from the native soil kindles the imagination, the fantasy of love creates a super-reality: a Puerto Rico invented by the writers, the Utopia of poets such as José Gautier Benítez or Luis Lloréns Torres that continues in many of the poets living in New York City since the beginning of the twentieth century.

Through language and movement the style of a culture dating from pre-Columbian days acquires the depth and the breadth which struck the first visitors and chroniclers with awe and amazement. In the mountainous region of the central towns—Maricao, Jayuya, Lares, Barranquitas—folklore remnants of these roots abound in the tales about the dead that roam the fields after sundown, guarding hidden treasures buried long ago in secret places. On the coast, the ghosts of pirates roam the towns and the sandy beaches echo the roar sound of the waves and the chains of heavy treasure chests. The *Carimbo* irons burn the tongue of *décima* singers who improvise lyrics to tell the infamy of slavery and the struggle for freedom. Witchcraft and fairy tales blend in a lunatic fantasy whenever writers create a world of dreams and transform the island and the life of its people to give a dimension of unreality to the vibrant reality of ordinary life. The pervading force of history in the tropics through the centuries, the menace of heavy rains, devastating floods, swarms of mosquitos, thunder and lightning, earth tremors, and mysterious beings with long hair, pale faces, and moaning voices: all these enlighten the metaphors and the rhetoric of the Puerto Rican writer. All the supernatural and historical factors, combined with the everyday experience of social, economic, spiritual, and physical strains contribute to the rich and varied world of literature. The totality of the cultural manifestations has been shaped by the nutrient sap of the Spanish vernacular.

The first people who heard Indian folktales and retold them to others were the conquerors and settlers from the Iberian peninsula, and the first witnesses who captured the saga of the island's entry into the New World concept were soldiers and priests like Juan de Castellanos (1522–1607) and Fray Damián López de Haro (1581–1648). The Taíno heritage remained dormant until very recently. The anthropologist Ricardo Alegría has done much to awaken the poets and the dramatists who are now incorporating this dormant aspect of the culture in their work. Lilliane Pérez Marchand, Luis Hernández Aquino, Juan Antonio Corretjer, and many others echo the *areyto* (Indian celebration) and pay homage to the herbs, the trees, the flowers, and the historical sites of Taíno culture in Puerto Rico. The oral literature of the island offers glimpses of pre-Columbian Indian poetry in anecdotes, proverbs, and legends. Most relevant of all, the Taíno heritage is preserved in everyday language. The most sophisticated poets faithfully and even reverently choose words of Indian extraction. Glimpses of the *bohío* (native hut), the *casabe* (a type of bread), the *güiro*, the *batey* (courtyard in an Indian dwelling), appear in sketches and lyrical compositions. The desire to recover the spirit of the primitive *Borinqueños* is also visible in pottery, in painting, in music, and in dance. As a tribute to the Taíno culture a native ceremonial center has been restored at the Caguana district of Utuado.

The vocabulary of Taíno origin gives a special flavor and color to the Spanish language by recalling the prehistory of the Caribbean. When saying *quimbobó* (okra), Jájome, Coamo, Humacao, Guayama, or Tayaboa (names of towns), distant national roots are affirmed and a subtle relationship is established between the Spanish language and the vernacular of the first inhabitants of the land. The names of rivers, of mountains, of so many geographical and historical spots on the map of Puerto Rico are a delight to the ear and the mind that rejoices in the persistence of the Indian ancestry. The Spanish philologist Tomás Navarro Tomás believes that the language of the Taínos became extinct toward 1550 in

Puerto Rico and Santo Domingo, but he points out the possibility that in Puerto Rico, "because of the isolation of certain mountainous zones, and perhaps due to the greater density of the population, there were nuclei of Indian families that maintained consciousness of their origin till the end of the eighteenth century." Navarro also alludes to the evident presence of the indigenous element in the districts of Indiera Fria, Indiera Baja, and Indiera Alta, situated in the mountain range of San Germán, in the western part of the island. The distinguished Spanish scholar suggests a line of speculation:

In the mountains of Maricao, where the Indieras are enclaved, is where the greater part of the legends and traditions of Puerto Rico folklore on the themes of mystery and marvel are located: caves with unknown houses; girls transformed into streams; men turned into *ceibas,* people petrified in the mountains, deeds of sorcerers and giants, hidden treasures.

The suggestive lines of Agueybaná (Taíno chieftain) lamenting "the good of the good we lost" and the songs of grief and protest interwoven in the quest for liberty and the clamor for love and endurance to achieve immortality, flow without interruption from the early *cantos* of the sixteenth century to the most recent outbursts of passionate existentialist neoromanticism. These voices utter their laments or their insults, their frustrations or their denunciations of social and political evils on the literary front everywhere. In plays and in fiction, in poetry and in essays, the Puerto Rican writers in the island and in the *barrios* (neighborhoods) of New York, Chicago, and other places, have revived the memory of the hidden Taíno stamina to strengthen the path towards the future.

From the Enchanted Garden to the Lost Eden

The writers who left letters, verses, and diaries describing the landscape, the flora and fauna, the customs, the "great heat and shade of the coconut trees," and that gentle and refreshing breeze hailed in a seventeenth century sonnet were fine observers of the environment. Puerto Rico had by then established a close relationship with Mexico, then known as New Spain, and two men from the island became known in the Mexican literature of the period. One was the poet Francisco de Ayerra y Santa María, a famous Latin scholar whose intricate and elegant style was admired by his contemporaries. The other, Alonso Ramírez, was a carpenter's son whose adventures and misfortunes are the theme of a novel by Sigüenza y Góngora. Another interesting relation with Mexico was established when the eminent Spanish writer Bernardo de Balbuena came to Puerto Rico after having lived in Mexico, bringing with him a library that became the research and intellectual symbol of the church in San Juan, and was destroyed by the Dutch attack in 1625. The brilliance and the glory of Balbuena, who wrote some of his books in Puerto Rico, were exalted by Lope de Vega in his *Laurel de Apolo* (Laurel of Apollo). He considered that Puerto Rico was never as rich as Balbuena made it in the Golden Age.

By the eighteenth century the painter José Campeche (1752–1809) had left a graphic testimony of portraits and landscapes, descriptive tableaux of customs, and traditional sketches.

The Nineteenth Century: The Flowering of a Tradition

At the end of the eighteenth century came the publication of the first complete history of Puerto Rico, written by Fray Iñigo Abbad y Lasierra and entitled *Historia geográfica, civil y política de la isla de San Juan Bautista de Puerto Rico* (Geographic, Civil and Political History of the Island of St. John the Baptist of Puerto Rico) (Madrid, 1788). The history is not only an important document as such but a beautiful and inspiring "literary" work also. Abbad y Lasierra loved nature and folklore and wrote wonderful descriptions of the landscape and the towns.

The impulse given to the creative urge by the traditional folklore brought by the settlers from the different regions of Spain, the religious elements inspired by the church rituals, and the remnants of the Taíno heritage which survived in some places, besides the magical charm embodied in the dances and songs of the Negro slaves and their descendants, mingled together and bloomed in the literature of the nineteenth century. From 1843 until 1898 the development of Puerto Rican literary talent was accelerated and enriched by the men and women who shared in the awakening of an artistic endeavor that has never abated. Poetry and prose expressed the dreams and longings of the whole nation, and the writer became the interpreter and the personification of the struggle for liberty and redemption. The use of a term that became a symbol in the works of some writers around the first half of the nineteenth century, which appears in newspapers and in the title of Alonso's masterpiece, *El Jíbaro* (1849), opened the door to a sort of mythology and social symbolism to represent the human and spiritual entity that was considered the substance of Puerto Rican culture. According to the best Puerto Rican lexicographer at the beginning of the twentieth cen-

tury, Augusto Malaret, the *jíbaro* is "the white Puerto Rican peasant."
This debatable definition has gone through a series of transformations
and many authors have written important essays on the *jíbaro*. Nevertheless, the idea of such a symbol has survived. The two parallel currents
which did not always flow harmoniously side by side from the beginning
of cultural self-expression, are the *criollista* (Creole or typical) national
theme, to which the image of the *jíbaro* is vital, and the so-called exotic
or outlandish trend, which disregards or belittles the former. The authors
of the first *Aguinaldo Puertorriqueño* (Puerto Rican Christmas Poems)
(1843) adopted a sophisticated pseudo-intellectual attitude that has persisted through the literary history of the country. The poet Francisco
Matos Paoli, in the introduction to the 1946 edition of the *Aguinaldo*,
says that the authors "aspired . . . to direct our literature through the
ways of a higher culture than the one offered by the oral source of folklore." The letter by D. Francisco Vasallo, the father of one of the young
writers whose naive poetry appears in this collection, reminded readers
that "the traditional customs of our fathers" must be respected and honored. The exciting pantomime by René Marqués, *Juan Bobo y la Dama de
Occidente* (John the Simpleton and the Lady of the West) (1956) is the
most recent work dealing with this significant approach to the cultural
self-expression of the artist and the poet. Marqués cunningly develops
the idea of a ballet to express the comical, the intellectual, and the human
factors involved in the dualism of the very life of the people of Puerto
Rico. The frontiers between the two trends were traced without malice
in the nineteenth century, but at present there is more bitterness and
passion, since the artist of today is concerned with the survival and the
integrity of the country's personality. In the prologue to *Juan Bobo y la
Dama de Occidente,* Marqués expounds this idea, shared by most contemporary writers:

We belong to the West, but as members of our cultural nationality. Only from
our national roots can we make a contribution in art, literature and thought, to
Western civilization. To delve into our Puerto Rican heritage as a universal value,
we need not become narcissists nor be hypnotized by our past. But in order to
emphasize our connection with the West, we should not destroy our Puerto Rican
essence, nor blindly scatter its particles in an unheard, artificial nirvana, created
by those who called themselves members of Western culture.

The nineteenth century has been labeled the golden age of cultural
life in Spanish colonial Puerto Rico, and some of the most eminent
patriots and writers of that century continue to be esteemed as spiritual

and ideological leaders for twentieth-century Puerto Ricans. Three of the best lyrical romantic poets of that period were José Gautier Benítez (1851–1880); El Caribe, whose real name was José Gualberto Padilla (1829–1896); and Lola Rodríguez de Tió (1843–1924). Among the best prose writers, who cultivated the essay, the novel, and the drama, and contributed to historical research, are: Alejandro Tapia y Rivera (1826–1882), Eugenio María de Hostos (1839–1903), and Salvador Brau (1842–1912). Among the composers of the nineteenth century all music lovers praise the *danzas* and other compositions by such artists as Julián Andino (1845–1920), Julio Arteaga (1867–1923), Braulio Dueño Colón (1854–1934), Manuel G. Tavárez (1843–1883), José I. Quintón (1881–1925), and Juan Morel Campos (1857–1896). In the fine arts, besides José Campeche, who belongs to the eighteenth century, the two outstanding painters in the later nineteenth and early twentieth century are Francisco Oller (1833–1917) and Ramón Frade (1875–1956?). Besides works by individual writers, musicians, and painters, there is a wealth of anonymous artistic expression embodied in the folklore of the island. The accumulation of the wisdom of the illiterate peasants and the poor who inhabited the remote mountain regions, the villages, and the small towns constitutes a huge bibliography of *décimas, coplas* (couplets), *aguinaldos, seis chorreao, Bombas* (typical folk dances), the stories of *Juan Bobo*, and a large number of religious and popular tales and proverbs.

Another source of information for the beginning of cultural self-expression, from the early nineteenth century until the end of Spanish colonial rule in 1897, is the written testimony of foreigners who lived in Puerto Rico. George Dawson Flinter, the author of a report published in London in 1834, describes the life and customs of the Puerto Rican peasant in the mountains and depicts the general condition of the island According to Flinter, the peasant enjoyed many advantages, a positive view that coincides with the image projected by such romantic and realistic Puerto Rican authors as Alonso in *El Jíbaro* (1849), or the skit writer Manuel Méndez Quiñones, whose comic sketches are full of happy endings. Among his plays, the one entitled *Los Jíbaros Progresistas* (The Progressive Peasants), presents a gay picture of a fair in Ponce in 1882. The emotion of Flinter, a regimental commander, on describing a visit he made one rainy day to a peasant's house, expresses his esteem for the humble, generous, and hospitable folk who welcomed him to their *bohío*. Another foreigner, Charles Walker, describes the customs and character of the island's inhabitants in letters written from Puerto Rico between 1835 and 1837; and he demonstrates a fine sensibility to rural life in

Guayama, including a wake for a young child and a day at the town market. In the years when Flinter and Walker visited the island, learned Puerto Ricans and poets were forging their ideal image, with the substance of speech, the traditional inheritance, and the perception of the human qualities of the people of Borinquen. Santiago Vidarte sang to the idealized peasant woman surrounded by her treasures: the hut, the palm tree, coconuts, lemons, the *mamey* fruit, and the rose bush in bloom. The physical and moral portrait of man and woman became a common theme for the poet and painter.

But there is another view of peasant life. A vigorous naturalistic novel, *La Charca* (The Stagnant Pool), by Manuel Zeno Gandía, documents the painful existence of the rural society at the traumatic end of the nineteenth century. Published in 1894, the novel denounces social conditions in the last of the "colonial jewels." By casting herself down a ravine towards the Río Grande of Arecibo, the female character, Silvina, becomes the decadent symbol of the image that had been idealized by the romantic writers of an earlier period, since the beauty of paradise lost and abolished through destructive misery was a tragedy. The magical nature of the river, "a living being, with a past hidden in the abrupt hills, with a nonconforming present . . . with an uncertain future," seems a premonition of the perplexities that would face the people of Puerto Rico in the aftermath of the conflict of 1898 and the first years of the country's experience under the flag of the United States.

The Twentieth-Century Cultural Struggle

The sudden and dramatic change in the course of history resulting from the Spanish American War placed Puerto Rico in a very difficult situation. By virtue of the Treaty of Paris, which disregarded the fact that the colony had been granted autonomy in 1897, it became a possession of the United States. As such, a period of readjustment to fit into this political status characterized the first two decades of the twentieth century.

Puerto Rico is today a complex and homogeneous society that has grown to more than 3 million inhabitants since 1898, when the population amounted only to about one million. This demographic reality has become a challenge to a world full of economic ills, and it has been a major concern of all the political parties in Puerto Rico. United by a deep feeling about the need to safeguard a common heritage, the cultural struggle during the twentieth century has been marked by a defense of the national identity. The core of the silent hopes and fears can be studied and analyzed through literature and art as well as through the reports and documents of government divisions and political parties. Faced with the imposition of English by the dominant political power, the proud and consistent defense of the Spanish vernacular has become a weapon of resistance and a force of cultural significance in education, business, and politics.

Literature of the Twentieth Century

The years between 1898 and World War I were of dramatic suspense in the cultural life of Puerto Rico. The mature writers realized with great awe that their country had come under the influence of a different language and new traditions and beliefs, foreign to the Hispanic sources on which they had been nurtured. Their reaction was both pathetic and heroic. The literature of those years often tells of the process of trial and error the country faced during its adjustment to its new role. The Puerto Rican writer kept the romantic spirit alive during that trying period to safeguard his heritage and the most cherished loyalties to religion, language, and patriotic creed. The poetry and prose of those years illustrate the pathetic and heroic resistance of the people to the tactics of colonialism and absorption into the overpowering U.S. mold.

José de Diego (1867–1918), considered by some critics as a precursor of Puerto Rican modernism, and by others as its initiator, was a leader in the transition years from 1898 until his death. His poetry and speeches carried the message embodied in the flag, the coat of arms, the historical and legendary past, and the dream of independence. While the Nicaraguan Rubén Darío was proudly proclaiming the liberation of Latin American poets from the shackles of traditional Spanish versification, thus becoming an inspiration for all writers, the creative José de Diego was undergoing the trauma of 1898. Thus the Puerto Rican man of letters was faced with the task of survival, not as an ordinary person, but as the personification of this significant moment in the homeland: the metamorphosis of the island from what Américo Castro, the Spanish essayist, has termed the "vital dwelling" to a strange house of immense and empty galleries where the native tongue, Holy Spirit of all literary creation, was neither spoken nor heard. The cultural struggle since then has centered around the dread of extinction of the country's language and mores, giving its basic strength to forceful literary output of the present century.

Luis Lloréns Torres (1877–1941) and Nemesio Canales (1878–1923) added their voices to those of other intellectuals and politicians who defended the integrity of Puerto Rican ideals and the personality of their birthplace. The excellent magazine that appeared in 1913, *Revista de las Antillas* (The Antilles Review), brought fresh and daring esthetic manifestos to the fore, balanced by a deep patriotic concern for the land and its destiny. Among the contributors, such famous Latin American poets as Rubén Darío and Santos Chocano (who visited Puerto Rico) enriched the review, and the island writers became known in Spain and Latin America. Modernism meant action and compromise in the works of Lloréns, Canales, and their contemporaries, a heroic effort to overcome the regional and spiritual limitations of the colony as such, and to help channel the anguish and despair of the generation of 1898 in Puerto Rico through the expressions and dreams of these exceptional minds. It is fitting to mention that Lloréns shaped his theories as a poet and as a patriot with historical and philosophical knowledge. Puerto Rico and the Caribbean region were to him a vast and unified entity that had to be inseparable. In *Alturas de América* (The Heights of America) (1940), he gathered a selection of his life's work in which he included the famous *Canción de las Antillas* (Song of the Antilles) (1913) and "Mare Nostrum" (1940), representing the point of departure and the climax of his favorite theme: a hymn of glory to the cradle of New World civilization, a grandiose song to the Caribbean. If Lloréns represents the first important new wave in the contemporary cultural panorama, his counterpart in prose was Nemesio Canales, author of *Paliques* (1913), a collection of newspaper articles in which he penetrates the most subtle problems confronting Puerto Rico and mankind with irony, freedom of ideas, and very keen intelligence. As the novelist and critic Enrique Laguerre stated in 1942, the writers of the *Modernista* (modernist) movement were responsible for the "awakening of the Puerto Rican conscience"; the "enthusiasm for culture"; the "explorations of our nature"; the "love of our language, our traditions and the roots of our origin"; and a "healthy universalism."

Virgilio Dávila (1869–1943), author of *Aromas del Terruño* (Aromas of Homeland) (1916) and *Pueblito de Antes* (Little Town of Old) (1917), reveals in his works a complete disregard for fashion and the conventions of literary taste. His main concern is his alertness to the sentiments of love, death, and grief in the homeland, captured in simple descriptions of daily life unashamed of being romantic and realistic. His son, José Antonio Dávila (1898–1941), also a renowned poet, translated into

English all the sonnets of *Pueblito de Antes,* a masterpiece of Puerto Rican literature. It has the charm of a play like *Our Town* by Thornton Wilder or Dylan Thomas's musical poem *Under Milk Wood.* The simple actions and feelings of ordinary people and the natural phenomena of life and death are raised to a high poetic realm.

These few examples are representative of the writers' dedication to the cultural struggle from the early twentieth century until World War I. That same impetus is still alive after eighty years of a relationship with the United States. After 1918 the younger poets ventured in the vanguard, following new trends in the American and European literature of the period. The first current, *diepalismo,* was invented by Luis Palés Matos and José I. De Diego Padró. The emphasis is on the function of sounds as versification reveals the musical value in the poetic process. A lyrical pentagram pleasing to the ear had its maximum expression in the famous *Tun Tun de Pasa y Grifería* (1937) by Luis Palés Matos, acclaimed as one of the leading interpreters of Negro rhythms in the Caribbean region and the world. Expressing their will to search for the new and to exalt metals and mechanical instruments, another group of poets came forward in 1923, proclaiming *euforismo* (euphoria) as their ideal. The combined credo of physical wellbeing, the capacity to resist pain, and the desire to imitate the Italian futurists, gave the poetry of Vicente Palés, Tomás L. Batista, and their friends, the "euphoria" of *mens sana in corpore sano,* touched with a sparkle of vitality and the scorn of sentimentality. The No Group created the movement called *Noismo,* a doctrine of negation which made its official appearance in 1925. The names of Vicente Géigel Polanco, Samuel R. Quiñones, Emilio Delgado, and Vicente Palés are linked to it. They aspired to find philosophical support for poetry, and their approach to style is comparable to Tristán Tzara's Dadaism combined with the imagery of the Spanish *Ultraístas.* The No Group had a deeper impact on the poetic trend on the island than the preceding vanguard attempts. In 1929 the *Atalayistas* entered the scene with great success. Some of the writers responsible for this trend assumed eccentric attitudes reminiscent of the Bohemian French poets of the Parnassian and Symbolist movements in the late nineteenth century, combined with shocking dress and loud manners. They favored grandiloquent expression with a deep concern for pure lyricism, aspiring to exalt the individuality of the poet and the sensations of the moment in the creation of a new reality. For about six years, until 1935, this *pléyade de atalayistas* was the dominant attraction in San Juan. Clemente Soto Vélez and Graciany Miranda Archilla, who later moved to New York and have lived there permanently, were prominent members of the group and were involved as well in Nationalist activities under Pedro Albizu Campos. The vitality and authenticity of numerous poets whose works are considered of the highest value in contemporary Puerto Rican literature emanated from the *Atalayista* movement. Among them are Samuel Lugo, Luis Hernández Aquino, José Joaquín Rivera, and Joaquín López López.

The vanguard movements, all short-lived but impressive in their theories and manifestos, were very meaningful in the cultural struggle. Despite the flashes of passing literary fashion, the ever-present *criollismo* or *boricuismo,* reflecting the inner self of Puerto Ricans as a people with a clear awareness of their own character and destiny, dominated twentieth century literary expression until the 1930–1940 generation. One of the poets most admired by critics in the vanguard years developed his work independently, and his sojourn in Spain from 1919 to 1924 gave his language and poetry the vigor and enthusiasm to spur the cultural atmosphere of the island under the spell of the Ultraists he had known in Madrid. This poet was Evaristo Ribera Chevremont (1896–1974). He published articles about the vanguard movements, and, above all, proclaimed the need to kill "eloquence, the high tone, the grave and the theatrical." Rooted in the Spanish classical tradition of the Golden Age, Ribera Chevremont achieved an intellectual balance between universality and *criollismo,* and wrote about the city and the working class without sacrificing the esthetic credo and the Parnassian structure of his sonnets and his varied approach to poetic excellence, as can be appreciated in his *Antología Poética* (Poetic Anthology) (1924–1950), *La Inquietud Sosegada* (Restlessness Appeased) (1946–1956), and *La Llama Pensativa* (The Pensive Flame), 1954.

The wave of essays, novels, plays, short stories, and poems with Puerto Rico itself as a theme started emerging around 1934, the year that marks the appearance of the most influential essay about the cultural spectrum of Puerto Rico after thirty-six years of American domination, entitled *"Insularismo"* and written by Antonio S. Pedreira (1899–1939), professor and chairman of the Department of Hispanic Studies at the university. Pedreira's critical approach to social, political, and artistic problems helped release the energy of the intellectual circles towards research and introspection with a serious and creative attitude. The generation of 1930, led by Pedreira, initiated the study of the essence and substance of the cultural struggle. The following generations have continued this search with different emphasis and a new style, while the literature of Puerto

Rico has been inspired by the landscape, the people, the traditions, and the personality of the Puerto Ricans. The urban setting has gained importance as a literary subject, leaving behind the *jíbaro*. The economic and political dilemma, including language as the spirit of survival, has become the center of educational and intellectual debates in meetings, seminars, books, newspapers, and every other means to express the ideas the Puerto Ricans consider vital to the unending cultural struggle which started after 1898 and is still very much alive. Such concepts as colonialism, statehood, independence, socialism, Marxism, and democracy are common words in everyday conversations in Puerto Rico. The first novel by Enrique Laguerre, *La Llamarada* (Flash of Fire), the fine essays and short stories by Miguel Meléndez Muñoz and by Abelardo Díaz Alfaro, author of *Terrazo,* the historical summary by Tomás Blanco, *Prontuario Histórico de Puerto Rico* (Historical Compendium), are a few of the main books of this century that give a vivid testimony of the concerns of the people as interpreted by the writers. Although lyric poetry has been dominant during the twentieth century, the short story and the drama were cultivated with great success after 1940. The plays by René Marqués and Francisco Arriví and the poems by Julia de Burgos have received extensive recognition in the island and in many foreign countries. Artistic and literary activities have been part of the daily life of the *Ateneo*, the Institute of Puerto Rican Culture since 1955, and the universities located in all the important cities and towns, such as Ponce, Mayagüez, Río Piedras, San Germán, San Juan, Humacao, Cayey, and others.

The currents in this overall picture from 1898 until the present show a vitality and depth which proves beyond any doubt the significance of Puerto Rico in Spanish American letters. The trauma of the early twentieth century has been channeled gradually into a vigorous awakening of the vital seeds dormant in the inner self of the people. In the political, economic, and social structure of the country, as well as in literature and art, the generations of 1930, 1940, and 1950 are responsible for the great creativity of the island as a response to the cultural struggle.

It is of crucial significance to recognize the persistence of the defense of Spanish as the language of the land through the struggle for identity during the Americanization of Puerto Rico. Poems on this theme best express the emotional and psychological impact of the imposition of English on the school system until 1948, when Commissioner of Education Mariano Villaronga declared Spanish the language of instruction while English was to be studied as a second language. Two examples of the inspiration of the poets are the poem by José Mercado (1863–1911) and the one by Evaristo Ribera Chevremont (1896–1974). The title of both poems is "The Castilian Language." Mercado expressed his sentiments in this manner:

> Immortal tongue, my Borinquen land
> is united forever to your existence.
>
> The cannon roared, foreign soldiers
> set here their bold foot,
> and an inexorable law was fulfilled,
>
> and Spain wept its great misfortune
> with the same bitterness and sadness,
> filled with bereavement and heartache,
> that another misfortune one day wept
> the last Moorish King of Granada.
>
> This knot, which force yesterday broke asunder,
> tie it, my Castilian tongue.
>
> For a flag can be changed,
> but never sentiments!

Years later we still hear the echoes of this chant in the voice of Ribera Chevremont:

> The language that dressed my cradle with words
> is the language born in the Castilian soil . . .
>
> The language—voice of the centuries—joins my word.
> They shall not destroy it, for it is the best part
> . . . The substantial, the eternal—of the whole of my race.
>
> And my race is, in all, faith, sorrow, love, art.

The novels of Enrique Laguerre (1906–   ), represent the most coherent and extensive body of fiction from 1935, when he published *La Llamarada* (The Flame), until 1976, when *Los Amos Benévolos* (The Benevolent Masters), his last book, appeared. Laguerre has been consistent in his literary search for the inner threads of his country's history. Through his novels one can see rural and urban societies, the life and death of the coffee and sugar cane plantations, the strife of a rising middle class in a cauldron of prejudice and economic hysteria, the echo of folklore and the saga of the Puerto Rican exodus. Other well-known novelists are Pedro Juan Soto (1928–   ) and Emilio Díaz Varcárcel

(1929–   ). Soto, who lived in New York for fifteen years and became a teacher of English, is the product of a bicultural situation that gives his fiction a dramatic and poignant feeling for social and language changes in the culture of his birthplace. Among his best works are chosen *Spiks* (1956) and *Usmaíl* (1958). He is now writing a novel about his son, Soto Arriví, who was killed for political reasons during a tragic encounter with police. The works of these writers have already been studied by critics and doctoral students at colleges and universities in Puerto Rico and in the United States. Their books have been translated into different languages. Díaz Varcárcel became widely known in Spain when he wrote, while living in that country, *Figuraciones en el mes de marzo* (Imagery in the Month of March) (1972). He is considered the best fiction writer on the participation of Puerto Rican soldiers in the Korean War, which he has developed in many short stories and in *Proceso en Diciembre* (Suit in December) (1963). Recently he published a novel about the mosaic of cosmopolitan life called *Harlem todos los Días* (Every Day Harlem).

Music and Art: A Creative Force in the Cultural Struggle

As soon as Puerto Rico became a possession of the United States in 1898, the island started to celebrate the Fourth of July, and other traditional U.S. festivities such as Thanksgiving, Labor Day, Memorial Day, etc.

Lincoln's and Washington's birthdays were also celebrated in schools and in public and official gatherings. July 25 is a significant date in a new calendar of events. Besides being the traditional Spanish feast of St. James the Apostle, the patron saint of the towns of Aibonito, Fajardo, Guánica, and Santa Isabel, at Loíza Aldea it is celebrated in a colorful and artistic festival in which the African and Spanish roots are blended in religious pageantry, folklore, costumes, rituals, dances, and popular parades.

July 25 is also the date on which U.S. troops disembarked at the Bay of Guánica in 1898. This act of war gave a sad connotation to the day of St. James the Apostle until 1952, when the Constitution of the Commonwealth of Puerto Rico was approved on July 25. The date acquired new luster and prestige, and official government ceremonies on that day, known as Constitution Day, are held every year. The transformation from Spanish to American ways in the early decades of the century brought about a decline in social life. According to Pedreira in *Insularismo:*

Long ago, innumerable towns on the island maintained an exquisite social life, in which there alternated concerts, soirées, open-air band programs, patron saint's *fiestas,* groups of aficionados, gatherings in homes and religious solemnities. Humacao, Guayama, Juana Díaz, San Germán, etc., so imbued with the culture of old, are today mere municipalities. Mayagüez, the center of innumerable cultural events, is today a factory town. Only Ponce gently resists this annihilating contamination.

In spite of this somber view by the master of the 1930 generation, Dr. Pedreira, Puerto Rico's musical and artistic life since 1950 has been rich and varied. The establishment of the Institute of Puerto Rican Culture in 1955 ushered in theater festivals, art exhibits, concerts, and popular compositions of diverse modalities. The presence in Puerto Rico of the renowned cellist Pablo Casals gave luster to musical and social life and the Casals Festival, celebrated every year, attracted many famous musicians to the island. The Conservatory of Music became a center of action and the island musicians expanded their activities. Among the most prominent twentieth-century names in music, in the island and abroad, are the pianist Jesús María Sanromá and the composers Héctor Campos Parsi, Amaury Veray, and Luis Antonio Ramírez. Popular music has grown and expanded, musical education has improved, and the Symphony Orchestra has presented excellent programs. One of the most significant aspects of artistic creativity among the Puerto Ricans of the twentieth century is the existence of two prominent families whose members are all dedicated to music, among them eminent interpreters of the piano, the violin, the cello, and the viola. The families are the famous Figueroas and the Hutchinsons. José Narciso and Kachiro Figueroa and their daughters, sons, and nephews are a great honor to music, as are violinist Henry Hutchinson and his wife, a pianist, whose son, Henry Hutchinson, Jr., is also a well-known violinist.

Of all the popular compositions, the most distinguished and most elegant is the Puerto Rican *danza,* which has a graceful and pleasing quality that evokes the leisured life of the late nineteenth century. Nevertheless, it has survived the turmoil of the present, and *danzas* are still played in concert halls while people dance to their rhythms at every level of society. The famous composers of *danzas,* such as Morel Campos, Tavárez, and Quintón are still considered among the masters, and there are new *danzas* by modern composers such as Narciso Figueroa.

Besides this favorite musical composition and dance, the folk culture of the island has been enriched with new modalities and some contemporary singers already figure in the annals of popular culture. Rafael

Pablo Casals rehearsing with the Casals Festival orchestra.

Hernández is one of the most prominent composers of popular songs, such as *Lamento Borincano* (Puerto Rican Lament), which some Puerto Ricans consider a national hymn as significant as *La Borinqueña*, the national anthem. Noel Estrada, author of *En Mi Viejo San Juan* (In My Old San Juan) is also well known. The words and the music of both *Lamento Borincano* and *En Mi Viejo San Juan*, among the best-known songs by Puerto Ricans of the twentieth century, are a sentimental contribution to the national struggle for identity.

Parallel to the development of music is the development of the plastic arts. The great monuments of Puerto Rico are the fortresses and walls of the old city of San Juan, whose artistic value and historical significance began to be appreciated anew after the Institute of Puerto Rican Culture was created in 1955. The survival and reconstruction of some churches, monasteries, and palaces, as well as the private houses reconstructed in Old San Juan and in other cities are a testimony of the deep desire of the present generation to retain the character of the traditional colonial architecture of Spanish days. Although there is excellent modern architecture, the country is proud of the heritage represented by the Castle

A present-day view of one of the sentry boxes in the fortress of El Morro.

of San Felipe del Morro, the Castle of San Cristóbal, the Fort of San Jerónimo, the Fortaleza Palace, the ancient gates of San Juan, and the whole city of San Juan, with its Christ Chapel, the Cathedral, El Convento Hotel, the Casa del Libro, St. Joseph's Church, and other buildings restored or in the process of restoration. They preserve an era that links Puerto Rican architecture to that of other Latin American nations from the sixteenth to the nineteenth century.

Of all the plastic arts, painting has flourished the most. The paintings of José Campeche (1752–1809), Francisco Oller (1833–1917), and Ramón Frade (1875–1954) represent significant accomplishments in the artistic expression of the island. Campeche produced magnificent portraits and historical and religious paintings. Oller brought to his art lively regional scenes and his oils were coveted by private collectors in Spain. His renowned *El Velorio* (The Wake) has a place of honor in the history of Puerto Rican art. Frade became a master of Impressionism and his figures and landscapes are the first examples of the early alertness of Puerto Rican art to twentieth century esthetics. In museums and galleries opened since 1960 one can appraise the amalgam of the influence of Cubism, surrealism, and abstract art on Puerto Rican artists. The visual reality and ideological essence of Puerto Rican culture permeate the posters, engravings, oils, and all the graphic arts, whatever the style or theme.

During the last twenty-five years several foundations have granted scholarships to Puerto Rican writers and artists, and the Department of Education, the University of Puerto Rico, the Institute of Puerto Rican Culture and other branches of the local and federal government have sponsored study trips to Europe, Mexico, and the United States for painters and sculptors, besides employing several artists and sponsoring a program of graphic arts which has produced excellent work. The most important private museum of the island, located in Ponce, holds a rich collection of works by famous artists of the world and Puerto Rico. It is one of the cultural centers sponsored by the Ferré Foundation. The *Museo de Ponce* has attracted the attention of collectors and museums in the United States and Europe. A series of galleries in San Juan, devoted to the treasures of Puerto Rican culture, are part of the work of the Institute of Puerto Rican Culture. The following short list of well-known artists is neither exhaustive nor ordered by rank: Lorenzo Homar, Rafael Tufiño, Myrna Báez, Julio Rosado del Valle, Juan Hernández Cruz, Epifanio Irizarry, Olga Albizu, and Francisco Rodón, whose portraits of outstanding men such as Betancourt of Venezuela, Muñoz Marín of

An international art exhibit in Puerto Rico.

Puerto Rico, and the Argentinian writer Jorge Luis Borges, among others, have been acclaimed by critics both in the island and abroad as great artistic works.

Popular sculpture, represented by the *santeros* (religious wood carvers), is characterized by refined polychrome pieces carved mainly in wood by the artisans of different towns. The Cabán family and the venerable Don Zoilo Cajigas (1855–1961), a native of Aguada, have excelled in this art. The themes of the Nativity, the Three Magi, the Holy Trinity, the Immaculate Conception, the Virgin of Monserrat, the Divine Providence, Our Lady of Perpetual Help, Saint Rita, Saint Barbara, and the Virgin of Carmen are some of the images most often represented in a variety of styles.

The passing of time has developed in the Puerto Ricans a faith in the roots of their identity in spite of the twentieth century propaganda about the American way of life and the benefits of American citizenship. The political divisions show three major ideals among the people: statehood, autonomy, and independence. The cultural struggle, however, is a strong element of unity among the people of all social and economic strata. In 1980 this struggle gained momentum with the creation of AFAC, the Administration for the Development of Arts and Culture. A group of prominent intellectuals opposed the law creating the AFAC and argued in favor of the Institute of Puerto Rican Culture, in existence since 1955. Although this has recently become a very important local political issue, the strong and prolific seeds of art, music, poetry, and folklore are so healthy and potent in twentieth-century Puerto Rico that this type of disagreement does not affect the climate of the arts or the efforts of the artists. The extremist argument that all educational and artistic woes are insoluble while Puerto Rico remains a colony of the United States, has been strong during the twentieth century. Yet Puerto Rico, as a colony of Spain from 1493 until 1897 and a territory of the United States from 1898 until the present, has always been able to progress in the arts. This land has expanded its horizons beyond the limits of the dependency that exists in economic, social, and political problems. The creativity of the people, their intellectual and artistic achievements express a strong and independent culture. The cultural struggle within and outside the island, and the labor of students, teachers, writers, painters, and singers, continue to spur the creative abilities of the new generations.

The Rise of the Outer Community

Puerto Rico and the Puerto Ricans have their own strong identity notwithstanding their social, political, and economic relationship with the United States. New York, Philadelphia, Chicago, Washington, Los Angeles, Miami, and other urban centers have large numbers of Puerto Ricans of different generations, all of them active and creative in the struggle for identity.

The social and ethnic background of the Puerto Ricans in the U.S. cultural mosaic reflects the dominant characteristics of the island's culture pattern and historical destiny. Every Puerto Rican who has exchanged his birthplace for any of the metropolitan centers of New York, New Jersey, Pennsylvania, Illinois, or California has to learn to adapt his body, mind, and soul to the realities of a new environment. He also remains attached to his homeland in many ways. His language continues to be Spanish. His preference for native food is evident in the existence of many stores catering to his tastes, where one can buy tropical produce such as *plátanos, yautías, aguacates, achiote, bacalao, pasta de guayaba,* and many other common items in the daily diet of the island of Puerto Rico. The ties of migrants to the towns where their ancestors were born and raised are extremely strong and emotional. When Hurricane Donna—known as San Lorenzo in Puerto Rico since it hit the island on that saint's day—caused severe damages in the Caribbean some years ago, the New York Puerto Ricans rallied immediately behind the newspaper *La Prensa* and collected more than $50,000 to help the island's victims. This has been repeated every time a major disaster has struck Puerto Rico. When three children arrived in New York years ago and the authorities decided to shelter them in an institution far away in California, the editorial of *La Prensa* expressed its concern with typical Puerto Rican flavor: the three children should have been accommodated with their aunt in New York City instead of being sent away to an unknown place, even if it offered better physical conditions than the home of a relative. For the people of Puerto Rico at all social levels—the poor and the wealthy, the illiterate and the intellectual, the peasant and the town and city dweller—the concept of *mi casa, mi patria, mi tierra* (my home, my land, my soil) is an inseparable trilogy. Home is where parents brought up their children; even after marriage the parents' house is referred to as "home." In the lifetime of any Puerto Rican, no matter how many moves and changes are made, the first "home" is never forgotten. Old grandparents, aunts, nephews and nieces, godfathers and godmothers, neighbors and friends, make a great and unending chain that is Puerto Rico itself, the macrocosm of the extended family. The words *compadre* and *comadre* (the terms used for godfather and godmother but literally meaning co-father and co-mother) best symbolize the relationship established between friends through the ceremony of baptism, a significant link in the social structure of the family cultural pattern in Puerto Rico. The treatment of *compadre* and *comadre* is extended to old friends, and every Puerto Rican feels a moral responsibility to his or her fellow beings embodied in the idea of fatherhood, motherhood, and brotherhood.

The psychological and ethical standards of the Puerto Rican people reveal a deep belief in God and a Christian faith that gives the concepts of love, life, and death a special meaning. It is difficult to trace any atheism among the writers of the island. Even the Marxist and revolutionary protest literature of the twentieth century presents a philosophy of life that emanates from the mystery and power of the Almighty in the ethical and cultural pattern of Puerto Rican society. Of course, the roots are found in the Spanish heritage, in which the Catholic religion was the core of the family. Even Puerto Ricans who have adopted other faiths may reveal in their conduct and innermost sentiments the indelible imprint of Catholicism.

Puerto Rican migrants to the United States may hear descriptive terms such as WASP and see a varied religious panorama. The Jewish synagogues and the human diversity in creeds and traditions may change the views they held before leaving the island. However, for every Puerto Rican and his or her descendants, Catholicism is the spiritual and moral guide that shapes their understanding of evil and goodness and all the actions and reactions of human beings.

Language and art in the Puerto Rican community outside the island offer a substantial subject for research and understanding. The language of Puerto Rico is Spanish, even for Puerto Ricans who live in the continental United States. The artistic expression of the Puerto Rican in poetry, painting, sculpture, and all the popular derivations of the island's musical folklore are also related to the ideas derived from a common heritage in which the Spanish, Indian, and African roots merge. Even abstract artists show evidence of this tradition in poetry and the plastic arts, in the sense of color and form, in the semantic derivations of imagery, and in the essential creative urge to assert essence, being, eternity, through the eternal truths and transitory meanings coupled in *ser* and *estar,* two verbs of primary importance in the Spanish vernacular.

Puerto Ricans frequently establish the difference by making the statement *"No son todos los que están ni están todos los que son."* (Not all those who really are, are here; nor all those who are here, really are.) This play of words based on *ser* and *estar* may express the distance between ideologies or the mere absence or presence of people at a specific time in a specific place. The phrase cannot be conveyed properly in English. Thus, it is important for the Puerto Rican migrants to determine the difference between "to be a man" and "to be here," "to be good" and "to be well" (*ser hombre, estar aquí, ser bueno, estar bien*).

One of the most unjust and prejudiced criticisms made in the United States is that the language of the Puerto Ricans is an inferior brand of Spanish. THIS IS NOT SO. Spanish is a universal language spoken by millions in Spain, Latin America, the United States, and the Antilles. In every country, as with the English language, the vernacular is interspersed with colloquial expressions and local words to designate certain flowers, trees, animals, birds, foods, and geographical and topographical phenomena. Some segments of society have been influenced by a foreign tongue used in the locality. The character of the language as such remains intact in Puerto Rico and the Puerto Ricans who live in the United States remain loyal to the Spanish of their elders. Most scholarly experts have asserted that Spanish as spoken in Puerto Rico has remained free of adulteration in spite of the bilingual system of education, which gives English a superior and even exclusive importance in some schools. The people of Puerto Rico use Spanish in daily life, and their songs and poetry are written in Spanish. To pronounce a C or a Z as S, to change a final or intervocalic R into L or to give a double L (*elle*), the sound of a Y, are phonetic transformations that exist in most Spanish-speaking countries. The shorter forms of *nada* (nothing) and *para* (for) (*na, pa*) are also common in Spain as well as in Mexico, Argentina, and Peru. The flavor of the language spoken by Puerto Ricans of all cultural levels, its melody and its magical powers, carries the emotional and spiritual personality of a national entity within the linguistic realm of the Spanish language. The eminent Puerto Rican lexicographer, Augusto Malaret, is the author of two important dictionaries: *Vocabulario de Puerto Rico* and *Diccionario de Americanismos*. The Spanish scholar and professor of phonetics and philology at Columbia University, Tomás Navarro Tomás, wrote the first important book on *El Español en Puerto Rico,* and many other studies and essays deal with this aspect of Puerto Rican culture in the twentieth century. The interference of English in the oral and written expression of the Puerto Ricans in the United States is considered a natural phenomenon and does not alter the essential respect and defense of the vernacular. When the New School for Social Research in New York announced a course entitled Spanglish, all the Puerto Ricans rallied against this attempt to insult and humiliate the Puerto Rican community. The educated and intellectual classes in the island and in the United States combat this distorted propaganda. A large percentage of the people of Puerto Rico who migrate to the United States represent the poorest and least educated inhabitants of the island, although there is a well-educated working class in business and factories. There are artists, writers, and professors in all the important cities and the Puerto Rican leadership includes lawyers, physicians, architects, engineers, and politicians of high rank. The theater, ballet, opera, and electronic media, as well as newspapers and other media are beginning to use a high percentage of Puerto Rican talent.

Although 1950 has been considered the peak year for migration to the United States, Puerto Ricans had been coming to New York since the nineteenth century. Arthur A. Schomburg (1874–1938) was born in San Juan and came to New York as a young man, becoming part of the life of the country and participating in many of the activities affecting the Puerto Ricans in the early part of this century. His famous collection of art and books on African culture, now known as the Schomburg Center for Research in Black Culture, is a branch of the New York Public Library. Eugenio María de Hostos and other patriots and writers spent years of struggle in New York before Puerto Rico became a possession of the United States in 1898. A revolutionary poet, Pachín Marín, who died fighting for Cuban independence, wrote his love poetry in New York. Before World War I and the granting of citizenship in 1917, Puerto Rican families were established in the United States. Around 1918, Jesús Colón and other workers looking for jobs to improve their economic condition came to work in factories, and spent their whole lives there. When Luis Muñoz Rivera became resident commissioner (1910–1916), he brought his family with him; his son, Luis Muñoz Marín, (1898–1980), was educated in the United States, where he wrote poetry and lived the Bohemian intellectual life of a journalist and writer in his youth. The impact of the Puerto Rican involvement in the cultural life of New York, Washington, Chicago, and Philadelphia is known everywhere. Journalists like Luisa A. Quintero of *El Diario-La Prensa,* performers like Miriam Colón and José Ferrer, scholars and writers, educators and poets from Puerto Rico, are representative of the advancement of the Puerto Rican community outside the island. A younger generation active in New York since 1970 has had an impact on the Hispanic arts. *El Museo del Barrio,* besides having organized exhibitions by Puerto Rican artists, has been a center for poetry readings and workshops. Theater training is offered to talented Puerto Ricans by the traveling theater sponsored by the actress Miriam Colón.

Puerto Rican poets in New York belong to different generations. Some came from the island a half century ago; others arrived as children and have grown up in Manhattan, Brooklyn, the Bronx, and other sections of New York State and as far away as the Midwest or the southern and western coasts of the United States. Probably there is no region of the country where the mark of the Puerto Rican presence is not felt. Hawaii has a very important Puerto Rican community that has grown through several generations without losing its identity. The voice of this mass of people scattered here and there is heard in the music and the poetry that express the yearnings, expectations, and frustrations of the Puerto Ricans, "exiled" not for political and religious reasons, as often happens with immigrants, but primarily because the island cannot cope with the economic demands of its population. The poets born in the United States, children of Puerto Rican parents and even the offspring of mixed marriages, continue to identify themselves as Puerto Ricans. Among them are many differences of poetic language and style, as is to be expected from their varied ages, inclinations, sensitivity, and esthetic influences. Juan Avilés is a traditionalist who maintains a balance between a taste for modernism and Vanguardism. Among his favorite themes is the coffee plantation of his youth in the town of San Sebastián and the learned language of his poems preserves the flavor of the most colorful words of *jíbaro* origin. Pedro Carrasquillo brought to New York a legacy nurtured by rural reminiscences mixed with his hard life and his social protest against inequality and injustice. Víctor Hernández Cruz reconstructs mental pictures in collage style and writes verses and prose poems in which the Latin neighborhoods of the Puerto Ricans in New York harmonize with the vignettes of the island far away, interspersing Spanish and English words in a bilingual combination of great charm. Literature constitutes a document of varied humanistic faces to study the Puerto Rican journey from the mountain to the town, to the slums, to the cities of the United States. Spanish and English wage a battle in Puerto Rican cultural and educational spheres. In the complex life of the Puerto Ricans when they settle in the United States, the struggle becomes dramatic. Spanish and English grasp the disturbed and humiliated human being who does not surrender his cultural identity. His spiritual refuge will continue to be the vernacular tongue; his defense will be the language learned in the streets, the factories, and the schools, while he continues to communicate with sign language, gestures, cries, and silences. His drama has inspired poets and prose writers. With the least possible rhetoric, José Luis González (born in Santo Domingo, raised in Puerto Rico, and at present an active Marxist and Mexican citizen) has written excellent short stories about this type of life. Pedro Juan Soto, well known both in Puerto Rico and in the United States, is a unique creator of short stories, novels, and experimental dramas in which the language struggle between Spanish and English becomes a real experience. *Spiks*, published in 1956, reveals the torturing nightmare of the violence of existential reality for the people who have left the homeland to search for a better life in the slums of New York. In one of his novels, *Ardiente Suelo, Fría Estación* (Burning Earth, Cold Season) (1959) and in a short story dated 1960, *"Esa antigua fragancia"* (That Old Fragrance), he considers the future of the outer Puerto Rican community and its relation with history. These words represent his point of view:

The national and personal identity crisis of the Puerto Rican in New York is not solved with money. The clash with an anonymous lifestyle is very deplorable. The colonial Puerto Rican goes to New York without knowing who he really is, where he comes from, and towards what future he is moving.

La Carreta (The Oxcart), a three-act play by René Marqués, can be considered the apotheosis of the economic plight that caused the migration to the United States. Besides being written with spelling and phonetics that imitate the rural speech of the *jíbaro*, the play presents the ravages of displacement and the plight of the Puerto Rican who abandons the countryside for the slums of San Juan and from there flies to New York, where the last act takes place. The hope of returning to the homeland is optimistic, a dream of possible happiness in searching for the original roots.

Second, third, or fourth generation Puerto Ricans, who know English better than Spanish, express in song and poetry the uncertain future of their people, and denounce the evils of American prejudice and the tragic sense of life of the Puerto Rican community. Language becomes a weapon: English interspersed with darts of Spanish nouns, adjectives, and interjections, slang with the flavor of the native language of their elders, sayings, vulgarity, and obscenities in both English and Spanish to hurt the reader and the audience, all with a flair for originality and wisdom, in a theatrical and sometimes burlesque style. Two well-known poets of this character are Pedro Juan Pietri and Jesús "Papoleto" Meléndez. Of all the cries of outrage of the younger *barrio* writers of New York, none is better known than the *grito* (protest) of Pedro Pietri (1944–   ) whose *Puerto Rican Obituary,* a tragic and moving poem, begins with this statement:

> They worked
> They were always on time
> They were never late
> They never spoke back
> When they were insulted
> They worked
> They never went on strike
> Without permission
> They never took days off
> That were on the calendar
> They worked
> ·Ten days a week
> And were only paid for five
> They worked
> They worked
> They worked
> And they died
> They died broke
> They died owing
> They never died knowing
> What the front entrance
> Of the first national bank
> looks like

"*Grandma, Please Don't Come,*" a story by Jesús Colón, a writer of an older generation, is a delicate and sentimental preview of Pietri's *Obituary.* His message becomes a pathetic plea, with his "grandmother" a symbol of his people in the tropical homeland. These are Colón's words:

All people, North Americans and Puerto Ricans alike, are looking to the day when they can spend the last years of their lives on a tropical isle—a paradise on earth surrounded by clear blue sea imprisoned in a belt of golden beaches. A land perfumed with nature's choicest fragrances. For many of us this is a dream that will never be realized. The boasted "American way of life" has taken out of us the best of our energies to reach that dream.

Grandma, you are there on that beautiful isle. You were born there. You have been there all your life. You now have what most people here can only dream about. Don't let sentimental letters and life-colored photographs lure you from your island, from your nation, from yourself. Grandma, please, please! DO NOT COME!

In 1964, Jaime Carrero, a professor and writer who has contributed important poetry and experimental plays to Puerto Rican contemporary literature, published the first poem in which the concept of Neo-Rican-ism appears. The poem is the lament of a Puerto Rican on an airplane between New York and San Juan. The selection is entitled *From Vuelo D (Conversación IV)* (From Flight D—Conversation No. 4).

Lamento 2:
I was born in New York new blood.
I was born in New York.
I am not a Jones Act Puerto Rican
yeah?
I am a Neo-Rican man . . . new flash.
yeah?

I know what I know no Jones Act man
yeah?

what was that?

Lamento 3:
This Puerto Rican is silent
This Puerto Rican is sad

to be silent and sad
I feel something big
or low
or dark
is going on
in the back
of the mind, man.

This Puerto Rican is silent and sad.
The color no white man dares to ask.

Piri Thomas, the renowned author of *Down These Mean Streets* (1967), recalls in his novel the countryside, the rain, the little birds, the way of life and the lay of the land that the voice of his mother bequeathed to him in Spanish, contributing to Piri's mental bilingualism and his peasant-like attitudes in style, although he writes in English and is considered one of the most effective contemporary North American writers. Considered by some critics the chronicler of *barrio* life in New York, Piri Thomas tells "how not only the people, but their dreams, are suspended in between the worlds of memory and reality." In his later work, *Savior! Savior!* (1972) "the seeds of urban *barrio* culture flower in aesthetic richness."

The words of Piri Thomas's mother in "Puerto Rican Paradise," a chapter of *Down These Mean Streets,* reveal the secret struggle of many migrants from the island to the land of freedom and opportunity:

Bueno hijo, you have people everywhere who, because they have more, don't remember those who have very little. But in Puerto Rico those around you share *la pobreza* (poverty) with you, because only poor people can understand poor people. I like *los Estados Unidos,* but is sometimes a cold place to live—not because of the winter and the landlord not giving heat but because of the snow in the hearts of the people.

Notes

CHAPTER 8: *1898: The Hope and the Trauma*

1. The story of the bombardment is told in the authoritative account by Angel Rivero Méndez, *Crónica de la Guerra Hispanoamericana en Puerto Rico* (Madrid, 1922), pp. 125–144.
2. Rivero, *Crónica*, pp. 181–186.
3. Robert T. Hill, *Cuba and Porto Rico with the other Islands of the West Indies* (New York, 1898), pp. 148–149.
4. George D. Flinter, *An Account of the Present State of the Island of Puerto Rico* (London, 1834).
5. Hill, *Cuba and Porto Rico*, pp. 158–169.
6. The proclamation is found in the *Annual Reports of the War Department*, Washington, D.C., 1902), vol. 1, pt. 13–15. Reprinted in *Documents on the Constitutional History of Puerto Rico*, 2d ed. (Washington, 1964), p. 55.
7. *Documents*, pp. 56–57.
8. Hanna to Day, San Juan, December 3, 1897, *State Department Consular Dispatches*, vol. 19 (Transcription, Historical Research Center, University of Puerto Rico), p. 314.
9. Hanna to Day, San Juan, January 8, 1898, *Dispatches*, p. 315.
10. William E. Curtis, *Trade and Transportation Between the United States and Spanish America* (Washington, 1889), p. 26.
11. George F. Kennan, *American Diplomacy, 1900–1950* (Chicago, 1951), p. 17.
12. E. E. Morison, John M. Blums, and John J. Buckley, eds., *The Letters of Theodore Roosevelt* (Cambridge, Mass., 1951), 1:607.
13. *Letters*, 1:717.
14. *Letters*, 2:83.
15. *Selections from the Correspondence of Theodore Roosevelt and Henry Cabot Lodge, 1884–1914* (New York, 1925), 1:299–300.
16. Ernest R. May, *Imperial Democracy* (New York, 1961), p. 247.
17. Alfred T. Mahan, *Lessons of the War with Spain* (Boston, 1918), p. 29.
18. For the official correspondence, see *Spanish Diplomatic Correspondence and Documents, 1896–1900* (Washington, 1905), pp. 211–227.
19. McKinley to the Commissioners, Washington, August 26, 1898. This communication is found in the manuscripts belonging to General Brooke, available at the Historical Society of Pennsylvania, Philadelphia. Quoted hereon as *The Brooke Papers*, 1898.
20. Richard Harding Davis, *The Cuban and Porto Rican Campaigns* (New York, 1898), p. 360.
21. *Informe Sobre el Censo de Puerto Rico, 1899* (Washington, 1900), pp. 41, 44, 45, 61.

22. *Informe*, pp. 132, 145.

23. *Informe*, pp. 152–154.

24. The point was made by José Ramón Abad in a thoughtful study, *Puerto Rico en la Feria Exposición de Ponce en 1882,* new ed. (San Juan, 1967), pp. 252–254.

25. For a study of the Puerto Rican views, see Paul Nelson Chiles, *The Puerto Rican Press Reaction to the United States, 1888–1898* (Philadelphia, 1944).

26. See the revelation in De Diego's speech of March 12, 1913, in Néstor Rigual, *Incidencias Parlamentarias en Puerto Rico* (San Juan, 1972), 1:74.

27. Rivero, *Crónica,* pp. 533–574, contains a vivid narration of the last days of Spanish rule.

28. Albert G. Robinson, *The Porto Rico of Today* (New York, 1899), p. 222.

29. Rivero, *Crónica,* pp. 208–218.

30. Quoted in Luis M. Díaz Soler, *Rosendo Matienzo Cintrón: Orientador y Guardián de una Cultura* (Río Piedras, 1960), 1:163.

31. Díaz, *Rosendo Matienzo Cintrón,* 1:168–169.

32. The activities of Henna and Hostos are described in *Memoria de los Trabajos Realizados por la Sección Puerto Rico del Partido Revolucionario Cubano, 1895–1898* (New York, 1898).

33. Hostos's views and experiences are recorded in his diary, "Madre Isla," *Obras Completas,* vol. 5 (Havana, 1939).

34. Lidio Cruz Monclova, *Luis Muñoz Rivera: Los Primeros Diez Años de Su Vida Política* (San Juan, 1959), p. 707.

35. Luis Muñoz Rivera, *Obras Completas, Septiembre-Diciembre 1895* (San Juan, 1960), p. 236.

36. See the version in Cayetano Coll y Toste, *Boletín Histórico de Puerto Rico* (San Juan, 1926), 13:355–358.

37. Brooke to the Adjutant General, San Juan, November 30, 1898, *The Brooke Papers.*

38. See Edward J. Berbusse, *The United States in Puerto Rico, 1898–1900* (Chapel Hill, 1966), p. 85.

39. Brooke to Adjutant General, San Juan, November 30, 1898, *The Brooke Papers.*

40. Brooke to Adjutant General, San Juan, November 30, 1898, *The Brooke Papers.*

41. Berbusse, *United States in Puerto Rico,* p. 87.

42. Berbusse, *United States in Puerto Rico,* p. 88.

43. Berbusse, *United States in Puerto Rico,* pp. 88–89.

44. Berbusse, *United States in Puerto Rico,* p. 91.

45. Berbusse, *United States in Puerto Rico,* pp. 90–92.

46. Henry to McKinley, San Juan, January 23, 1899, *The McKinley Papers,* reel 4, ser. 1, Manuscript Division, Library of Congress.

47. Henry to McKinley, San Juan, February 28, 1899, *The McKinley Papers,* reel 6, ser. 1.

48. Berbusse, *United States in Puerto Rico,* p. 94.

49. Henry to McKinley, San Juan, February 28, 1899, *The McKinley Papers,* reel 6, ser. 1.

50. Henry to Adjutant General, San Juan, March 10, 1899, *The McKinley Papers,* reel 6, ser. 1.

51. Telegram to Henry, Washington, March 11, 1899, *The McKinley Papers,* reel 6, ser. 1.

52. Henry to McKinley, San Juan, April 8, 1899, *The McKinley Papers,* reel 6, ser. 1.

53. Henry Wells, *The Modernization of Puerto Rico: A Political Study of Changing Values and Institutions* (Cambridge, Mass., 1969), pp. 76–79.

54. See the text of the circular in *Documents,* pp. 59–63.

55. See Elihu Root, "The Principles of Colonial Policy," in his book, *The Military and Colo-*

nial Policy of the United States. Addresses and Reports (Cambridge, Mass., 1916), pp. 163–165.

56. For several descriptions of this hurricane, see Luis A. Salivia, *Historia de los Temporales de Puerto Rico (1508–1949)* (San Juan, 1950), pp. 255–277.

57. Davis to Secretary of War, San Juan, August 11, 1899, *The McKinley Papers*, reel 7, ser. 1.

58. Root to McKinley, Washington, August 18, 1899, *The McKinley Papers*, reel 7, ser. 1.

CHAPTER 9: *The Rise of Colonial Tutelage*

1. *Report of Brig. Gen. George W. Davis on Civil Affairs in Puerto Rico* (Washington, 1900), p. 545.

2. Elihu Root, "The Principles of Colonial Policy," in his book, *The Military and Colonial Policy of the United States. Addresses and Reports* (Cambridge, Mass., 1916), pp. 165–171.

3. *Report on the Island of Porto Rico, its Population, Civil Government, Commerce, Industries, Productions, Roads, Tariff and Currency, with Recommendations by Henry K. Carroll, Special Commissioner for the U.S. to Porto Rico* (Washington, 1899). See especially pp. 48–59.

4. Berbusse, *United States in Puerto Rico*, pp. 151–165.

5. Quoted in José A. Cabranes, *Citizenship and the American Empire* (New Haven, 1979), p. 39.

6. Philip C. Jessup, *Elihu Root* (New York, 1938), 1:378–379.

7. Cabranes, *Citizenship*, pp. 42–44.

8. See the text in *Documents on the Constitutional History of Puerto Rico*, 2d ed. (Washington, 1964), pp. 64–80.

9. Lyman J. Gould, *La Ley Foraker: Raíces de la Política Colonial de los Estados Unidos* (Río Piedras, 1975), pp. 94–96.

10. For an analysis of the evolution of American policy in this regard, see Rexford G. Tugwell, "Report on the Five Hundred-Acre Law," *Puerto Rican Public Papers of Rexford Guy Tugwell* (San Juan, 1945), pp. 291–347. Also see the scholarly study by Enrique Bird Piñero, "The Politics of Puerto Rican Land Reform: A Study in the Dynamics of Legislation" (Master's Thesis, Chicago, 1950), pp. 45–52.

11. *Downes v. Bidwell*, 182 U.S. 244, 341. For a scholarly analysis of the legal problems involved, see José Trías Monge, *Historia Constitucional de Puerto Rico* (Río Piedras, 1980), 1:235–272.

12. Trías, *Historia Constitucional*, 1:235.

13. Reece B. Bothwell, *Puerto Rico: Cien Años de Lucha Política* (Río Piedras, 1979), 2:117–120.

14. Bolívar Pagán, *Historia de los Partidos Políticos* (San Juan, 1959), 1:60–62.

15. Quoted in María Dolores Luque de Sánchez, *La Ocupación Norteamericana y la Ley Foraker* (Río Piedras, 1980), pp. 96–97.

16. Luque de Sánchez, *La Ocupación*, pp. 98–99.

17. Luque de Sánchez, *La Ocupación*, p. 138.

18. Berbusse, *United States in Puerto Rico*, pp. 173–175.

19. Luque de Sánchez, *La Ocupación*, pp. 141–142.

20. Berbusse, *United States in Puerto Rico*, pp. 177–180.

21. Gordon K. Lewis, *Puerto Rico: Freedom and Power in the Caribbean* (New York, 1963), pp. 87–88.

22. Luque de Sánchez, *La Ocupación*, p. 148.

23. Pagán, *Historia de los Partidos,* 1:85.

24. See the text in Bothwell, *Puerto Rico,* 2:191–197. For Matienzo's conversion, see Luis M. Díaz Soler, *Rosendo Matienzo Cintrón: Orientador y Guardián de una Cultura* (Río Piedras, 1960), pp. 203–254.

25. Díaz Soler, *Rosendo Matienzo Cintrón,* 1:279–287; Pagán, *Historia de los Partidos,* 1:102–113.

26. Pagán, *Historia de los Partidos,* 1:113.

27. James D. Richardson, *A Compilation of the Messages and Papers of the Presidents* (Washington, 1906), 11:1176.

28. Luis Muñoz Rivera, *Campañas Políticas* (Madrid, 1925), 2:136.

29. Díaz Soler, *Rosendo Matienzo Cintrón,* 1:340.

30. See the text in Néstor Rigual, *Incidencias Parlamentarias en Puerto Rico* (Río Piedras, 1972), 1:15.

31. E. E. Morison, John M. Blum, and John J. Buckley, eds., *The Letters of Theodore Roosevelt* (Cambridge, Mass., 1951), 3:678–679.

32. *Letters,* 4:262.

33. *Letters,* 3:152.

34. *Letters,* 4:1110.

35. *Letters,* 5:501–503.

36. *Message From the President of the United States Relative to his Recent Visit to the Island of Porto Rico* (Washington, 1906), p. 5.

37. Rigual, *Incidencias,* 1:17–27.

38. Rigual, *Incidencias,* 1:32.

39. Rigual, *Incidencias,* 1:34–45.

40. *Register of Porto Rico for 1910* (San Juan, 1910), pp. 140–141.

41. *Register,* pp. 190–191.

42. G. M. Fowles, *Down in Porto Rico* (New York, 1910), pp. 81–169.

43. *Register,* p. 145.

44. *Register,* p. 190.

45. Fowles, *Down in Porto Rico,* p. 134.

46. Carmelo Delgado Cintrón, "Historia Política de Puerto Rico," *La Gran Enciclopedia* (Madrid, 1976), 2:108–109.

47. The crisis is studied in Truman R. Clark, "President Taft and the Puerto Rican Appropriation Crisis of 1909," *The Americas,* vol. 26 (October 1969), pp. 152–170.

48. See the full text in Fowles, *Down in Porto Rico,* pp. 171–186.

49. Clark, "President Taft," p. 163.

50. Clark, "President Taft," p. 164.

51. National Archives, Record Group 350, Bureau of Insular Affairs, War Department, Record Card, Civil Government in Puerto Rico, pt. 1, p. 1. From hereon quoted as BIA / WD.

52. BIA / WD, Record Card, pt. 1, pp. 9–10.

53. *Inaugural Address of Governor George R. Colton* (San Juan, 1909).

54. Colton to Secretary of War, San Juan, December 6, 1909, BIA / WD, file 858-13; Dec. 8, 1909, file 858-14.

55. Fowles, *Down in Porto Rico,* pp. 154–156.

56. BIA / WD, Record Card, pt. 1, pp. 41–42.

57. BIA / WD, Record Card, pt. 1, pp. 46–47.

58. BIA / WD, Record Card, pt. 1, pp. 39–40.

59. The article was summarized in BIA / WD, Record Card, pt. 1, p. 156.
60. BIA / WD, Record Card, pt. 1, pp. 159–160.
61. Colton to Muñoz Rivera, San Juan, April 1, 1910, BIA / WD, file 127-6.
62. Colton to Edwards, San Juan, January 11, 1910, and his cable of April 16, 1910, BIA / WD, files 126-92, 126-47.
63. Muñoz Rivera, *Campañas*, 3:118–121.
64. Muñoz Rivera, *Campañas*, 3:125.
65. Stimson to Muñoz Rivera, Washington, March 29, 1912, BIA / WD, file 127-14.
66. Muñoz Rivera to Stimson, Washington, March 30, 1912, BIA / WD, file 127-14.
67. For an analysis of this testimony see Arturo Morales Carrión, "The Historical Roots and Political Significance of Puerto Rico," in A. Curtis Wilgus, ed., *The Caribbean: British, Dutch, French, United States* (Gainesville, 1958), pp. 146–148.
68. See Morales Carrión, "Historical Roots," p. 148.

CHAPTER 10: *The Wilsonian Era in Puerto Rico*

1. See the Bureau Reports for 1914 and 1916. BIA / WD, files 119-14, 119-102, and statement, file 119-129.
2. Bailey W. Diffie, *Porto Rico: A Broken Pledge* (New York, 1931), pp. 46–50.
3. For a review of the 1900–1920 period see Juan José Osuna, *A History of Education in Puerto Rico* (Río Piedras, 1949), pp. 1–257.
4. Ismael Rodríguez Bou, "Significant Factors in the Development of Education in Puerto Rico," in *Status of Puerto Rico. Selected Background Studies* (Washington, 1966), pp. 157–160.
5. See the introduction in A. G. Quintero Rivera, *Lucha Obrera en Puerto Rico* (San Juan, n.d.), pp. 14–15.
6. Igualdad Iglesias de Pagán, *El Obrerismo en Puerto Rico: Epoca de Santiago Iglesias (1896–1905)* (Valencia, 1973), pp. 21–43.
7. Iglesias de Pagán, *El Obrerismo*, pp. 46–49.
8. Iglesias de Pagán, *El Obrerismo*, pp. 47–48.
9. Iglesias de Pagán, *El Obrerismo*, p. 51.
10. Gonzalo F. Córdova, *Santiago Iglesias: Creador del Movimiento Obrero en Puerto Rico* (Río Piedras, 1980), pp. 40–41.
11. Santiago Iglesias Pantín, *Luchas Emancipadoras (Crónicas de Puerto Rico)* (San Juan, 1929), 1:137–141.
12. Iglesias, *Luchas*, pp. 191–192.
13. For Iglesias's early contacts with Gompers, see William G. Whitaker, "The Santiago Iglesias Case, 1901–1902: Origins of American Trade Union Involvement in Puerto Rico," *The Americas*, vol. 24, no. 4, (April, 1968), pp. 374–393.
14. Samuel Gompers, "Address before Federación Regional," in *American Federationist*, vol. 11, no. 4, (April, 1904), p. 298.
15. "President Gompers Speaks to Workingmen," *American Federationist*, 11:304.
16. Whitaker, "The Santiago Iglesias Case," p. 380: Iglesias de Pagán, *El Obrerismo*, p. 162.
17. The events are summarized in Whitaker, "The Santiago Iglesias Case," pp. 389–393; Iglesias de Pagán, *El Obrerismo*, pp. 166–180.
18. "President Gompers in Porto Rico," *American Federationist*, 11:293–306; also "In Porto Rico," *American Federationist*, vol. 11 (May 1904), pp. 391–394.
19. Iglesias de Pagán, *El Obrerismo*, p. 277.

20. The report is found in "President Gompers' Report," *American Federationist,* vol. 15, no. 13 (December 1908), p. 1070.

21. *American Federationist* vol. 15, (December, 1909), p. 1079.

22. Iglesias to President Taft, Washington, November 27, 1909, BIA / WD, file 3377-5.

23. Pagán, *Historia de los Partidos Políticos* . . . (San Juan, 1959), 1:164.

24. Fernando Bayrón Toro, *Elecciones y Partidos Políticos de Puerto Rico (1809–1976)* (Mayagüez, 1977), p. 144.

25. Pagán, *Historia,* 1:170.

26. See "Porto Rico: Her Present Conditions and Fears for the Future," *American Federationist,* vol. 21, no. 5 (May 1914), pp. 377–389.

27. Pagán, *Historia,* 1:184.

28. José Cabranes's book, *Citizenship and the American Empire,* (New Haven, 1979), while strong on the strictly legal field, is woefully lacking in an insight as to the complex Puerto Rican background.

29. See Woodrow Wilson, "The Ideals of America," *The Papers of Woodrow Wilson* (Princeton, 1972), 12:221–222.

30. *Papers of Woodrow Wilson,* 12:223.

31. *Papers of Woodrow Wilson,* 12:225.

32. "Address at Vassar College," *Papers of Woodrow Wilson,* 12:362.

33. Muñoz Rivera to Wilson, January 14, 1913, *Wilson Papers,* Mss. Division, Library of Congress, ser. 2, reel 39.

34. The formula was explained in Edwards to Colton, November 22, 1911, BIA / WD, file 1286-22.

35. Edwards to Colton, January 10, 1912, BIA / WD, Record Card, pt. 4, file 3377-167. Cabranes is mistaken when he writes that it was not until 1914 that Muñoz Rivera made his views known. Cabranes, *Citizenship,* p. 73.

36. Colton to Edwards, January 17, 1912, BIA / WD, file 1286-38.

37. Cable from McIntyre to Colton, May 30, 1912, BIA / WD, Record Card, pt. 2, file 3777-177.

38. Hamilton to Wilson, Mobile, March 12, 1913, *The Wilson Papers,* ser. 4, reel 192, case files ff. 131317.

39. Quoted in Frank Otto Gatell, "The Art of the Possible: Luis Muñoz Rivera and the Puerto Rican Jones Bill," *The Americas,* vol. 17, no. 1 (July 1960), p. 6.

40. Garrison to Wilson, War Department, October 6, 1913, *Wilson Papers,* ser. 4, reel 192, case files 38896.

41. See José Celso Barbosa, "Indecisiones y Desconciertos" in *Orientando al Pueblo* (San Juan, 1939), pp. 81–96.

42. Pagán, *Historia,* 1:156–157.

43. Sebastián Dalmau Canet, *José De Diego* (San Juan, 1923), pp. 30–31; José De Diego, *Nuevas Campañas* (Barcelona, 1916), pp. 141–151.

44. Muñoz Rivera, *Campañas Políticas* (Madrid, 1925), 3:139, 148–151.

45. Gatell, "Art of the Possible," pp. 5–6.

46. Yager to McIntyre, November 25, 1913, BIA / WD, Record Book, pt. 2, 3777-185.

47. Quoted in Cabranes, *Citizenship,* p. 72.

48. Muñoz Rivera, *Campañas Políticas,* 3:257–261.

49. Bureau Memorandum, December 8, 1913, BIA / WD, Record Card, pt. 2, file 3377, pp. 188–189.

50. McIntyre to Yager, December 26, 1913, BIA / WD, Record Card, pt. 2, file 3377, p. 193.

51. BIA / WD, Record Card, pt. 2, file 3377, pp. 205–206.

52. BIA / WD, Personal File—Luis Muñoz Rivera, p. 127.

53. See, for instance, his letter to Barceló, April 14, 1914, *Campañas Políticas*, 3:179–181.

54. Muñoz Rivera, *Campañas Políticas*, 2:266.

55. McIntyre to Yager, April 17, 1914, BIA / WD, Record Card, pt. 2, file 3777, p. 237.

56. BIA / WD, Record Card, pt. 2, p. 256.

57. BIA / WD, Record Card, pt. 2, p. 260.

58. Gatell, "Art of the Possible," p. 11.

59. Gatell, "Art of the Possible," pp. 11–12.

60. Pagán, *Historia*, 1:157–164.

61. Muñoz Rivera, *Campañas Políticas*, 3:201.

62. See the *bases* in De Diego, *Nuevas Campañas*, pp. 300–306.

63. Muñoz Rivera, *Campañas Políticas*, 2:287–341.

64. Muñoz Rivera, *Campañas Políticas*, 3:206; Gatell, "Art of the Possible," p. 15.

65. *The State of the Union Messages of the Presidents*, 1790–1966, 3:2562–2569.

66. McIntyre to Yager, December 10, 1915, and Yager to McIntyre, December 17, 1915, BIA / WD, Record Card 3377, pt. 4, files 283, 229; also Cabranes, *Citizenship*, p. 80.

67. Wilson to McIntyre, January 28, 1916, in BIA / WD, Record Card, pt. 4, file 3377, pp. 301–2.

68. Gatell, "Art of the Possible," pp. 17–18; See the texts in Muñoz Rivera, *Campañas Políticas*, 2:342–357.

69. Gatell, "Art of the Possible," p. 18.

70. Muñoz Rivera, *Campañas Políticas*, 3:215.

71. Muñoz Rivera, *Campañas Políticas*, 3:220–221.

72. Muñoz's last days are recounted by E. Martínez Acosta, *Luis Muñoz Rivera* (San Juan, 1948).

73. See the letter in BIA / WD, Record Card, pt. 4, file 3377, p. 386.

74. Yager to McIntyre, December 10, 1916, BIA / WD, pt. 4 file 3377, p. 387.

75. Cable from McIntyre, December 20, 1916, BIA / WD, pt. 4, file 3377, p. 389.

76. Memorandum to the Secretary of War, July 20, 1916, BIA / WD, pt. 4, file 3377, pp. 348–349.

77. See note, BIA / WD, pt. 4, file 3377, p. 366.

78. The best study of the purchase is C. C. Tansill, *The Purchase of the Danish West Indies* (Baltimore, 1932).

79. See Article 6 in Tansill, *Purchase*, pp. 532–533.

80. Fred L. Israel, ed. *The State of the Union Messages of the Presidents, 1790–1966* (New York, 1966), 3:2578–2579.

81. Baker to Shafròth, February 16, 1917, BIA / WD, Record Card, pt. 5, file 3377, p. 413.

82. Memo to Secretary of War, March 21, 1917, BIA / WD, pt. 5, p. 433.

83. Yager to McIntyre, February 28, 1917, BIA / WD, pt. 5, p. 429.

84. *Report of the Chief of the Bureau of Insular Affairs* (Washington, 1917), p. 21.

CHAPTER 11: *The Aftermath of the Jones Act*

1. Antonio Fernós Isern, "From Colony to Commonwealth," *The Annals of the American Academy of Political and Social Science*, vol. 285 (January 1953), pp. 16–22.

2. For a summary of the Puerto Rican war effort see Knowlton Mixer, *Porto Rico: History and Conditions* (New York, 1926), pp. 92–95.

3. McIntyre to Secretary of War, June 30, 1918, BIA / WD, file 9, pp. 119–10.

4. See the speech in José De Diego, "El Plebiscito," in *Obras Completas* (San Juan, 1966), pp. 523–549.
5. For a summary of events, see Truman Clark, *Puerto Rico and the United States, 1917–1933* (Pittsburgh, 1975), pp. 31–35.
6. Bolívar Pagán, *Historia de los Partidos Políticos* (San Juan, 1959), 1:183.
7. For an introduction to Barbosa's political thinking see his *Orientando al Pueblo* (San Juan, 1939).
8. Pagán, *Historia de los Partidos Políticos*, 1:187–200.
9. Arthur Yager, *Twenty Years of Progress in Puerto Rico* (San Juan, n.d.), pp. 10–11.
10. Clark, *Puerto Rico and the United States*, pp. 48–49.
11. Quoted in Bernard Bailyn et al., *The Great Republic* (Boston, 1977), p. 1058.
12. Todd's recollections of Harding are in Todd, *Desfile de Gobernadores* (San Juan, 1943), pp. 65–84.
13. Clark, *Puerto Rico and the United States*, pp. 51–53.
14. Clark, *Puerto Rico and the United States*, p. 63.
15. Clark, *Puerto Rico and the United States*, pp. 67–73.
16. Arturo Morales Carrión, "The Historical Roots and Political Significance of Puerto Rico," in A. Curtis Wilgus, ed. *The Caribbean: Dutch, French, United States* (Gainesville, 1958), p. 158.
17. Todd, *Desfile de Gobernadores*, pp. 88–89.
18. Clark, *Puerto Rico and the United States*, pp. 87–89.
19. Memo by McIntyre, March 28, 1924, BIA / WD, Record Card, pt. 4, file 3377, pp. 509–511, 518. Also, Clark, *Puerto Rico and the United States*, p. 90.
20. See the text in Pagán, *Historia de los Partidos Políticos*, 1:227–234.
21. "Report of the Treasurer," in *25th Annual Report of the Governor of Porto Rico* (Washington, 1926), pp. 146–148.
22. *Annual Report*, pp. 510–513.
23. *Annual Report*, p. 35.
24. Clark, *Puerto Rico and the United States*, pp. 95–100.
25. Pagán, *Historia de los Partidos Políticos*, 1:268–275.
26. *En Defensa de Puerto Rico* (Asamblea Legislativa, n.d.).

CHAPTER 12: *The Plight of the 1930s*

1. Luis A. Salivia, *Historia de los Temporales de Puerto Rico (1508–1949)* (San Juan, 1950), pp. 316–328.
2. The Roosevelt governorship is aptly studied by Truman Clark, *Puerto Rico and the United States, 1917–1933* (Pittsburgh, 1975), pp. 133–148.
3. See Walter Lippmann's "Introduction" to Theodore Roosevelt, *Colonial Policies of the United States* (New York, 1937), pp. 11–13.
4. Roosevelt, *Colonial Policies*, pp. 117–118.
5. Clark, *Puerto Rico and the United States*, p. 139.
6. For Padín's ideas see his book, *Personas Sobre Cosas* (San Juan, 1951).
7. Víctor S. Clark, *Porto Rico and Its Problems* (Washington, 1930), p. 21.
8. Clark, *Porto Rico and Its Problems*, p. 496.
9. Bailey W. Diffie, *Porto Rico: A Broken Pledge* (New York, 1931), pp. 46–50.
10. Clark, *Puerto Rico and the United States*, pp. 147–148.
11. Clark, *Puerto Rico and the United States*, pp. 84–85; Pedro Albizu Campos, *Obras Escogi-*

das, 1923–1936 (San Juan, 1975), 1:8. The compiler, J. Benjamín Torres, does not mention Albizu's service in the army.

12. Albizu Campos, *Obras Escogidas,* p. 15.

13. Albizu Campos, *Obras Escogidas,* p. 19.

14. Albizu Campos, *Obras Escogidas,* pp. 29–31.

15. The best book on Muñoz's life during this period is Carmelo Rosario Natal, *La Juventud de Luis Muñoz Marín* (San Juan, 1976).

16. Luis Muñoz Marín, "Porto Rico: The American Colony," *The Nation* (April 8, 1925), pp. 379–380.

17. Luis Muñoz Marín, "The Sad Case of Porto Rico," *The American Mercury* (1929), pp. 138–139.

18. Pagán, *Historia de los Partidos Políticos* (San Juan, 1959), 2:44–46.

19. Thomas Mathews, *Puerto Rican Politics and the New Deal* (Gainesville, 1960), p. 54. This is the best and most scholarly book on the subject.

20. Mathews, *Puerto Rican Politics,* pp. 61–66.

21. Mathews, *Puerto Rican Politics,* p. 70.

22. The writer was a witness to many of these events.

23. Mathews, *Puerto Rican Politics,* pp. 111–113.

24. For a description of PRERA, see Earl Parker Hanson, *Transformation: The Story of Puerto Rico* (New York, 1955), p. 64 ff; Rigual, *Incidencias Parlamentarias en Puerto Rico* (Río Piedras, 1972), 2:142–145.

25. Quoted in Mathews, *Puerto Rican Politics,* p. 151.

26. Mathews, *Puerto Rican Politics,* pp. 155–159.

27. Besides Mathews, *Puerto Rican Politics,* pp. 162–186, see the good summary in Welles, *The Modernization of Puerto Rico* (Cambridge, Mass, 1969), pp. 115–118.

28. Albizu Campos, *Obras Escogidas,* 1:254–268.

29. Mathews, *Puerto Rican Politics,* pp. 249–250.

30. Mathews, *Puerto Rican Politics,* pp. 254–255.

31. Hanson, *Transformation,* pp. 156–157; see also Frank Otto Gatell, "Independence Rejected: Puerto Rico and the Tydings bill of 1936," *The Hispanic American Historical Review,* vol. 38, (February 1958), pp. 25–44.

32. Robert J. Hunter, "Historical Survey of the Puerto Rico Status Question, 1898–1965." *Status of Puerto Rico: Selected Background Studies* (Washington, 1966), pp. 92–93.

33. Memorandum to the Solicitor General, Washington, March 31, 1936, *The Cummings Papers,* Manuscript Department, University of Virginia, Accession 9973, box no. 84.

34. Roberto Rexach Benítez, *Pedro Albizu Campos: Leyenda y Realidad* (San Juan, 1961), p. 16.

35. See the statements in J. Benjamín Torres, *El Proceso Judicial contra Albizu Campos* (San Juan, 1979), pp. 37–38.

36. Hanson, *Transformation,* p. 158.

37. Pagán, *Historia de los Partidos Políticos,* 2:114.

38. Mathews, *Puerto Rican Politics,* pp. 275–277; Hanson, *Transformation,* pp. 160–163.

39. Ismael Rodríguez Bou, "Significant Factors in the Development of Education in Puerto Rico" in *Status of Puerto Rico: Selected Background Studies* (Washington, 1966), pp. 162–163.

40. Mathews, *Puerto Rican Politics,* pp. 272–273.

41. *The Secret Diary of Harold Ickes* (New York, 1953), 2:5–6.

42. Federico Ribes Tovar, *Albizu Campos: El Revolucionario* (New York, 1971), p. 67.

43. Mathews, *Puerto Rican Politics*, pp. 310–313.
44. Mathews, *Puerto Rican Politics*, p. 314.
45. Ribes Tovar, *Albizu Campos*, pp. 87–88.
46. Hunter, "Historical Survey of the Puerto Rico Status Question, 1898–1965," *Status of Puerto Rico: Selected Background Studies*, p. 97.
47. Rexford Guy Tugwell, *The Stricken Land* (New York, 1947), p. 39.
48. Blanca Silvestrini de Pacheco, *Los Trabajadores Puertorriqueños y el Partido Socialista (1932–1940)* (Río Piedras, 1979), pp. 121–125.
49. Córdova, *Santiago Iglesias: Creador del Movimiento Obrero en Puerto Rico* (Río Piedras, 1980), p. 129.
50. Pagán, *Historia de los Partidos Políticos*, 2:144–145.

CHAPTER 13: *The Forging of Consensus*

1. For some significant facts, see Félix Mejías, *Condiciones de Vida de las Clases Jornaleras de Puerto Rico* (Río Piedras, 1946).
2. Daniel Creamer, *The Net Income of the Puerto Rican Economy, 1940–1944* (Río Piedras, n.d.), pp. 21–22.
3. Earl S. Garver and Ernest B. Fincher, *Puerto Rico: Unsolved Problem* (Elgin, Ill., 1945), pp. 22–23.
4. For the early history of the party see Olivo de Lieban Córdova, *Siete Años con Muñoz Marín, 1938–1945* (San Juan, 1945).
5. Muñoz Marín to Ruby A. Black, San Juan, August 11, 1939, in Reece B. Bothwell, *Puerto Rico: Cien Años de Lucha* (Río Piedras, 1979), 3:207–209.
6. Luis Muñoz Marín, "Development through Democracy," in *The Annals of the American Academy of Political and Social Science*, vol. 285, (January 1953), p. 3.
7. See the party's platform in Bothwell, *Puerto Rico*, 1:613–624.
8. For the 1940 elections, see Pagán, *Historia de los Partidos Políticos* (San Juan, 1959), 2:149–162.
9. Stetson Conn and Byron Fairchild, *The Framework of Hemisphere Defense* (Washington, 1960), pp. 5–7.
10. Conn and Fairchild, *Framework*, pp. 11–13.
11. *Thirty-ninth Annual Report of the Governor of Puerto Rico, Honorable Blanton Winship* (San Juan, 1939), pp. 17–18.
12. *Fortieth Annual Report of the Governor of Puerto Rico, Hon. William D. Leahy* (San Juan, 1940), pp. 17–18.
13. Conn and Fairchild, *Framework*, pp. 17–18.
14. Conn and Fairchild, *Framework*, pp. 30–36.
15. Rexford Guy Tugwell, *The Stricken Land* (New York, 1947), pp. 95–97.
16. Conn and Fairchild, *Framework*, pp. 53–54.
17. Bothwell, *Puerto Rico*, 1:623.
18. Tugwell, *Stricken Land*, pp. 76–77.
19. Tugwell, *Stricken Land*, p. 71.
20. "Inaugural Address," *Puerto Rican Public Papers of Rexford Guy Tugwell* (San Juan, 1945), pp. 7, 11.
21. Thomas Aiken, Jr., *Poet in the Fortress* (New York, 1964), pp. 153–154.
22. Henry Wells, *The Modernization of Puerto Rico: A Political Study of Changing Values and Institutions* (Cambridge, Mass., 1969), pp. 136–140.

23. Charles Goodsell, *Administration of a Revolution: Executive Reform in Puerto Rico under Governor Tugwell, 1941–1946* (Cambridge, Mass., 1965), p. 21.
24. Tugwell, *Public Papers*, p. 149.
25. Tugwell, *Public Papers*, pp. 159–180.
26. Creamer, *Net Income*, p. 38.
27. Creamer, *Net Income*, p. 31.
28. Goodsell, *Administration*, pp. 55–59.
29. Bothwell, *Puerto Rico*, 1:643–645.
30. Pagán, *Historia de los Partidos Políticos*, 2:223.

CHAPTER 14: *The PPD Democratic Hegemony (1944–1969)*

1. Memorandum of Roy D. Davenport, Deputy Under Secretary of the Army, "Puerto Ricans in the Armed Services," September 8, 1965, pp. 10, 26, 62–63. Copy provided by Salvador M. Padilla, former adjutant general of the P.R. National Guard.
2. Davenport, "Puerto Ricans," pp. 2, 117–139.
3. Tugwell, *The Stricken Land*, pp. 670–671.
4. Tugwell, *The Stricken Land*, p. 595.
5. *Forty-Sixth Annual Report of the Governor of Puerto Rico, Honorable Rexford G. Tugwell*, vol. 1 (San Juan, 1947).
6. *Forty-Sixth Report*, p. 80.
7. *Forty-Sixth Report*, p. 80.
8. "Message to the Sixteenth Legislature. First Regular Session," *Puerto Rican Public Papers*, p. 264.
9. For the events described, see Surendra Bhana, *The United States and the Development of the Puerto Rican Status Question: 1936–1968* (Wichita, Kans.), pp. 94–97.
10. Bhana, *Status Question*, pp. 97–98.
11. Bhana, *Status Question*, pp. 60–62.
12. For the text, see Antonio Pacheco Padró, *Puerto Rico: Nación y Estado* (San Juan, 1955), pp. 24–25.
13. Pagán, *Historia de los Partidos Políticos*, 3:228–231.
14. The documents are found in Bothwell, *Puerto Rico*, 3:419–427.
15. Bhana, *Status Question*, pp. 77–83.
16. Bothwell, *Puerto Rico*, 3:454.
17. Bothwell, *Puerto Rico*, 1:661–666.
18. "*Muñoz Marín Recapitula Desarrollo del Pensamiento Político Sobre el Status*," a speech at Barranquitas, July 17, 1951.
19. Antonio Fernós Isern, *Estado Libre Asociado: Antecedentes, Creación y Desarrollo Hasta la Epoca Presente* (Barcelona, 1974), pp. 66 69.
20. David F. Ross, *The Long Uphill Path* (San Juan, 1969), pp. 77–105.
21. Fernós, *Estado Libre Asociado*, pp. 69–80; Bhana, *Status Question*, pp. 100–103.
22. Earl S. Pomeray, "Election of the Governor of Puerto Rico," *The Southwestern Social Science Quarterly*, vol. 23 no. 4 (March, 1943), pp. 355–360.
23. Fernós, *Estado Libre Asociado*, pp. 93–94.
24. For an analysis see "Mensaje II" in Luis Muñoz Marín, *Mensajes al Pueblo Puertorriqueño* (San Juan, 1980), pp. 30–54.
25. Muñoz Marín, *Mensajes*, p. 9.

26. National Archives, Record Group 126, Office of Territories, Department of Interior, 9–6–8, box 862, pt. 6.
27. *Documents on the Constitutional History of Puerto Rico,* 2d ed. (Washington, 1964), p. 153.
28. Bhana, *Status Question,* p. 127.
29. Fernós, *Estado Libre Asociado,* pp. 108–112.
30. Aiken, *Poet,* pp. 188–189.
31. See the communications in National Archives, Record Group 48, Department of Interior, Office of the Secretary, 9–8–2, box 3696, pt. 8.
32. Office of the Secretary, 9–8–2, box 3696, pt. 8.
33. See Resolution 23 in *Documents,* pp. 166–167.
34. Bhana, *Status Question,* pp. 148–164, has a good summary.
35. Carl J. Friedrich, *Puerto Rico: Middle Road to Freedom: Fuero Fundamental* (Cambridge, Mass., 1959), p. 41.
36. Emil J. Sady, *The United Nations and Dependent Peoples* (Washington, 1956) is a useful book on the subject.
37. Bhana, *Status Questions,* pp. 171–174.
38. Fernós, *Estado Libre Asociado,* p. 354.
39. Personal information.
40. Davenport, "Puerto Ricans in the Armed Services," pp. 21–23, 85–86.
41. Harvey S. Perloff, *Puerto Rico's Economic Future: A Study in Planned Development* (Chicago, 1950), p. 394.
42. For a study of this period, see Ross, *The Long Uphill Path,* pp. 129–168.
43. Rita M. Maldonado, "Why Puerto Ricans Migrated to the United States in 1947–73", *Monthly Labor Review,* U.S. Dept. of Labor (Sep., 1976), p. 10.
44. Muñoz Marín, *Mensajes,* p. 172.
45. Bayrón Toro, *Elecciones y Partidos Políticos de Puerto Rico (1809–1976)* (Mayaguez, 1977), pp. 215–217.
46. Robert W. Anderson, *Party Politics in Puerto Rico* (Stanford, 1965), pp. 93–117.
47. Anderson, *Party Politics,* pp. 90–91.
48. For an exposition of the program see the statement by the Commonwealth Under Secretary of State in *Hearings Before a Special Subcommittee on Territorial and Insular Affairs, H.R., 86th Congress First Session H.R. 9234* (Washington, 1960), pp. 47–57.
49. Luis Muñoz Marín, "Puerto Rico and the U.S., Their Future Together," *Foreign Affairs* (July 1954), pp. 541–551.
50. Federico Ribes Tovar, *Albizu Campos: El Revolucionario* (New York, 1971), pp. 140–159.
51. Fernós, Estado Libre Asociado, pp. 371–382; on Bentley's reaction see Bothwell, *Puerto Rico,* 4:195–196.
52. Pagán, *Historia de los Partidos Políticos,* 2:350–351.
53. Pagán, *Historia de los Partidos Políticos,* 2:390.
54. Muñoz Marín, *Mensajes,* pp. 155–161.
55. Fernós, *Estado Libre Asociado,* pp. 422–432.
56. See the documents in Fernós, *Estado Libre Asociado,* pp. 488–493.
57. Bothwell, *Puerto Rico,* 1:276–325.
58. Bayrón Toro, *Elecciones,* pp. 231–239.
59. Luis Muñoz Marín, *An America to Serve the World,* April 7, 1956 (San Juan, 1956).
60. John F. Kennedy, *The Strategy of Peace* (New York, 1961), p. 177.
61. Arthur M. Schlesinger, Jr., *A Thousand Days* (Cambridge, Mass., 1965), pp. 732–733.
62. *Documents,* p. 206.

63. Fernós, *Estado Libre Asociado*, pp. 549–550.

64. Welles, *Modernization*, pp. 253–254.

65. Welles, *Modernization*, pp. 253–254.

66. See the text in Fernós, *Estado Libre Asociado*, pp. 356–357.

67. Fernós, *Estado Libre Asociado*, p. 556–557.

68. *Status of Puerto Rico: Report of the United States-Puerto Rico Commission on the Status of Puerto Rico* (Washington, 1966), p. 3.

69. For additional data on elections and parties during the 1964–1968 period, see Bayrón Toro, *Elecciones*, pp. 240–244.

CHAPTER 15: *A Postscriptum: The End of Consensus*

1. For the 1968–1979 elections, see Fernando Bayrón Toro, *Elecciones y Partidos Políticos de Puerto Rico* (1809–1876) (Mayaguez, 1977), pp. 245–274.

2. For an analysis of this compact, see *Compact of Permanent Union between Puerto Rico and the United States. Report of the Ad Hoc Advisory Group on Puerto Rico* (October 1975).

3. For a discussion of recent political and legal issues, see Arnold Leibowitz, *Colonial Emancipation in the Pacific and the Caribbean* (New York, 1976), pp. 34–63; Roberta Ann Johnson, *Puerto Rico: Commonwealth or Colony* (New York, 1980); and Angel Calderón Cruz, "Las Relaciones Exteriores del Estado Libre Asociado de Puerto Rico," *Contemporary Caribbean Issues* (Río Piedras, 1979), pp. 29–54. Also Gordon K. Lewis, *Notes on the Puerto Rican Revolution* (New York, 1974).

4. *Economic Study of Puerto Rico* (Washington, 1979), 1:13.

5. *Economic Study*, 1:14–15.

6. For some additional observations, see Economic Study, vol. 1, no. 5 and Eliezer Curet Cuevas, *El Desarrollo Económico de Puerto Rico: 1940 a 1972* (Hato Rey, 1979), pp. 360–372.

7. *Informe al Gobernador del Comité para el Estudio de las Finanzas de Puerto Rico (Informe Tobin)* (Río Piedras, 1976).

8. *El Desarrollo Económico de Puerto Rico: Una Estrategia para la Próxima Década* (Río Piedras, 1976).

9. *Puerto Rico's Political Future: A Divisive Issue with Many Dimensions* (Washington, March 2, 1981).

Suggestions
for Further Reading

CHAPTER 1: *An Island is Settled*

For a general introduction to archaeological studies in Puerto Rico see Ricardo E. Alegría, "Los Estudios Arqueológicos en Puerto Rico," *Revista / Review Interamericana,* vol. 7, no. 3. (Fall 1978): 380–384. The origins of the Archaic tradition are studied in Ricardo Alegría, H. B. Nicolson, and Gordon R. Willey, "The Archaic Tradition in Puerto Rico," *American Antiquity,* vol. 21, no. 2. (October 1955): 113–121. Another fixed chronology is by Alegría and Irving Rouse, "Radiocarbon Dates from the West Indies," *Revista / Review Interamericana,* vol. 8, no. 3. (Fall 1978): 495–499. For the relations with other aboriginal cultures, see Alegría, "La población aborigen antillana y su relación con otras areas de América," Congreso Histórico Municipal Interamericano, San Juan, 1948, pp. 233–246. Some excellent books by U.S. scholars include Irving Rouse, "Puerto Rican Prehistory," in *Scientific Survey of Porto Rico and the Virgin Islands,* pts. 3 and 4 (New York Academy of Sciences, 1952); Froelich Rainey, *Porto Rican Archaeology* (New York, 1940); and the earlier, pioneer book by Jesse W. Fewkes, *The Aborigines of Porto Rico and Neighboring Islands* (New York, Reprint, 1970).

For more information on the Arawaks, see Rouse, "The Arawaks," *Handbook of South American Indians,* vol. 4. (Washington, 1945). Ball games are discussed in Alegría, "The Ball Game Played by the Aborigines of the Antilles," *American Antiquity,* 14, no. 4 (April 1951): 348–352. A recent bibliography written in Spanish has been published by Jalil Sued-Badillo: *Bibliografía Antropológica para el Estudio de los Pueblos Indígenas del Caribe* (Santo Domingo, 1977). See also his *La Mujer Indígena y su Sociedad* (Río Piedras, 1979).

CHAPTER 2: *The Outpost of Empire*

For the early development of Puerto Rican history, the author has drawn heavily on her original research in the *Archivo General de Indias* (General Archives of the Indies) in Seville; particularly the sources found in the sections *Audiencia de Santo Domingo, Escribanía de Cámara,* and *Contaduría.* Additional Information on Puerto Rico's early role in Caribbean history is found in Salvador Brau, *La Colonización de Puerto Rico* 3d ed. (San Juan, 1966); Arturo Morales Carrión, *Puerto Rico and the Non-Hispanic Caribbean* 2d ed. (Río Piedras, 1971); Enrique T. Blanco, *Los Tres Ataques Británicos a la Ciudad de San Juan Bautista de Puerto Rico* 2d ed. (San Juan, 1968); Adolfo de Hostos, *Historia de San Juan,*

Ciudad Murada (San Juan, 1966); and Fernando Géigel Sabat, *Balduino Enrico* (Barcelona, 1934).

The author has prepared a sourcebook in Spanish on Puerto Rico's first centuries: *Antología de Lecturas de Historia de Puerto Rico (Siglos XV–XVIII)* (San Juan, 1971). Interesting English sources on Cumberland's expedition are listed in Morales Carrión, *op. cit.*, 26–27. Also see "A large Relation of the Port Ricco voiage; written, as is reported, by that learned man and reverend Divine Doctor Layfield, his Lordships Chaplaine and Attendant in that expedition; very much abbreviated" in *Purchas His Pilgrimes* vol. 14. (Glasgow, 1906): 44–106.

CHAPTER 3: *Organization of an Institutional and Social Life*

Besides the sources mentioned for Chapter 2, which have been widely used, the author also used the works by Vicente Murga Sanz, *Cedulario Puertorriqueño*, 2 vols. (Río Piedras, 1961–1964), *Historia Documental de Puerto Rico* (1956), and *Juan Ponce de León* (Madrid, 1959). An earlier printed source, Alejandro Tapia, *Biblioteca Histórica de Puerto Rico* (Puerto Rico, 1854), was also used. For church history, see Antonio Cuesta Mendoza, *Historia Eclesiástica de Puerto Rico* (Ciudad Trujillo, 1948) and his *Los Dominicos en el Puerto Rico Colonial* (Mexico, 1946). For economic and social history, the author used Arturo Morales Carrión, *Albores Históricos del Capitalismo en Puerto Rico* (Río Piedras, 1972). On municipal and local history, see Aida Caro Costas, *El Cabildo o Régimen Municipal Puertorriqueño en el Siglo XVIII* (San Juan, 1965) and her book on *Villa de San Germán: Sus Derechos y Privilegios Durante los Siglos XVI, XVII y XVIII* (San Juan, 1962).

CHAPTER 4: *The Eighteenth Century Society*

In preparing this chapter extensive use was made of primary and secondary sources, most of which are readily available. Some primary sources include Fray Iñigo Abbad y Lasierra, *Historia geográfica, civil y natural de la Isla de San Juan Bautista de Puerto Rico* (San Juan, 1970), the first island history, originally published in Madrid in 1788. Abbad also wrote *Viaje a la América* (Caracas, 1974), the first part of which deals with Puerto Rico. This is the diary Abbad kept during his travels as secretary to Bishop Manuel Jiménez Pérez; it served as the basis for his *Historia,* although there are differences between the two works. Another reference used in this chapter was Pierre Ledrú and Nicolás Baudin, *Viaje a la Isla de Puerto Rico, 1797* (San Juan, 1957). Ledrú, a French scientist who visited the island as part of a botanical expedition, provides a vivid description of Puerto Rico and its society at the end of the century. Fernando Miyares, in *Noticias Particulares de la Isla y Puerto de San Juan Bautista de Puerto Rico* (Río Piedras, 1955), written in 1755, provides a descriptive account of Puerto Rico which antedates Abbad's *Historia* by a decade.

Among the documentary collections the most important are: *Actas del Cabildo de San Juan Bautista de Puerto Rico* (San Juan, 1949–1970), edited by Aida R. Caro and Francisco M. Zeno, a valuable edition of the proceedings of the *cabildo* from 1730 to 1817; Cayetano Coll y Toste, *Boletín Histórico de Puerto Rico*, 14 vols. (San Juan, 1914–1927), the most important documentary collection of Puerto Rican history; and Alejandro Tapia y Rivera, *Biblioteca Histórica de Puerto Rico* (San Juan, 1945), originally published in 1854, which contains important documents on eighteenth century Puerto Rico, chief among them Alejandro O'Reilly's *Memoria.*

Some useful secondary sources are: Aida Caro Costas, *El Cabildo o Régimen municipal puertorriqueño en el Siglo XVIII,* 2 vols. (San Juan, 1965), a detailed study of the municipal government in Puerto Rico; Arturo Morales Carrión, *Historia del Pueblo de Puerto Rico* (San Juan, 1968), which traces the island's history from its beginnings to the eighteenth century and, by the same author, *Puerto Rico and the Non-Hispanic Caribbean* 2d ed. (Río Piedras, 1971), a documented study on the decline of Spanish exclusivism; Bibiano Torres Ramírez, *Isla de Puerto Rico (1765–1800)* (San Juan, 1968), which deals primarily with the last third of the eighteenth century and is based on documents found in the *Archivo de Indias* in Seville; and Juan M. Zapatero, *La Guerra del Caribe en el Siglo XVIII* (San Juan, 1964), a history of the struggles among the European powers for the domination of the Caribbean basin.

CHAPTER 5: *Puerto Rico in a Revolutionary World*

The material in this chapter has been heavily based on the author's unpublished doctoral dissertation, presented at the University of Chicago in 1953, "Early Relations between the United States and Puerto Rico, 1797–1830."

A. *The Bourbon Reforms:* A basic study is Bibiano Torres Ramírez, *La isla de Puerto Rico, 1765–1800* (San Juan, 1968). For a contemporary vision of the insular social milieu at the end of the century, see Andé Pierre Ledrú, *Viaje a la isla de Puerto Rico en el año de 1797* 5th ed. (San Juan, 1971), originally published in 1863. See also Arturo Morales Carrión, *Puerto Rico and the Non-Hispanic Caribbean* 2d ed., Rio Piedras, 1971): 93–99.

B. Fin de Siécle—*A War Interlude:* For the diplomatic background the author has relied on Morales Carrión, *Puerto Rico and the Non-Hispanic Caribbean,* pp. 103–113. For an extended treatment of the British attitude, especially its military and strategic aspects, see Enrique T. Blanco, *Los tres ataques británicos a la ciudad de San Juan Bautista de Puerto Rico* 2d ed. (San Juan, 1968) and José Manuel Zapatero, *La Guerra del Caribe en el Siglo XVIII* (San Juan, 1968): 46–485.

C. *The Development of Legalized Foreign Trade:* For trade and economic activity in the Caribbean during this period, the reader is referred to Manuel Moreno Fraginals, "El comercio azucarero cubano entre 1790 y 1819," in *Santiago* (Santiago, Cuba, June-September, 1974): 32 *et seq.* See also the same author's notable book, *El ingenio, complejo económico y social cubano del azúcar,* 3 vols. (Havana, 1978). For the development of American trade, see Roy F. Nichols, "Trade Relations and the Establishment of United States Consulates in Spanish America, 1779 1809," *Hispanic American Historical Review,* vol. 12. (August 1933). With regard to Puerto Rico, see Morales Carrión, *Puerto Rico and the Non-Hispanic Caribbean,* pp. 119–120. References to the triangular trade between the Spanish West Indies, the United States, and the Baltic region are found in Emory R. Johnson *et al., History of the Domestic and Foreign Commerce of the United States,* vol. 2. (Washington, 1922): 14–19. The trade with the Spanish West Indies is studied in Dorothy Bourne Goebel, "British trade to the American colonies, 1726–1823," *American Historical Review,* vol. 49. 1938, and Samuel Eliot Morison, *The Maritime History of Massachusetts, 1783–1860* (Boston, 1921). For the opposition of the Caracas merchants to Spanish trade concessions, see Eduardo Arcila Farias, *Economía colonial de Venezuela* (Mexico, 1946). The socioeconomic history of Puerto Rico during this period is analyzed in the scholarly notes by the Puerto Rican historian José Julián Acosta to the third edition (San Juan, 1866) of Iñigo Abbad y Lasierra, *Historia geográfica, civil y natural de la isla de San Juan Bautista de Puerto Rico;* statistics and contemporary data can be found in Pedro Tomás de Córdoba, *Memorias geográficas, históricas, económicas y estadísticas de la isla de Puerto Rico,* 6 vols. (San Juan, 1831–1833); the politico-administrative process is adequately treated in Lidio Cruz Monclova, *Historia de Puerto Rico, Siglo XIX*, vol. 1, 1808–1868 (Río Piedras, 1952). For relations and parallelisms with contemporary Cuba, see Jacobo de la Pezuela, *Historia de la isla de Cuba*, 4 vols. (Madrid, 1868–1878), and Ramiro Guerra y Sánchez, *Manual de Historia de Cuba (Económica, Social y Política)*, 2d ed. (Havana, 1964).

D. *Puerto Rico and the Latin American Struggle for Independence:* On the general background, see John Lynch, *The Spanish-American Revolutions, 1808–1826* (London, 1973). For the reception of news in the island and the early reactions, see: Pedro Tomás de Córdova, *Memorias geográficas, históricas, económicas y estadísticas de la isla de Puerto Rico*, vol. 3. 2d ed. (San Juan, 1968): 469 ff., and Lidio Cruz Monclova, *Historia de Puerto Rico (Siglo XIX)*, vol. 1. (Río Piedras, 1962). The initial manifestations of separatist feelings are studied in Francisco Morales Padrón, "Primer intento de independencia puertorriqueña, 1811–1812," *Caribbean Studies*, vol. 1, no. 4. (January 1962): 11–25. For convenient summaries of West Indian privateering during this period, see José Rafael Fortique, *El Corso Venezolano y las revistas de Irvine y de Perry en Angostura* (Maracaibo, Venezuela, 1968); Charles C. Griffin, "Privateering from Baltimore during the Spanish American Wars of Independence," *The Maryland Historical Magazine*, vol. 25. (1940): 1–25; Lewis W. Bealer, *Los Corsarios de Buenos Aires* (Buenos Aires, 1937): 1–50 *passim;* and Fernando S. Géigel, *Corsarios y Piratas de Puerto Rico, 1819–1825* (San Juan, 1946): 23–34. American interest in the area is studied in Charles C. Griffin, *The United States and the Disruption of the Spanish Empire* (New York, 1937); and Arthur P. Whitaker, *The United States and the Independence of Latin America, 1800–1830* (Baltimore, 1941). For naval operations, see Gardener W. Allen, *Our Navy and the West Indian Pirates* (Salem, 1929), and Dudley Knox, *A History of the United States Navy* (New York, 1936): 139–140. References to the Ducoudray Holstein expedition are based on H. L. V. Ducoudray Holstein, *Memoirs of Simón Bolívar, President Liberator of the Republic of Colombia and of his Principal Generals; Secret History of the Revolution and the Events which Preceded It, from 1807 to the Present Time* (Boston, 1829: 298 ff.; also see the author's doctoral dissertation.

For biographical data on Valero, see Mariano Abril, *Antonio Valero, un Héroe de la Independencia de España y América* 2d ed. (San Juan, 1971).

CHAPTERS 6 AND 7: *The Last of the "Colonial Jewels" (1818–1868) and The Challenge to Colonialism.*

The following primary and secondary sources were used in the preparation of these two chapters and are recommended for further reading. A major work dealing with conditions in Puerto Rico up to the third decade of the nineteenth century is by Pedro Tomás de Córdova, *Memorias geográficas, históricas, económicas y estadísticas de la isla de Puerto Rico*, 6 vols., 2d ed. facsim. (San Juan, 1968). Also useful and by the same author is *Memoria sobre todos los ramos de la administración* (Madrid, 1838). *Diario Económico de Puerto Rico 1814–1915*, compiled and edited by Luis E. González Vales (San Juan, 1972), is an important source for assessing the work of Alejandro Ramírez, Puerto Rico's first intendant. George Flinter is the author of *An Account of the Present State of Puerto Rico* Reprint, (San Juan, 1971) which describes conditions in Puerto Rico during the third decade of the nineteenth century. The only major account of the *Grito de Lares* is found in José Pérez Moris and Luis Quijano, *Historia de la Insurrección de Lares* (Barcelona, 1872), written from a pro-Spanish viewpoint. *El Proceso Abolicionista en Puerto Rico: documentos para su Estudio*, edited by Arturo Morales Carrión, 2 vols. (San Juan, 1974) is a valuable collection of documents from European and

American archives on the institution of slavery in Puerto Rico. The early development of political parties in Puerto Rico under the Spanish regime is discussed in Francisco Mariano Quiñones, *Historia de los Partidos Reformista y Conservador de Puerto Rico* (Mayagüez, 1889). For the position taken by the island representatives at the *Junta de Información* (1866) on the question of slavery, see Segundo Ruiz Belvis *et al*, *Proyecto para la Abolición de la Esclavitud en Puerto Rico* (San Juan, 1959).

Secondary sources useful for the study of nineteenth century figures in the island's history include Luis Bonafoux, *Betances*, 2d ed. (San Juan, 1970); Lidio Cruz Monclova, *Luis Muñoz Rivera (Diez Años de su Vida Política)* (San Juan, 1959); *Baldorioty de Castro* (San Juan, 1966); and Luis E. González Vales, *Alejandro Ramírez y Su Tiempo* (San Juan, 1978). Some books that are essential to understanding the rise and development of the autonomist movement in Puerto Rico are *De Baldorioty a Barbosa* (San Juan, 1957); *La Comisión Autonomista* (San Juan, 1957); and *El Ensayo de la Autonomía* (San Juan, 1975), all by Pilar Barbosa de Rosario. The standard history of Puerto Rico in the nineteenth century is by Lidio Cruz Monclova, *Historia de Puerto Rico en el Siglo XIX* (San Juan, 1972). Two important books on the slavery question are by Luis Manuel Díaz Soler, *Historia de la Esclavitud Negra en Puerto Rico* (San Juan, 1953); and Arturo Morales Carrión, *Auge y Decadencia de la trata negrera en Puerto Rico (1820–1860)* (San Juan, 1978). For a history of the *compontes* and the governorship of Gen. Romualdo Palacio, see Lidio Cruz Monclova, *Historia del Año de 1887*, 3d ed. (Río Piedras, 1970). An important work for the study of the workers' class in Puerto Rico is Labor Gómez Acevedo, *Organización y Reglamentación del Trabajo en el Puerto Rico del Siglo XIX* (San Juan, 1970). See also Fernando Picó, *Libertad y Servidumbre en el Puerto Rico del Siglo XIX* (San Juan, 1979). Isabel Gutiérrez del Arroyo, *El Reformismo Ilustrado en Puerto Rico* (Mexico, 1953), is the standard work on the impact of Enlightenment on the island. For a history of the development of journalism in Puerto Rico, see Antonio S. Pedreira, *El Periodismo en Puerto Rico*, 2d ed. (Río Piedras, 1969). The closing days of the nineteenth century are ably dealt with in Carmelo Rosario Natal, *Puerto Rico y la Crisis de la Guerra Hispano-Americana* (San Juan, 1975), a fine study on the Spanish American War and its impact on Puerto Rico.

CHAPTER 16: *A Special Voice: The Cultural Expression*

The author has used some material already published in her writings on the culture of Puerto Rico. See particularly: *Jornadas Literarias. Temas de Puerto Rico* (Barcelona, 1967), *Borinquen: An Anthology of Puerto Rican Literature*, co-edited with Stan Steiner with an introduction by María Teresa Babín (New York, 1974); *The Puerto Ricans' Spirit: Their History, Life and Culture* (New York, 1971); *Panorama de la Cultura Puertorriqueña* (New York, 1958); and *Puerto Rican Authors* (Metuchen, N.J., 1974), co-edited by Marnesba O. Hill and Harold B. Schleifer, with an introduction by María Teresa Babín.

For some additional useful sources, consult, for example, on the early manifestations: Alejandro Tapia y Rivera and others, *Biblioteca Histórica de Puerto Rico* (1854), which contains early documents from the discovery of Puerto Rico until 1797; Tomás Navarro Tomás, *El Español en Puerto Rico* (San Juan, 1948), a basic study of the oral and written language of Ponce de León and the early Spanish settlers in Puerto Rico; Arturo Morales Carrión, *Historia del Pueblo de Puerto Rico* (San Juan, 1968); and Luis M. Díaz Soler, *Historia de la Esclavitud Negra en Puerto Rico* (Madrid, 1953).

For the nineteenth century, see: Augusto Malaret, *Vocabulario de Puerto Rico* (New York, 1955), a contribution to lexicography in Spanish America; Manuel A. Alonso, *El Gíbaro*

(Barcelona, 1849), of which a new edition was published in Río Piedras in 1949, with a prologue by Manrique Cabrera; María Cadilla de Martínez, *La poesía popular en Puerto Rico* (Madrid, 1933); Cayetano Coll y Toste, *Leyendas Puertorriqueñas* (San Juan, 1953); Juan José Osuna, *A History of Education in Puerto Rico*, rev. ed. (Río Piedras, 1949); and Manuel Zeno Gandía, *La Charca* (San Juan, 1894), the most important novel of the nineteenth century, describing the economic plight of the peasant population of the island. Many editions of this masterpiece have been published.

For Puerto Rican history, see Tomás Blanco, *Prontuario Histórico de Puerto Rico*, 6th ed. (San Juan, 1970); Antonio S. Pedreira, *Obras Completas* (San Juan, 1969); Luis Muñoz Rivera, *Obras Completas* (San Juan, 1968); René Marqués, *Ensayos* (Rio Piedras, 1966); and Arturo Morales Carrión, *Ojeada al Proceso Histórico y Otros Ensayos* (San Juan, 1971).

Among the extensive work in fiction, poetry and theatre, see: Emilio S. Belaval, *Cuentos para Fomentar el Turismo* (Barcelona, 1967); Guillermo Cotto Thorner, *Trópico en Manhattan* (San Juan, 1967); Abelardo Díaz Alfaro, *Terrazo* (San Juan, 1967); Enrique A. Laguerre, *Obras Completas* (San Juan, 1962–1964); Concha Meléndez, *Literatura de Ficción en Puerto Rico: Cuento y Novela* (San Juan, 1971); and Pedro Juan Soto, *Spiks* (Río Piedras, 1970). Other significant works include Luis Lloréns Torres, *Obras Completas* (San Juan, 1967–1969); Luis Palés Matos, *Poesía, 1915–1956* (San Juan, 1968); René Marqués, *La Carreta*, translated into English by Charles Pilditch as *The Oxcart* (New York, 1969); and *Borinquen: An Anthology of Puerto Rican Literature* (New York, 1974), edited by María Teresa Babín and Stan Steiner.

Besides the works included in the sources already quoted or used by the contributing historians, an extensive bibliography is readily available in English and Spanish on the history of Puerto Rico and related subjects. Some titles are included here for the reader who may want to pursue further studies. Helpful aids in this endeavor are: Enrique R. Bravo, *An Annotated Selected Puerto Rican Bibliography* (New York, 1972); Eugenio Fernández Méndez, *The Sources on Puerto Rico Culture History: A Critical Appraisal* (San Juan, 1967); and Paquita Vivó, *The Puerto Ricans: An Annotated Bibliography* (New York, 1973).

A good general introduction is found in Kal Wagenheim, *Puerto Rico: A Profile* (New York, 1970). For Marxist interpretations see Manuel Maldonado Denis, *Puerto Rico: A Socio-Historic Interpretation* (New York, 1972) and Adalberto Lopez, ed., *The Puerto Ricans: Their History, Culture and Society* (Cambridge, Mass., 1980). Also, for an overall, non-Marxist view, see Eugenio Fernández Méndez, *Historia Cultural de Puerto Rico, 1498–1968* (San Juan, 1970). Sociological studies of interest to historians include: Sidney Mintz, *Worker in the Cane: A Puerto Rico Life History* (New Haven, 1960); Julian Steward et al., *The People of Puerto Rico* (Urbana, 1956); and Melvin Tumin and Arnold Feldman, *Social Class and Social Change in Puerto Rico*, 2d ed. (Indianapolis, 1971). Good studies on the history, the society, and the economy are found in *Status of Puerto Rico: Selected Background Studies Prepared for the United States-Puerto Rico Commission on the Status of Puerto Rico* (Washington, 1966).

An essential book on the government of Puerto Rico is Carmen Ramos de Santiago, *El Gobierno de Puerto Rico*, 3rd ed. (San Juan, 1976). On present political history, see Juan M. García Passalacqua, *La Alternativa Liberal: Una Visión Histórica de Puerto Rico* (Río Piedras, 1974); Kenneth R. Farr, *Personalism and Party Politics: Institutionalization of the Popular Democratic Party* (Hato Rey, 1973); and Reece B. Bothwell, *Trasfondo Constitucional de Puerto Rico* (Río Piedras, 1966). For the study of the Spanish language in the island, see: Manuel Alvarez Nazario, *El Elemento Afro-Negroide en el Español de Puerto Rico* (San Juan, 1961); Samuel Gili Gaya, *Nuestra Lengua Materna* (San Juan, 1965); Luis Hernández Aquino, *Dic-*

cionario de Voces Indígenas (Bilbao, 1969); and Rubén del Rosario, *La Lengua de Puerto Rico*, 7th ed. (Río Piedras, 1971).

Although this book deals primarily with the history of the island of Puerto Rico, mention should be made of the extensive literature available on the migration experience and the life of Puerto Ricans in the United States.

An essential contemporary study is by the U.S. Commission on Civil Rights, *Puerto Ricans in the Continental United States: An Uncertain Future* (Washington, 1976). Other useful studies are Kal Wagenheim, *A Survey of Puerto Ricans on the U.S. Mainland in the 1970's* (New York, 1975) and National Puerto Rican Forum, *The Next Step Toward Equality: A Comprehensive Study of Puerto Ricans in the United States Mainland* (New York, 1980). A few titles in the migration literature are: Clarence Senior, *The Puerto Ricans. Strangers—Then Neighbors* (Chicago, 1965); Elena Padilla, *Up from Puerto Rico* (New York, 1958); Joseph P. Fitzpatrick, *The Puerto Rican Americans* (New Jersey, 1971); C. Wright Mills, *The Puerto Rican Journey* (New York, 1948); and Clara E. Rodríguez et al., eds., *The Puerto Rican Struggle: Essays on Survival in the U.S.* (New York, 1980). Recent Marxist interpretations are: Manuel Maldonado Denis, *Puerto Rico y Estados Unidos: Emigración y Colonialismo* (Mexico, 1976); and Centro de Estudios Puertorriqueños, *Labor Migration Under Capitalism: The Puerto Rican Experience* (New York, 1979). On the return migration to the island, see José Hernández Alvarez, *Return Migration to Puerto Rico* (Berkeley, 1967); and Celia Cintrón and Pedro Vales, *A Pilot Study: Return Migration to Puerto Rico* (Río Piedras, 1974).

Index

375